HER NAME IS GRACE

The Battle of Two Kingdoms

Ingrid Herrmann

Ark House Press
arkhousepress.com

© 2025 Ingrid Herrmann

All rights reserved. Apart from any fair dealing for the purpose of study, research, criticism, or review, as permitted under the Copyright Act, no part may be reproduced by any process without written permission.

Scripture quotations from The Authorized (King James) Version. Rights in the Authorized Version in the United Kingdom are vested in the Crown. Reproduced by permission of the Crown's patentee, Cambridge University Press

Some names and identifying details have been changed to protect the privacy of individuals.

Cataloguing in Publication Data:
Title: Her Name Is Grace
ISBN: 978-1-7641362-4-2 (pbk)
Subjects: REL012170 RELIGION / Christian Living / Personal Memoirs; REL012040 RELIGION / Christian Living / Inspirational; BIO018000 BIOGRAPHY & AUTOBIOGRAPHY / Religious.

Typeset by initiateagency.com

WITH IMMENSE GRATITUDE TO:

Editor: Linda Cloete (née Schumann)

Linda Cloete has a D Phil (Library and Information Science) degree. Her career includes positions as librarian, lecturer and freelance consultant in Library and Information Science. Her achievements comprise numerous academic publications.

Co-editor: Lucia Geyer

Lucia Geyer has a Master's degree in Library and Information Science. Her career includes positions as librarian, lecturer, freelance consultant in Library and Information Science and editor of various academic and other publications.

Graphic Designer: Martin Howard

Cover Design by Martin Howard, who is not only a skilled graphic designer but also serves as a volunteer facilitator at the Sycamore Project. This innovative program invites crime victims into prisons to share their experiences and discuss the profound effect of crime, fostering understanding and rehabilitation among inmates. Ingrid was able to share her story in prison on several occasions and experienced the benefits of the experience first-hand.

sycamorevoices.org
http://bio.link/martinhoward

And to all the wonderful family and friends who have encouraged, supported and literally carried me over the finish line – I could not have done it without you. I love you all!
Blessings
Ingrid

TABLE OF CONTENTS

List of Abbreviations vii

Forward: A Sinner Saved By Grace xi

Introduction... xv

Part I: The Huguenots of France and the Clash of the Titans................ 1

Part II: The Lutherans of Germany and the Controlled Opposition....... 24

Part III: Deepest Darkest Africa.. 75

Part IV: The Puzzle Pieces Coming Together.. 167

Part V: Ingrid Solveig Herrmann 312

Part VI: Her Name is Grace 360

References 473

Appendix A: Gevers Genealogist Diagram 481

Appendix B: Gevers Plaat 483

Appendix C: Statte Van Die Zoeloe-Konings.. 485

LIST OF ABBREVIATIONS

ANC	African National Congress
BBC	British Broadcasting Corporation
BMS	Berlin Missionary Society
DM	Deutschmark
CESA	Church of England in South Africa
CIA	Central Intelligence Agency
COSAS	Congress of South African Students
EKD	Evangelical Church of Germany
FCCC	Front Line COVID-10 Critical Care Alliance
FRELIMO	Frente de Libertação de Moçambique (Mozambique Liberation Front)
HMS	Hermannsburg Mission Society
ICU	Intensive Care Unit
IUEF	International University Exchange Fund
Lt. Gov.	Lieutenant Governor
MPLA	People's Movement for the Liberation of Angola (Portuguese: Movimento Popular de Libertação de Angola)
NCC	National Church Council
NKJV	New King James Version
NWO	New World Order
PAC	Pan Africanist Congress of Azania

POW	Prisoner of War
PPS	Post-Postscript
PS	Postscript
PTSD	Post-Traumatic Stress Disorder
RN	Registered Nurse
SACBC	South African Catholic Bishops Conference
SACC	South African Council of Churches
SEQCC	Southeast Queensland Corrections Centre
SWAPO	South West Africa People's Organisation
TFP	Tradition, Family, Private Property
UCA	United Christian Action
UN	United Nations
UNO	United Nations Organization
UNTF	United Nations Trust Fund
USA	United States of America
USSR	United of Soviet Socialist Republics
WCC	World Council of Churches

Our Father which art in heaven, Hallowed be thy name.
Thy Kingdom come, Thy will be done in earth, as it is in heaven.
Give us this day our daily bread.
And forgive us our debts, as we forgive our debtors.
And lead us not into temptation, but deliver us from evil:
For thine is the Kingdom, and the power, and the glory, for ever.
Amen.

~ KJV

FORWARD: A SINNER SAVED BY GRACE

I was first given the vision of writing this book not long after I came to living faith. I clearly heard God urging me to write my personal story. Although there had been numerous attempts to write this book, I consistently struggled and eventually gave up. My family, particularly my mother, encouraged me to write the book, but I was young and lacked the confidence and emotional maturity required for such a task. Apart from that, the project seemed overwhelming, and it was difficult to find information at the time.

Although I grew up with many of the family anecdotes captured in this book, intensive research was required to verify and fully develop them. I was also hindered by my own conscience and keenly aware of certain topics that needed to be addressed with great sensitivity. However, in His absolute grace and kindness, God's mercies are new every morning, and He embarked on this journey with me, which spanned some 30 years, and used that time to work a great deal of healing in me. He tenderly revealed Himself to me, guiding me and eventually bringing me to the point of complete surrender to Him in obedience.

After meeting my second husband, Willem Herbst, we got involved in missions and studying theology. I was given a gift of seeing and understanding the "bigger picture", and I loved Ethics, Church History, Biblical Theology, and the study of world views. Through my formal studies, I learned to read for research and to write. Many of the concepts that I was taught were so deeply embedded in me that they had become a part of this book. My upbringing had taught me analytical thinking or critical thinking. Both Willem and I were avid readers, and we could easily spend time together in silence, just reading. I devoured numerous missionary biographies, often rereading them several times and mulling them over.

It was during this time that I became aware of a "brooding darkness". It was as though some of the fog was being swept away and, for the first time, I could see a deep evil simmering within the nations of the world, boiling their people like frogs. This experience still influences the way I look at the current world situation and systems. In hindsight, I can see that I was being "awakened". The Lord used the next 30 odd years to prepare me, teach me and mould me to understand this "brooding darkness", and its threads are included in my story. This part of my story, which is covered in this text, involves the struggle of two kingdoms and how it plays out in our history, countries, nations and our souls.

It is important not to overlook the sovereignty of God in this struggle. – *God rules over the affairs and destiny not only of Israel, but also of all other nations. The words God has spoken will be fulfilled.*

Willem's favourite author was Arthur Pink (1886–1952) and his expository books. It was Willem's hobby of genealogy that got me started on researching my side of the family. Initially, it was just something nice we could do together, but it soon became an obsession for both of us. He taught me the value of source documents and travelling to various cities, to sit for hours on end, scanning through death certificates. My research has taken me down numerous rabbit holes and, although I have solved some puzzles, some of them still remain unanswered. That is what makes writing a book so enjoyable and interesting. I often ran the risk of staying in research mode and eventually I had to take the plunge and write the book. There were still times during which I got side tracked and had to refocus.

In this process, I came to have a clear vision of what the Lord wanted me to do – to write my story through the lens of my family and relatives and in the context of our lives and beliefs. It is the story of how we became Christians generations ago, and how we left Europe to become pioneers in South Africa. Finally, it is the story of how the Lord saved me and brought our family to Australia.

This book covers the lives of several generations and different family groups in my family tree. Some were missionaries and others were colonists. They faced famine, impossible challenges, persecution, war, death and migration into unexplored countries and continents. These are the men and women who shaped me. Their tenacious faith and resilience remain a constant encouragement to me and my family and, hopefully, to all those who read this book. My narrative is written within the context of history – not only in geopolitical terms, but also in socio-economic and philosophical ideology. It captures the history of our nations of origin and the history of the nations of our "new" countries and, most importantly, how we navigated history through faith and the way in which the lack of faith sometimes shaped our choices. As observed by King Solomon in Proverbs 14:12: "There is a way that seems right to a man but it's end is the way of death" (*Holy Bible. New King James Version (NKJV)*, 1982).[1]

Willem loved this proverb and often quoted it to us. In Arthur Pink's biography, he read how this same verse was instrumental in Arthur's conversion. My husband was an absolute character, but on this one thing he was immovable and that was his faith in the Lord Jesus Christ. He did not care who you were and even rallied to write to the Prime Minister of South Africa to plead the case of Christ for the nation.

For the courage of his convictions, I dedicate this book to my late husband, Willem Herbst. It was an honour to know you and serve you as your wife.

---

[1] From here on, referred to as "NKJV (1990)".

To my mother and my brother: thank you for setting an example with your zeal for Jesus, for your immense encouragement and support, and for your unwavering belief that I could do this.

To my children, who taught me unconditional love and forgiveness: you have made my life worth living. You are the apple of my eye. Thank you!

Above all, to the Lord Jesus Christ, who chose to take me, a simple farmer's daughter, by the hand and to pull me out of the depths of the mire and placed my feet on the unshakable ground of The Rock. To You dearest Lord, I surrender all. To You be the honour and the glory for ever and ever.

A Sinner Saved by Grace

INTRODUCTION

Early morning always finds me in one of my favourite spots – in the kitchen, by the kettle when I am making myself an early cup of coffee, or at the sink by the open window. The sash windows face east and across an old paddock, which is in serious need of mowing. Through a gap between the trees, I can see horses grazing and swishing their tails. I can stand there for hours, dreaming or simply looking at God's beautiful creation, admiring the works of His hands. Sometimes, when I get up early enough, I can watch the sunrise, but today it is overcast, and the sun is hidden behind the clouds. This reminds me of my own life, not so long ago, when the Son did not feature in the scenery of my everyday life at all.

Life was dark and full of suffering, some due to circumstances and some … hmm, oodles due to my own fault. The day I got saved was fraught with dark clouds and enough self-pity to fill an ocean. All hope had fled and there did not seem to be any point in living. This day, I got my first lesson in the existence of the spirit realm and the true meaning of spiritual warfare. At the window of my bedroom, I could see a dark and evil presence that appeared incredibly powerful. At that moment, when I walked through the bedroom door, I knew that this shadow was intent on ensuring my death that night. The magnetic pull from this demonic being was so powerful that I instantly considered jumping out the window, three floors below and onto the concrete car park. Sheer terror swept over me in icy, suffocating, crippling waves.

At this point, I was crying uncontrollably. Hopelessness mingled with terror and fear made me glance at the bedside table, looking for something to hold onto, so as to withstand this powerful pull to jump. I saw my Bible on the bedside table and the words, "Thou shalt not kill" shot through my head. I hesitated for an instant and then threw myself onto the bed, clinging onto the sides for dear life. Crying out to the Lord, '*God if You truly exist, let me live, but if You do not, let me die tonight.*' All my anger and rage poured out, mixed with the realization that I could not save myself; that I never could. In that moment, I surrendered and handed over the reins of my life to the King.

I cried myself to sleep, not knowing if I was going to wake up the next morning, but I did. And it was wonderful. It was my first day of being alive, of truly living! The peace in my heart was so astonishing and I knew without a shadow of a doubt that Jesus had come to fill my heart. The atmosphere was clear and bright, filled with light as I had never seen before. Where there had only been despair and loss, joy now burst through, and it was beautiful.

The Lord flooded me with knowledge and an insatiable hunger for His Word. Slowly, He led me through the next 33 years, opening my eyes to see things I had never seen before. He made it clear that He wanted this story to be told to the world. As I am writing, I am experiencing an intense spiritual attack. I am reminded of just how weak I truly am; that even though so much growth has occurred in the last years, I am weak, but He is strong!

This is the story of how God gave me the culture and heritage, the love for history and the ability to see "the bigger picture". We are already in 2024, and time is running out. All over the world, things are wildly out of control. People are filled with fear for the future. I am here to tell you that there is hope. There is always hope, if you are willing to soften your heart and surrender. Please, whatever you do, do *not* wait!

People say you can choose your friends, but you cannot choose your family. So true. For a long time after that fateful day, I had wondered what the tug and pull was that brought me to this point. I have recently learned about generational blessings. Previously, when I was looking in the mirror, observing my green eyes staring back at me, I knew that my eyes came from my mother, whereas my nose comes from the Schumann side of the family. My daughter inherited her great grandmother's hair and the features of her two times great grandmother and her tender heart. Apart from the obvious benefits from his father's side, my son has a remarkable resemblance to the Herrmann family, including his love for war.

From as far back as I can remember, I have been fascinated by our family photographs that my mother lovingly kept in old shoe boxes on top of their bedroom wardrobe. This was in Empangeni days, and, as a three-year old, I had much time on my hands. I had learned to climb, and the old mango tree outside the kitchen door was no longer much of a challenge and neither was the wardrobe. I could often be found sitting on the top of the wardrobe, with the open boxes of photographs, studying the family photos with much interest. It was here that I discovered that I had an older sister who had passed before I was born, and a photo of our beloved dog, Nooky, before he had died. There were photographs of mama's brothers and sisters, her parents and there were numerous photographs of our life on the farm in Scheepersnek, before we moved to Empangeni. I wanted to know them all. And so started my love for our family and their history – a quest that became very important to me – particularly in more recent years.

I was already married to my second husband, Willem, when the two of us were managing the Christian Book Shop attached to our church in Pinetown. A stream of ministers would come in and spend time with Willem at what we called the *Stamm Tisch* – a round table conveniently set next to Willem's desk in the far corner, away from other shoppers. One of these visitors was the head of the Bible Society in KwaZulu Natal. The two of them would chat over copious amounts of tea. I regret that I do not have a photo of Doc, as we called him. He was such an interesting person. He had studied in Germany under Ratzinger and loved telling us all about it; particularly since Ratzinger had just become Pope Benedict XVI. I think he was the only evangelical in Ratzinger's class. All the lectures were in German and Doc did not speak German. One day, he asked me about my background, and I told him that I was a direct descendant of the Hermannsburg Missionaries, who came from Germany to South Africa.

As part of his duties with the Bible Society, Doc would travel and visit the churches all around the province. These travels also took him to the German Lutheran churches and that was when he made a remarkable observation. He had noticed that all the descendants of the missionaries and their colonial settlers had done rather well for themselves, as if they had been blessed by their forbears. Thinking about this, I could see that he was right. I looked at all my uncles and aunts and all my cousins and it was clear that he was, indeed, right. All of them could hold their heads high and had done their families proud.

> "And His mercy is on those who fear Him from generation to generation" (Luke 1:50).

Not long before this episode, I got hold of a couple of books written by my second cousin, Carine Nel, about the Fröhling and Schumann side of my family. Prior to that, my mother gave me more books about the colonists, "*Die Klingenbergs in Südafrika*" and the history of the Hermannsburg Mission to Africa, as narrated by Hedwig Schütte in *Aus dem Leben unser Voreltern* ("From the lives of our forefathers"). On the inside of the book cover, Hedwig had written: "An Ursula Gerritz von Hedwig Schütte in Dankbarkeit für die Tipparbeit: Zweieter Versuch ins Galloland, 1858". How remarkable to know that my mother had helped Hedwig by typing this book. While I was at college, this book had helped me with an assignment in Church History. I found it fascinating to say the least.

However, as wonderful as these stories may be, I wanted to know more about the lives of my ancestors in Germany. I wanted to know what had motivated them as missionaries to leave their families in Europe and to cross oceans in a sailing ship to another, largely unexplored continent, all the way around the Cape of Good Hope to Natal, where the only inhabitants were the African people and wild animals. I wanted to establish what it was about these magnificent and courageous characters that shaped me into who I am. Where did they get the resilience to survive so much hardship as pioneers?

"Our Savior says: "You shall know the truth and the truth shall make you free" (John 8:32). As an understanding of the soul in its natural state, spirituality is sick; in a state of error and ongoing self-deception. The truth sets us free from our self-imprisonment, from the bondage of our illusions, so that we may be healed, transformed and made new.

However, knowing the truth is more volitional than it is cognitive. – It is revealed in our decisions and actions, and not merely in holding to a "true opinion" or assenting to a "true creed". Knowing the truth permeates the entire person – *bekhol levavkha* – and accepts all the consequences of its decision and passion. There is danger here, friends. Even learning Scripture and studying theology may become untruth, if it is devoid of the fear of the Lord. "How many have asked, 'What is truth?' and at bottom hoped that it would be a long time before the truth would come so close to him that in the same instant it would determine what his duty was to do at the moment?" (Kierkegaard, 2009).

"The deeper question is whether you actually want genuine freedom, since many are content to "exist" in the cold comfort of their resentments, in the desert of the self-serving ego, and in the wasteland of anger and fear... Self-deception is enticing because it provides an excuse to be mediocre; it justifies a victim mentality and abnegates personal responsibility. It is far easier to blame others for your life than to own the truth about yourself, to walk in the truth, and to seek the blessing of truth. Spiritual freedom means being awakened and empowered to choose the Eternal by denying the present moment's demand to be made absolute. It offers no peace to the natural desire for the soul to return to its sleepy state but calls and rouses the heart to wake up and confront the demands of eternity ...

In heaven, there is only the language of truth, and truth is the language of heaven. "If we ask according to his will, he hears us ..." (1 John 5:14). This means that words find their traction only in honesty of the heart, in the midst of our deepest need. Only in "fear and trembling" can we talk with God, though when we pray fervently, our words may trail off until we become silent ... But it is there, in the silence of the soul, that we may learn to listen to the Spirit and to hear God's voice. When we seek first the Kingdom of God, we will lay aside everything else, quiet our hearts, and focus our will. Seeking God in this way is an end in itself, for whatever else we may seek must be subordinated to this greater seeking. "You will seek me and find me, when you seek me with all your heart" (Jer. 29:13). Anonymous

PART I

THE HUGUENOTS OF FRANCE AND THE CLASH OF THE TITANS

THE GEVERS FAMILY OF FRANCE

"At some time or the other most of us will have tried to put a jigsaw puzzle together; baffling little pieces that in the end form a clear coherent picture of a landscape or whatnot. The hardest thing about it is the beginning. The more pieces that get put into place, the clearer and more comprehensible the whole picture becomes. Many people never get past the beginning and in frustration give up.

It is rather like that with most of us in our attempts to make something of political events in the world. We can see only the separate bits, which often make no sense. And we are astounded at what seems to us the ignorance of many politicians displayed by their attitudes and responses to certain things, so that in our amazement we are compelled to wonder how such fellows could ever have reached high office" (Fragments of a World Revolutionary Drama) (Vaqué, 1989).

Heritage, as expressed in traditions, language and culture, forms a big part of who we are, as do our choices and the choices of those who have gone before us. The life of each person lies in the blood, and we inherit our genetic legacy through our bloodline. I am rather proud of my heritage. Perhaps everyone is. It certainly explains the strong sense of patriotism that most of us have. As far as I can establish, all my ancestors came from Germanic background, with the exception of one part of the family, who is possibly French, possibly Basque. The origins of the Gevers are shrouded in obscurity. There are Gevers near Lüneburg, Germany, in France and in Holland. The information that has been handed down to me, reflects an intriguing story that has fascinated me since childhood. My mother had either inherited The Gevers Book or bought her own copy, which had gone missing. In Germany, there is a *Geschlechter Buch* ("Gender Book") available on disc, with the Gevers family on it. This should certainly solve some of the mystery of what I am about to tell you.

The Gevers family was apparently quite wealthy in Germany, and I have it in my mind that, somewhere down the line, one of them was Bishop of Lüneburg/Braunschweig. And this is where it becomes interesting, but I digress. Two inter-related groups of German Gevers migrated to South Africa.

Prior to that in 1783, Paul Gevers from Rotterdam, Holland, arrived in the Cape. However, he returned to Holland after a short time. Then in 1880, two brothers of the first group of Gevers arrived in the Cape. Before his migration, the oldest brother, Heinrich, changed his name from Gevers to Gebers to prevent confusion between the two family lines. The younger brother, Johan Jurgen Friedrich Gevers, born on 30 March 1861 in Reimerdingen in Schneeverdingen, married into the Meyer family from Harburg. He was my great grandfather. His daughter became my grandmother, Ida Marie Sophie Gevers.

Getting back to Lüneburg in Germany: I discovered fascinating insights from photographs and photocopies of various source documents of German origin. I found these in an old, brown envelope. I believe they were collated by my aunt Brunni and passed on to my mother. It took much reading and deciphering to make head or tail of the documents and in the process, I discovered a possible link between the Gevers and the Bourbon Dynasty. A deeper investigation into the genealogy of the kings and dynastic houses shows connections between the French and the Germans, which resulted from the Francs moving into Germany under the rule of Charlemagne and Catholicism going on a spree of baptising the local population, willing or unwilling, into the Catholic faith. They set up monasteries for the crusader knights and dukedoms often followed. Although the exact link is unknown, the names of the Gevers are linked to the Dukedom of Braunschweig, which fell under the Fiefdom of Lüneburg. A relative, Bernhard Gevers, detailed research into the Gevers origins from Coburg Germany and discovered that the names of the Gevers were linked to the Bourbon Dynasty.

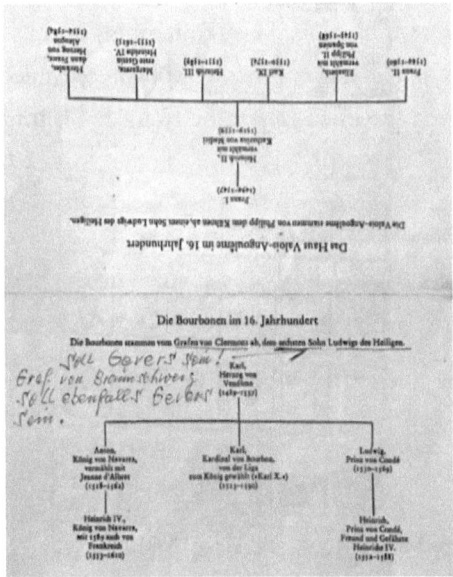

Found in the 'brown envelope' with the researcher's handwritten notes of his findings. There were many supporting documents, but it is difficult to make the connections without understanding how the researcher (Onkel Bernhard Gevers) made his suppositions. He had employed a history professor in France, according to Hogard Gevers, but I do not have access to all his research.

In his own handwriting, my relative asserts that the Count of Clermont, the sixth son of Ludwig des Heiligen (Louis the Holy or Louis the Pious), ought to be Gevers and that they are of the Bourbon Dynasty. He further explains that the Duke/Count of Braunschweig, therefore, ought to be Bourbon as well! That means that we are somehow related to King Henry IV, who took over the throne of France as the first Bourbon King. It could therefore be entirely possible that the Gevers family has French origins, which may explain why the surname in the armorial is spelled Gevres or Gesvres. I would obviously love to conclude all the speculation with more facts and evidence, but in the following paragraphs, I capture the information that I did manage to unearth.

When Robert, Count of Clermont, sixth and youngest son of King Louis IX of France, married Beatrix of Burgundy in 1272, he also married the heiress to the Lordship of Bourbon and member of the House of Bourbon-Dampierre. Her grandfather was Hugh IV, Duke of Burgundy. Robert's son, Louis I, le Boiteux, was a French *Prince Du Sang*, ("Prince of the Blood"), Count of Clermont-en-Beauvaisis and La Marche, and First Duke of Bourbon. In this way, Robert inherited the Lordship of Bourbon from his wife. This is interesting and I saw it occurring quite often in my research. The descendants of Robert continued for a further few generations and I noted the inclusion of the Fleur de Lis into the coat of arms.

In the Rietstap Armorial General, of which I have a photocopy, the Coat of Arms is registered.

Blazon of Coat of Arms – GEVERS	
Shield:	Azure Blue
Charge:	A Fleur-de-Lis (Lilly) in argent (Silver)
Helmet:	Esquires or Gentleman's Helmet
Crest:	A Fleur-de-Lis
Mantling:	Argent (Silver) and Azure (Blue)
Significance:	The Colours: Azure = Blue The Metals: Silver/Moon/Pearl = Composure, Calmness, Nobility The Charge: Fleur-de-Lis = One of the flower charges.

Legend has it that it was first used by the Frankish King, Clovis I (466–511AD). A hermit beheld an angel, holding an azure shield emblazoned with three gold lilies. The hermit was ordered to give the shield to King Clovis, who would be victorious in battle from then on.

Gevers means "generous giver ", and "Semper Idem" in the Crest means "Always the Same", as in the biblical "Christ, the same yesterday, today & forever" (Hebrew 13:8)[2]

During the Second Crusade in 1150, Louis VII of France used the Fleur-de-Lis on his royal seal and on his banner. This Iris flower was called Fleur-de-Louis (flower of Louis), which was eventually modified to Fleur-de-Lis." (Volker, [s.a.])

---

[2] New information passed down by Hogart Gevers. Reference https://www.youtube.com/watch?v=QE5uRp1v9Q8&t=25s

Cover page of a document in the 'brown envelope'. Recorded coat of arms of the Gevers Family in France.

Second page of the above. Shows the Fleur de Lis for the Gevers Coat of Arms. Unfortunately, the researcher did not photocopy the Potier family coat of arms as well. The researcher had travelled to France and Germany to obtain this information.

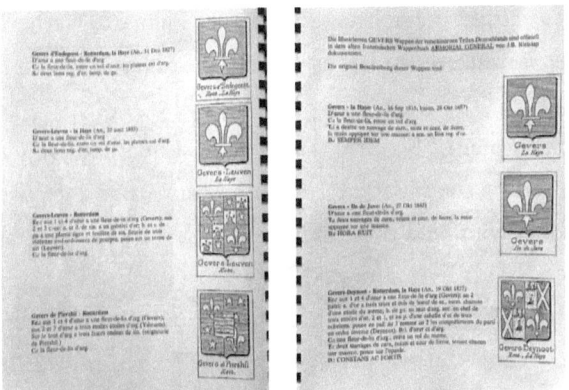

From Walter Volker's Gevers. The Gevers/Potier crests in Holland with explanation.

Getting back to the genealogy, we fast forward to Charles de Bourbon, who was a French *Prince Du Sang* and later became Duke of Vendome. His son, Antoine de Bourbon, was the fourth child, Duke of Vendome and King of Navarre through his marriage to Queen Jeanne III in 1548. Jeanne d'Albret (Joana in the Basque language) was the daughter of King Henry II of Navarre and Margaret of Angouleme. Henry had strong sympathy with the Huguenots and was fluent in both French and Spanish. In 1526, he married Margaret of Angouleme, who became known as Marguerite de Navarre. Her brother became King of France, Francis I. She was the ancestress of the Bourbon kings of France, being the mother of Jeanne d'Albret, whose son, Henry of Navarre, succeeded as Henry IV of France, the first Bourbon King. As an author and a patron of humanists and reformers, she was an outstanding figure of the French Renaissance.

After her public conversion to Calvinism in 1560, Jeanne joined the Huguenot side. She received recognition as a spiritual and political leader of the French Huguenot movement, and a key figure in the French Wars of Religion. During the first and second wars, she remained relatively neutral, but in the third war, she fled to La Rochelle, becoming the *de facto* leader of the Huguenot controlled city. She negotiated a peace treaty with the French Queen Mother,

Catherine de Medici, and arranged the marriage of her son, Henry to Catherine's daughter, Marguerite. Her son succeeded her as Henry III of Navarre, who later became the first Bourbon King of France, known as Henry IV.

Jeanne was the last active ruler of Navarre. Her son inherited her Kingdom, but as he was constantly leading the Huguenot forces, he entrusted the government to his sister, Catherine, who held the regency for more than two decades. In 1620, Jeanne's grandson, Louis XIII, annexed Navarre to the French throne.

Henri de Bourbon, Prince of Conde, was a friend and cousin of Henry of Navarre and attended the wedding at the palace Louvre in Paris. And this leads us to that fascinating little story that I mentioned before.

According to family legend, a cousin of Henry of Navarre was a part of the body count at the St Bartholomew Massacre. However, two of his boys were rescued and smuggled out of Paris amid great danger and taken in stages to Rotterdam in Holland. However, the Gevers connection is still something of an enigma, although there are documents that show that there were Gevers' at the court of Henry IV. It may be from these Gevers' that the splinter group fled France to Holland, as Henry IV was also later assassinated. Documentation of this group exists in the armorial, as well as in the archives from Holland.

"Van dit voormals Fransch geslacht, dat zijne bezittingen * had in de Brie Champenoise aan de oevers de Ourcq, heft sich ten tijde van *Philips, Herzog van Bourgondie*, Graaf van Champagne en van Brie, een tak hier te lande nedergezet, aanvankelijk te Delft, later ter Rotterdam, alwaar de afstammelingen bijna zonder uitzondering hebben gewoond tot in het begin der 19de eeuw.

*Deze gingen in het begin der 16de eeuw, *door het huwelijk van Jeanne Francoise Ceuillette de Gevres,* over aan een tak van het geslacht Potier, welks leden ze als Baron, enz., later als Hertog de Gevres, bezeten hebben tot 1794, toen de laaste overgeblevene ge guillotineerd en het kasteel verwoest werd. Die ruine ligt op den rechter Ourcq-oever, niet ver van het dorpje Gevres."

The translation of the above text reads as follows:

During the time of Philip, Duke of Burgundy, Count of Champagne and Brie, a branch of this former French family, which had its possessions in the Brie Champenoise on the banks of the Ourcq, settled here in this country, initially in Delft, later in Rotterdam, where the descendants lived almost without exception until the beginning of the 19th century.

*These passed at the beginning of the 16th century, through the marriage of Jeanne Francoise Ceuillette de Gevres, to a branch of the Potier family, whose members they owned as Baron, etc., later as Duke de Gevres, until 1794, when the last remaining ones were guillotined, and the castle was destroyed. The ruins are located on the right bank of Ourcq, not far from the village of Gevres.

(De la Chesnay Desbois (1774); De Courcelles (1826)

Added to this document (Appendix B) is the genealogy of the Gevers family in Holland from which no doubt the afore-mentioned Paul Gevers from Rotterdam came to visit the Cape in South Africa.

Through John Calvin (1509–1564), a large group of nobles came to faith, as well as all their family members and all those who were under their protection – the estates, the town and the villages. Like the rest of France, Catherine de Medici, being a dedicated Catholic, was in an absolute uproar and so was the Medici's in Italy, I would imagine. The Huguenots had to be stopped.

Catherine de Medici's son, Charles IX, saw the culmination of decades of tension between Protestants and Catholics. After several unsuccessful attempts at peace and the Massacre of Vassy in 1562, Charles arranged for the marriage of his sister, Margaret to Henry of Navarre, a major Protestant nobleman in the line of succession to the French throne. Facing hostility, Catherine de Medici, who influenced most of Charles's decisions, instigated him to oversee the massacre of thousands of Huguenot leaders, who gathered in Paris for the Royal wedding. This event, which is known as the Bartholomew Day Massacre, was a significant blow to the Huguenot movement.

The mass killings caused Charles's physical and mental health to deteriorate, and he died. Soon after his death, it is estimated that 10 000 Huguenots were killed in Paris alone. Charles's last words on his deathbed were, "What bloodshed! What murders! What evil council I have followed! Oh my God forgive me – I am lost! I am lost!" To his mother, "Who but you is the cause of all this? God's blood, you are the cause of it all"! Charles's brother took the throne, but he did not last long and soon we had the first Bourbon King on the throne of France: King Henry IV of Navarre.

Although Martin Luther (1483–1546) emerged as the fiery pathfinder of the Protestant cause, other scholars had also been questioning the practices of the church. In France in particular, men were re-examining the Scriptures and reaching conclusions similar to those of the German monk. Their ideas spread and inspired several small, pious communities tucked away in the remote provinces of the country.

The Catholic French monarch, Francis I, acted against these communities, with his harshest blow being struck against the Vaudois or Waldenses, who were an inoffensive society living in a series of scattered hamlets in the Southern Alpine regions of *Piedmont* and Provence. The rebels were ruthlessly hunted down, thousands put to the sword or burned at the stake. The number of survivors was tragically small.

This massacre was to set the pattern of events in France for the next century or more. When the persecution intensified, it was resisted ever more firmly, until what had started as peaceful religious disagreements became outright revolution. The battle lines were drawn. By the year 1560, the protestants in France numbered between 400 000 and one million, and from about this time they came to be known as "Huguenots". Despite ruthless persecution, the French Protestant population survived and grew, forming strongholds in various parts of the country.

At the start of the Huguenot wars in the early 1560s, the battle lines had been drawn. The reform movement was located in areas bounded by the rivers Rhone and Loire, the Bay of Biscay and the mountains of the Pyrenees, with outlying fortresses in Normandy and Dauphine. Their numbers were less significant than their leadership: it is estimated that, although the Huguenots made up about 3% of the total population of France, a third of the nobility had embraced the reformed faith. They were well disciplined and managed to establish their own state within France. They raised armies, negotiated with foreign powers and fought a sporadic civil war from 1559 until the proclamation of the Edict of Nantes in 1598. The civil war in France began shortly after Charles IX ascended to the throne in 1560. The wedding between Margaret and Henry Navarre offended the Catholics and in a diabolical way played into the hands of Catherine de Medici.

Nothing as nefarious as this massacre is planned in isolation and by one person. Behind the scenes, powerful people were at work. The darkness could not allow hundreds of years of power to be thwarted. The sooner we realise that we live in a world of no liberty, the sooner we will be able to take up the battle cry for freedom.

The Jesuits were created by the Holy Roman Empire, in particular by the Benedictine Order, in response to the Reformation.

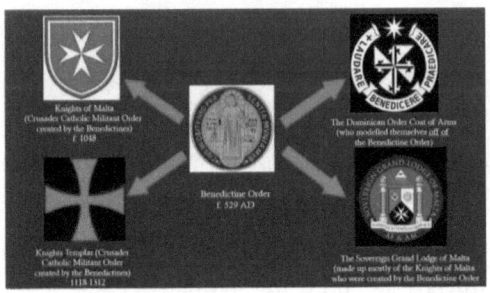

The diagram clearly illustrates the influence of the Benedictine Order and their esoteric background. Ultimately also responsible for the establishment of the Jesuit Order. The Benedictine Order was established 529 AD.

"The Jesuits by their very calling, by the very essence of their institution, are bound to seek, by every means, right or wrong, the destruction of Protestantism. This is the condition of their very existence, the duty they must fulfil, or cease to be Jesuits.

... They must be considered as the bitterest enemies of the Protestant faith; in the second, as bad and as unworthy priests; and in both cases, therefore, to be equally regarded with aversion and distrust" (Nicolini, 1854).

Prior to the Bartholomew Day Massacre, the Jesuits had been trying to infiltrate France, but they were repelled. A National Council was convened at Poissy to put an end, if possible, to religious dissension, and heal the wounds of the Church. Catherine de Medici whose favourite maxim was, *divide et imperia* ("divide and rule"), showed herself impartial in this contest, thinking to retain the obedience of one party by the fear it had of the other. Although the Roman Catholics had a large majority, the eloquence – particularly that of Beza – was so overpowering that the National Council broke up without any result. Before breaking up and after a great deal of debating, the assembly decided that the Jesuits should be admitted into France on the condition that they submit to the laws of the nation. However, they had to renounce all their privileges and take another name other than "The Society of Jesus" or "Jesuits".

However, these monks were able to adapt to every contingency, that they may succeed in their undertakings. No sooner had they set their foot in France than they began to spread rapidly over the country, soon aspiring to enter the universities and monopolise the entire education of the youth. However, the universities would not allow them entrance. The Bishop of Clermont had bequeathed them a large amount of money, but, notwithstanding this and all their intrigues, they contested the decision of the universities and won their day in court.

In 1572, Catherine de Medici turned to the Guises for help. On 23 August, Guise attended a secret meeting, where the Massacre of Saint Bartholomew's Day was planned. Guise personally supervised Coligny's murder, thereby avenging his father's death. He soon became the head of the Catholic Party. Catherine de Medici came to depend on him with the intrigues of her sons and that of Henry of Navarre. At dawn on 24 August 1572 – the eve of St Bartholomew's Day – royal troops went into action. On that day, between 2 000 and 3 000 Huguenots were massacred in Paris alone, while another 20 000 (estimates vary) died in other parts of the country. Remorse for the massacre deprived Charles IX of his reason and sent him to an early grave.

His brother, Henry III, who succeeded him, was occupied with his own pleasures, allowing the same protestants whom he had defeated as Duke of Anjou at Moncontour and other places to live in peace. Henry's indolence favoured the ambitious views of the Duke of Guise, who aspired as nothing less than the throne of France. He and his partisans, particularly the Jesuits, stirred up the fanaticism among the citizens against the king, who, although an observer of all those external practices of the Roman Catholic faith, was considered by the Church a bad Catholic.

A remedy had to be found, lest France turned into a Protestant country. A league was formed that included Philip of Spain and Henry of Guise. He had the audacity to enter publicly into a confederacy with Philip II of Spain. The Articles of the Alliance purported, "that a confederacy, offensive and defensive, was entered into between the king and the Catholic princes on behalf of themselves and their descendants, in France as well as the Low Countries: and on the death of King Henry III, to take measures that Cardinal de Bourbon should be appointed his successor; the heretic and relapsed princes being forever excluded from the right of succession." (Nicolini, 1854).

Henry III's position became highly precarious. The Guises were in possession of several of the chief towns and Duke Henry of Guise was the idol of the people.

The balance of success was in favour of the Holy League with the Guises at the head, but Henry of Navarre had received financial aid from England and won the Battle of Coutras. On the other hand, the Duc de Guise was too strong for the Protestant Germans, who had marched into France to join the Huguenots, and he defeated them. This subdued King Henry III, who was forced to accept the terms of The League. He signed the Edict of Union (1588), in which he named Guise Lieutenant General of the kingdom and declared that no heretic could succeed to the throne.

Unable to endure the humiliation, Henry III had the Duke and the Cardinal of Guise assassinated that same winter and many leaders of the League arrested. Priests and Jesuits from every pulpit poured out curses upon that tyrant, who deserved to be swept from the face of the earth. The Duc de Mayenne entered Paris on behalf of The Legue and declared open war on Henry III, who, after some hesitation, threw himself under the protection of his cousin, Henry of Navarre in the spring of 1589. (These two were cousins – one a Roman Catholic and the other a Protestant!). The Germans once more entered northeastern France and the Leaguers were unable to make headway either against them or against the armies of the two kings. They fell back on Paris, and the allies hemmed them in. It appeared as if the royalists would soon destroy the last stronghold of the League, when King Henry III was suddenly slain by a priestly assassin.

On 1 August 1589, King Henry III was stabbed to death by Clement, a Dominican Friar, at St Cloud. No matter what The League or the Jesuits tried to connive, they were unable to prevent the ascension of Henry of Navarre – a Protestant – to the French throne. From it's very beginning, the Jesuits were the most ardent promoters of the League. The portrait of the assassin was displayed on the altars to public veneration, and they even proposed to erect a statue of him in the cathedral of the Notre Dame. Henry of Navarre (known as Henry IV) reigned in France to the dismay of the Catholic people. The greatest achievement of his reign was restoring peace to a divided country and issuing the decree of the Edict of Nantes.

This edict granted freedom to all the protestants throughout France. They received the right to public worship, to trade and practice the professions, as well as the right to print books without having to apply for permission from the Catholic authorities. However, as soon as Henry IV was assassinated by a Catholic fanatic, the country was plunged into turmoil once more and, what is more, saw the rise of Cardinal Richelieu to power in the Catholic Church. During those years, assassinations, massacres, turmoil and wars bore the fingerprints of the Jesuits, who became a part of the Illuminate at a later stage. Absolutely nothing has changed – neither then, nor now.

While Christianity was forced by threats from the Papacy, a new era was emerging in which there was choice taken from people's lives. You can see the pull and tug of the splintering. Biblical truth was being watered down in Roman Catholicism due to the infiltration of ancient Gnostic mysticism and no longer important as Kingdom truth. The Reformation emphasized Biblical Truth: 'Sola Scriptura', which became extremely important. Neither party was keen on tolerating the other and both became highly judgemental. The golden thread of the True Sovereign Kingdom was being splintered. As both sides fell into a reactionary mode, they lost sight of the Kingdom of God as it is expressed in Scripture. Both began to rely heavily on church tradition. R.C Sproul (2009) expresses the Sovereignty of God very well in this statement: "The kingdom of God is not of the people, by the people, or for the people. It is a kingdom ruled by a King, and God does not rule by the consent of His subjects but by His sovereign authority. His reign extends over me whether I vote for Him or not." Satan has always tried to place himself in the position where only God is meant to be. He uses the tactics of divide and conquer as well as deceit very effectively in his attempt to destroy the Truth.

We see this same model at work in modern day Ireland. The nefarious dark forces, that brooding darkness, were quick to pick up on this schism – that is if they had not engineered it themselves – and by means that they have mastered early on, manipulated either side through finances and war. Every war incurs a cost and our 'little black fellows' (the nefarious dark forces and the black nobility who were also very involved in ancient banking systems) had absolutely no scruples in promoting one side or the other, or even both simultaneously, if it suited their purpose. The foolishness was that the parties involved were so short-sighted that they failed to see that they were borrowing from the same sources to fund their wars. Moreover, they began to depend on these sources and the convenient honey pot was ever so obliging. One can literally hear the cackles of laughter as the black noose pulled tighter and tighter. Give someone enough rope …

King Henry IV thought he was doing the world a great favour by establishing peace; particularly for the royal coffers. However, peace at the cost of True Kingdom Truth is no real peace. Without realising it, the Cardinal's death knell to all Protestants was a death knell to freedom of choice.

> "We fence in our minds any invasion of ideas we don't want to consider at all" (Edith Schaffer).

Gesvres/Gevers and the Potier Family in France

The Gesvres/Gevers and Potier families were *Gentilhommes ordinairs du Roi*. Forming the Kings Bodyguards (*Gards du Corps du Roi*). Unlike other units of the royal household, such as the French Guards and the Swiss Guards, the *Gard du Corps* was an exclusively aristocratic corps.

Captains du Corps – The reign of Francis I crested in 1447.

- **Francois Potier de Gesvres (1612–1646)**: Marquis de Gesvres
- **Leon Potier de Gesvres (1620–1704)** Duke of Gesvres

    The title of Baron of Gesvres first came to the Potier family with the marriage of Jacques Potier to Francoise Cuillette, daughter of Jean, Seigneur de Freschines et de Gesvres. Their son, Louis, inherited this title.
- **Rene Potier de Tresmes (1579–1670)**, first Count, then Duke de Tresmes, Peer of France, Marquis de Gandelu, was a French soldier and politician of the 17th century and Captain of the Kings Bodyguards.

    Rene was the oldest son of Louis Potier, Baron de Gesvres, Secretary of State and nephew of Nicholas III Potier de Blancmesnil. The Count of Tresmes was bailiff and Governor of Valois from the year 1599. He had been made *Gentilhommes ordinaires du Roi of King Henry IV*. He was appointed on 31 January 1608 and on 20 October of the same year, he was appointed as the governor of the town and Castle of Chalons. *The dutchy-peerage of Tresmes (in Crouy)* was renamed *de Gesvres 1670* in honour of the Mance family stronghold. He married Marguerite de Luxembourg, Princess de Tingry (d1645), and became the favourite of King Henry IV of France and is said to have received sums from the Royal Exchequer for work being carried out on his chateau and a church at Tresmes. Louis Potier had inherited the land from his father, and it was raised to a Marquisate for him in 1626. On his death in 1630, the land and title passed to his son, Rene. His marriage to Marquerite was so unequal, that it caused a scandal which had not been forgotten even by Saint Simon's time and no less scandalous was Rene's promotion to the rank of Duke, which seemed to have taken place in 1648. The estate and title were inherited by his third son and remained in the family until the execution of the last Duke during the Revolution (1794). The contents of the Chateau, including the large collection of paintings from the long gallery and even the fish in the moat, were then sold and the beautiful Chateau was destroyed in the early years of the 19th century. In his advanced years, Rene had commissioned the famous architect, Mansart, to restore his father's Chateau. It was Rene's grandson, the third Duke, who, according to Saint Simon, proclaimed that all the "crucifixions" at Versailles had been painted by Inri Rene. Like his brother, Bernard, and his two short-lived elder sons, Rene was a soldier. Some minor ruins of the Chateau survive the grim massacre.

- The splinter group in Holland (from the Potier/Gevers family) survived quite well, marrying into families of standing, amassing a small fortune and holding prestigious positions. Some, if not all of them, may have been involved in the Illuminism that was sweeping across Europe at an alarming rate.

The House of Potier. The splinter group went to Holland under the name of Gevers. This diagram displays the hidden hand of Illuminism.

Source:
https://en.wikipedia.org/wiki/House_of_Potier

House of Potier
House of Bourbon
Charles, Duke of Vendôme
Gardes du Corp du Roi (France)

The House of Potier was a noble house in Ancien Régime France. Members of the Potier family were Nobles of the Robe who gained their prominence through serving the King of France.

- Since writing the above history and shortly before publication, I received some startling information from Hogart Gevers in South Africa. He mentions that the original research was done by Bernhard Gevers, from whom he learned much of our French connection. Bernhard garnered the help of a French history professor at considerable expense. This is where all the research papers come from in the little brown envelope. It is true that the Gevers family at Givry in Burgundy was summoned by Catherine de Medici to attend the royal wedding festivities in Paris. However, because the parents did not trust Catherine, they sent the children away from France to Germany. As it turns out their fears were well grounded; they were brutally murdered at the St Bartholomew Massacre. This is how the family arrived in Germany. Perhaps the Gevers daughter who married into the Potier family was from Givry. There is still much research to be done but what rings out loud and clear is this – we were French Huguenots![3]

The Huguenots in South Africa and the Fouché Family

God is Sovereign and God is good. People put their faith in man's inerrant goodness – based on what, exactly?

---

[3] New information passed down by Hogart Gevers. Reference https://www.youtube.com/watch?v=QE5uRp1v9Q8&t=25s
https://www.youtube.com/watch?v=17vcHOXCzu8&t=65s

Cognitive dissonance is created when our beliefs are challenged, or when two beliefs are inconsistent. It is human nature to try to hold our beliefs in harmony with our world view and avoid disharmony (or dissonance).

The exodus of the Huguenot families from France started around the middle of the 17th century. Originating as a trickle, it turned into a flood with the abolishment of the Edict of Nantes in 1685. Reform church services were prohibited; schools and seminaries were closed; and synods were forbidden to meet. Protestants were excluded from government positions, and numerous of the unrepentant and those clinging onto their beliefs were sent to the gallows, broken at the wheel or sentenced to serve as galley slaves. Despite the death penalty for attempting to escape from France and the vigilance of Cardinal Richelieu and his Jesuit spies, the exodus continued. Refugees crossed the frontiers into Switzerland and Germany, and large numbers escaped to England, Scotland, the Channel Islands and North America.

Others fled to the Netherlands, where they were received with kindness and hospitality. It is estimated that France lost more than a million of her most industrious citizens during the second half of the 17th century, most of them in the years following the revocation of the Edict of Nantes. This massive outflow devastated the intellectual and economic core of France.

The Protestants' self-discipline and capacity for hard work had made them a powerful force in trade, industry and in the public life of the country. Their strong faith, combined with a commitment to unselfish labour, made them a tough and self-sufficient community. The Dutch recognised the value of the refugees. Their qualities of thrift, piety and devotion to the Protestant cause would clearly make a worthy contribution to the wealth and stability of the Netherlands. However, the vast and sudden influx had placed a strain on the resources of an already populous nation. It is estimated from 75 000 to 100 000

French Protestants settled in Holland. The Dutch authorities encouraged a portion of them to seek homes in overseas Dutch settlements. One such settlement had been established in the Cape of Good Hope, at the southernmost point of Africa. Their relocation coincided with the Commander at the Cape, Simon van der Stel (1630–1712) requesting more settlers from the Dutch authorities.

The Cape was an outpost of the powerful Dutch East India Company – a highly prosperous federation governed by seventeen directors, who reported to those little nefarious men. In order to encourage agricultural production, they resolved to send a large number of colonists to the Cape of Good Hope, which was in serious need of fresh produce for the crews of passing ships. Those to be sent to the Cape of Good Hope included French Refugees – particularly those who were cultivators of the vine, and those who understood the processes of making vinegar and distilling brandy. About 200 individuals took up the offer.

Simon Van der Stel's predecessor, Jan van Riebeeck (1619–1677), had released a number of Dutch residents from the Company, so that they could set themselves up as independent farmers. These men, known as *free burghers* ("free citizens"), pioneered the expansion of the Cape colony. However, two decades later, the vast majority of the land was still under-cultivated and too thinly populated. Simon Van der Stel wrote to the Dutch East India Company: "… all this place needs is people to make it the most fruitful place on earth" (Theron & Joyce, 1987:8).

The first French refugees arrived at the Cape of Good Hope in 1688 in seven ships, destitute after leaving all their belongings in Europe. At their arrival, they were given basic building materials and provisions for a few months. Only their skills and determined spirit would ensure their survival and prosperity and as predicted, many of them were able to fulfil the desires of the Company by laying out vineyards. They built homesteads in the Cape Dutch style, many of which have survived to this day, and the vineyards still produce excellent wines.

The instructions were to distribute the Huguenots throughout the settled areas and among the Dutch-speaking landowners. The French families soon integrated with the Dutch people, and it was not long before their language gave way to Dutch/Afrikaans from French. Today, the area where the French families settled in the Cape is known as Franschhoek ("French Corner"). Some of the most important people in the South African story originated from these Huguenots, who excelled as military leaders, politicians, lawyers, artists and writers. When the British arrived at the Cape in 1795, numerous French families joined the Burghers in the "Great Trek" during 1835 – 1846 away from the Cape and in search of a place where they could live free from the British rule.

Among the French immigrants who arrived at the Cape of Good Hope, was the forebear of my second husband, Willem Herbst. His mother was a descendent of Philipe Fouche, who arrived with his wife, Anne, his son, Jacques, and two daughters aboard the *Voorschoten* in 1688. At a later stage, the Fouche (Foucher) family was included in the great exodus inland, which came to be known as the *Groot Trek* ("Great Trek").

The Fouche family was the focus of my late husband's research, which spanned several decades. Eventually, he solved a well-known conundrum that other genealogists were unable to figure out and that was the connection of Willem Herbst's Fouche ancestors to Jacobus Johannes Fouche, also known as J.J. (Jim) Fouche. He was a South African politician who served as the second State President of South Africa, from 1968 to 1975. He was awarded the South African decoration for Meritorious Service and the Paraguayan National Order of Merit. Fouche was also Honorary Colonel of the Regiment President Steyn.

Willem handed over all his research to the Huguenot Museum in Franschhoek, which made it available to the University of Stellenbosch in the Western Cape. Together with his Protestant faith, this is the significant legacy he left for his family.

Huguenot Memorial Museum Cape Town. Photographer unknown.

There are two reasons why this seemingly unrelated piece of history is included in this book. Firstly, the Protestant faith of the Huguenot Protestants and the Dutch formed an intrinsic part of the culture and way of life in South Africa. At a later stage, large numbers of my relatives joined as German Lutheran missionaries and colonists. It is the protestant faith and European culture that was the glue that kept them together. The Germans identified easier with the Afrikaners, who were mostly farmers in the areas surrounding the German farms and hamlets. When the Anglo Boer War (1899–1902) broke out, most of the German settlers sided with the Boers and joined their local commandos to fight against the British. In his historical account, Dieter Lilje narrates that most Germans remained neutral, explaining that relatives were often set against one another, as some sided with the Boers and some with the British.

Secondly, this story provides the backdrop to another theme of intrigue and betrayal, one that is revealed as puzzle pieces slowly fall into place, and the evidence of the brooding darkness spreading its tentacles across South Africa and beyond becomes clear. See Part III for more information.

PART II

THE LUTHERANS OF GERMANY AND THE CONTROLLED OPPOSITION

A BRIEF HISTORY OF CHRISTIANITY IN GERMANY – DIETER LILJE

The history of the early Christianisation of Northern Germany is summarised from the following two narratives: *Goldene Äpfel in silbernen Schalen (Golden apples on a silver platter)* by J.M. Gehrig and *Heimatgeschichtliche Erzählungen* by L. Harms, compiled by T. Harms.

I love this part of my history. These are the stories I have been looking for my entire life. At last, I see where my entire family and all my relatives come from. In this way, I have managed to obtain a deeper understanding of my faith and the subtlety of deception. The trouble with people who have been displaced from their homeland, whether by migration or by force, even generations later, is their enduring sense of displacement and loss – as if an anchor in their very

DNA has been lifted, never to find rest again. I am not sure if others have found this to be true. While briefly living in Mauritius, I did come across a lady who was studying this phenomenon at university. Up until then, I did not know that it was even a thing. What really brought it home to me was when Willem took me on my first European holiday. We landed at München airport and hired a car to drive through Europe. From the moment that I took my first steps on German soil, I was struck by the realization and feeling that this was home; that I had come home. I have never forgotten that moment. Unfortunately, the closest we came to Hermannsburg, was Lüneburg. My dream is to return to the Lüneburger Heide one day to visit all the villages from which my family originates and where the story of our forefathers had been written.

The mighty Romans were afraid of our brave Germanic ancestors, with their imposing physiques and their shining blue eyes. They were well known for their trustworthiness and keeping their word, their hospitality, and for their aversion to prostitution and adultery. They were heathens, who served their pagan gods and sacrificed human beings. During their numerous battles and wars, they distinguished themselves as enthusiastic and highly skilled warriors, plunderers and robbers. They also came together to enjoy their drinking orgies. They wore only animal skins and diet mainly consisted of meat from their hunting expeditions, roots, acorns and nuts. These were the Saxons from Northern Germany, who conquered England, where they first encountered Christianity. Some of them returned to Germany later to preach the Gospel to the people in the northern parts of Germany. And so it happened that Winfried returned to Germany and baptised more than 300 000 Germans. After him, the two Ewald brothers also came back, but they both died as martyrs. They were murdered by our heathen forefathers and were sacrificed to their gods. There were other missionaries who continued this work among the Saxons – people like Willehad und Liudger, who were supported by the pious Emperor, Charlemagne the Great (died 814 AD), who was Christian.

The Saxons in northern Germany

The northern part of Germany was known as the land of the Saxons and Low-German (Plattdeutsch) was the mother tongue of the inhabitants of this region.[4] The Saxons were subdivided into three sections: the western part, to the west of the Rine River was known as Westfalia; Eastfalia – to the east; and between those two, the Engern or the Anglos. The people from Lüneburg region belonged to Eastfalia. The name originated from the pale colour of their hair, which was called "fal". During the reign of Emperor Charlemagne, the Great (768–814 AD), the Saxons were still heathens. The name "Saxon" is derived from their battle-axe, which was called a "Sachs" – an iron axe attached to a wooden handle. The Saxons loved nothing better than to fight and they were courageous and fearless warriors.

The Saxons worshipped Wodan, who was one of the most prominent gods in Anglo-Saxon mythology. Known as the god of war, wisdom and poetry, Woden played a significant role in the Anglo-Saxon culture, as well as in the Viking culture, where he was known as Odin, Allfather. However, Woden differs significantly from Odin, firstly in that he has both his eyes,[5] while other features about his characterization do not match his Norse prototype.

In this way, Wodan can be viewed as an Anglo-Saxon god, and his story appears to be his own. Unfortunately, no detailed account of Woden and his mythical adventures survives, and some have debated if he was even a god. The earliest English chronicles from the 8th, 9th and 10th centuries claim that he was the father of the Anglo-Saxon peoples, but despite this, Woden was still discussed in the 11th century after the Norman Conquest.

---

[4] My mother tried to teach me a little of the Plattdeutsch she had learned from her grandfather. However, I never got any further than saying, "Hallo, how are you"?
[5] In the Norse mythology of the Viking culture, Odin is known to have stabbed out one of his eyes to gain wisdom and knowledge that was hidden from him.

As a powerful god in Anglo-Saxon mythology, particularly known for his role as the god of war, Wodan was worshipped for centuries. Wodan's name is derived from the Proto-Germanic word "Wōdanaz", which means "fury" or "raging". He was originally a god in the Germanic pantheon. He was associated with other gods, such as Tiwaz (whose Norse analogue is known as Tyr), who was the god of war and justice, and Thor, the god of thunder and strength. Woden was also associated with the goddess Frigg, who was his wife and the goddess of love and fertility. Wednesday is drawn from his name and through this, he has even been associated with the Roman God Mercury.

The earliest written record of Woden is found in a runic inscription of a 7th century brooch located in southern Germany. His next mention comes from Bede in the 8th century, where he is claimed to have been the father of the Anglo-Saxons, whereas Paul the Deacon claims that Woden was worshiped by all the nations of Germania. His name can be seen across the landscape in modern England. Places such as Wednesbury, Woodnesborough and Wednesfield all indicate a link to Woden. Although there are likely many more, the older names have been lost in the record.

> Christianity offers a different set of values and beliefs than those of Woden and the other (pagan) gods. People often found these Christian values more appealing, in that they were not violent and focused on war, but rather focused on forgiveness and clemency. However, this was not an easy transition (Readman, 2023).

It was to Wodan that many people were brutally sacrificed on stone altars, their heads cut off with knives made of flint-stone. To this day, one can still see the so-called "seven stone-houses", built in a square with eight granite rocks, with four entrances and a huge covering rock on the top, roughly 12 km from

Hermannsburg. On such stone altars people were sacrificed, when, for example, the Saxons returned victoriously from war. They would sacrifice up to ten percent of their captives to Wodan and, if they had suffered great losses, they would sacrifice them all.

Charlemagne the Great reigned as a pious Christian Emperor over the middle and southern parts of Germany, France and Italy, which was called Frankenland. Along his northern border, was the land of the heathen Saxons, the archenemies of Christianity. The Saxons continually attacked and invaded the southern borders, looting, murdering and destroying the churches and killing the priests. Charlemagne launched a full-scale war against the Saxons, firstly to protect themselves, but also to convert the Saxons to the Christian faith by force. That is how the terrible war started that lasted for 33 years. The Saxons had two influential leaders, dukes (*Herzöge*) as they were called, because they led their people from the front – Duke Wittekind in Westfalia and Duke Albion in Eastfalia.

In spite of this war, the Saxons did not let up with their invasions, which angered the Emperor, who knew that he needed to teach them a lesson, for peace to return in that part of his kingdom. At the battle at Verden, by the river Aller, he struck and killed 4 500 Saxons, but it was not enough to subdue them. Wittekind and Albion immediately gathered a powerful army to avenge the terrible loss and at Osnabrück and Detmold, they drove the Emperor back in a bloody battle and took 4 000 prisoners along. All of these were sacrificed on the stone altars. We can hardly fathom the horror and the bloodshed, the terror griping the captives and the hysteria spreading like wildfire.

A sudden turnabout occurred in the year 785 AD, when both Duke Wittekind and Duke Albion were converted to Christianity and baptised. At last, there was peace in those areas controlled by the dukes. In other areas of Saxony, the wars and battles continued until 805 AD, when the entire Saxony submitted to the Emperor's authority and converted to Christianity. The Emperor was not only concerned about the Saxons' submission but made sure that his subjects were educated by establishing episcopates and churches. That is how the episcopates of Minden, Osnabrück, Verden, Bremen, Münster, *Paderborn*, Halberstadt and Hildesheim came about. At these centres, mission institutions were established from where the Catholic priests moved throughout the region to preach the gospel to the heathen Saxons. Two leading and loyal missionaries in the service were Willehad and Liudger. Willehad became bishop of Bremen and Liudger bishop in Münster and, in this way, they can be regarded as the apostles of Saxony.

DER HEILSBOTE LANDOLF (LANDOLF, MESSENGER OF SALVATION)

Liudger lived for a long period at Minden and had a profound influence on the local mission institution, which brought about great missionary enthusiasm. One of the monks or priests was Landolf, who was taught and converted to Christianity by Liudger. Having originated from Eastfalia, he decided to return to his home country to preach the gospel to his own people. When he received permission from his superiors, he travelled alone on the river Weser towards Eastfalia.

He took his Bible with him, as well as a prayer book, his fishing net and some supplies of food. When he reached the site where the Aller River flowed into the Weser, he turned into the Aller and rowed north towards Verden and on to the site where Charlemagne had killed 4 500 of his Saxon countrymen, to pray for those who had been murdered there. From there on, he intended to go to the stone-houses, where so many people were sacrificed to the pagan gods. Therefore, he travelled on the river Oertze and ate fish that he caught in the rivers. The direct route would have been much shorter, but very cumbersome, as the interior of the country was thick with forests and deep swamps and very difficult to cross on foot. He had also been told that, when he wanted to visit the stone-houses, he should first visit the Billing, who lived at "Harms ouden Dorp" at the River Horz. This little river is actually the Oertze River that flows through Hermannsburg. As this river seems to jump from one side to the other, like a horse, it was called *Horz* (Oertze), meaning "horse".

Horses were regarded as the wealth of the people, which were not only used for their military expeditions, but the meat was part of their special food diet. A horse with a spotless white coat was considered as holy. These horses were kept in the holy oak forests and used for prophesying purposes by the pagan priests. They interpreted the horse-neighing to foretell whether they would be successful or if they would fail in what they had planned to do, e.g. waging a war. As horses played such a significant part in the lives of the Saxons and in the Lüneburg area, two wooden horses were attached to the apex of most houses, thereby displaying their significance, and from old, a jumping horse was included in the coat of arms.

LOWER SAXONY STATE FLAG

Lower Saxony State flag.

Source: https://img.freepik.com/premium-vector/germany-state-lower-saxony-vector-flag-design-template-lower-saxony-flag-independence-day_471203-1843.jpg

The Billing was the custodian of the law. The word "Bill" is the Low-German and Saxon word for "law". This Billing from the Horzsachsen (Horse Saxons) was called Harm – i.e. Hermann – and he lived in the *Harms Oude Dorp*, which means "Hermann's old town". Today, this is agricultural land, but the farm kept its name.

Back to Landolf's travels: at this point, he was on his way to *Harm 's oude Dorp,* where he was received warmly. Hermann Billing's house was a large hut that was surrounded by an enclosure for the cattle – particularly for the horses – which could graze on the meadows along the Oertze River.

Hermann Billing was not a nobleman, but a so-called "free man" (*Frieling*) and owner of seven big estates. Landolf stayed with the Billing family for some time and preached the gospel to them. When he expressed his desire to preach the Gospel to the entire neighbourhood, Hermann Billing told him that they would first have to discuss this at the annual meeting of the freemen, where such permission had to be agreed upon. He stayed with the Billings throughout the winter and waited for the meeting to take place, which was only scheduled for spring. In the hut on the main estate, the family and all the workers regularly gathered around the fire, where the head of the house told the stories about the old heroes and of their brave forefathers. On such occasions, Landolf was given permission to tell them about Christianity. His joyful witness to his faith touched their hearts. He prayed and sang to them the songs he had learned. Later, some of them would even join him in prayer and singing.

The annual meeting was to take place at the *Sieben Steinhäuser* ("seven stone-houses"). Landolf went to the meeting, being protected by his host, Hermann Billing. The first day they did not get very far, as they gathered at the deep stone quarry (*Tiefen Bruch*), where Landolf witnessed the cruelty and barbarism of his countrymen. At midday, all the free men gathered at the stone altar. The young warriors brought two prisoners whom they had captured during a previous battle. They had to move close to the altar. Two priests came forward with a mistle branch and a sharp knife, made of flint-stone. Mistle plants, which are found in birch trees, are considered as holy. As they did not grow in the ground, people believed that their seed came down from heaven.

After some prayers were sung and directed to the gods Wodan and Thor and to the goddesses Hertha and Hela, the prisoners were laid on their backs on the rock, so that their heads were hanging down at the side and the priests cut off their heads with their knives. When the bodies had bled out, they were thrown into the quarry, where they disappeared into the swamp. Never had Landolf witnessed such a horrifying deed, although he had been captured as a young man and taken into the neighbouring France.

This horrendous human sacrifice was followed by another dreadful scene. Some of the young men brought braid-work (*Flechtwerk*) made from fir branches, which they laid down in front of the altar. They soon returned with a man and a woman, who were accused of adultery. The Billing asked the accused whether the accusation against them was true. When they affirmed the accusation, the family came forward and spat into their faces, after which the man was stripped of his armoury and their hands and feet were tied, before they were thrown into the mirey quarry. The braid-work was placed on top of them and the family, followed by the others would step on it to drown the adulterers in the swamp. Hermann Billing later told Landolf that there were three offences punishable in this way: adultery, lying and cowardice. People guilty of these offences were not worthy of dying by way of a weapon.

Landolf was deeply affected by this experience and said to the Billing, "If you have such a hatred of wickedness and sin, how much more could become of you, once you would convert to Christianity?" On this day, as also on other occasions when human offerings were made, the proceedings ended with a drinking orgy. When everybody was drunk, a big fight broke out. Everyone had his own battle-axe and joined in the fighting and soon several dead bodies were lying on the ground. These bodies were burned and the ashes were buried. The killers were not accused of murder. On the contrary, this was considered as honourable acts that called for respect. Landolf witnessed it all and it spurred him on to preach the gospel of the One True God to these people.

The next morning, after the big feast, Landolf and Billing and the freemen continued their journey to the meeting place at the "seven stone-houses ". A huge crowd that included pagan priests, noblemen and free men had gathered there. After more sacrifices had been executed – fourteen people in total – the relationship between the Saxons and the Franks was discussed.

As Billing's guest, Landolf stood up and requested permission to proclaim the Christian message in this area. Immediately, many stood up in anger and distrust, with some grabbing their battle axes threateningly. On hearing the word "Christian", they were immediately reminded of the neighbouring Franks, who were still their enemies. However, Billing stood up in Landolf's defence and spoke to the crowd, informing them that Landolf was no Frank; that he was actually one of them – an Eastfalian. He went on to explain that Landolf was taken prisoner during the war with Frankenland, where he converted to Christianity and had been a scholar of Liudger, who was known to all as a leader of the Saxon people. Six months earlier, he came from Westfalia, all by himself, returning to his homeland and he had been a guest in his house, he told them. He gave Landolf permission to proclaim the Christian message in his house. He suggested that Landolf should inform the meeting what he wanted to convey to his people. His huge body, noble, courageous and fearless appearance made a deep impression on the big crowd and, in total silence, they listened to him – the first Christian sermon that was held in that region.

Landolf told them how, roughly 100 years ago, around 690 AD, two Christian priests, the white and the black Ewald, came to preach the gospel to their fathers. They were also descendants of the Saxon people and had come from England, but they were not permitted to preach, and they were murdered. They were killed on these stones as a sacrifice to your god, Wodan. They had murdered their brothers, friends and guests, although they had done nothing to deserve death. He continued to tell them that God was still angry with them and that his anger would only subside once they had turned to Christianity. "Your gods are worth nothing. They can't help you", he told them. Where is your oak tree[6] ded-

---

[6] This particular oak tree stood in Verden, next to the Aller River.

icated to your god Wodan? Charlemagne the Great, had destroyed it. Where are your brave Dukes Wittekind and Albion? They are now Charlemagne's friends, Christians. A higher power, the God of the Christians, defeated them". He went on to tell them about the experience of Wittekind and Albion, when they visited Charlemagne the Great in Aachen; how they listened to a priest's sermon about Jesus in the huge church. They witnessed the Emperor walking into the church, taking off his crown and kneeling at the altar and prayed. In the church, they heard the wonderful songs, praising God. Wherever they went, they experienced great love and hospitality from the Christians, which overwhelmed them. The same applied to the Emperor, who even showed his love towards the beggars. He invited Wittekind and Albion to his castle. Fourteen days later, they were baptised by the priest to whom they had listened in the church.

All that and much more, Landolf told the gathering of men. "I am also a priest", he told them and, "I would love to teach you about the Gospel of Jesus Christ, he who forgives and cleanses us from our sins. Will you allow me, to preach to you or do you want to kill me also, just as you have killed the two Ewalds? Here I am in your midst, I am in the hands of God".

Everybody was silent. Hermann Billing stood up and supported Landolf's request, stating that Landolf had been a good guest in his house, and he would love to hear more from him. He encouraged the meeting to give Landolf permission to preach. An old man with long white hair stood up and said, "Throw the lots"! Seven square bars, made of oak wood, were prepared, each with a marking on one side. A priest took these bars, shook them in his hands and threw them into the air. While these bars were being prepared, Landolf prayed to the Lord on his knees: "Lord, let us win this, so that these people may get to know you." The seven bars fell onto the ground, six of them landing face-up and the markings pointing upwards and only one with the markings pointing downwards. Everyone at the meeting was informed about the result, and they shouted: "The God of the Christians won"! Billing went to Landolf and told him: "Now you may go throughout this whole region, and no one will hinder you proclaiming the name of your God. But also come back to my house, I want to become a Christian too".

On their way back to Billing's house, they passed the stone blocks where Landolf witnessed the sacrifice at the deep quarry. He informed Hermann Billing, "Here I want to build my first church". In response, Billing gave him permission to do so, telling him that he would like to be the first person to be baptised in this church. The rocks of the heathen altar were to be thrown into the quarry to destroy all signs of paganism. After three months, the wooden church was finished. On the day that it was dedicated, Hermann was baptised, together with his five sons, three daughters, a big group of his blood relatives and his labourers. The water for the baptism was taken from the Oertze River.

This church no longer exists it was burned down by the heathen Wenden people. A big church has taken its place. This church was dedicated to the apostles Peter and Paul. Together with some helpers supporting him, Landolf continued to live and work loyally in this region, until the years 830–840 AD.

One hour on foot north of Hermannsburg, where the Oertze and Wietze Rivers meet, lies an oak forest where the pagan god, Thor, was once venerated. Landolf built a chapel there to counter and overcome the idolatry. The town Müden established itself around this chapel. Landolf built several similar chapels, where other pagan gods were venerated and, in this way, several villages were founded, including Munster, Wietzendorf, Bergen, etc. Although agriculture was still unknown to most people, Landolf and his people were highly skilled farmers, and he introduced agriculture to the region wherever he went. In this way, Landolf became a benefactor in the entire region – for both the spiritual and the physical needs of the people.

Hermann Billing

Around the year 940 AD – approximately 100 years after Landolf's death – a thirteen/fourteen-year-old boy was tending his father's cattle just outside Hermannsburg, when a magnificent procession of proud knights came along on horseback. When they suddenly left the road and crossed the meadow, approaching him, he was upset, as the meadow was no road, and it belonged to his father. After thinking for a moment, he marched straight up to the knights and told them, "Go back, the road is yours, but the field is mine"! The knight leading the procession, riding high and majestically on his horse, looked down at the boy, surprised that he dared to stand in his way. He halted his horse, delighting in the courage of boy.

"Who are you, boy?", he enquired.

The boy replied, "I am Hermann Billing's oldest son", the boy replied, "and my name is also Hermann, and this is my father's field, and you may not cross it"!

"But I want to," the rider responded threateningly, lifting his spear, "or I will knock you down"!

The boy remained standing fearlessly and replied, "What is right must remain right and you may not cross this field, unless you want to ride over me".

"What do you know about what the law is, boy"?

The boy replied, "My father is the *Billing* ("Guardian of the law") and one day I will be his successor, and no one may transgress the law before a *Billing*"!

The rider responded even harsher: "Is that right, boy, not to obey your king? I am Otto, your king".

"Are you Otto, our king, of whom my father told me so much, Otto Heinrich, the Saxon's son? No, that can't be," the lad continued, "because Otto the King, protects the law, but you are breaking it. That Otto would never do, my father told me".

"Take me to your father, brave young man", the king responded, his face reflecting friendliness and kindness.

"There is my father's courtyard, there you can see him," Hermann said, "but these cattle here, my father entrusted to me, I may not leave them and cannot accompany you. But if you are really Otto, the King, then turn around back onto the road, because the King protects what is right".

King Otto, known as Otto the Great, obeyed the young man, because he was right. He paid a visit to the boy's father, saying to him, "Billing, give me your oldest son. I want to take him along to rear and educate him at my court, he will be a loyal man, and I need such loyal people". Which true and loyal Saxon could reject such a request from his king? When the young Hermann was called from the field, he agreed to go with the King, who reared him as a loyal and capable servant.

King Otto the Great was friends with the pious and well-educated archbishop Adaldag from Bremen, who was known for spreading the Christian faith with great passion and zeal among the then heathen Danes and Normans. King Otto entrusted Hermann in the archbishop's care, and he could not have selected a better teacher. In Bremen, the young Hermann grew into a pious young man. As a reliable and trustworthy adviser of King Otto, Adaldag trained Hermann in statecraft, managing state business, and in handling different weapons.

When King Otto took Hermann to his own court, he realised what a courageous and intelligent young man he had become, just as the King had anticipated. Hermann was also a humble man who showed gratitude and loyalty towards his King; so much so that the King called him "his" Hermann, his most loyal friend, and even his son. What was particularly special about Hermann was that he did not forget his origins and his past. He remained caring and friendly towards the poor and the people in humble circumstances, thereby gaining the respect and love of both the nobility and the less important at the King's court. Climbing the ladder step-by-step, Hermann was made a knight, and he accompanied the King on his many journeys and campaigns. The King even entrusted him with the education and upbringing of his two sons, Wilhelm and Ludolf. Later, he managed the government services to the satisfaction of his King, and he often travelled as Earl – i.e. as judge – through the Saxon country.

The judgement over life and death (capital punishment) was exclusively entrusted to the King and those that he had commissioned to act in his authority. During specific times of the year, the royal judges travelled throughout the country, holding criminal courts, which included capital punishment. The Earl would hold these courts during the day and in the open, with the sentence being carried out immediately.

A story is told about Hermann Billing's honest and upright character that was demonstrated when he was acting as Earl. During one of his journeys as earl and judge, he came to his hometown, *Harms Ouden Dorp*. His father had died some time ago and, as the new head of the family, he leased his seven farms, partially to his brothers and partially to other family members. However, they extended their boundaries unjustly and at the expense of their neighbours, expecting that no one would dare to complain, as they had such a powerful brother and relative. However, when Hermann held his court of justice (half an hour from Hermannsburg), a free man called Kuonrat stood up and accused Hermann's family of having taken half of his land. Deeply saddened and solemnly, Hermann instructed that his family members to be fetched. Kuonrat's accusation proved to be true, and Hermann's family admitted their deceit and guilt. When Hermann heard this, he was moved to tears.

Being a strong and sovereign man, Hermann cried out, "You could do that, although you bear the name Billing?" He fell silent, folded his hands and began to pray. Then he continued, "My brothers and my family members, reconcile yourselves now with God. Today we will see one another for the last time. You are condemned to death. You will have to die. You deserve your death in a twofold way, as you are members of the Billing family". The priest, who was always present at these criminal courts, came forward and listened to their confession. After their contrite confession, he gave them absolution and holy communion. Reconciled with God, the seven men returned to the place of court, where Hermann prayed with them again. After he had committed them to God, Hermann had their heads cut off in his presence.

He spent a sleepless night, fasting and praying on his own farm at the Oertze River. He kept this up, until he was consoled by a priest the next day. Hermann promised God that he would build a church on his farm, which he would dedicate to the apostles Peter and Paul, just as the first church was built at the quarry by one of his forefathers. In the year 958, the foundation stone of the new church was laid. Due to the strict and unbiased way in which he performed judgement and execution – as a man with a soft and pious heart – the people respected and adored Hermann and, when he returned to the King's court, he was received with deep admiration. Otto the Great embraced him and called him his most loyal knight, who served his God and his king with equal loyalty.

In the year 960, King Otto decided to go to Italy in an attempt to settle some disputes caused by the godless Pope John in Rome. However, his beloved country and homeland, Saxony, was situated right in the northern region of Germany, where it bordered the territories of the recently conquered Danish and Slavic people, who had partially become Christians, some in name only, with some remaining heathens and hating Christianity. When he had to decide who was to rule Saxony in his absence, which could take some years, King Otto selected Hermann, who was appointed as the Duke of Saxony and King Otto's representative.

The next year, King Otto began his journey down south. In Rome, he deposed the godless pope John from his office and appointed the pious Leo as the new pope. Otto stayed in Rome for five years. In 962, Leo crowned King Otto as Emperor of the Holy Roman Empire, recognising him as the secular head of Christianity.

One of the Slavic tribes, the *Wenden* ("Wends"), who were still heathens, were known for their severe hatred for Christians. After the Christians had conquered them under the leadership of Otto, their hatred only intensified and, wherever they went, they burned and destroyed everything in their way. Their main goal was to destroy the Christian churches and chapels and to kill the Christian priests. During this time, Landolf's first church, which he had built at the quarry, was reduced to ashes. Eight priests were murdered right there, with others being dragged to the altar at Radegast, where they were sacrificed to the heathen gods.

During Otto's absence, the Wends boldly launched a raid in Saxony, leaving utter destruction in their way. Hermann was in Bremen, when he received the message of the destruction caused by the Wends. With great haste, he gathered his soldiers and attacked the marauding and murdering Wends at Hünenburg. It was only after he had defeated them and pursued the retreating Wends into their homeland, that the Wends surrendered and called for peace. They declared to keep order and to accept Christianity. Hermann began restoring the churches and the chapels that had been destroyed and appointed new priests.

In order to protect the country more efficiently against further invasions and attacks, Hermann built strong fortresses in Saxony, also in Hermannsburg, around which the people, who had managed to escape from the Wends, started to re-establish themselves. That is how Oertzenburg, Wietzenburg and other villages were built. Before his death in 972, Hermann had the great joy of having the newly built church for which he had prepared the foundation on his own farm, dedicated on Peter and Paul day. This church is still standing today, although with some alterations.

In the year 973, Hermann's greatest friend and benefactor, King Otto, died, and later in the same year, Hermann Billing also died. Together with his tithing, he bequeathed almost half of his agricultural fields and meadows towards this church and the parish. King Otto II appointed Hermann Billing's son, Benno/Bernhard, as the Duke of Saxony.

It is from this point that we pick up the story of the Hermannsburg Mission many years later.

THE CRUSADES AND THE HIGH MIDDLE AGES

In order to link the foregoing history to the beginnings of the Hermannsburg Mission, we should look into the Medieval history of the period 1096–1300 CE. During the majority of the so-called High Middle Ages, the Crusades occurred, which were in essence, military expeditions initiated by the papacy to seize the Holy Land from Muslim control. However, prior to the 11th century, the endorsement of warfare was not at the top of the Vatican's agenda. Therefore, it is fair to ask how a dramatic shift in policy came to pass that the popes moved from denouncing bloodshed to demanding it in the Name of God.

The extended military raids[7] stemmed from changes that were taking place outside Europe before the age of the Crusades – primarily the growth and expansion of Islam. Indeed, Christian Holy Wars such as these bear a striking resemblance to the Muslim custom of Jihad, which, by then, had become a highly successful Islamic institution. By translating the idea of a "holy warrior" into Christian terms, the Papacy created a "Knight for Christ".

I am a believer and I believe the Bible is incredibly important. From beginning to end. Have you heard of the Book of Enoch? I'll

---

[7] This is partially clarified by the quotation on the council of Laodicea but also on the previous history i.e. the 33 years of war. All of Charlemagnes military expoilts were in the name of Chirstianity and may not have been openly sanctioned by the pope but not stopped either, as these raids and wars 'were promoting Christianity' albeit at the point of the sword.

explain this to you. The Book of Enoch was well known throughout the Middle East until the [8]*Council of Laodicea. That's when it was excluded from the Canon. At the Council, there were some decisions that took place that were science and government based. Unfortunately, they wanted the book excluded not because of any theology issues. The book of Enoch tells a story, a very important one that is relevant today. One that you're under the heel of today. The Council of Laodicea is also when* [9]*the killings began. It is also in government and those who would wield religious power, were very cruel*[10]*. It is also when they did not act on the words of Christ out of kindness, but they began to kill people who would dare to seek relationship with God by themselves. See, a lot of people don't know that! In other words, they wanted to rule the faith of the world and they took books out that would cause a person to be independent. In fact, in those times, the priests set the policies, and if you thought differently from the priests, you were killed. God expressly forbids the killing of anyone because they didn't believe. So, they tried to revert the 'error of grace' and mercy. We don't take people out anymore and stone them. They tried to bring that back, the old law,*

---

[8] "The Council of Laodicea was a regional Christian synod of approximately thirty clerics from Asia Minor which assembled about 363–364 in Laodicea, Phrygia Pacatiana. The council took place soon after the conclusion of the war between the Roman Empire and the Persian Empire, waged by Emperor Julian. Julian, the last Constantinian emperor, attempted a revival of paganism." (https://en.wikipedia.org/wiki/Council_of_Laodicea.)

[9] Christians killing anyone that disagree with them – Holy wars

[10] The leaders of the church were no longer practicing as Christians with a personal relationship with the Lord Jesus Christ, but rather as wealthy nobles – more a political thing.

circumventing Christ so that they could be Christ on earth. People don't know that.

How can anyone be pleasing to the Most High God? To walk by faith is incredibly important ... those were dark times. Priests were going around cursing people's graves, trying to rule people in death as well as in life. No one was allowed to have a personal relationship with the Lord Jesus Christ. You had to have a relationship with the priest and then the priest would manage your relationship with Christ.

When a man has the power to crush another person, that's the only time they seem to feel like they're empowered. – Anon (Source: Direct quotation from an anonymous podcast).

The Crusades were more than just military exploits, in that they shaped nearly every aspect of life. The popes who promoted the Crusades gained authority to muster an army and send it on a mission. In the end, their venture into military affairs and the employment of armed forces caused more harm than good, ultimately damaging the prestige of the Papacy. By the time of the last Crusade, Europe had come to regard the Pope as just another warmongering king – not as the guardian of souls.

A fundamental change that arose from the Crusades was the growing desire for expansion. Europe was experiencing a population explosion and globalisation was not far behind. Another very important development that followed, was that of banking. Old banking families in Europe and in the Middle East were quick to get involved and expand their trade. Noteworthy here is the establishment of the Knights Templar, who managed the transfer of funds across Europe, financing the various armies and military campaigns. On the negative side, travel resulted in the exposure to new ideas and ideologies, which were brought back to Europe. The esoteric side of Islam, witchcraft and Eastern philosophies, including Alchemy, became popular and spread through Europe like wildfire.

When the Crusades came to an end, new opportunities had to be found for the vast armies of knights, which no longer served a purpose. Greed for wealth and resources, the Crusades, the lavish lifestyle of the Teutonic Knights[11] and the pursuit of their conquests had faded into the past. Crusades were launched in northern Germany and Lithuania, where Catholics were still forcing people to convert or die. The Popes and Emperors of this period often maintained debauched lifestyles. Land grabs were the order of the day and endless squabbles ensued over territory and religion, such as in the Spanish Inquisition.

The English Knights got involved, as did the knights from across Europe. They would travel in large entourages and on their way up north, they would stop at their favourite town or city, where they would spend money, often on artworks, to grace their castles and palaces. The Crusader tourist industry was in full swing, which concluded with a bout of spirited fighting. Afterwards, the weary warriors would make their way back south, or across the channel to their homes, recounting tales of their exploits, until the next year's campaign. These crusades taking a year to complete, from beginning to end, resulted in the origin of the modern day "gap year". The sons of rich noblemen would embark on their own "gap year" adventures abroad, sowing their wild oats, but with far less bloodshed.

However, some young men who could not leave this happy state of affairs to continue. Some of them – including Martin Luther (1483–1546), John Calvin

---

[11] The Teutonic Order is a Catholic religious institution founded as a military society c. 1190 in Acre, Kingdom of Jerusalem. Its members have commonly been known as the Teutonic Knights, having historically served as a crusading military order for supporting Catholic rule in the Holy Land and the Northern Crusades during the Middle Ages, as well as supplying military protection for Catholics in Eastern Europe (https://en.wikipedia.org/wiki/Teutonic_Order).

and Jan Hus (1369–1415) – stirred up a political and religious riot. The popes in Rome did not take kindly to this, because they were caught red-handed, so to speak, and their lavish refurbishment schemes and grand building designs had to find alternative patronage. They could no longer obtain large amounts of lucre from the poor, uneducated masses scattered across the Holy Roman Empire. Luther made great inroads into the German speaking people by translating the Bible from the original Hebrew and Greek into German.

> *As early as 1517 Luther had already translated parts of the Bible, such as the penitential psalms, the Ten Commandments, the Lord's Prayer and the Magnificat. Melanchthon was astounded by the quality of the translation and persuaded Luther to do a more systematic job. In 1521, while he was forced to stay in Wartburg, Luther translated the* **New Testament** *based on Erasmus's second edition (1517) from the original Greek and inspired by some of the choices made by this humanist in his translation to Latin.*
>
> *In 1523, he translated the Pentateuch, and, in 1524, the Psalms based on the Hebrew* **Old Testament** *and the Greek translation of it – the Septuagint.*
>
> *Then, with a group of translators (Caspar Cruciger, 1504–1548; Justus Jonas 1493–1555; Mattaüs Aurogallus, 1490–1543; who met weekly, he translated all the other books in the Old Testament, including those the Hebraic Canon had not kept because they were not written in Hebrew, but in Greek or Aramaic: The Deuterocanonical books. This great work was completed in 1534. The first edition was soon sold out. Many more followed in Luther's lifetime, among which one was illustrated by Albrecht Dürer and another by Lucas Cranach the Elder. In 1546, 500,000 copies of the whole Bible, published in 93 cities, were in circulation. The average*

price was two florins. (Musée virtuel du protestantisme. Musée protestant. [s.a.] – Martin Luther, Translator of the Bible)

The newly invented printing press[12] proved very useful and made the distribution of the translations faster and easier than the response from Rome. Because they were becoming educated, people were changing for the better and they were no longer illiterate slaves. The greater part of the nobility had a wonderful time under Catholicism: they acknowledged Rome with a nod, while continuing to live exactly as they pleased, making more money and becoming more powerful as they went along. However, let us pause for a moment, because things were about to change dramatically. Because of developments like the reformation movement and the invention of the printing press, there were nobles who not only aligned with Luther but, more importantly, sincerely believed in his message. These noblemen reformed their morals and beliefs, as well as their lifestyles.

However, trouble was brewing in paradise. With the help of the Benedictine Order, Rome plotted its backlash with the creation of the Jesuits and, while Luther and the other reformers were establishing churches throughout greater Europe, the scheming men of Rome were spreading their poison. The introduction of the Jesuits in northern Europe signalled the powerful reaction against Protestantism. The papacy not only halted the progress of Protestantism but, more remarkably, revived an obsolete doctrine – the temporal supremacy of the Roman Catholic Church. This doctrine, which governed almost the entire Europe for centuries, had fallen into decline. How was this possible?

The Jesuits had numerous tactics and strategies, such as the admirable unity of purpose, versatility of character, unscrupulous pliability of conscience, the confessional, the pulpit and the conviction that their first success depended on

---

[12] In 1440, the German goldsmith and inventor, Johannes Gutenberg (died 1468) invented the movable-type printing press, thereby starting the Printing Revolution.

the duration of their order. However, above all, the focus was the education of the youth. They infiltrated every university and established their own schools. They established schools for the poor and arranged modes of instruction suitable for children, while enforcing the practice of catechising.

In 1551, the Jesuits established themselves in Vienna and, soon after that, they obtained the management of the university. Vienna was followed by Cologne and Ingolstadt and, from those three principal points, it spread all over Germany. Their ambition was to rival the fame of the Protestants. In more modern times, similar tactics are being used by the communists, as clearly demonstrated by the forceful distribution of the woke agenda all over the world.

Other, much more horrendous events were also occurring that would have disastrous effects – not only for Germany, but also for the entire world. This will be explored in more detail later in the book.

For the moment, a new challenge emerged to vex the Jesuits – in Hermannsburg!

PASTOR LOUIS HARMS : YOUTH AND WORK (CONTINUED FROM DIETER LILJE)

It was during the time of rationalism that Louis Harms was born on 5 May 1808 at Walsrode, a friendly country and a monastery city in the Lüneburg Heath, Germany. His father was the second local pastor. In the year 1817, Louis Harms was transferred to the village of Hermannsburg. In this famous little village, influenced by the history of the Saxons and the Billing family and, particularly, the courageous and loyal Saxon Duke Hermann Billing, Louis Harms lived as child. At the time, the village did not have a great reputation. The congregation had become wild: alcohol abuse, immorality, quarrelling and fighting ruled their lives and destroyed the time-honoured customs and the lives of the farmers.

Louis Harms was the second of ten children. He had a strong personality and demonstrated a strong determination to achieve his goals. He loved German history – particularly the book *Germania* of the Roman Tacitus, which he took with him on his long walks during which he dreamed of the past. He would sacrifice his sandwich to the Germanic God, Wodan, on a tree trunk. Later, he studied medieval history, focusing on the local history. As a very active child, he had exceptional physical strength, and his mental strength also surpassed that of his peers. He learned to play the piano by drawing a keyboard with chalk on a table, as no piano was available. He had a bright mind and an excellent memory. His mother was a great storyteller, a gift that he inherited from her. He was proud of all these gifts with which he was blessed. One day, he fell victim to a devastating accident. He was skating on the frozen Elbe River, when suddenly the ice collapsed beneath him, and he fell into the freezing water, after which he took ill. He never fully recovered from the consequences of this accident, and he never quite regained his physical strength.

Louis grew up under the strict supervision and guidance of his father and the kindness and love of his mother. His father was a serious theologian, who understood the Bible as God's Word, but did not preach faith in Christ, whom he himself did not know, but rather the rationalistic understanding of religion – i.e. to live out the Christian virtues like honesty and truthfulness. In other words, his father's theology did not leave room for faith in Jesus Christ, the Saviour, and the redemption of a sinner by faith and by grace. These notions were weaned out of the seminaries and universities by the nefarious little men in Rome. Jesus was understood as the teacher of morals – not as the Son of God. This theology of Rationalism was taught by Louis's father. Louis was taught to be obedient, truthful and hardworking and, therefore, he grew up as a motivated, intelligent and hardworking pupil. Louis was tutored at home by his father.

During the years 1824–1827, Louis attended the high school (Gymnasium) at Celle and, until 1830, he attended the University at Göttingen and the University of the Kingdom of Hannover. He was a brilliant student, and he did not only study Theology, but also European literature, the ancient holy writings of Hinduism, the Classics from ancient Greece and Rome, and Philosophy. In order to widen his studies, he also became literate in ten languages. He loved history and studied the sciences of Biology, Physics, Astronomy and Mathematics. He had an excellent memory and accumulated vast amounts of knowledge in numerous study fields.

He participated in one sport only and that was fencing (sword-fighting) – a sport that would allow him to defend his cherished honour. He studied day and night, sometimes not even attending the Sunday services. He studied alone, as the other students' progress was too slow for him. He hated superficiality and he loved science. His achievements, commitment and his virtuous life made him proud. At a later stage, he made the following comment about his pride: "It is terrible, how a human being can deceive himself! Because he did not murder, nor steal or lie, or commit any other immorality, because he lived an honourable and righteous life, he foolishly thought, he was no sinner …". Towards the end of his studies, Louis experienced a turning point. He wrote about this time as follows: "When I realised, looking at the Ten Commandments and through the enlightenment of the Holy Spirit, that I had indeed sinned against God", and that he was a lost and condemned sinner, he wept endlessly, like a child. Only then, did he seek God's forgiving grace and recognized it in the One, sent by God, his Son Jesus Christ, the Saviour.

The realization of Louis can be expressed in the following words: "Salvation is found in no-one else, for there is no other name under heaven given to men, by which we must be saved, but alone in the name of Jesus Christ" (Acts 4:12). This experience opened the way for him to face other believers, leading the way for him to evangelize the lost. His entire life became the fruit and witness of his faith, a full commitment to his Lord, and a renunciation and denial of this world and his own ego. He held on to the Word of God as it speaks in law and gospel and with firmness, preached repentance. People accused him of being legalistic and following the Commandments too closely. He countered such accusations by saying: "If I would preach, that man could earn his salvation by keeping the commandments, or if I would set up new self-conceived rules and commandments, then I would be a false preacher. But I preach nothing but Jesus Christ, the Crucified, for your salvation, and that the fruit of your faith and the proof of your love and gratitude towards the Lord demands of you, to strictly live according to what the Bible teaches and not what human beings have conceived or invented for themselves". This he would continue to proclaim, until his very last breath and that it was the devil that was trying to tempt one to be disobedient and undisciplined, to live contrary to God's Word and so seek to rob you of your salvation.

Louis's love for the Lord governed his entire life. His heart was enriched through his love for Jesus, and he reached out to numerous people. Based on his deep love for and empathy with the poor and the sick, the prisoners and the lost, he sought, visited and assisted them personally and, wherever he could, he cared for their physical and spiritual needs.

The day when the words from Acts struck his soul – "Salvation is found in no-one else, for there is no other name under heaven given to men by which we must be saved, but alone in the name of Jesus Christ" – Louis could not sleep. He continued to hear a voice addressing his soul: "What have you done to assist so many lost people?" The next day, he went to other believers, begging them, "We have to do something for the poor heathens". That was the beginning of the Lauenburg Mission Society. Starting in Lauenburg, followed by Lüneburg and Hermannsburg, Louis's enthusiasm lit a fire for the heathen mission. He almost became a missionary himself. On 27 March 1844, he wrote, "I wanted to go to the heathens, but twice the Lord prevented me from going"[13].

For 14 years, he remained an intern. This time of waiting and testing served as a personal process of cleansing and verification. He mastered the art of

---

[13] Quotations from Louis are from his memoirs.

patience and did not lose trust. In the spring of 1844, the Church Council in Hannover declared him a supporting preacher to his father in Hermannsburg. By the decision of this Council, Louis could stay at his home, where God had called him for a greater service.

In 1849, after the death of his father, Louis was inducted as pastor of the Hermannsburg congregation, on the 21st Sunday after Trinity. Everything he thought and did was influenced by one question: "Lord, what do you want me to do? What can I do for you?" In this way, the Hermannsburg Mission began – the mission that (in the words of Pastor Harms) was unwanted, uncontemplated and invented, not formed, having at its source faith in and a deep love for Jesus Christ.

THE FINAL DAYS OF LOUIS HARMS

The last years of Louis Harms's life were marked by hardships, but such times serve to deepen and strengthen the faith. For the Mission Society, these hardships had a strengthening effect: like a tree in a gale-force wind, it deepened its roots to secure itself. It had become necessary for the missionaries to learn this, under the leadership of the new superintendent, because their spiritual father (Louis Harms) had become so weak that he, as everybody else, had to think of his imminent death. In 1862, he wrote to his friend, "Since 4–5 weeks I am so weak, that I can only continue with my work without much effort and I am no longer in a position to travel …". His rheumatic fever had advanced, affecting his brain. However, after a few days, his condition improved considerably.

Despite his illness, Louis continued to perform his duties, even at the time when he was bed-ridden with smallpox (*Blattern*). To the very end, he remained closely and compassionately connected to everything that the missionaries experienced – their work and struggles, their joys and sorrows. It remained of utmost importance to him that the missionaries kept to and remained loyal to the goal of the mission. In his last letters to the missionaries, he continued referring to the dedication to the missionary goal and, in this way, he managed to write to Superintendent Hohls on 29 June 1865: "I have already written too much; I no longer cope because of my weakness; so I finish off and commit all my treasured children, big and small, black and white, man and woman, into the loyal hand and heart of our highly-praised Lord Jesus Christ. O, children, children, believe, love, be loyal and obedient; let everything you do, be a total commitment of your heart! May God give you his Spirit of Grace and of prayer"!

In his last letter to the missionaries, dated 27 July 1865, Louis wrote: "I do not want to hide from you, that I am becoming very weak and that my strength has deteriorated greatly. Yet, I do still hold all services and God bestows His grace on me for that. My mental strength is not yet broken. I can no longer walk to church and need to be pushed there on a wheeled cart. I have reserved the right to appoint my successor in the Council of the Mission, without anyone interfering. So, I inform you that, when I have passed on, I have appointed my brother, Pastor Theodor Harms from Müden, as my successor....". In closing, he said, "Should I have, which I don't believe, wronged anybody, then may he/she please forgive me, as I forgive with all my heart everyone that has hurt or grieved me ... Now I commit you to God our Lord and into the hand of His grace. I want to pray for you until my very last breath as a loving father for his children and pray you will not forget me in your prayers. I greet and kiss you in the name of the Lord Jesus Christ. Jesus Christ yesterday, today and the same in eternity!"

After a brief improvement in his condition, he managed to write the following to Hohls on 30 October: ".... Now I can no longer; my hand does not want to hold the pen; and it is already late. My faithful God bless you all, my dear children, all of you, young and old, white and black! May God make you loyal, loyal, loyal – in the large and small matters ... God make you humble that you do not seek your own, but that which is Jesus Christ's! And God give you sincere love, that you may remain at peace with one another, for the Lord's sake, who is a God of peace! God bless you all in body and soul, now and forever! Amen".

He preached on the following Sunday and, after conducting a funeral on Monday, he performed his last service on Wednesday. After this, he could no longer serve, and his strength deteriorated fast. The strenuous work and the serious ailments of rheumatism and asthma, smallpox and, finally, dropsy (*die Wassersucht*) had consumed his body. His last heard prayer was: "Help us always, O God, make us ready for everlasting joy and bliss. Amen". He passed away at 3:30 AM on Tuesday, 14 November 1865.

On 17 November, Louis Harms was buried at the Hermannsburg cemetery. The General Superintendent and Oberkonsistorialrat, D. Meyer, from Celle held the liturgy in the Church and Oberkonsistorialrat, D. Niemann of Hannover, sent by the King, held the first sermon on Phil. 1:21. The congregation of Hermannsburg, so he said, was mourning a faithful pastor; the church was mourning a brave warrior; and the mission, one of its first leaders. A large crowd of children felt orphaned: their dear father had to be buried. His brother, Theodor Harms, delivered a heartfelt funeral sermon based on John 17:3; a scripture that was to become the guiding light of his new life.

After the funeral, the Abbot, D. Uhlmann, wrote the following about Harms: "Louis Harms, through his mighty sermons, started a spiritual awakening or revival within his own congregation and far beyond, as Northern Germany had not seen before". In his essay on Louis Harms in *Real-Encyclopaedia for Protestant Theology and Church*, Uhlmann wrote: "the Hannoverian Church has been richly blessed by Harms' activity ... His self-sacrificing love in his service to the Lord was the secret of his life, and the strength of his work"[14].

---

[14] As described by Dieter Lilje – original source not available.

Establishing the Mission and Mission Seminary

The Beginnings: 1844

After initially supporting his father as assistant preacher in Hermannsburg, Louis Harms became the full-time pastor of the congregation after a few years. He knew how to address his parishioners in such a way that the coldness of Rationalism was scattered like chaff from the wheat, so that they willingly listened to and followed him. He never needed to ask support for the poor and needy, as they gave him everything, without prompting. However, he was ridiculed by the ministers of the neighbourhood, who followed Rationalism. Even the administrator of this district urged his superiors to get the police to stop the people from attending the worship services, so that the congregations would not become impoverished. This was, of course, in vain. More and more people came from far and wide to listen to the preacher. "And what kind of man did they find? A large, gaunt figure, with traces of serious battles on his face, with a taciturn mouth, and wonderful eyes, that penetrated deep into one's soul. Plain and simple, straight and rough, firm and unequivocal and yet, of mild kindness and winning love, enabling simple folk to soon trust him and the kids running up to meet him and hang onto his hands". In the evenings, he gathered his community in his thatched home or, in summertime, outside the window of his study. There, he would read to them from an ancient Low German Bible, addressing them in either Low or High German, while they all listened intently, because he was a such master storyteller.

Since the congregation had been awakened to a new level of holiness, sending missionaries into the heathen world followed almost automatically. Numerous gifts were sent to Hermannsburg for this purpose. For example, a farmer donated his farm, so that Louis Harms could establish a mission institution in this house.

His brother, Theodor Harms, took over the training of the young mission students. As sons of farmers and artisans, most of them came from the Heath, and they were deeply gripped by the desire to preach Christ to the heathens. Their rigorous education alternated between physical and spiritual work. Apart from languages, religion, geography, masonry, carpentry and gardening, their studies also included music – particularly the playing of brass instruments, which were practiced zealously. As the teacher, Theodor Harms participated in everything, including the physical tasks. This was how the first missionaries were schooled, so as to prepare them to be sent off after a few years.

Louis Harms had to face the problem of how to send the missionaries into the mission field. The costs of travelling from one continent to the other were exorbitant. The Harms brothers received a proposal from a shipbuilder at Bremerhaven to build a fully equipped brig[15] for an amount of 14 000 Thaler. This ship would make it possible to transport the missionaries and, during the intervening time, cargo could be transported to earn money. This was accomplished, but not without considerable controversy and criticism. The beautiful brig was named the *Kandatze* (Candace), a name that was purposely chosen to endear it to the Muslims in East Africa, considering that Louis Harms's main vision was sending the missionaries to the Galla people.[16] It would be interesting to establish if this was the first ever purpose-built mission ship.

---

[15] A brig is a sailing boat with two masts that was big enough to take 20–30 men and their luggage.
[16] The Galla (Oromo) people are a powerful Hamitic ethnic group, native to the region of Ethiopia and parts of northern Kenya.

The Candace Ship 1835-1871 for the Hermannsburg Mission. Painting by Alexander Scherzer.

Source: German South African Resource Page. Ship's Passenger Lists Hamburg to Africa. https://safrika.org/schiff_en.html

The Hermannsburg Mission was the personal creation of no other than Pastor Louis Harms in Hermannsburg. The roots of his decision lay in the circumstances and events of his time and was related to the decline of the North German Mission. The Mission House of the North German Mission had closed and the attempt to have it transferred to Bremen had failed. That was most likely one of the reasons for Harms's suggestion to open a mission house in Hermannsburg. Although his Lauenburg friends also encouraged him to do so, that was not the main and actual driving force behind his decision. The real driving force was his life of faith and the loving response of his congregation. As they offered gifts of love, thereby increasingly filling his hands, more and more young Christians made themselves available for the mission work with the heathens.

THE MISSION HOUSE

In his first annual report, dated 20 July 1851, Louis Harms wrote, among other things: "See, we needed a mission house here; for the Lord had called so many young men from our own congregation, and from far and near, for missionary service, that we could not withhold our helping hand from them, to prepare them for this service and to make them proficient, by teaching and by practical experience, within the congregational life. How could we then prevent the Lord?

No! We had to thank and praise Him and realize that this is the way, how the Lord reveals to us his salvation and to put our hand to the plough and not look back ...".

Harms had approached various mission institutions, requesting them to recruit and train his young students, but to no avail. One evening, the twelve young men were gathered in Harms's room, where he told them that they had been refused admission at the last institution where he had requested admission for them. They responded and said, "God knows that we have a burning desire to become missionaries to the heathens; why don't you see to it that we are instructed and then sent out?" For days and nights, this idea did not leave Harms with any peace. Finally, he decided to buy a mission house with God's help, or if he could not buy one, to build one that could accommodate the young students and to have them instructed in the mission work.

The church, school and parsonage are located on the western shore of the Örtze River. At that time, there were only a few farms for cultivation on the eastern side. Because of the quiet and peaceful surroundings, it was an ideal location for the mission facilities. Beyond the drift, through the Örtze and across the long wooden footbridge, which spanned the river, the landlord, August Witte, had a farm with a suitable new residence. Harms bought this house with the farmland, garden, fruit farm and the moorland in Sunderfelde – a total of 20¾ acres – for 4 000 gold florins. There was only one problem: Harms had no money. He said to himself, "As I said in my heart, I want to buy the house; may God provide the money". God gave him the congregation to help to provide. On 10 May 1850, Harms paid the last instalment with 200 Thaler gold and, on 9 December 1850, he was able to buy another two morgen heath-lands for 160 thaler from the widow Witte. Typical of its era, the farmhouse featured a central living room, flanked by smaller rooms. The layout included a centrally positioned stove, a wastewater drain and a connecting passage to the barn.

The house was probably suitable for a farmer, but it would not serve well as a mission house, and the interior had to be reconstructed. The refurbishment would be done by the students, under the guidance of their teacher. Because the students were not able to move into the house yet, they boarded with the Witte family. Over the front door, the pupils painted a cross and, under the cross, they wrote: *In hoc vinces* ("Under this sign, you will become victorious"). With the exception of Bading, Ludwig and Hansen, all the students were children from the Lüneburg Heath. The others were Müller, Schütze, Schröder, two Hohls brothers, Kohrs, Stegen, Meyer and Struve.

Louis Harms appointed his younger brother, Theodor Carl Friedrich Harms, as inspector/instructor at the Mission House. Like his brother, Hermannsburg was Theodor's native village, which he loved very much. Theodor was born on 19 March 1819. His father had prepared him for the high school/gymnasium. During Easter 1835, he moved to Lüneburg for his tertiary studies. On 15 March 1839, he passed his matric examination, after which he continued his studies in Theology in Göttingen, until 1842. As a schoolboy, he had already become a believer. From 1842 to 1849, he was a home tutor at the Forestry Inspector Ohrt in Lauenburg. In 1852, he married Ohrt's daughter, Charlotte.

On 12 October 1849, when Louis Harms was inducted as pastor of the Hermannsburg congregation, the Mission House was also dedicated and, as the instructor, Theodor Harms moved in the next day.

The conditions for acceptance at the Mission House were as follows: The student had to be between the ages of 22 and 25; he had to be free from military service and had to have parental consent for missionary service. However, the main conditions were that he should be a believer with his whole heart; devoted to the Lutheran Confession; and he had to have the "necessary gifts". Harms also expected each student to stay in the local congregation for one or two years, prior to their studies, so that he could get to know them personally and establish their suitability for the missionary service. During this time, the student had to earn his own living.

The first Mission House began with a vibrant and joyful sense of community. The students reconstructed the house and, when they could move in, their daily life became an intimate, blessed and joyful one. In the biography of his brother, Theodor Harms (p. 79) writes as follows: "I, (T. Harms) had the task to teach the pupils in Scripture, the Confessions of the Church and the elements, which were to serve the understanding of Scripture, and to alternate their studies with physical labour, to keep them healthy and to help them to enable themselves in the land of the heathens. The only foreign language that I had to teach was English, as almost no missionary could manage without this language. Many shook their heads and said: 'What effect will our simple farmer boys have as missionaries? But we did not let ourselves be misled; we trusted the living God and knew the strength and ability of our Lüneburger Heath farmer boys. It gave me huge pleasure to share the physical work with my students. While working, we discussed, learned by repetition, and sang!" (Harms, [s.a.]b).

The timetable for the mission seminary for the first year is available. At 6 AM, it was time for morning worship, followed by personal chores until 8 AM time. Every Monday and Friday, 8–9 AM, were dedicated to the interpretation of Romans; on Tuesday and Thursday, Genesis was studied; and Wednesday and Saturday were dedicated to the study of Dogma. From 9–10 AM, for five days, Church History was studied, and on Friday, the German language was studied. For two days, 10–11 AM, German was studied, and for three days English was studied. On Wednesdays, a worship service was held, and during the time of Lent, the service was held on Fridays. The time leading up to lunch at 12 PM was designated for personal chores. After lunch and until the so-called Vesper bread, the students had to do physical work in the garden, on the fields, in the house, or in the workshop. The workshop was established with a workbench and a forge for wrought-iron work. At 4 PM, teaching resumed, with two hours being reserved each of World History, Geography, Arithmetic and practicing a brass band instrument.

Supper was at 7:30 PM. From 8:30–10 PM was dedicated to either singing practice, reading and speech practice, or Bible study and, on Fridays, time was set aside for an open fraternal meeting. Saturdays were reserved for the interpretation of either the Gospel or the Epistle of the Sunday to come. In the first year, there were numerous History lessons. In the following years, there was a greater emphasis on Bible interpretation and Dogma, followed by practical theology. They also had to practice preaching and giving catechism classes.

Concerning the theological basis of the training at the Mission House, Harms said: "With our mission house, we stand on the solid ground of our Lutheran Church, whose cornerstone is the Lord". In his second mission report, he emphasized that the missionaries should leave, as "Lutheran Christians and servants of the Church, to bring the glory of our worship, the pure doctrine and the pure sacrament of our Church and the power of our song, to convey these priceless treasures of our Church, to the heathen brothers". Being closely associated with it, Harms always placed the justification by faith in the foreground, as well as the correct doctrine of the sacraments, the Holy Baptism as the cleansing regeneration and the Holy Communion as the true Body and Blood of Jesus Christ.

On 16 February 1861, Louis Harms wrote to a missionary friend, "The Church is nothing but a communion of believers, and everyone across the world who believes in Jesus Christ, belongs to her and will certainly be saved, whoever it is. While we now, on the one hand, hold on to general brotherly love as part of the one holy Christian Church with all its believers, we also, on the other hand, hold on to the orders and regulations of our particular church." He wanted to hold on to brotherly love, because they were all of one faith, although not of the same denominational confession.

The students participated in all church services, Bible studies and Mission hours. In the teaching of Catechism, they were expected to stand among the youth in the Church and answer the questions. On Sunday evenings, they attended meetings or visited in the homes of the congregation. Members of the congregation often visited the Mission house and brought gifts, food and bedding, at times even participating in the choir practices, conducted by Inspector T. Harms. The playing of brass instruments was of great importance and particularly favoured by Theodor Harms. As something entirely new in the Lüneburg Heath, it made a significant contribution to the upliftment of the community and spiritual life; particularly during Mission hours and at Church festivities.

The students did not live a secluded life in the Mission house. They not only learned from books, but also from life and experiences, getting to know the great diversity of people, groups, classes and ranks. They learned to communicate with them and how to behave in different groups. Through the ecclesiastical customs and discipline and their faithful prayers, the community supported them in their training. It was a rare community of faith and love, worship and prayer; of work and celebration; of joy and suffering.

In their second year of studies, Hansen, one of the students, fell ill and died in September 1851. In April 1853, another student, Stegen, died from tuberculosis (*Schwindsucht*). Two students were asked to leave the Mission house, because they refused to comply with the rules of the house. After four years of training, the students had to take their examination, which also served as a test of the capabilities and efficiency of the training at the seminary at Hermannsburg.

With great tension and apprehension, the Harms brothers, their students and all the friends of the Mission anticipated the results of the examination, which was conducted at the Church Council in Stade, as the Hannoverian Church Council could not accommodate the examination. The students submitted their written work, which was followed by the oral examination on 14 and 15 September 1853. What great joy there was when all eight students passed! The examiners commented highly positively on the examinations and training at the seminary. They expressed the following verdict: They received a true theological education. Consequently, every student was granted an honourable certificate. All could return to Hermannsburg with a joyful heart. The ordination of the first missionaries – six for preaching ministries and two for the catechetical ministries – was held on 16 September 1853 in the St. Wilhadi Church in Stade. After Pastor Harms held a sermon on the mission work, the ordination was led by D. Koester, assisted by Pastors Eickenrodt and Westphalen.

Sending out the first missionaries

On 20 October 1853, the first eight missionaries and eight colonists were sent out on the Candace. Immediately thereafter, the second group of young students stood ready to be taken up for their preparation as missionaries in the Mission house. Twelve candidates were chosen, although many more had availed themselves. With these 12 male students, the Harms brothers went to Church. After a sermon based on Romans 10:13–15, held by Louis Harms, he told them that he was their father now and they were his children. He asked them warmly to become engaged with the Lord Jesus for as long as they were in the Mission house; to avoid thinking of any other betrothals, but to focus on how they need to prepare themselves for the service of the Lord. At the altar, they vowed before the two Harms brothers with a handshake that they wanted to fulfil their obligations in loyalty, love and obedience, with the help of the Lord. They knelt, prayed together and were blessed.

In 1857, as the second group of students was in training, the Mission encountered a severe setback. – The Müden congregation called Theodor Harms to be their pastor, because their pastor, who had become very old and ill, wished to go on pension. The Church Council in Hannover agreed to this request, and Theodor Harms felt obliged to accept this calling.

Despite Theodor's departure being such a great loss to the Mission, Louis honoured his brother's decision, although he would have preferred him to stay, and he was of the opinion that Theodor himself would have liked to stay too. The students were grieving as they had not completed their studies. As the pastor of the Müden congregation was still well enough to continue with his work, Theodor did not have to move to Müden immediately. In this way, the lectures could proceed, and the students could complete the course under his leadership. After passing the examinations and after their ordination, these students, together with the colonists, were sent out on the *Candace* on 2 November 1857.

By 26 November 1857, the third group of students had already been enrolled at the Mission. *This third student group included my Great-Great Grandfather, Johannes Friedrich Theodor Fröhling.* This third intake included more students, as Louis Harms did not wish to turn away any applicants. Therefore, he took in 21 students, to which three students were added later. With a total of 44 people living at the Mission house, the household was huge. Louis Harms called on Baustedt, the rector and assistant preacher from Rodeburg in Schaumburg, who was closely linked to the Mission, to become the new inspector/lecturer of the Mission.

By the end of 1857, Louis Harms had bought an additional 80 acres of land from the Meyer brothers. At this point, Harms had collected enough money to make the full payment of 4 000 thaler gold for the land. His intention was to use the purchased land to establish a refuge for released convicts. The plight of prisoners had deeply touched his heart, and he intended to provide them with work and pastoral care. The establishment of this refuge for the released prisoners filled Harms with great joy. No mission funds were used for this new development, and it was not long before the refuge could almost maintain itself.

After passing their examination and having been ordained, the third intake of students was sent out with the Candace on 13 November 1861. Immediately, 24 new students were accepted for the fourth intake, although this number did not reflect all those who had volunteered. Numerous volunteers had to stand back. *From this group, the following students are persons who will be mentioned in the reports of JHC Lilje: Leisenberg, Stoppel, Flygare (Sweden) and Hansen.*

The Second Mission House

In the early days of the Mission, the students were mainly sons from the Lüneburg Heath. However, by 1861, young people were streaming to Hermannsburg and to the Mission from all over the country. This strong inflow urged Louis Harms to consider how he could accommodate these large numbers of applicants. Because the annual surplus provided the funds for building, a second Mission house was built, where an additional 24 students would be trained, just like those in the old Mission house. A new teacher was employed, and 48 students were being trained simultaneously, which made it possible to send out a student group every second year. Some viewed Louis Harm's expansion of the Mission as madness and fanaticism. However, Louis was convinced that he had made the changes because God instructed him to, and because financial gifts made it possible to build the new Mission house. – "God gave it to me, so I built it". In 1862, the students could move into the new Mission house. The older students moved into the new house, and the young brothers were placed in the old house, under the supervision of the more experienced inspector, Baustedt.

In 1882, my Great Grandfather, Friedrich Beherends Schumann from Nesse in Ostfriesland entered the ministry. He was destined for the Zulu Mission, and he arrived in South Africa in 1887 to assist the ailing Missionary Fröhling.

This brief yet captivating history of the birth and founding of the Hermannsburg Mission clearly portrays the distinctive German influence on life in South Africa – attending church, listening to the brass bands playing at special occasions, the food, the language, the culture. It was such an integral part of our life and our celebrations. As a child, I would read the Scriptures with my mother every night, before going to bed. I was fascinated to read that Louis Harms was so keen on prison ministry; yet I never saw any of that back home in South Africa. Harms was a pioneer in numerous way. I would love to have sat at his feet and listen to his stories; to find out more about this ministry and what had become of it. I have a strong personal interest in prison ministry, but I will get back to that in my personal story.

My grandfathers were only teenagers at the time, but after meeting Harms and listening to his services, they were already contemplating missions to Africa. Harms offered a renewed sense of hope at a time when the Industrial Revolution (1760–1840) had deprived so many artisans and farmers of hope. No wonder folk came from near and far to Hermannsburg, where they were offered the possibility of an adventure into a brave new world where they could make a difference. Apart from offering the opportunity to be well educated, the Lüneburger Heath was alive with the Gospel and loaded with potential. The toll on parents, who lost their sons, and so many in a single community, is almost incomprehensible. Most of them would never see their children again. Yet, for the sake of the Gospel, these parents freely gave their permission for their children to go. I still wonder how many mothers cried quietly in their pillows at night.

I have a book entitled *Hermannburger Missionare in Südafrika* ("Hermannsburg Missionaries in South Africa"),[17] which lists 221 missionaries with mini-biographies and photographs, in alphabetical order. This number should be multiplied two or even three times to include all the colonists who came with them. Although those stories are not listed or narrated, they are a part of my history. Without them, the mission would not have been successful. These missionaries were distributed across 126 missions – from Natal to as far North as Botswana.

---

[17] Pape, H. 1986. *Hermannsburger Missionare in Südafrika: 221 Lebens und Arbeitsberichte mit Bildern: ein Beitrag zur südafrikanischen Missionsgeschichte.* Eigenverlag.

If we include the women who came from Germany to marry the missionaries, we add another large number of families who greeted their beautiful daughters at Hermannsburg or Osnabruck, never to see them again. Most of these women were chosen as wives for the missionaries by the Mission, and they had to undergo some form of training before they were sent out on the missions. Most of them had not met their prospective husbands before. They wrote loving letters to one another, until their ships sailed. Those who died in childbirth were replaced by other willing brides from Germany. It is not clear how many grandchildren were born in Africa, who never met their grandparents in Germany. Each family counted the personal cost and made peace with it.

The spiritual awakening that swept through Lower Saxony, kindling a deep personal relationship with their Saviour, our Lord Jesus Christ, was profound, Yet, unfortunately, the wider world remains largely unaware of it. A missionary organisation originated that was ahead of its time, with its own seminary, purpose-built ship, prison ministry and the willing support of a nation. Descendants of this mission have written numerous biographies and accounts, the sheer abundance of material being far too extensive for the scope of this book. Later, the mission expanded to other parts of the world, including Central Africa, America, India and *Australia*. Everywhere they went, they made a lasting impact. University students study them and refer to them in dissertations and theses dealing with religious and cultural impact on nations. No, the end of this mission is nowhere in sight, as the stories are still unfolding, even to this day. Doc was right when he told me that day in the bookshop that every subsequent generation is adding to its richness.

> "Practical atheism is **believing** God exists but **behaving** like He does not" – Vlad Savchuk (https://x.com/vladhungrygen/status/1779192833842589976).

Question: Do you suffer from God amnesia, or do you suffer from world amnesia? To suffer from either is very dangerous. – My own thoughts.

Thanks to my cousin, Carine Nel, these beautiful stories have been collated and preserved. She had direct access to the memoirs, diaries and letters of both Fröhling and Schumann which were carefully collated by her mother. She travelled to Germany, where she expanded her research at the Mission House Archives in Hermannsburg. She also travelled to Nesse to meet with the Schumann family. Her mother had lovingly preserved so much rich material that she could write [18]two books – books that I am happy and very proud to have in my possession. Over the years, I have read both texts from cover-to-cover, and one of them is beginning to fall apart now. I am very happy to share some of these life stories with you. These are the stories we grew up with, in the shadow of two giants of the faith.

Johannes Friedrich Theodor Fröhling – Lüneburg Germany

Friedrich Fröhling, my two times great grandfather, grew up in a small hamlet close to Lüneburg in the Lüneburg Heath. Carina introduces him as "A Missionary – A Messenger of the Gospel in Zululand, 1862–1887." He was a prolific writer of letters, journals and reports, which gives one a keen idea of his thinking.

---

[18] The books are listed in the list of references.

Missionary Fröhling. Image supplied by Carine Nel.

"Lüneburg was first mentioned in medieval records in a deed signed on 13 August, 956 AD, in which Otto I, Holy Roman Emperor granted "the tax from Lüneburg to the monastery built there in honour of Saint Michael". An older reference to the place in the Royal Frankish Annals for 795 states: ad fluvium Albim pervenit ad locum, qui dicitur Hliuni, i.e. "on the river Elbe, at the location, which is called Hliuni" and refers to one of the three core settlements of Lüneburg; probably the castle on *the Kalkberg which was the seat of the Billunger nobles from 951.* The Elbe-Germanic name Hliuni corresponds to the Lombard word for "refuge site" (Wikipedia 2024).

The family was of humble, farming background. His mother, Katharina Dorothea Fröhling née *Meyer*, who came from Hamburg, appeared very strict and imposing. I am not at all sure if she was related to the Meyers on the Gevers side of my family. Although the Meyers pop up repeatedly in my family tree, I know very little about them. In the photograph that I have of him, Friedrich's father, Heinrich Peter Friedrich Fröhling, looks a kindly gentleman.

Friedrich was born on 25 September 1834 in Lüneburg. His parents loved the Lord with all their heart and guided their son in the ways of a quiet, pious life. They loved their son and wanted only the best for him. Being brought up as a Lutheran, he writes in his journal, "The Lord showed me or rather kept me in faith and grace from my youngest childhood onward and I can truly say 'His mercies are new every morning'. He continues, "Praise the Lord O my soul, and do not forget the goodness He has shown you" (Psalm 103:2).

Friedrich grew up in a loving household of two girls and two boys of which he was the oldest. Their days started and ended in prayer, and they were instructed in the Word from a young age. His father enjoyed reading to them and teaching them, telling them stories, and having discussions with them. Friedrich and his siblings were taught the value of obedience, and they were put to work around the house, each performing their share of the household chores. Their parents were, in one word, strict: no back-chat or rebellious behaviour was allowed. It was a matter of doing as you are told and, where possible, before you were told. If you knew what it was that you had to do, you should do it, without being told to. This was one of the greatest blessings for Friedrich and for his adult life.

The Lord, Jesus Christ, was his all and everything, and his love for the Lord consumed his life. He walked with the Lord from the time he woke up in the morning until he dropped his head on the pillow at night. Sometimes, it felt as if the Lord had his arms around him as he walked through the day.

Another great influence in Friedrich's life was Pastor Harms, who, at that time, was ministering in Lüneburg and would often come to visit his parents. Young Friedrich was taught the way of a surrendered life in prayer. It was during school that things would go awry and there came a time of falling away. In the course of his college studies and in his career, he had to face numerous temptations and trials. It was his parents, Pastor Harms and the Hermannsburg Mission conferences that kept guiding him back to the right path.

It was in the summer of 1853, when he attended the Missions Conference at Hermannsburg, that the message of evangelism to the nations hit him so hard that he could not shake the deep conviction of becoming a missionary. He began to pray, asking the Lord to show him the way. The next year, he arrived at Hermannsburg for the Easter celebrations and spoke to Pastor Harms about missions for the first time. Pastor Harms immediately saw it as an interview for application, which was actually beyond the scope of what Friedrich had in mind on that day. However, Harms pressed on and reminded Friedrich that he needed to be free from all military conscription and have the consent of his parents. It took another three years for everything to be worked out according to plan.

When God has his hand in it, you must know for sure that nothing, none of Satan's plans, will be able to derail it. I have seen this in my own life too. It may take time. It may take a long waiting period in the school of hard knocks, as our Bishop Bell in Pinetown was so fond of calling it, but you can bet your bottom dollar that it will materialize. If God has ordained it, that is the end of it and you may as well surrender, because the trips around the mountain can be very painful. I know!

On 26 November 1857, Friedrich started his training. After passing his examinations, he was ordained on 29 October 1861 in Hannover, and on 27 November of the same year, barely a month after his ordination, he boarded the mission ship the *Kandatze* ("Candace"), which had undergone extensive renovations, in order to negotiate the sandbanks of Port Natal harbour on the east coast of Africa.

> "Through Jesus, victims become victors, misfits become messengers, and slaves become soldiers" (Vlad Savchuck).
>
> "Truth is like seeds. We can shoot or sow, hit people on the head or plant in their hearts, Truth has to be served with grace" (Vlad Savchuk).

Friedrich Behrends Schumann – Nesse Ostfriesland, Germany

"Very close to the North Sea, the village Nesse is located on a 5.76 m high mound. During excavations in 1958, they discovered that the wharf had been built by hand. It is elongated and similar to an oversized dike. This is surrounded by a limestone marsh, the Nessmer Marsh. Nesse was founded in the 9th C as a trading settlement. It is thought that the original name was Nas, meaning 'headland'. The current name Nesse appears first in 1408. Today Nesse is in part a rural community and a holiday destination because of its lovely climate and proximity to the beaches. What I found interesting was that it has Ostfriesland Meadow sage – Salvia Nemorosa growing wild. Two such shrubs are growing in my back yard. Who would've thought!" (Wikipedia, 2024).

My Great Grandfather, Friedrich Schumann, came from Nesse. – Thekla Heynke, Carine's mother, wrote a short biography about his life as an introduction to the book *Friedrich & Johanne Schumann: Arbeiter im Weinberg Gottes im Zululand 1887-1923 (workers in the Vineyard of God in Zululand, 1887–1923).*

Missionary Schumann. Image supplied by Carine Nel.

Friedrich, who was born on 7 February 1857, was baptised by non-other than Pastor Harms on 8 March 1857. Like all good folk originating from Ostfriesland, Friedrich was proud of his homeland and culture. His childhood and youth were hard and filled with deprivation, which is why he remained extremely modest and frugal in his personal needs throughout his entire life.

In his biography, Friedrich writes that his father was a worker, but my mother (Ursula Schumann) said he was a grave digger. I am not sure how they came to be in such an impoverished state, but I suspect that the downturn in the German economy after industrialisation had something to do with it. His father was Jan Behrends Schumann, and his mother was Elsche/Gesche Friedrichs Lohmeier (spelled Lohmeyer in some texts). She was the second wife of her husband. Friedrich had three older half-brothers, three sisters and another brother from his mother of which he was the second oldest. They were eight children in all.

His parents worked hard to provide for their large family. Friedrich was sent to school, but at the age of 14, he was removed to help provide for the family on a full-time basis, However, while he was still at school, he would work in the fields in the spring, and he would do the weeding for other neighbours.

In summer, he assisted in bringing in the harvest for the local farmers and in autumn, he herded the cattle. These were his jobs as a young lad before and after school.

He had developed a love for reading since a young age, but because he did not have the financial means to buy books, he availed himself of the local minister's library. He particularly enjoyed the reports and biographies of missionaries. Among these, one stood out – a book that spoke about seven Rheinische missionaries who had been murdered. He was apprenticed to the baker, Hattermann, in Norden and attended the Technikon twice a week. Because he had to get up very early in the mornings and work gruelling hours during the day, he often did not feel like studying at night. The following year in February, his father passed away and a month later, he was confirmed. He continued working at the bakery for a further three years, and in 1877, he joined the Missions Society in Hermannsburg. Apart from attending classes, he was also employed as a worker in the printing press. He had to wait six years before he was sent out as a missionary to Africa.

The waiting taught Friedrich the lessons of patience and submission. His waiting period started as a young boy, when he was already writing letters to Pastor Harms, requesting to join the Mission. However, as previously mentioned, he was the primary breadwinner of his family and Pastor Harms could not take him away from his family commitments. It appears that it was only when Pastor Harms was satisfied that his mother, whom he knew well, was taken care of that he sent Friedrich out. However, this moment came suddenly.

News came from Africa that Pastor Fröhling was very ill and would not survive his illness. He had requested someone to be sent from Germany to assist him. Schumann was bundled onto the first available ship and sent post haste and without examination or ordination, to Natal, where Pastor Fröhling was dying of cancer. On his arrival, Friedrich Schumann was ordained in the church in Hermannsburg, Natal.

Before I continue with the story of Friedrich Schumann's life and work in Natal, South Africa, it is necessary to provide some historical and political context to provide a better understanding of what missionaries experienced in South Africa.

PART III

DEEPEST DARKEST AFRICA

THE ZULU AND THE HISTORICAL AND POLITICAL CONTEXT – DIETER LILJE

In the year 1497, around Christmas, the Portuguese seafarer and explorer, Vasco da Gama (1459–1524) landed on the East African coast as the first European, discovering the land which he would call "Natal". It was only in 1652 that the Dutchman Jan van Riebeek (1619–1677) and Administrator of the Dutch East India Company, took possession of Table Bay, thereby founding Cape Town. Dutch people came to settle in the Cape Colony, followed by the French Huguenots by the end of the century, with whom they mixed. The Afrikaners (the "Boers") had their origin in the union between the Dutch and the French, although their language was closely related to Dutch (Flaams).

In the war between England and France,[19] the Dutch supported France. The Cape became English in 1806 and, in 1814, it became known as the Cape Colony. After the new British government abolished slavery in 1834, large

---

[19] England and France were at war – on and off – from 1689 to 1815. The war only ended when England defeated Napoleon at the Battle of Waterloo on 18 June 1815.

crowds of Boers, who did not accept this new law,[20] migrated to the north in different treks. One of the migrating groups, under the leadership of Piet Retief and *Gert Maritz*, trekked over the Drakensberg into Natal. When Piet Retief attempted to sign a contract with the Zulu King, Dingane, in the King's city on 6 February 1838, Dingane murdered Retief and his men. In 1838, Dingane attacked the Boers, who had roughly 1 000 ox wagons, at Mooi River and violently murdered roughly 700 men, women and children. Because of the intense sorrow and crying, the Boers named the founded settlement Weenen.[21] The Boers soon received reinforcements and assistance from other families who were moving north. On 16 December 1838, Andries Pretorius led them in the battle of Blood River, where they took revenge on Dingane. The battle led to the dethronement and subsequent murder of Dingane, after which his brother, Mpande, was made the new king of the Zulu people. After the Battle of Blood River, Natal was free to be occupied by the Boers.

First arrivals F.G. Farewell (1793-1829) & Henry F. Fynn (1803-61) Port Natal 1824.

---

[20] They viewed the blacks as the children of the Biblical Ham and, therefore, cursed to remain servants and slaves.
[21] The name Weenen means "Place of weeping".

Although there had been British merchants in Port Natal since 1824, they initially showed no interest in this establishment – a situation that changed later. In 1839, the Boers founded the city of Pietermaritzburg and declared the land a Republic, which they named Natalia. However, this republic was not acknowledged by the British and, in 1842, they occupied Port Natal under the leadership of Captain Smith. They regarded the land as British property and the Boers as their subjects, similar to those in the Cape Colony.

Durban Port Natal postcard as it would look like when the settlers arrived.

Although Natal was initially under the authority of the Cape, it was declared an independent colony in 1856, granting it near-sovereign power to govern itself through its own governor, who was appointed by England. As the colonies were governed well, more and more Europeans settled there – particularly Boers, English and German people. During the middle of the century, there were roughly 2 000 white settlers in the Natal colony. In 1848, a ship from Bremen brought approximately 200 Germans, who settled in a colony to farm with cotton in an area that they called New Germany. During that time, approximately 5 000 English settlers arrived in Natal, where they founded cities and towns like Durban, Richmond, Estcourt, Ladysmith, Newcastle, Dundee, Greytown, Stanger and others.

While the Zulu kings were extending their power in Natal, another influential Zulu, Mzilikazi (ca. 1800–1868), was born. Mzilikazi later established the Matabele nation, and became their king. After initially serving under King Shaka (1787–1828), Mzilikazi left with approximately 20 000 supporters and fled north over the Drakensberg. During the period 1824–1830, he waged war against the local tribes, mainly the Tswana people, between the Vaal and Limpopo Rivers, subdued one tribe after the other and widely extended his bloody kingdom.

Because the numbers of the Sotho and Tswana peoples were greatly reduced during Mzilikazi's wars, it became easy for the Boers, of whom some groups had moved north, to penetrate into this territory. Although Mzilikazi fought back and defended his territories, the Boers had superior weapons, and they managed to defeat Mzilikazi in 1836/7, occupying their land. In this way, the indigenous people lost their land and became dependent on the Boers. The large numbers of Boers forced Mzilikazi to move north, beyond the Limpopo River, where he established the capital of the Matabele kingdom, Bulawayo, in the present Zimbabwe.

The missionaries, Moffat and Livingstone, approached Mzilikazi, but they were not allowed to establish a mission station on his land. The Boers established a republic – which they named Orange Free State – on the land between the Orange and the Vaal Rivers that they had acquired in 1848. In addition, four other republics were established in Potchefstroom, Utrecht, Lydenburg and Zoutpansberg. Each of these free states had its own government and president. In order to protect them against external enemies, they founded a federation and, for any necessary matters of mutual importance, a general council.

Britain was not really concerned about them, as their business interests did not suffer in any way. In 1852, a contract was signed in which the Boers were permitted to govern themselves, according to their own rules, laws and regulations and without interference from British government. Before they unified, the republics did not always agree on all matters, which eventually resulted in a civil war. It was only in 1864 that President Pretorius was accepted by all parties, and only then the unified South African Republic of Transvaal was born. The city of Pretoria was founded and made the capital of the new state. It was during this time that the Hermannsburg Mission Society established itself in Natal and Bechuanaland.[22]

> "My grace is sufficient for you, for my power is made perfect in weakness" NIV. In effect Paul is declaring, 'I have complete proof of the reality of the power of Christ, because I know how very weak, I am, and in what an impossible situation I am for continuing my work. In the middle of my physical pain, the onslaught of insulting criticism, the weakness that reduces me to exhaustion, the difficulties in every part of my life, still I find strength to go on, and I know it is not my strength."
>
> "The reality in the life of an evangelist, 'or teller of the Truth', is not pointed out as a series of miracles which remove all sickness, hardship, and fatigue from that person, but a series of hard slogging days of work during which a sufficient amount of the Lord's strength has become evident in the human being's weakness" (Edith Schaeffer 1993).

This beautiful passage has been an enormous comfort to me during this personal trial I am facing, but my momentary affliction is nothing compared to the trials and afflictions faced by those early pioneers.

---

[22] On 30 September 1966, Bechuanaland became the Republic of Botswana.

If there is one book that I heartily recommend to all those who are faced with suffering, it is this one by Edith Schaeffer.[23] She opens her book by quoting a following beautiful poem, written by the martyred missionary, Betty Stamm, before she and her husband were sent out to China:

Afraid? Of what?
To feel the spirits glad release?
To pass from pain to perfect peace
The strife and strain of life to cease?
Afraid of - that?
Afraid? Of what?
Afraid to see the Saviours face,
To hear His welcome, and to trace
The glory gleam from wounds of grace
Afraid of - that?
Afraid? Of what?
A flash, a crash, a pierced heart;
Darkness, light, O Heaven's art!
A wound of His a counterpart!
Afraid of – that?
Afraid? Of what?
To do by death what life could not –
Baptize with blood a stony spot?
Till souls shall blossom from the spot?
Afraid – of that?

---

[23] Schaeffer, E. 1993. *Affliction: a compassionate look at the reality of pain and suffering*. Baker Books.

The Migration from Europe to Natal

From the mid-eighteenth to the late nineteenth century, thousands of Europeans found their way to Southern Africa as part of the mass European exodus to America, Africa, New Zealand and Australia. However, the mass influx of Germans was not enough for the language and culture to survive in a foreign land. In fact, early immigrants had little reason to maintain contact with their fatherland, where they had borne the brunt of political and religious instability, economic crises and the consequences of the Industrial Revolution. Within a generation they were absorbed into their new environment. For example, the Cape was home to German and Dutch settlers and, as previously mentioned, smaller groups from other nations included the French Huguenots.

This assimilation was equally evident in Natal. In 1840, 12 German men settled in Pietermaritzburg, the capital of the Voortrekker Republic of Natalia. However, all of them were married to non-German women and their children did not speak German. If groups of Germans found it difficult to preserve their language, it was even more difficult for individuals. One of the first known individuals was H.E.C. Behrens, nephew of the Hanseatic Consul to the Cape, Maximilian Thalwitzer. Behrens arrived in Natal in 1841, hoping to pursue agricultural interests. When Britain annexed Natal in 1843, Behrens moved into colonial service as an interpreter. He was soon placed in charge of the finance office and in 1850, he became the Secretary of the Natal Fire Assurance and Trust Company. Later he was to become a leading figure in the Natal Bank and Colonisation Company, which became Barclays Bank, currently trading as the First National Bank of South Africa. Behrens's farm, *Perseverance*, would become the headquarters of the Hermannsburg Mission Society in South Africa. (HMS).

Apart from German officials whose primary concern was trade, few immigrants maintained contact with the German states. However, stimulated by an upswing in German classicism and romanticism in the early 19th century, accompanied by the expanding nationalism and patriotism of the post-Napoleonic era, a German national identity began emerging. This was entrenched by the liberal revolutions of the 1830s, but its initial effect was limited to those living in Germany.

Colonialism became a major factor in transferring nationalist sentiments to communities around the world, but the brief colonial experience (1880–1945) of Germany was never a major consideration in British-oriented Natal. In fact, Germans encountered considerable opposition and generally remained neutral during the conflicts between Germany and Britain. Besides, the foundations of German communities had already been laid by this time. The question is: how did the German language and culture survive in a foreign and even hostile environment?

The answer to this question lies in the rise of mission societies; particularly those conducted by Lutherans. "The most powerful factor in the cultural life of the Germans in Natal is the Lutheran Church", W. Bodenstein wrote in 1937 (Lutherans, Germans: Hermannsburgers, 1992). "It stands in the foreground, determining and shaping the essence of that cultural life, permeating the whole fabric as a religious life energy". Various missionary societies were sent to Natal of which the Hermannsburgers, who arrived in 1854, were by far the most prominent. They maintained close contact with their home church, and the ongoing ordination of missionaries insured a fresh influx of German and Scandinavian blood to Natal.

Pastor Louis Harms was particularly concerned with the need to connect the missionary society to the church and to establish an "indigenous church" that would be the counterpart of the home church in terms of doctrine, liturgy, organisation and church discipline. Harms's vision included the eventual establishment of an independent African-controlled Lutheran church, while the HMS approach to the mission ensured the establishment of German communities.

Not all missionary societies assisted in the building of German culture. The Roman Catholics, for example, were more interested with spreading Catholicism than national culture. Furthermore, being celibate, the clergy and members of religious orders had no descendants and were unable to pass on their language from parent to child. Consequently, although valuable work was done in Mariannhill Monastery near Pinetown, this did not lead to the establishment of German communities.

Ironically, the arrival of German Lutherans and the establishment of the German communities in Natal occurred more by accident than design. The HMS, with its unique concept of colonial and communal mission derived from the medieval monastic mission to the Saxons and was destined for the Galla people of East Africa (This was Harm's dream). But for the existence of a tiny German Community on the Natal coast, the HMS may never have entered Natal.

"Life in the sunshine of the old Colony of Natal was an affair made insular and self-centred, if only through the very isolation of place. Few ships called, and those that did were only small coastal traders from the Cape. There was little business, and such agriculture as was practiced, was tentative and exploratory; for none knew what crops the land could most profitably yield, or what manner of livestock would flourish best.

There were not more than 3000 Europeans in all the land at the beginning of 1846, and there seemed to be greater incentive for people to leave the country than to come into it. When Lt. Gov. West landed in Durban, he found 400 Voortrekker family's resident in Natal as subjects. But twelve months later all but 60 of these had wandered away, back across the Drakensberg to Republican freedom in the vastness of the central plains. The British government prejudiced by European style of small, fertile, well-watered farms, it was hard for them to understand a man in faraway Natal who complained of receiving only 2000 acres" (Bulpin 2014).

INGRID HERRMANN

THE BERGTHEIL GERMANS/ COTTON GERMANS OF NATAL (*DIE BAUMWOLLDEUTSCHEN VON NATAL*)

"Europe in the early 19th century was a turmoil as a result of the aftermath of the French Revolution, Napoleonic wars, the effects of the Industrial Revolution and sweeping socio-political changes – which all resulted in a period of uncertainty and intense unrest. The new machines which had begun to revolutionize agriculture and industry resulted in poor health and working conditions for those who had work, but for many others the result was unemployment and starvation. All over Europe, the new technological age had broken the traditional paradigm that had existed for centuries. The result was a radical change in the day-to-day life of every European" (Volker 2006).

Walter Volker (2006) continues as follows: "With new scientific and medical discoveries and improved applied technologies, a population explosion occurred. Diseases which had previously kept population levels reasonably stable, were being overcome, while at the same time infant mortality decreased and lifespans increased with better sanitation, better medical care, broader access to education and higher standards of living".

Not only are my family direct descendants of the Hermannsburg Missions to Natal, but we are also direct descendants of this small splinter group of Germans, who arrived before the missionaries in early 1848. Their story is characterized by great courage, hardship, tough character, perseverance, faith and hope. This demonstrated, as Walter Volker (2006) puts it, "the characteristics of true pioneering people". They, among others, were to lay the foundation of what was to become a highly prosperous developed settlement.

Painting Zulu Beehive Huts.
Source unknown.

As I progressed with the research of this book, I found that God never does things in isolation: He is to be found in the details of everything. I cannot stress this enough in the wake of history being splintered into unrelated pieces of the jigsaw puzzle: divide and conquer is not God's battle plan; it never was. It has always been about Him and His Kingdom. Therefore, we should not be surprised if what we perceive as a remarkable, fortuitous event, has, in fact been orchestrated by God from the start. Take, for example, the French Revolution (1789–1799) mentioned earlier. Very few people know that it was, in fact, a planned event by the nefarious little black men, with the intention of annihilating the French nobility. It is my personal view that all of it was a reaction against the Huguenots. The French nobility had been highly effective in maintaining unity among the people. The actual origin of destabilisation can be attributed to the elitist bankers and Zionist masons/Jesuits, who destabilised Europe for their own ends. However, God used all their evil plans to spread the Gospel into previously unreached places. That is the way of persecution and the extension of God's Kingdom.

How do I know that I am on the right track? Apart from a lifetime of listening to the Holy Spirit, reading and researching, the testing of my faith has been so intense that it ought to have derailed me completely and destroyed my witness. However, the overpowering love of God and His mercies are new every morning, and He lifts me with His mighty right hand every day.

The trouble with some missionary biographies is that they do not always show or recount how much the ordinary man/woman still suffers from intense temptations and trials. Why? For the benefit of those who will face similar trials and tests. This assurance allows us to appreciate the full extent of God's love and grace, enabling us to understand that God truly never leaves us or forsakes us.

> "The parish of Bramsche, which is part of the district of Berensbruck, is located in the Hanoverian jurisdiction of Osnabruck. As part of the domain of Vorden, it used to belong to the ancient bishopric of Osnabruck which after the Thirty Years War ruled in turn by a Catholic and then again by a Lutheran Bishop (*the latter exclusive from the house of Brunswick-Lüneburg*). It changed hands several times in between but after Napoleons defeat was returned once more to become a part of Prussia" (Volker 2006).

This was certainly true for the Bergtheil colonists who ventured into unexplored territory with great uncertainty. Did they have misgivings, fears and anxieties? Absolutely! It is easy to portray their journey as courageous in hindsight; particularly if you are not the one facing the challenges. Apart from enduring a hell-raising voyage around the Cape of Good Hope, most of them travelled with families, including women and children. It is not faith in yourself and in your own strength that keeps you from breaking down. No, it is a faith in something far greater. It is a faith in knowing that your Heavenly Father is the true Sovereign of this world and that He has everything under control and holds you in the palm of His hand.

This little band of German Lutherans came from Northern Germany, fed and watered in Lower-Saxony. The family names listed include at least five whom I can identify as being directly or indirectly part of my family tree – Fortmann, Erfmann, Freese, Meyer, Dinkelmann and possibly Rabe and Schafer. The towns from which they originated, were:

Achmer – Erfmann
Engter – Dinkelmann (Kalkiese) and Meyer (Kalriese/Schleptrup)
Epe – Dinkelmann
Hesepe – Fortmann and Meyer
Westercappeln – Freese and Meyer

That little German community owes its existence to the opposition of the British government to the immigration scheme of a Bavarian Jew, Jonas Bertheil, who established the Natal Cotton Company. He saw the potential of a European settlement along the Natal coast and, when the British and Bavarian government rejected him, he went to the Kingdom of Hanover for support. Approximately 188 people from the Osnabruck-Bremen district accepted his offer. After being supplied with full outfits of suitable clothing donated by an influential and benevolent individual citizen of Bremen, they sailed from Bremerhaven on the *Beta* on 21 November 1847. The ship arrived at Port Natal on 23 March 1848. Durban was hardly an inspiring sight, with its single sandy track into town, about 60 wattle-and-daub houses[24] among the bushes and trees and one building with a flag, which was the abode of the port captain. They settled near

---

[24] Wattle-and-daub" houses are a traditional building style that uses a combination of materials for construction, including wooden sticks or branches and "daub", which is a mixture of clay, straw and sometimes animal dung.

Port Natal and named their new home Bergtheil, later to be renamed as Neu-Deutschland (New Germany).

Bergtheil's cotton scheme failed after the first crops were ravaged by bollworm[25] and, furthermore, the ginning machinery he had ordered from England never arrived. The settlers soon abandoned the cotton in favour of market gardening. Walter Volker (2006) goes into detail of this period in his book. It appears that cotton was not a crop that should have been taken on by poor immigrants, and a warning pertaining to this had been published in Cape Town. When the farmers' five-year contract came to an end, many did not renew them. The fledgling community may well have floundered within a generation, since the immigrants did not maintain contact with Germany and had no vision of a distinctly German community. The arrival of a Berlin Missionary Society (BMS) ensured that the language and religion would continue – for the time being.

Original Lutheran Church.
New Germany Natal.
Now a national monument.
Source unknown.

---

[25] Bollworm is a type of moth that attacks the cotton boll.

Founding Plaque of the New Germany Lutheran Church. Source: https://kznpr.co.za/wp-content/gallery/pinetown-new-germany/New-Germany-Lutheran-Church-Posselt-Road-M32-S-29.47.53-E-30.53.17-Elev-316m-4.jpg

Pastor Carl Wilhelm Posselt (1815–1885) agreed to care for the congregation in New Germany (near Pinetown), on condition that he would be allowed to continue his missionary work. On 19 November 1848, he consecrated the first chapel of the BMS in South Africa. On his arrival, he had to marry four young couples and baptise the babies born on the voyage. He conducted missionary work among the farm labourers in the Valley of a Thousand Hills and, in 1854, he established a second station, Christianenburg, which he named after his first wife, Christiana. This settlement is now part of Clermont, adjacent to New Germany. He also taught Scripture in the little German school that the settlers had established.

However, the influence of the Berliners in shaping the character of the German settlement in Natal pales in comparison to the Hermannsburgers. The BMS did nurture German culture in New Germany, which, in turn, played an important part in bringing the Hermannsburg Mission Society (HMS) to Natal.

THE LIFE OF AN EARLY SETTLER

Posselt briefly reports on this period briefly as follows:

> "At the time that I came to the German congregation, its members were to a large extent very unbridled, among whom many big sins prevailed. Of the sanctity of the Sabbath, they had no inkling. I considered myself forced, with great seriousness and complete determination, to act against the prevailing sacrilege, and the congregation bowed before the Holy Word, if not immediately then at least gradually".[26]

It was a rough, tough life. The settlers had to fashion their own hand-made tools and implements with which to start working the land before Bergtheil arrived a month later with cotton seed. They lived in tents, although they soon started building tiny homes, mostly comprising of three rooms with a kitchen outside. They laid out and planted small gardens with potatoes and other vegetables from seed they had brought with them. They purchased cattle and built *kraals* (enclosures) and fenced pastures for them. Problems arose almost from the start. Large areas of land had to be cleared of thick bush and much of the terrain proved to be unsuitable for cotton. On the positive side, the bush provided valuable supplies of fuel and building materials.

It is at this point that the idyllic part of the story began, which is almost too good to be true. These settlers also had to contend with the animal world and, in those days, wildlife was prolific. All Zululand lay open before the adventurers, and hunters from all over flocked to Natal to go on safaris into the bush to kill … and to be killed.

---

[26] Source undetermined/ verified.

Mpande ka Senzangakhona (1798–1872), who was king at the time, allowed white men to do pretty much as they pleased, resulting in that a slaughter of wildlife ensued. It was a honey-coloured moon that lit the ten thousand hills in a golden age for hunters.

> "Across the Thukela an eager company travelled to explore a wonderland of scenery and game. Their wagons rolled onwards though the bush and the grass, with the crisp air of the morning breezes wiping the last memory of their dreams from the traveller's thoughts. Now a bushbuck would go crashing through the tall grass, crossing the track and vanishing again into the undergrowth beyond. Then a herd of frisky antelopes would scamper away over the distant hills, turning around with an inquisitive look and a whisk of their tails before they disappeared over the summit" (Bulpin 2014).

It is hard for me to imagine the area between Durban and Pietermaritzburg full of animals. In just under 200 years, it has become a sprawling metropolis with farms dividing the capital city of Pietermaritzburg from Assegai in Hillcrest. The Kloof gorge saw its last leopard in the late 1970s.

> To continue: "Flocks of pigeons' wheel overhead, and beautifully coloured birds sailed from bush to bush with their plumage flaming and flashing in the rays of the sun. Here and there a troop of monkeys would peep down from the top of the trees, while hawks and vultures hovered high in the air, and the great crested eagles blinked and plumed themselves on the decayed branch of some bare trunk.

All day the adventurers hunted and traded and explored. It was a carefree careless kind of life, full of excitement and surprise, and the nights were a delight. Then beside some friendly campfire, the wanderers lazed beneath the stars. There they yarned and swapped their tales of triumph and disappointments, with the air full of the smell of tobacco and the African night, their faces ruddy in the fire glow, and the tongues of the hunting dogs red in the light.

Then it was easy to forget all troubles, prosaic inhibitions, wars, peace and politics. Was not the world as vast as the night? Were not the heavens but the product of all the smoke of all the campfires that were ever burnt, with the stars a few lingering sparks? So, they would yarn and roll over and sleep until the first morning star came to knock at the door of night and wake them up. Then the bustle and the packing and the hasty eating would start all over again, so that with Venus, the second star of morning (the lifter up of the shadows and sleepers from the ground), they were ready and eager to be off.

Around these wanderers their lived an animal world of surpassing variety and number. The huge, formidable buffalo would come out of the bush and stand in the trails watching the wagons and the straining oxen with interest and amusement. The Zulu say, 'The buffalo is enquired about from those ahead." It is a proverb of prudence, meaning "forewarned is forearmed". The hunters found him a character to be reckoned with and more than one disturber of the peace of the animal world came to grief on his horns" (Bulpin 2014).

There are endless stories and hunting tales and I would encourage the reader to read *Natal and the Zulu country* by T.V. Bulpin[27] from whom I took the foregoing extracts.

It would not have taken long for the settlers to take to the hunt, just as many farmers did. I have fond memories of my family gathering on my uncle's farm *Tussen Bay* in Zululand, the men decked out in their khaki outfits with leather belts and veld hats. My uncle, Vic *Freese*, was particularly fond of the hunt and smoking fragrant cigars. Oom Solly Maritz (of the famed Voortrekkers) would sink into his favourite armchair after dinner, the paraffin lamp shooting little plumes of black smoke up towards the ceiling, and the rest of the men sitting or standing around, sipping ice cold beers recalling their success or failure.

There would also be memories of snakes of which South Africa has an abundance – *puffadders, rinkhals/cobras, boomslange*, green and black mambas, to mention a few. These would be unwelcome guests to the settlers and for us, even to this day. You had to learn fast how to deal with them, as most of their bites were fatal.

It was on *Tussen Bay* that my mother would take us to visit her sister – particularly during the winter holidays. I think it was late one afternoon, when my brother Eddie, who was a young lad at the time, walked the path through the orchard to the little wooden hut that served as the privy. He had just made himself comfortable when he spied the snake. He shot through the door all the way back to the farmhouse, hardly touching the ground.

The birds are always the first to let you know of an unfriendly intruder, followed by the dogs, who barked like crazy at the sight of a snake. On this particular occasion, it was a *Boomslang* in the gum trees just outside the yard. Panda, my cousin's old English sheep dog, was running up and down, barking, while the birds in the tree were going hysterical. Out came the rifles and the snake was

---

[27] Bulpin, T.V. 2014. *Natal and the Zulu country.* Hatfield, Pretoria: Protea Boekhuis.

soon disposed of. Just imagine the old wattle and daub huts of the settlers and the poor protection they provided against the snakes.

In summer, mosquitoes would swarm, carrying malaria and other dangerous viruses. Ticks abounded in the long dry grasses and numerous settlers succumbed to tick bite fever.

THE FIRST HERMANNSBURG MISSIONARIES IN NATAL

After a long-needed respite in Cape Town, the missionaries from Hermannsburg sailed towards Durban. The winds were favourable and, with the Madagascan current not hindering, they soon made headway on the Indian Ocean. Some of their brothers had their little brass band going full tilt with a beautiful Lutheran chorus on deck. As they approached the harbour, they sailed past a ship with Jesuits.

Suddenly, they heard someone shouting from the shore: it was a man who had hitched a ride with the port pilot, and he came on board to introduce himself. It was a fellow German from the Hanoverian district! Initially, he thought they were Jesuits, but when he heard the brass band playing that chorus, he knew they were Lutheran Germans from home. He invited them to their little settlement and most of the brothers went along, leaving only a few behind on-board ship.

Schröder recounts: "We could not believe that the Lord had provided us such joy as we were welcomed by a fellow countryman in Port Natal. It was also the first time that we saw the native African people and we were confronted by their lack of attire and then saddened at the plight of these fellow German settlers in their very humble circumstances in New Germany".[28]

---

[28] Original source of Schröder's quotation unknown – as found in D. Lilje's document.

When the missionaries arrived, the Hanovarians had already been in Natal for six years and, after the cotton failure, they were planting sugar cane. The missionaries were confronted with a culture shock, and they required time to reach a full understanding of the cultural differences between Africa and Europe. It was a humbling experience, to say the least. They began to understand the reason for their training and what it actually involved to be a pioneer. However, at this point they did not think that they were going to stay in Natal, as they had originally been destined to the Muslim-dominated coastal-belt of the Galla people, up the East Coast of Africa, near Zanzibar.

This is evidence that man may make plans, but God has His way! I have seen it often enough in my own life; particularly with our first call to missions. God firstly seeks a surrendered heart, after which He moulds you and, only then He can truly use you for the plans He has for your life. You become like soft, refined putty in the hands of the Master Potter.

The attempt of the missionaries to penetrate the Galla people and Zanzibar was rebuffed, and they were turned back to Port Natal. They had already met Posselt on their previous visit, and it made sense to settle in that little German settlement in Natal, with the Zulu people.

> "Never forget that you are Lutheran missionaries and have undertaken to teach according to the Lutheran confession and using pure Lutheran sacraments. Also never forget that you are Germans and must cling to German language and traditions as a jewel given to you by God. And as Hermannsburg missionaries you may never become lords but must remain servants" (Harms (1857), as quoted in Oschadleus (1992:27).

With the assistance of Posselt, the HMS bought Behrens's 6 000-acre farm, *Perseverance*, and founded what was to become the centre of German culture in Natal.

Because of its origins on the Lüneburg Heath and the rural background of its missionaries, the HMS was widely regarded as a *Bauernmission* ("farmers mission"). The founder, Ludwig (Louis) Harms, was an intellectual man, a classically educated village preacher in Hanover who strangely commingled romanticism, evangelical fervour and chiliastic (millennialism) expectations. Harms was particularly fascinated by the christianisation process used by monks when converting barbaric Saxons to Christianity. He regarded this event as particularly important to the later development of central Europe. The monks established self-sufficient Christian communities, which would serve as practical examples of Christian living, thereby attracting others. As he explained in an 1851 article, *Zeitblatt für die Angelegenheiten der lutherischen Kirche,* this was the approach that Harms selected for the HMS.

> "The first twelve missionaries shall live in one place and settle there. They will meet their own needs as they are to be proficient in agriculture. Here they will attempt to convert the local population and at the same time educate them in cultural affairs, just like the Anglo-Saxon missionaries converted and educated the German ancestors. Once a local African congregation has been formed, two or three missionaries shall remain there, while the rest move.... two at the most three miles further and repeat the process" (Harms, [s.a.]b)

The farm *Perseverance* was renamed *Neu-Hermannsburg* and the missionaries participated in the physical labour involved. Even as seminarians, they were not permitted to shirk manual labour of erecting buildings to be used by the Mission

Society. On the mission field they led by example when it came to hard work. They consciously attempted to recreate their homeland in Africa and, therefore, they used the distinctive architecture found on the Lüneburg Heath. They also planted groves of trees around the buildings. Having been brought from agricultural and trade backgrounds, they immediately built a smithy. As more missionaries, colonists and their families arrived in 1858, 1862, 1866 and 1867 and then at regular intervals, the station rapidly developed into a thriving community that could start sending missionaries and colonists into Zululand.

Peter Paul Church Hermannsburg Natal by L. Klingenberg 1961.

Source: Schütte, H. 1967a. Die Klingenbergs in Südafrika.

In 1857, a German school was established for the settlers' children at Hermannsburg, and it became the leading boarding school in the colony. Famous figures, such as Louis Botha (the Boer General and First Prime Minister of the Union of South Africa), Sir Charles Saunders (a famous colonial Administrator, who was knighted in 1906), Sir George Leuchars and Sir Fredrick Moor (the last Prime Minister of the Colony of Natal) received their early schooling here. Hermannsburg School was also the first to establish a cadet corps in 1871. Later, my mother and most of her siblings attended school there.

Hermannsburg is situated in the Umvoti County, near the Natal/Zululand border. It was to serve as a launching pad into the independent Zulu Kingdom and, with the help of Bishop Schreuder of the Norwegian Mission Society, the HMS was able to expand into Zululand. Stations were soon established at Ehlanzeni, Enyezane, Etembeni, Emlalazi, Emhlangane, Emvutjini, Emlangubo, Ekombela, Entombe and Endholvini. The skills of the colonists were particularly useful in securing the permission of the Zulu king, Mpande, to conduct mission work.

At the express request of Andries Pretorius (1798–1853) of the Zuid-Afrikaansche Republiek, a leader of the Afrikaner Big Trek, the HMS expanded its work into Bechuanaland and the western Transvaal in 1857. Within years, Hermannsburg missionaries were also heading to India, Australia and the United States of America.

> "We go to prayer to be with God – not to find Him. Prayer isn't about finding God; it's about being with Him. Let's seek His presence, not just His answers" (Vlad Savchuk, 2024)

Missionary Friedrich Fröhling – continued

Friedrich Fröhling arrived in Port Natal a broken-hearted man. Shortly before sailing from Germany, he received the news that his betrothed, Marie *Behrens*, had passed away, and he was unable to attend her funeral. Once the ship had left Glückstadt, Germany, there were more challenges before they finally managed to reach open sea. They celebrated Christmas Eve on board ship and, in the new year, they travelled around the Cape of Good Hope towards Port Elizabeth, where they had a stopover, instead of in the Cape.

Unfortunately, there is no record of this trip in Fröhling's own hand, as his first diary had gone missing. However, a letter was delivered to him in Port Elizabeth from his sister. They shared his grief and, in his reply, he writes that he spent many hours in tears, privately grieving over his loss.

As they approached the harbour of Port Natal, rough seas awaited them and tremendously strong winds prevented them from entering the harbour. Everyone was instructed to remain in their cabins, but Fröhling and another brother could not stand remaining in their cabins for long, and decided to go on deck. However, on deck, they had to hold on for dear life, with the raging storm and winds ripping at them. They decided to go back down below deck and immediately smelled smoke coming from somewhere. There was a fire! They ran around, trying to locate the fire, which turned out to be in the captain's lounge, with him being busy on deck. It appeared as if his hot pipe was left lying on the sofa, smouldering on the upholstery. Fortunately, they were able to put it out, thereby preventing a major disaster. It took 14 days of being flung about in the rough weather before a tugboat was sent to assist them safely into port.

Shortly after they had laid anchor in Durban on 28 March 1862, a group of friends from the Cotton Germans in New Germany arrived to greet them. In those days, New Germany was approximately four hours by horseback inland. Fröhling was immediately confronted by the difference in culture. He met some of the local Zulu people of whom one was able to speak English. When he wanted tobacco, Fröhling gave him a cigar. As soon as he had received the cigar, he asked for alcohol too. It did not take long for tobacco and alcohol to become widespread. In the Natal archives, I came across a directive from England, forbidding the selling of alcohol to the natives. This led to the establishment of the early *shebeens*.[29] However, the Zulus had been brewing their own beer called

---

[29] Shebeens are uniquely South African local taverns. Although the *shebeens* are a vibrant part of the community and social life today, they used to be illegal.

umqombothi, which was made from maize, maize malt, sorghum malt and yeast, as well as *amaHlewu*, which is a fermented drink from maize.

What is clearly evident from Fröhling's journals and Carine Nel's book about Fröhling, is his total dependency on God in prayer: rough weather – prayer; hardship of any kind – prayer; arriving safely in a new country – prayer and praise! God was never far from him.

He enjoyed his new surroundings as if they had been dropped into the most beautiful garden, even if the sand from the dunes covered his shoes. A large part of the land offshore consisted of sand dunes. They could pick wildflowers as much as they wanted, which, in Germany, could only be found in pots. These, I imagine, are the native geraniums and pelargoniums. I suspect that what he called a "cactus with an amazing crown" would be the beautiful prehistoric cycads that are so highly prized and an endangered species today. There were no hotels, guesthouses or shops. Yet, barely 100 years later, Durban is a big harbour city, with hotels lining beautiful beaches. There are universities, many schools and department stores with all the luxuries one could wish for.

Oxen wagons were sent from Hermannsburg to collect those arriving by ship, with all their luggage. The British built a small chapel, which was standing alone in the sand. From missionary Hans Schröder, we learn that they travelled up to Hermannsburg on 2 April 1862 and arrived at their destination on 15 April 1862. This two-week trip now takes approximately three to four hours by car. After a month at the mission station, Fröhling was sent out with six mission brothers to Zululand, where they arrived on 24 May 1862. Fröhling, Kaiser and Muller started the new mission at Enhlangubo, three and a half hours west of Emlalazi. In the New Year (1864), Fröhling was transferred to Enyezane. In these two years, he learned to speak Zulu and possibly a little Afrikaans/Dutch too. On 7 January 1864, he was inducted into the Zulu ministry by Prigge.

With Kaiser's help, Fröhling began to plough the land. He had also employed a couple of Zulu men to help. As they began ploughing, they came across the largest black mamba he had ever seen since his arrival in South Africa. This one measured 10 feet. Fröhling was steering the plough and Kaiser, who was driving the oxen, saw the snake coming out of the grass before it caught the plough. In response to Kaiser's loud warning cry, "Snake!", everyone ran for cover in all directions.

Mambas are known for their speed, but this snake was still trying to uncoil itself from the plough. With a well-aimed crack from Kaiser's long whip, the snake was momentarily lamed, and they were able to get close enough to kill it. The two Zulus returned hesitantly, their eyes as big as saucers, amazed that the missionaries had been able to kill the snake so quickly. Not many years later, a black mamba was responsible for another terrible tragedy in Fröhling's life.

I might have been about six years old when our dog, Fuchs, a cross between a Doberman and a German Shepherd, sounded the alarm in the late evening. My father took his *sjambok*, a heavy leather whip traditionally made from hippo hide, and laid into the snake with a vengeance. It was a young mamba of about 2 meter long. I assure you: I have a healthy fear of snakes.

Life on a mission station involved hard labour and establishing vegetable gardens and fruit orchards – labour at which Fröhling was particularly good. Soon, he also got some pigs, chickens, which prized for their eggs and their meat, some cattle and about eight cats. The cats kept the rodent population under control, and they kept snakes away too. The fruit trees included oranges, lemons and bananas. The vegetables, depending on the time of year, included beans, peas, potatoes and sweet potatoes, which was something new for him. Water had to be carried in buckets from the river by hand, or by means of a yolk around the shoulders, with a bucket on either side. Milk was provided by the cows, and butter was churned by hand. Other staples came from the mission station in Hermannsburg or from the ship in Durban, when she docked after a trip to Europe.

Numerous visitors, who came to the station to stay overnight, were always welcomed. Often, it would be a fellow brother or two from a neighbouring mission station, or travellers on their way into the interior or up the coast. The most welcome visitor was the mission wagon arriving from Durban, bringing supplies and letters from Germany, which were delivered by *The Candace*. These visits were always a time of celebration and chatting deep into the night, often accompanied by music and singing.

A New Bride for Fröhling

Fröhling had been in negotiations with his father to find him another bride. They got to know one another via letters every six months or so, and Fröhling was longing to meet his new bride-to-be. However, he first needed to expand his mission house, which involved making the bricks by hand. Missionaries from the neighbouring stations came out to help. Some of his furniture arrived from Germany, and he bought strong stuffing[30] to make mattresses for the new beds. He went to pick up a large heap to take to the house, but decided against it, thinking that it would be easier to fetch the ticking, rather than walking to and fro with armfuls of grass. No sooner had the pile of grass landed on the ground, than a couple of snakes emerged of a kind he had not seen before. After grabbing a spade and killing the snakes, more and more emerged from the grass bundle, all of which he was able to kill quickly with the spade. When he was satisfied that there were no more snakes in the grass, he sat down and praised God for sparing him from deadly snake bite. He had been holding this mass of snakes in his arms!! With hard work, Fröhling soon had the mission house ready for his new bride, with enough room for all the guests that come by.

---

[30] At that time, the mattress stuffing was made from the cut grass that had been drying in heaps on the fields.

Pastor Harms was not impressed with the fact that Fröhling had bypassed him on the bridal selection process, because Harms would have liked to do the honours himself. Imagine that. The disagreement nearly derailed the arrival of his bride and Fröhling was devastated. Between his father and Harms things got sorted out and, in 1864, Sophie Dorothea Beutin from Lauenburg, just across the Elbe River in Schleswig-Holstein, travelled to South Africa to meet her new husband. She became my two times great grandmother. According to her photograph, she was of slender build, with dark hair that she kept pinned up. Did she know what was awaiting her on the other side of the world in deepest, darkest Africa? Many of the young missionaries brought their brides with them, while others had to wait for their brides to come on another voyage. So, it came that, as Fröhling turned 30 years old in September, he was still waiting patiently for his bride. Christmas came and went.

Sophie Beutin.
Image supplied by Carine Nel.

On Tuesday, 17 January 1865, Fröhling wrote in his diary: "We had only just got up this morning when a messenger arrived with a letter. The message being that the ship, *The Candace*, has arrived in Port Natal. That was good news indeed because we have been waiting a long time for this news. Prigge will be going to the ship in Durban and fetch our brides"!

Almost a month later, on 15 February 1865, he wrote: "The most strenuous and at the same the best day of my life. We had much still to do in preparation for the arrival of Sophie and the rest of the guests. We expected them to arrive in the evening or even the following morning. Things were in a bit of a shambles trying to get everything perfect".

Just after lunch, Fröhling tried to lie down and take a nap, but could not settle down. He got back up and glanced out the window. There, in the distance, he saw the wagon coming over the crest of a hill between the long grass and thorn trees. With only an hour before the wagon would roll in, what still needed to be done, had to happen in great haste and with pounding heart.

Prigge went ahead of the wagon and greeted Fröhling with a message from Sophie, requesting him to wait in the lounge, where she would like to meet him. Soon, the wagon arrived and, with it, the long-anticipated moment of their meeting. Prigge got up and, after welcoming Sophie, he quietly excused himself, leaving the couple alone. Reaching out with his hand, Fröhling gave her a brief kiss on her lips. She was so beautiful and slender, glowing with a lovely outgoing nature. Her eyes were sparkling with anticipated joy. I can just imagine the tension of longing and yet he restrained himself and they both knelt in prayer to thank the Lord for this extraordinary day. Do men like this still exist – men of character and full of loving gentle kindness? After praying, they emerged as a couple ... as two old friends who were meeting again after a long separation, as though no time had passed, comfortable in each other's presence. They were no longer two strangers who had only met and had barely exchanged ten words with each other.

They joined the other brides and guests and together, enjoyed an excellent afternoon of coffee and cake with much celebration. Prigge announced that he needed to carry on with their journey to deliver all the remaining brides to the anxiously waiting missionaries in the further outlying mission stations.

Friedrich and Sophie stood side-by-side, with their arms around each other, greeting their guests, after which they spent the rest of the evening getting to know each other.

The following days were spent together, never far from each other's side. Fröhling never suspected that he would be so happy again. Both would have loved to have had their family there, so that they too could see how happy they were.

On 20 June 1866, the Lord blessed them with a beautiful little girl – my great grandmother, Maria JOHANNE Dorothea. The following year, Sophie gave birth to a lovely son, and they christened him Heinrich FRIEDRICH Wilhelm on 3 May 1867. Although he was a "premmy", he was quite strong. A year later, Sophie became very ill and, although she recovered well, she remained weak. It was decided that she should go to Hermannsburg for a time of rest and recovery.

Johanne Schumann née Fröhling.
Image supplied by Carine Nel.

Fröhling went over to Emvutjini to meet with Prigge and make the arrangements. He had just sat down to a refreshing cup of coffee, when a runner arrived, with a horrific message that Sophie had been bitten by a poisonous snake. Fröhling shot out the door and rode off on one of Prigge's horses, in the hope of seeing Sophie alive. The Lord gave grace that he was able to be with her for two hours before she passed away. She greeted him on his arrival. "The Lord is my Shepherd. I shall not want" (Psalm 23:1). He ministered to her until the end, and she was able to pray and comfort her children with a blessing and a kiss before she fell asleep in complete peace in the Lord. It was 24 November 1868 – barely three years and nine months since her arrival in Africa.

On the veranda, at the front of the house, stood a wooden crate with beans that had been harvested and were ready to dry. As Sophie turned around to go into the house, a black mamba, approximately ten feet long, struck her on her right leg, just above the ankle. She never saw the snake herself. The snake shot into the house, where it was killed in the lounge. Sophie immediately went to the kitchen and took glowing coals from the stove and seared the bite wound. Other remedies were tried, but nothing helped. She had no fever, swelling or fear. Grace abounded for her. She was buried the following day.

In all his grief, Friedrich chose to trust the Lord, his God. "He is God and He is still alive, and He is my Father". He wrote this beautiful poem for Sophie, even as she was dying. Every verse beginning with: "The Lord is my Shepherd", her favourite Psalm.

Der Herr ist mein Hirte!
Das ist der letzte gruss,
Den mir die Teure und Werte.
Mein liebes Weib zuruft.

Der Herr ist mein Hirte!
So sprach sie, als ich trat
Zu ihrem Sterbebette;
Geschlagen wie so hart!

Der Herr ist mein Hirte!
Mir schadet nicht der biss
Der Schlange, die mir heute
Ein bote Gotte ist.

The poem continues with a further 14 verses, one more beautiful than the next. Tears are streaming down my face, and I am no longer able to write further this afternoon. Such pain. Such loss!

In 1869, Fröhling got engaged again, this time to Bertha Johanna Valentina Riecke. In her memoirs of her father, my great grandmother writes: "Bertha was previously engaged to another missionary that was sent to Africa in 1861. He however absconded the mission with the treasury and has never been seen or heard of again. On her arrival in Port Natal, she was taken to Hermannsburg, where she helped with the little school. "This is also where my father fetched his new bride on the 9th of July 1869". Born on 9 January 1844, Bertha Riecke was 26 years old when she came from Hamburg. She became a loving and compassionate mother to Fröhling's little children. She taught them well: particularly singing and songs. Life at the mission station was filled with joy again, and Fröhling wrote more poems.

In 1870, a new little half-brother joined the family. He was named Peter. However, after Peter's birth, Bertha was not able to get up from her bed again. Eight days later, on 5 April 1870, she too departed to be with the Lord. She was buried at Enyezane too. That was a bitter pain for both father and children to bear. Fröhling composed this song:

Ein Weib wenn sie gebieret
So hat sie Traurichkeit,
Weil durch sie eingefuhret
Die Sunde und Bosheit.

Daher der Tod ist gekommen
Und so auch ihre Stund,
Da ihrem Leib genommen
Die Seel, oft Frisch, gesund.

Es wird das kind geboren
Zum Leben in den Tod.
Das Weib stirbt, auserkoren
Zum Leben ohne Not.
Da ist des Jammers Ende;
Da ist der Freude viel.
In Jesu Schoss und Hande
Ist das ersehnte Ziel.

All Angst is nun vergessen.
Sie denkt der Schmerzen nicht,
Weil ihr is zugemessen
Die selge Freud und Licht.
Die kann ihr nicht gewahren
Weder der Mann noch Kind
In der Zeit, da nur Zahren
An Tagesordung sind.

This poem too continues with a further six verses, with the two final verses:

Drum Angst und Traurichkeiten
Kommt her, ich acht euch nicht,
In euren truben Zeiten
Hab ich Freud, Trost und Licht

Mein Jesus will mich sehen.
Und das ist mein Gewinn:
Da mag die Welt vergehen,
Ich eil zu Jesus hin.

Da hab ich Freud und Wonne,
Da hab ich Trost und Ruh,
Da scheint mir die Sonne,
Stromt mir Erquickung zu.
Da schau ich ohne Ende
Sein holdes Angesicht;
Da küss sich seine Hande,
Hab ihn und lass ihn nicht.

A colonist's wife, Frau Kaiser, fetched baby Peter to care for him. Friedrich and Johanne remained behind with their father at the mission station, where Johanne remembers him teaching her how to knit. At the age of six, she was able to knit little booties for her new baby brother, Peter.

Johanne writes further: "One day we were outside in our father's beautiful flower garden with other children to play in the shade of the gazebo. Dinner time came and we were called to come inside, not once but several times! Because we were able to hear him well enough but had chosen to ignore him, my father took a stick with him to teach us a little lesson in obedience. He came into the garden, and there in the grass before the gazebo lay a big snake. By God's grace we were not meant to listen and obey our father at that moment! If we had, we would've been bitten. Fortunately, our father was able to kill the snake before anything could happen to us. That is how the Lord comes and helps! And with rejoicing we were able to go inside and eat".

Towards the end of 1871, Fröhling was called back to Germany. Fröhling, his children and several other passengers made the trip to Germany on the historic last voyage of *The Candace*, which was being decommissioned. She had sailed the seas as a missionary ship for the Hermannsburg Mission Society for 36 years. The Missionary Rossler came to run the mission at Enyezane in the absence of the Fröhlings.

Through all his pain, tragedies and suffering, Fröhling kept the faith. He and his children remained in Germany for two years, during which he met his third wife, Johanna Henrica DOROTHEA Andersohn, a relative of his mother. When they first arrived in Germany, she nursed little Peter in the Bethesda Hospital in Hamburg. She was one of the founding members of the hospital with two others and, when they heard that she was about to leave with Fröhling, they were very sad to lose her. Johanne remembers that she met up with her cousins from her late mother's side of the family, Dora and Henny, who recounted stories about her new stepmother and the tremendous work she was doing at the hospital. Fröhling and Dora got married at Hermannsburg before boarding the *Windsor Castle* to take up the ministry in South Africa again. They never had any children of their own, but she remained a loving, loyal wife to Friedrich and a mother to his children.

Fröhling family with Dorothea.
Image supplied by Carine Nel.

One thing that Johanne remembers is that the return trip seemed to be quite short. They had sat down to eat when the waiter arrived with steaming hot tea. He had moved behind Johanne, and she must have bumped him somehow, because the boiling hot tea was poured out on her. Rapidly, Dora rushed with Johanne to the cabin, where she treated her and lovingly nursed her, as if she were a doctor. It was in those moments that Johanne realised that she had been graced with a loving mother again.

During their absence, a new Zulu king, Cetshwayo (1826–1884) was crowned on 2 September 1873. He promised not to hinder the missionaries and their followers and for some years all went well at Enyezane. They had a lovely little church with a bell tower and Sundays brought numerous visitors, mostly from the Norwegian missionaries, who also preached in Zulu.

Johanne writes that more African people were being baptised, among whom were their faithful Petrus and Fidi, Joseph and his wife, Elizabeth, and their two children, as well as Johannes and his little girl.

The main road from the Tugela River up to Eshowe went over Enyezane. In the afternoons after church, they would take a stroll in Fröhling's big garden. It was pleasant in the cool of the day to sit under the gazebo eating fresh fruit picked directly off the trees in the orchard. Sometimes they would gather a group of friends and take long hikes up the nearest hill or mountain, where they would enjoy hot coffee and cake. This was always accompanied by much laughter singing and playing.

INGRID HERRMANN

The Zulu Wars and the Rape of Africa

"Our objective is to gain control of the two great treasure-houses on which the West is dependent: the energy sources of the Persian Gulf and the minerals of Central and Southern Africa."
– Leonid Brezhnev, Secretary General of the USSR (1971)[31]

Sir Bartle Frere, the British High Commissioner, had been sent to South Africa to promote confederation. An independent Zululand was not only contrary to his hopes, but an actual threat to them. On the issue of furthering high politics, he had resolved to destroy Zulu independence. From Frere's time and through it's commander-in-chief, General Thesiger, the British army in South Africa became entirely preoccupied with the idea that war with the Zulus was a possibility and, therefore, it must be prepared for as if it was a certainty, in professional soldier's dictum. Troops were steadily concentrated in Natal and the messes were full of speculation and boasting by subalterns as to the chances of a tilt at the renowned Zulu power.

Among the colonists, the sugar planters were the only group to have a lurking desire for war. This makes sense, given the fact that the coastal sugar plantations had been taken over by British colonists, with a very small number of Afrikaners and French from Mauritius.

The prospect of a defeated Zululand was attractive to them, as it held some hope of a chronically scarce plantation labour. The independent Zulus had hitherto never been prepared to leave their homes to work in foreign parts.

---

[31] This quotation appears in the following text: Hilali, A.Z. 2006. *Cold war politics of superpowers in South Asia* (p. 79). https://qurtuba.edu.pk/thedialogue/The%20Dialogue/1_2/4_Mr.%20Hilali.pdf

Steady warmongering started occurring among the politicians, their professional soldier servants and the missionaries, with the general public gradually being prepared for future events. The missionaries played an important part in this preparatory "cold war". Their efforts at converting the Zulus had not been met with conspicuous success. After 27 years of labour, the Norwegians had nine mission stations, with 100 Zulu converts. The English church had four stations, with about 20 converts, and the Hanoverians had five stations, with little other result for their efforts (Bulpin 2014).

The entire Zulu national way of life was opposed to the form of Christianity advocated by the missionaries at that time. To the Zulu, a man owed sole allegiance to his king – nobody else. He was, in duty, bound to give military service and obey the slightest order, even if it led to death. The few who were converted by the missionaries were suspect to the Zulu nation. The Zulus said that they were mainly criminals, runaway women, witches, or other rascals (*scabengu*), who had found sanctuary with the missionaries as a way of avoiding their responsibilities and punishments.

Sensational stories appearing in Natal newspapers, which Cetshwayo "suspected" were contributed by missionaries, also brought about mutual feelings of animosity. These stories, mainly of Zulu atrocities, with the usual ingredients of slaughtered babies in arms, were mostly plain nonsense penned by individuals who did not know the Fifth Commandment.[32]

Against this rising tide of propaganda, a few voices were raised in defence of the Zulu people. Bishop Colenso (Anglican) made some attempt, pointing out the absurdity of the more extravagant press reports and the responsibility of those disgruntled individuals, who were claiming that the godless despotism

---

[32] The Fifth Commandment reads as follows: *Honour your father and your mother, that your days may be long upon the land which the LORD your God is giving you* (Exodus 20:12).

of Cetshwayo must be overthrown by a recourse to war as a prerequisite of Christianity.

However, feelings became increasingly inflamed. In 1877, rumours had grown that Cetshwayo intended to kill all Christian converts. One convert was, in fact, killed at the mission station of Enyezane on the grounds of being a witch. A few days later, another was killed at Eshowe. The rest took flight and fled into Natal.

On 2 April, Durnford[33] wrote to his mother: "You will hear that as all missionaries have left Zululand, it is war. All bosh! These missionaries are at the bottom of all evil. *They* want war so that we may take the Zulu country and thus give them homes in a good and pleasant land. The Zulus do not want them, and I for one cannot see why we should cram these men down their throats".

After splitting the Zulu Kingdom into 13 parts, the British appointed John Dunn (1834–1895) as one of the Zulu chiefs. Dunn was vehemently opposed to missions and stations were only returned to the missionaries after considerable wrangling. Volker's station at Emlalazi was not returned: Dunn had long converted it as his personal possession.

Death at Enyezane

Back at Enyezane, one of Fröhling's new converts, Joseph, decided to build his own house for his wife and children. Fröhling was happy to help Joseph with the building and construction work and things were progressing. However, this idyll was not destined to last, as unrest was building up between the Zulus and the British. Cetshwayo wanted to put an end with God, and the missionaries would be caught in the middle of this unrest.

---

[33] Source of the quotation is unknown, but Lieutenant-Colonel Anthony William Durnford, a British Army Officer, served in the Anglo-Zulu War.

In the mornings, Johanne always took her father his coffee, before he started to preach. One morning, about 30 Zulus had surrounded Joseph's cottage. At first, Fröhling thought that they were looking for medicines, but then the Zulus began chanting and banging their sticks. He saw them take Joseph behind the pigsty, where they began to lay into him. There was nothing anyone could do against those numbers. They dragged him to the front of Fröhling's house, where they continued to lay into Joseph with much anger and hatred, accusing him of being a witch. Fröhling and his family had secured themselves in the house, although they had drawn the curtains, Johanne peeked out and saw everything. The Zulus took Joseph down to the Enyezane River, where they continued to hit him, until he died, after which they stuck his body into a crocodile hole, where the crocodiles did the rest.

The Fröhlings tried to hold it out at Enyezane as long as they could, but Dora could no longer stay. Fröhling arranged for a helper to come and load the wagon and to take Dora and the children with whatever possessions they could load across the Tugela River into Natal. A Christian Zulu came over from the Norwegian Mission in Eshowe to drive the wagon. Just as they were crossing the river, a runner came up to the wagon to tell Johannes that Cetshwayo's *impis*[34] had arrived to kill him – not long after he had left. "Now you are safe", he exclaimed! At first, he was not able to say much else, but after a few moments of silence, he began to praise and worship the Lord, who had made this miracle possible that day! They were escorted to safety in Hermannsburg and Johannes found refuge at another mission station.

In Hermannsburg, they were comfortably housed in the main mission house, and the children attended school. They had much to do, learning German, English and Zulu. The mission house was a single-story house with a thatch roof that resembled the farmhouses in Lower Saxony. It was 120 feet long and

---

[34] *Impi* is a Zulu word for a group of armed men, or warriors.

40 feet wide, with eight living rooms, 16 bedrooms and a kitchen. The passage resembled a hall and, before the church was built, they used it for their services. On three sides of the house, there was a verandah.

It was here that missionaries and colonists came to stay when they first arrived from Germany, before they were sent out. Each family received two bedrooms and a small lounge. When I think of the accommodation that married couples had as trainee missionaries with Operation Mobilisation (OM) in Boskop, Pretoria, I cannot help but notice the vast difference. I still have memories of rats creeping into our little room at night, from the gap under the door, and beds sagging in the middle to the floor.

Fröhling had stayed behind at Enyezane, but when the Zulu War[35] broke out, he packed up the rest of their belongings and sent them across the border. This was done in several trips and with much tension, as more and more missionaries were leaving and trying to cross the river. Fröhling freed the animals – particularly the 30 pigs, which were originally destined for *The Candace* – and managed to bring over a 100 head of cattle. The Zulus did not eat pork and used them for target practice with the guns they had received.

At first, the missionaries waited out the war just across the Tugela River, in the hope that it was going to be a short-lived skirmish. Fröhling rented a small cottage at Nonoti from a local farmer, Mr A. Colenbrander. As descendants of ministers, both Colenbrander and his wife originated from Holland, on the German border, and, therefore, they were able to speak good German. They were lovely hospitable people and Fröhling remained there, while Dora went to Hermannsburg with Peter for respite and care. Once he had recovered, they joined him at Nonoti. There was an abundance crocodiles, which tucked into one their dogs. Johanne and Friedrich stayed at Hermannsburg, where

---

[35] The Zulu War was fought in 1879, between the British Empire and the Zulu Kingdom.

they attended school. Two of Fröhling's baptised disciples later joined them at Nonoti, bringing their sister and mother with them, who were also baptised at a later stage.

However, against their hopes, the war ranged on for quite some time. All the missionary stations were plundered and destroyed, with one exception. While his bride was on the high seas, on her way from Germany, a young missionary, Schröder, was murdered. She would never see him alive again. After the Zulus had plundered Fröhling's little church in Enyezane and destroyed all the benches and the altar, which had been hand made by Fröhling, the British used the church as a horse stall.

The Mission Work

Delving into detail of all Fröhling's missionary exploits would require an entire book on its own, but here, I want to focus on what I have learned about the man and how he handled adversity. Fröhling's diaries and reports give detailed accounts about the hardships involved in evangelising the Zulu people. Both the cultural and spiritual misunderstandings were not easy to overcome. What was acceptable in one culture was not acceptable in the other, and time and patience were required to get to know and understand one another. Fröhling had to master the art of Zulu negotiation and cultivate strong relations with the Zulu people and heir monarch, who allowed them to establish their mission stations in Zululand to begin with. Although there were several squabbles and tense moments, most were eventually resolved. In the meantime, he remained close to the Lord and steadfast in prayer.

Fröhling saw the bones of those slain in battle, strewn without burial across the plains and, during a particularly severe drought, possibly in the 1860s, he witnessed the Zulu people collecting the bones of both humans and animals, grinding them up and eating the powder. Despite his intense efforts to feed the hungry and teach them agriculture, he had little success. Women were the farmers, and they planted maize, sweet potatoes and *amadumbe*.[36] However, little produce was preserved for difficult times.

The work was hard and yielded little fruit, often feeling like taking one step forward and three steps back. However, with perseverance, they eventually built a small chapel, where services were held in German and Zulu. What truly broke Fröhling's heart was the violence and bloody conflicts among those he had come to bring to Christ. Although new converts were baptised from time-to-time, they were severely persecuted by the local *sangomas*.[37] New converts were brutally tortured or killed, as a lesson to anyone who was considering conversion. At the time, the mission had not begun to appreciate the hold of witchcraft on this nation. This became clear to me as I was introduced to spiritual warfare decades later, but this information was not available to the missionaries, and it made winning souls for Christ very challenging.

Witchcraft and satanism are global phenomena that may have differences in language, design and structure, but essentially, they involve the worship of gods, other than the one true God, demi-gods and ancestors. Witchcraft and satanism distinguish themselves by collectively embracing a different worldview, whereas Christianity – despite its different denominations – still remains united under the Kingdom of God.

Sometimes we do not see the woods for trees. It has been like this from the beginning of time. Although it is mostly hidden, there is a counterfeit kingdom trying to establish itself on earth and in your heart by using whatever nefarious means at its disposal. Although unseen, it is continuously working at undermining and destroying the Creator's original design.

---

[36] *Amadumbe* is a small, edible root that is particularly popular in KwaZulu-Natal. I have eaten many over the years, and they were a favourite of my mother.
[37] *Sangomas* are traditional healers, herbalists or witchdoctors.

There is not a nation, tribe or people who have not been touched by its nefarious tendrils. Pretending that this brooding darkness does not exist, equals suffering from a type of amnesia, and not recognizing or knowing how to deal with it may be very dangerous. We fool ourselves if we think that the dark Venetian bankers, who established their first public bank in 1587, were not manipulating world finance as far back as even then and had not already taken over the entire British Empire, together with the Dutch East India Company and other such companies. Shrouded in impenetrable mystery, their guilds and secret societies span the entire globe: is the City of London not testament to their inviolability?

In the second half the 1800s, there was a certain amount of literature available on the subject, but it was not *readily* available and, if you had been taught not to look for it, you remained blind to its hold over nations and national affairs, let alone the individual. Although they knew they were dealing with a deep-rooted pagan tradition, steeped in ancestral worship, mystical practices and witchcraft, they struggled to find effective ways to guide the people to spiritual freedom.

While writing this book, I have done extensive research from historical resources, and I was often astounded by the plethora of strategies and designs employed across nations to impede the progress of Christianity, while advancing the agenda of the evil one. How brilliantly these evil, yet influential, figures manipulated public opinion through the media, with the ultimate goal of stoking tensions and igniting conflict – a conflict that would serve their interest. Their ultimate purpose was the subjugation of the Zulu nation, driven by an insatiable demand for cheap, slave-like labour.

Darkness is the absence of light and, if the Light does not expose the darkness, it remains free to continue. Therefore, it is the responsibility of all light bearers to do their jobs as originally intended. The satanic activity in the dark ages was so intense that the light of the Gospel was almost extinguished. The hatred towards all light bearers is brutal, with the evil one doing anything in his power to snuff it out. In South Africa, the missions were the target.

Where entire nations practice witchcraft or are under the control of witchcraft, the struggle against the darkness is always intense – particularly when people are beginning to respond to the Gospel.

In this way, the missionaries witnessed gruesome attacks on the converted souls, in an attempt to prevent them being baptised. Numerous lives were lost, some succumbing to their wounds and others falling victim to outright violence. Fröhlings diaries and reports record numerous incidents of where he was delivered from an attack or was able to intervene in time to save someone else from being attacked. Several of these events were spiritual in nature. The darkness hates the light.

(The Omnipresence of God)

Where can I go from Your Spirit?
Or where can I flee from Your presence?
If I ascend into heaven, you are there;
If I make my bed in hell, behold, You are there.
If I take the wings of the morning,
And dwell in the uttermost parts of the sea,
Even there Your hand shall lead me,
And Your right hand shall hold me.
If I say, "Surely the darkness shall fall on me,"
Even the night shall be light about me;
Indeed, the darkness shall not hide from You,
But the night shines as the day;
The darkness and the light are both alike to You.

Psalm 139:7–12 NKJV

There was another cultural habit that they had not considered, which was a severe hindrance for African people turning to Christ. When they are born, all children are handed over to the witch doctors or *sangomas* by their parents. The witch doctors make sure that the children in their village or area of influence receive incisions, either in the groin area or on another part of the body, after which fine pieces of bone are inserted into the wound. These are either bits of bone or herbs and powders with a curse attached to them. Although metal balls or bits are inserted in other parts of the world, the purpose of the the ritual is always the same – to dedicate the child to the ancestral spirits or demons.

Until they have been anointed, the victim may find it particularly difficult to accept the Gospel, or to listen to the name of Jesus. However, there was breakthrough, and many did come to know the Lord as their Saviour. In order to ensure the victory, you have to bind the strong man first! [38]

It was just past lunch time in the bookshop and Willem was busy on his computer. When an Indian gentleman entered, I went over to assist him. He requested reading material that would help him and his brother, who had just come to faith. It was a quiet day, and he started telling me the story about his brother and what he had gone through in the last six months. As a computer programmer, his brother was holding an excellent position when things started going wrong: he was losing weight, having fits and manifesting unusual mental health issues. Eventually, he lost his job.

He desperately tried to get help for his brother and counselling through the church, but there was not a church in the Pinetown area that was able or willing to try to help this gentleman. Eventually, he took his brother to an Indian minister in Shallcross, Durban, who had had a deliverance ministry, but the minister

---

[38] The phrase, "binding the strongman" is a reference to a passage in the book of Mark, where Jesus refers to Satan as "the strong man". In the parable recorded in Mark 3:27, Jesus says, "No one can enter a strong man's house and plunder his goods, unless he first binds the strong man. Then indeed he may plunder his house."

was unable to help him. His behaviour was becoming increasingly erratic, and the family was desperate. He was using drugs and alcohol, and his limbs were curling up in spasms. He had to wear diapers, and he was unable to get in and out his bed without assistance. They took him to a psychiatrist, who diagnosed him with schizophrenia and had him heavily medicated to stop him from harming himself or someone else. He was hospitalised in Wentworth Hospital on the Bluff, where he made little progress and continued to be heavily medicated. Eventually, his brother was able to take him home for visits over a weekend, but he was far from well and the family members were convinced that he was suffering from demonic oppression or even possession. They were extremely distraught and sad that the Church had failed them.

As a last resort, they decided to return to the deliverance minister in Shallcross, and, this time, he was able to help the poor man. He was tormented with evil spirits that were trying to kill him. Today, he is in his right mind and his good health has been fully restored. He is a born-again child of the living God, completely free – also from the heavy medication – and back at his job as a computer programmer. As we were talking in the bookshop, his brother showed me some before and after photographs. What a difference Jesus makes in the life of a sinner saved by grace. After talking for about two hours, we selected a number of good books to help him and his brother in their journey of discipleship. Although I did not see him again before we left Pinetown for Australia, I have never forgotten this powerful testimony. It touched me deeply and confirmed that some Christian churches are missing the boat, if not most of them.

"This world is enemy-occupied territory. Christianity is the story of how the Rightful King had landed and is calling us to take part in a great campaign of sabotage." – C.S. Lewis

THE ANGLO-ZULU WAR THROUGH DORA FRÖHLING'S EYES

AUGUST 1878

After lengthy negotiating for a new mission station in Hermannsburg, Fröhling was given the station at Entombeni, not far from Hermannsburg. After two weeks, he began to renovate the old farmhouse that the previous owners left on the property. A new house was to be built later. Peter and Dora remained at Nonoti for a few weeks. After Easter, Fröhling came to fetch them both to their new home. Dora writes that the farewell from the loving Colenbrander family, who had made them feel welcome and at home, was particularly difficult. Fröhling had done a good job with the renovations and Dora was very happy with their new home. There was even space for brother Hormann, who was a good bricklayer. Although there was still construction work to do on the rest of the building, they had a house-warming party on Dora's birthday in the renovated home down in the valley where it gets very hot in the summer.

The new house was being built about ten minutes from the original farmhouse, on the side of a hill, where they could enjoy the cooler weather and breezes, as well as protection from two high mountains on either side. From this elevated position, they could see other homes further afield and some of their new neighbours had come to introduce themselves. However, dark war clouds were gathering around them, and they were deep into a drought.

The memory of what had happened to their beautiful station at Enyezane was still very raw. Dora also mourned the loss of the dear Elizabeth, who got married off to a heathen after her Christian husband, Joseph, was murdered. Their children were like her own children, and she wondered what would become of them. Family members had come and taken her and the children away, across the Tugela River. All the chickens that Fröhling had saved from Enyezane were stolen by the Zulus. The drought brought sever starvation, and soon, the pigs started disappearing too. Thirty head of cattle had died, and the cattle that they had been able to save, were gaunt and sickly, not suitable to be used for transport. There was no milk for their coffee, and they ate their bread with schmaltz.[39] The land needed to be cleared and ploughed and, when Fröhling returned home at night, he was dead tired after the exhausting work.

Although it is very quiet in the valley, far from the bustle of main roads, the sounds of rebellion were becoming louder, with the Zulu nation and their king at the head of it. Nothing happens that has not been instigated and carefully planned in advance, and it was not clear which lies were fed to the Zulu king. Those in the Lüneburg station had already suffered severely at the hands of the Zulus. With an estimated number of 30,000 Zulu *impis* at the ready, troops were pouring in, and the word was that war would break out within weeks. As warriors, the *impis* had the reputation of being as fierce as tigers or lions. One could only imagine what would happen when they were completely taken over by violent rage. Although the border was fortified, it was not clear what was to become of the Europeans on the farms, if the *impis* were to break through. The Zulus in Natal were becoming highly unruly, doing just as they pleased. Many of them would walk up to farmers and give them an ultimatum to leave the farms or die. "Make that you get away, this is now my farm, Cetshwayo has given it to me". Two hundred armed Zulus marched up to a Swedish mission, where they abducted a Zulu girl by force. They took her down to the river and shot her at point blank.

An Englishman was caught smuggling wagon loads of guns into Zululand for Cetshwayo and his army. Who, on God's good earth, supplied him with all

---

[39] Schmaltz is any rendered animal fat, including goose or chicken fat and lard.

this weaponry? Was he not being handsomely paid? "Oh, what a tangled web we weave, when we first practice to deceive".[40]

December 1878

Things got worse progressively, and the borders were packed with soldiers. On hearing that 14 000 soldiers were to enter Zululand in January 1878, Dora feared that the Zulus were going to win and endanger their lives. They had to start making arrangements to safeguard themselves, although they did not know where to go. After recalling all the missionaries from Zululand, the HMS began cementing the doors and windows of the church in Hermannsburg, so as to create a refuge for the missionaries and their families during the worst times of the war. The only good news was that the drought had broken, and they welcomed the rains to help newly planted fields. The cattle and other animals would begin to thrive again.

In terms of the war, they were still living in a high state of anxiety. When thousands of Zulu warriors attacked, the soldiers were unprepared and many died. Within three to four hours, they could reach Hermannsburg. When in fear of your life, there is one answer and that is to pray, knowing that God is faithful. The natives with them were terrified and fled into the bush to hide. The men from the mission patrolled the perimeter of the church at night. They were in a constant state of readiness, prepared for any news of an invasion. However, the Lord does not give us more than we can bear!

---

[40] The quotation is from Sir Walter Scott's epic poem, *Marmion: a tale of flodden field*, which was published in 1808.

February 1879

The Zulus preferred to be dead than to be ruled by the English. The English, who had underestimated the Zulus apparently, believing that they were going to have an easy victory, did not have enough manpower to secure the borders. The missionaries kept getting false warnings of imminent attacks, sending their stress levels up a notch each time.

Women and children in remote homes would flee into the bush and sleep out under the stars. Wagons were prepared and taken to higher ground for the families to use when in flight.

When two riders in the authority of the local magistrate arrived with the warning to flee, Fröhling fled with his little family to the church, where several families were already living. More and more families arrived, with beds and food. The sick and bedridden were carried from their homes. They sang *Ein feste Burg ist unser Gott* ("A mighty fortress is our God") and the Superintendent read Psalm 91 to them. And they prayed and prayed. However, it turned out that the magistrate had been misinformed, and it was another false warning. Daylight came and nothing happened!

I have in my possession a lovely wooden plaque made by either my grandfather or great grandfather Schumann, (I forget which one). The church was their physical refuge, but their hearts, faith and lives were hidden in Christ: a mighty fortress is our God!

Schumann plaque:
Ein feste Burg ist unser Gott.

The success of the British at the Battle of Rorke's Drift (22–23 January 1879) resulted in sheer terror for retaliation from the Zulus. Lord Chelmsford crossed the Buffalo River into Zululand with 100 wagons with munitions and provisions, setting up camp and waiting a few days, but the Zulu appeared to be afraid of them. Unfortunately, Lord Chelmsford fell for the ploy and became more confident and at ease. No knowing Cetshwayo, who was a master warmonger, Lord Chelmsford did not suspect that the Zulu were planning to catch the English in a trap. They herded a large number of cattle high on a hill and, when Chelmsford saw the cattle, he left with a contingent of 1000 men and as many black soldiers, including officers, to get the cattle. These men included Shepstone's two sons of whom only one had survived, and Colonel Durnford, who was highly admired by both white and black. As Chelmsford neared the cattle, several miles away from the camp, 17 000 Zulu *impis*, who had been hidden in the bush and gullies, suddenly attacked from both sides. Firstly, they let loose with their guns, followed by their *assegais*. The English did try to fight back, and the infantry fired shots until their gun barrels burned their hands, but they suffered enormous losses and only a few survived.

The enemy came and stole all the cattle from the 100 wagons. As Chelmsford returned to camp, he witnessed the total devastation and loss. Bodies were piled high in the river, rendering the water undrinkable by the bloodiness of war.

When the Zulus set off towards them on 23 June 1879, the HMS sent out a warning and, again, they had to flee to the church. A day or two later, an official came by to report on the severe devastation in the vicinity of Fröhling's new mission. It was almost certain that the house had been destroyed; cattle were stolen and men woman and children were killed. Fröhling and his people went into the church to pray, thanking God that He had led them to the church and saved their lives. On another day, brother Hormann and a friend rode out to the mission to check everything out. On the following day, he reported back that the buildings had been left untouched. The Zulus did not make it up the mountain as far as the houses.

Fröhling, Dora and the children returned to their home, although, that night, they did not sleep well at all. As they were sitting down to breakfast the following morning, the word arrived that the Zulus had broken through the borders and were on the rampage. Dora and the children fled to their hidden wagon, and Zulu women and their children fled into the thick bush near the river. After a while, when things quieted again, Dora rushed back home, where she baked bread and collected more provisions. That night, they crept back to the wagon by the light of the moon. And thus, it continued for several days. Fröhling was encouraged by a Mr Cross to send Dora and the children back to Hermannsburg, but they did not want to be separated. A day or two later, Mr Cross appeared again, pleading with Fröhling to send Dora and the children away, because more Zulus had broken through. At Dora's request, Fröhling sent them to Nanoti, where Dora could connect with her dear friends again.

Meanwhile, another battle was raging. The English soldiers were battle weary and wagons were creeping along at a snail's pace, while the cattle were dying from exhaustion. Donkeys were roped in to perform the task, but they too were dying. Apart from the war costing large amounts of money, an estimated number of 1800 Zulus had been killed. The *kraals* of the king were burned down and Cetshwayo, who had fled in time, was not to be found anywhere. The war was becoming too costly and there was talk of peace. Moreover, another war was on the horizon, as the English had their sights set on the Transvaal Republic.

When they returned home, Dora and the family received the news of a young lad at the Lüneburg mission who had been killed by the Zulus. Along with several other young men from the missions, a man named Filter had been conscripted to fight with the English. As General Wood sneered at them, "You missionaries here in Lüneburg can pray like nothing on earth but you can't fight. You are just using the war to further your own ends". Later, General Wood would praise the young Filter for his excellent fighting ability, wishing that all soldiers could fight like him. Although Filter fought bravely, he was overrun by a hoard of Zulus, who had been hiding in the tall grass and bushes. His family witnessed it all: how they pulled him off his horse to capture him, dragging him away. Although they found the bodies of the dead Zulus, they never found Filter's body and they could only pray he was not tortured.

The foregoing is my paraphrasing and translation of Dora's letters to Germany. Not all the information in her letters has been included. Although I mainly concentrate on Dora and the effects of the war on women and children, Fröhling writes on the subject too.

It is evident that three different things were occurring simultaneously. Firstly, the English intended to subdue the Zulus and take their land from them and, secondly, the missionaries were to become the scapegoats of the war, as well as the supporters of the English in the war for fear of the Zulus. This was accomplished by propaganda, false flags, fear and Dunn, who despised the missionaries and whispered all kinds of enticing words in Cetshwayo's ears. Well played, your Majesty. Well played! All the shadowy characters in the City of London and across Europe lit their cigars, filled their snifters with South African brandy and smiled with satisfaction. It was not easy to repair the rift between the missionaries and the Zulus, and it was not possible to blame either side. It is only by looking at the bigger picture that it becomes evident that both sides had been played by a small group of chess players. It is my opinion that, in the heart of the people, the Zulu war never came to an end. What appeared to be peace for a while was merely an illusion. The war simply went underground, waiting for the right time to surface again, with the evil shadow figures working tirelessly in the background. And once more, we are reminded of Catherine de Medici's motto: Divide and rule.

I love the rendition found in one of Fröhling's letters of the underestimation of the English. This is taken directly from a high-ranking officer visiting the Fröhlings:

> "The English saw that the Zulu were not to be eaten at breakfast, as they first thought. The Zulus terrified and frightened them so much so that their knees trembled, and their loins quivered when the word Zulu was mentioned. Everywhere Zulus appeared to them as ghosts and demons, and if a daredevil crashed a wagon down a mountainside, the English officers heard loud gunfire and cannon thunder of the Zulu in it, and hastily saddled their horses and took flight".

I only imagine the two of them, puffing on their pipes, rolling their heads back, roaring with laughter.

Change in the HMS Natal

When Superintendent K. Hohls passed away on 20 February 1883, the HMS was divided into different districts, each with their own superintendent. Fröhling was called as bishop over the entire Zulu mission, and at the beginning of 1884, he was called to Hermannsburg, where he was ordained in 1885.

Dealing with administration and political matters in the aftermath of the Zulu wars, was particularly difficult for Fröhling. Additionally, he had to deal with the beginning of the split in the church. Although not all, most German churches were established after natural expansion. Congregations such as Wartburg, Neuenkirchen and Braunschweig owed their existence to a split in the Hanovarian Landeskirche (State Church).

It was not long before Fröhling had to write a very difficult letter to Germany. It was with a heavy heart that he wrote to the authorities in Germany on 29 April 1887 to inform them that he was suffering from cancer and that he was not going to recover. Fröhling writes as follows: "Everything that the Lord does is good. We must receive whatever He gives from His hand with thankfulness." And just like that, he switched to daily matters that had to be arranged and organised in the light of his announcement. He appealed for a young missionary to be sent from Germany as soon as possible to help him in his last days. Because Fröhling was already gravely ill at the time, Schumann's arrival was eagerly awaited. At the end of July 1887, Missionary Schumann arrived in Natal and, two weeks later, on 12 August 1887, Fröhling passed away.

Missionary Friedrich Schumann – Continued

Fröhling left his family a letter in which he exhorted his children to love their mother and to support her in all things. It was so beautiful to read this letter, seeing how gently he treated his beloved wife and honoured the years she dedicated to raising his children. It was truly a household characterized by love, respect and honour. He had a word for each child and encouraged them with these words: "Go comforted out into the world. God is with you! Never forget that in everything you do, think or contemplate, God sees it, God hears it, God guides it"!

After he left Germany and, in the weeks, following his arrival in Natal, Schumann barely had a moment to rest. He describes the two weeks he had with Fröhling as both wonderful and extremely sad. He got to love and respect the ailing bishop, and he was a rock of comfort to Dora and the children in the last days of Fröhling's life and in the difficult time after his death.

At the time of her father's death, Johanne was barely 21 years old, but in her short life, she had already endured so much loss, with both her mother and father gone. Before Fröhling married Dora, she acted as a little mother to her young half-brother, Peter. She always remained silently in the shadows, allowing the light to fall on those around her. As time progressed, Schumann and Johanne fell in love, and two years later, on 23 May 1889, they got married in Hermannsburg. Missionary Lilje performed the wedding ceremony.[41]

I have been already deeply touched by all these beautiful stories and it is such a privilege to share them with all of you. With each story, God is ministering my soul in different ways and according to my own need, teaching me so much. The skies have been overwhelmingly grey, both within and without. At times, my eyes well up. But was my question not: where did they find the strength and resilience? In his perfect timing, our Lord teaches us everything we need to know. All that is required of us is patience and humility, allowing the Potter to do his work.

There is more to come, though. So much more.

Mein Liebes Africa!

Ach ich bin viel zu wenig
Zu ruhmen seinen Ruhm;
Der Herr allein ist König
Ich eine welke Blum
Jedoch weil ich gehöre
Gen Zion in sein Zelt,
Ist billig, das ich mehre

---

[41] The great grandson of Missionary Lilje, Dieter Lilje, became the head of the Lutheran Church in Southern Africa and assisted me with this book by providing me with the early German history.

Sein Lob vor aller Welt!
Gott sucht Dich!
Gott liebt Dich!
Gott braucht Dich!

Johanne Schumann

With the blessing of the HMS leadership, Schumann was given the mission station at Emlalazi. The mission station, which had mostly been destroyed during the Zulu wars, had to be rebuilt and Schumann had to start all over with the mission work. One brave and loyal convert had remained at the mission to look after the gardens and to plant vegetables. Schumann's mother and sister were looking forward to travelling to South Africa, where they intended to live with Schumann, when they received the news that he had married a lovely girl whom he had met in Natal. Elsche Schumann was overjoyed at the news that her lovely son was happily married. Although Friedrich and his mother were never reunited – she passed away before she could make the voyage to Natal – his sister, Engel Schumann, travelled to Africa on her own to be with her brother and new sister-in-law.

His initial report captures the full extent of the devastation they faced upon arriving at Emlalazi. Blackened walls marked the ruins where the flames had destroyed everything. Apart from the large metal crosses, which were still all standing, the graveyard was in utter disrepair. Schumann had his work cut out for him: he had to clear the rubble and start building a new home: 40 ft long and 12 ft wide with a thatch roof.

Several young Zulus arrived to help with the work on the grounds and the building; 30 - 40 people started showing up for the Sunday services; and the loyal convert, who had looked after the buildings and the gardens during the war, came to learn at the mission station.

Schumann was still struggling with the Zulu language, but Johanne, who had a good grasp of the language, was an enormous help to him in this regard. In his follow-up report, he writes that great strides had been made and that a young girl had been baptised. The "Schumann" (meaning that he did not necessarily always accept the status quo) came out in him when she was given the name Christine for a Christian name. He questioned why people could not keep their own or names, which had meaning to them. Instead, they had to accept a name that was foreign to them and, with the Zulu accent sounded very strange.

Schumann preached the Gospel of salvation every Sunday, frequently urging the congregation to repent. However, their answer was always the same: they were considering it, but they feared that converting would lead to the loss of their wives and children. This was the cost of polygamy. If they had eight wives and they converted to Christianity, only one wife and her children could be accepted by the Lutheran church. Schumann requested the church to find another solution to this problem, which was a complex issue that required long-term attention and effort. The dispute between Christianity and culture was something that Schumann was prepared to debate without end. Ever the pragmatist, he was always looking for ways or improvement – if these were rooted in truth and not tradition.

His reports reflected the same problems as those experienced by the other missionaries in Zululand – taking one step forward and three steps back. Every step forward involved much debating, understanding and patience and, just as you were thinking that you had made a breakthrough, the Zulus were forced back to their kraals (settlements), and they had to start all over again. However, as time went by, larger numbers of people attended the lessons and were baptised. It was still a challenging road.

> "You are not only responsible for what you say, but also for what you do not say" ~ Martin Luther

If there is one thing I have learned from my great grandfather Schumann, it is how much harder he was on himself than on anyone else. If he suffered, as he surely did, he never felt sorry for himself and did not allow himself the luxury of grief. As a pragmatist, he took each day as it came, facing the challenges head-on. Accounts of him from others describe a man who tolerated no nonsense, although he often masked it with a sense of humour. This particular trait was passed down through generations; particularly to his grandson, Kurt. My uncle became well known throughout his teaching career for his sharpness, often delivering stern warnings with a touch of humour.

Schumann ran the mission station at Emlalazi from 1888 to 1903. It was during this time that the two Boer Wars were being fought.[42] Although this particular mission was not highly successful, he writes: "I have more reason to be grateful than to complain … It is by God's grace that I am still standing". He used to take long hikes to visit the Zulu *kraals* in the surrounding areas. He believed in pastoral care and he made sure to spend time with each community. He would often stay away from home for days at a time, staying with them in their *rondavel* huts. He not only offered a listening ear but also provided medical assistance whenever he could.

---

[42] The First Boer War (1880–1881) was fought between Britain and Transvaal. The Second Boer War – also known as the Anglo-Boer War – was fought from 1899 and 1902 between Britain and the two Boer republics: the Orange Free State and the South African Republic (Transvaal).

Schumann Family. Johanne and Pastor Schumann seated with Konrad on his lap. My grandfather standing middle back.

During their stay at Emlalazi, Johanne gave birth to ten children, followed by another two at a later stage. Only six of the twelve children – three boys and three girls – survived childhood. The oldest of the surviving children, Jann Wilhelm *Friedrich*, was to become my grandfather. Carine's book narrates the births and deaths of Johanne's precious babies, making you wonder how she managed to keep her sanity while facing that much loss and grief; not to mention her compassionate nature. This woman deserves a medal. Can you ever become desensitised to grief, I wonder? Where did they flee to during the Boer War with all their children? One child died of envenomation. Johanne was breast feeding when someone was bitten by a poisonous snake. Without hesitating she sucked out the poison and spat it out. But some must have entered the blood and from there into the milk from which the child died. The snake bite victim survived.

Below is a list of the names of Friedrich and Johanne Schumann's children:

1. Jann Wilhelm *Friedrich* Schumann: born 23 March 1890 at Emlalazi; became the teacher and headmaster at Glückstadt School.
2. Elsche Marie Dora Freese née Schumann: born 22 August 1891 at Emlalazi.
3. David Peter *Harm (Hermann)* Schumann: born 25 January 1893 at Emlalazi; became a tailor in Durban.

4. Johann Georg Heinrich Schumann: born 7 August 1894; died 2 April 1895 at Emlalazi.
5. Wilhelm August Behrend Schumann: born 17 November 1895; died 5 March 1896 at Emlalazi.
6. Itje Johanna Dora Schumann: born 5 February 1897; died 23 July 1898 at Emlalazi.
7. Louise Henrietta Bertha Sophie Lange née Schumann: born 6 June 1898 at Emlalazi.
8. Katharina Maria Magdalena Schumann: born 6 June 1900; died 22 October 1900 at Emlalazi;
9. Anna Katharina Sophie Volker née Schumann: born 20 July 1902 at Emlalazi.
10. Heinrich Paul Gerhard Schumann: born 29 August 1903; died 20 January 1907 at Emlalazi.
11. Anna Elisabeth Christine Schumann: born 9 June 1909; died 30 September 1907 at Bethel.
12. *Konrad* Heinrich Hermann Schumann: born 22 June 1909 at Bethel; became a teacher.

"Jesus said to her, "I am the resurrection and the life. He who believes in Me. Though he may die, he shall live" (NKJV John 11:25).

In her diary, Johanne writes: "I was suffering from heavy bleeding, and before the little ones could crawl towards the river I would hastily go and wash in the ice cold running water. After a brisk walk back, I would warm up again and feel refreshed enough to tackle the day's tasks ahead. But then one day I saw the natives farming on the other side of the river. I told my husband, who that same afternoon, went about to find a sheltered spot for me to bathe in. Hermann was about 5 years old and came with us to find the next bathing spot. Soon we found a perfect place and we had just turned around to go back home when Hermann came running up behind us shouting. 'Come quickly! I just want to show you something.' Oh! the disappointment! What did we see but a large nest of three crocodile eggs. We had never seen something like that before. How glad we were that the Lord was so gracious to warn us. All our good laid plans came to nothing. I then got the idea to have a cold bath at night with Bicarbonate of Soda. That did me the world of good. And see, today I am still healthy even though I am old".

The affair of Schumann's transfer from Emlalazi to Bethel was handled tactlessly and appeared to result from internal political maneuvering. It appeared that he was paying far too much pastoral attention to the Zulu people, while neglecting the Europeans. It was unclear to him how they could come to that conclusion: after all, the focus of his mission was ministering the Zulu people.

Sometimes, God works in mysterious ways: He is the one that closes some doors and opens others, although this may occur in unagreeable ways. Did He not say that in this life you will have trouble?[43] But see I have overcome the world! The missionary and the pastor must always be ready to go where the Master leads.

BETHEL; EKUHLENGENI; GLÜCKSTADT; SCHEEPERS NEK AND VRYHEID

From 1907 to 1914, Schumann stayed at Bethel, where he took over from Missionary Stallbom, while keeping the mission station at Ekuhlengeni under his wing as well. A year later, in 1908, he also took over the church at Glückstadt,

---

[43] John 16:33 "I have told you these things, so that in me you may have peace. In this world you will have trouble. But take heart! I have overcome the world."

where an exceptionally busy time started for Schumann, which was also to become the most productive part of his ministry.

Glückstadt Church. Photo by Jan van Wyk. Where the Schumann family ministered and worshipped for about three generations.

A young Zulu in the Bethel congregation, who had not done right by his fiancé, was not at all pleased that Schumann expressed an opinion about it. Seeking revenge, he decided to kill him. Although forgiveness is the language of Christ, revenge was the language of the Zulu people. Similar to the Saxons, forgiveness was not a cultural concept for the Zulus: it had to be taught. One Sunday afternoon, as Schumann was on his way back to Bethel from one of his long round trips, the young Zulu and a friend kept a careful watch, trying to find the right time and place to attack Schumann.

Several days later, the Zulu boy turned up at Schumann's house, asking Johanne, "Who were the two men that accompanied the missionary on his way back home"? He told her that he and his friend were hiding along the way with the intention of killing him. At this point, I would probably have fled in fear, but Johanne went to ask her husband who those men with him were, telling him the story. She then told the Zulu boy: "Pastor Schumann does not know of any men with him at all, but he does know that God sends his ministering angels to protect us during times of great danger".

Schumann might have been a man of few words, but he was not insular. The pastoral side of him was always open to listen and to help. Many children went through his house as boarders and, if the conversation at table became too animated, he would suddenly interject, "Don't you know that we have to give account for every unnecessary word we speak"? He might have said these words to my father, who was also fond to slamming his fist on the table, saying, "We can all sing together but we can't all talk together at the same time!" A moment or two of silence would follow, after which the conversation would begin again, but rather tentatively.

Being someone who preferred one-on-one interactions, Pastor Schumann found crowds suffocating and loud conversation bewildering. He avoided the mission conferences where possible and, if he did go, he would probably stand to one side – a man after my own heart. This behaviour often got him into quite a pickle with the Superintendent. However, when it came to weddings, it was another thing altogether and he very seldom allowed himself to miss the joyful celebration. After the wedding of Wilhelm and Emmy Meyer, he was heard saying, "Now that was a wonderful wedding!"

His grumpy frankness was probably one of his East Frisian peculiarities, but no one ever held it against him, because it was always accompanied by a cheeky grin. When Tante Bosser arrived during the week for a visit, he would ask, "What are you doing here? Don't you have any work to do?" Then Tante Bosse would tilt her head back and reply laughingly, "I want to come and visit you, Onkel Schumann". "But you are holding me up", he would respond. To which she would just laugh, while making herself at home. Schumann would then make himself comfortable and enjoy an hour chatting with her. When the peep toe shoes came into fashion, he wondered aloud if they were cheaper.

It was during World War I (1914–1918) that Schumann was appointed as the pastor at Glückstadt. My favourite photograph of my great grandfather is of him sitting on the veranda of his house with his hands clasped only by the tips of his fingers, his thumbs forming a type of pyramid on his lap. He sat there on Sunday mornings, making sure all his parishioners were getting ready for church.

Pastor Schumann at Glückstadt. Photo taken of the original image displayed in the Lutheran church foyer, by the author at the centenary celebrations.

I first saw this photograph in the Glückstadt Lutheran Church,[44] when it celebrated its 100th anniversary (1908–2008). My daughter, Candice arrived from Australia that day and, after picking her up from the airport in Durban, we drove straight to Glückstadt, several hours away up north. Poor Candice was utterly exhausted when we reached our destination. At Glückstadt, we were met by Carine Nel and her family. The church was packed to the rafters. The service

---

[44] It is noteworthy to mention that my great grandfather on my father's side, Gottlob Friedrich Wilhelm Hermann, was one of the founding members of the church.

continued for quite a while and the celebrations were finished off with a traditional South African *braai*⁴⁵ (barbecue), with the inevitable brass band without which the celebrations would not have been the same. Afterwards, we followed Carine back to their farm, where we met her husband and stayed overnight, drinking sherry and catching up on old family history. This was when Carine gave me permission to translate her books. Although I have not translated them, I have used them as reference sources in this book.

100 Years Glückstadt. DVD

The centenary publication of the Glückstadt Lutheran Church narrates the following story, written by my uncle, Fritz (my mother's eldest brother), entitled, *Ja Damals* ("Yes, back then").

> "We can compare life with a book. A book is made up of many chapters. When the one chapter is finished the next one begins. In my memoirs, the first chapter would be titled, *My Glückstadt Years*. We often hear of people talking about the good old days. That they were always good, is debatable. Even so, they have a nostalgia, that one would not like to forget. The number 100

---

⁴⁵ The *braai* is the South African version of a barbecue (BBQ), which traditionally involves outdoor cooking on a local wood fire, which gives the meat a distinct flavour.

has in cricket an important meaning but is also important in the life of a church building. So many memories of the earlier old days with old friends and the people of yester year.

Transport in those days was of oxen wagons, donkey carts, horse carts, and for those who could afford it a Spider.

In the early 20s, the first motor cars arrived like the Ford Tin Lizzies, 'in any colour as long as it was black'. I can still remember the whole congregation going out on day trips on oxen wagons to Hlonjane waterfall or to the Ntabankulu Mountain. The post would arrive in Glückstadt with the post coach and at the end of the 20s the new railway bus took over the service. On its first trip from Vryheid to the Black Umfolozi, the bus stopped at Glückstadt school and took the whole school population on a joy ride.

There was no doctor. When there was a birth, you could not expect any medical assistance. But it was obvious that when Tante Tschirpig moved in with a family, a new baby arrived. There were also storks, but they became fewer and fewer because Tante Tschirpig took over the business (typical Schumann humour). As children we ran about bare foot. The rule was that you got your first pair of shoes when you are being confirmed and that was usually in your teens. Sometimes on rare occasions you may be gifted a pair of second-hand shoes beforehand. It was therefore very often that one would stub one's big toe on a stone or rock. We understood very well the meaning of the verse "Behold I lay in Zion a stumbling stone and rock of offence …" (Romans 9:33).

In 1913, Pastor Schumann resigned from the missionary field altogether, in order to continue his far-reaching work of planting the sister churches of Scheepersnek, Vryheid and Leeunek. He would walk the long distances between each church before the Scheepersnek congregation gave him a horse and buggy, which he gladly accepted. On the first Sunday of every month, he would walk to Vryheid, where the little congregation met in different homes. After receiving the horse and buggy, he would leave on Saturday afternoon from Glückstadt and pass the Duvels on his way to Scheepersnek. This was a convenient short-cut, and he did not have to travel via Vryheid.

Lutheran Church, Scheepersnek KZN. Photo taken by André van Ellinckhuyzen for the author.

At Muller's Trees, he would leave the main road and travel along a farm road to the Duvels. At this point, the horse did not need whip or bridle, because it knew there was always a good feed waiting at the Duvels. Pastor Schumann enjoyed the pitstop and visiting with his old friends before continuing his journey. He would arrive at Scheepersnek in the evening and preach twice on the Sunday.

Before he received his own transport, the Duvels would try to meet him in the buggy to give him a lift. True to his character, he would chirp, "Herr Duvel, I want to warn you that one day maybe someone else will pick me up and take me to Scheepersnek". And so it happened that, one day, another farmer did pick him up along the way. "Ja, Herr Duvel, I warned you". "Good", retorted Duvel jokingly, "Then I won't come anymore either". On Mondays, he drove back to Glückstadt via Vryheid, where he did all the necessary shopping at the shop of his old friend, Mr Slerenski, a Jewish trader.

Pastor Schumann's daughter, Katrina, cannot remember if her father had ever been deterred by wind, rain or any bad weather. There were no bridges over the rivers and streams and, one day, after a heavy thunderstorm and heavy rain, the river before Dassiehoogte was in flood. However, Pastor Schumann thought that he could still cross the river. To his horror, the waters carried him, the buggy and horse downstream towards the White Umfolozi River, which was very full. Thank God, the horse managed to tread on solid ground and to pull the buggy, with pastor Schumann still in it, out of the water in time.

Pastor Schumann with Johanne in their retirement.

From 1930, the old couple stayed in a two bedroomed cottage near the school. Schumann still had an old yolk with a bucket on each side, like those used in the old days in Germany to carry water on his shoulders. He would go to the new well at Glückstadt every day to collect their daily water for the household and the garden. As he got older, he would only go as far as the school to get water from the tanks. The children could see him through the classroom windows, picking up dung from the children's horses and donkeys. One day, he came to the school with a wheelbarrow full of dung and a puffadder to show the children how to kill a snake. You take it by the tail and smash the head by bashing it hard on the ground several times.

In his shed and workshop, he had his own coffin stored in the rafters. At regular intervals, one of the local people would come and ask for the coffin, after which he would make another to take its place. No one knows how many coffins he had made before the coffin actually became his own.

Pastor Schumann was also proficient in both Greek and Latin and would read the Bible in all those languages. He worked together with the well-known Catholic priest, A. T. Bryant, on the translation of the Zulu-English Dictionary, that appeared in 1905. It remained for many years the standard for all translations. He was also known as the best scholar on Hebrew that the Hermannsburg mission had at that time (Nel, 2002:8).

In 1921, Scheepersnek received their own pastor – Pastor R. Drewes. The Vryheid congregation joined them. At the age of 65, Pastor Schumann (*inkonjane e tut udaga* – "calf stuck in the mud") retired the next year (1922), due to a throat illness. He died on 13 December 1947, at the ripe age of 91.

Both Friedrich and Johanne Schumann are buried at Glückstadt, in the cemetery of the little church, and only a short distance away, Schumann's eldest son (my grandfather), Jann Wilhelm Friedrich, is also buried.

Although you cannot really call Pastor Schumann an "original", because that is what we all are, he was certainly legendary – a type of an urban legend. That is why anecdotes are making the rounds about him in the German community to this day. The East Friesland motto, *Lever dod as sklav* ("Live as a slave") ran through his veins. In other words, work hard as slaves. That would explain why, when someone gifted him a barrow of chopped wood or manure, he saw it as an insult to his independence, rather than being happy to receive the gift. Every day, before breakfast and before dinner, he chopped firewood and collected manure (for the vegetable garden) himself. He kept his own vegetable garden and, two days before his death, he was still harvesting beans.

Wo de Nordseewellen trecken an den Strand (Friesenlied)

Wo de Nordseewellen trecken an de Strand,
wo de geelen Blömen bleuhnt int gröne Land,
wo de Möven schrieen hell int Sturmgebrus,
dor is miene Heimat, dor bin ick to Hus.

Well'n un Wogen sung'n mi all mien Weegenleed
und de hogen Diecken kennt mien Kinnertied,
kennt ok all mien Sehnsucht, as ich wussen weer
in de Welt to flegen, öwer Land un Meer.

Woll hett mi dat Lewen all min Lengen stillt,
hett mi allens gewen, wat min Hart nu füllt,
allens is verswunnen, wat mi quält un dreew,
hev dat Glück woll funnen, doch de Sehnsucht bleev.

Sehnsucht na min scheunet, grönet Marschenland,
wo de Nordseewellen trecken an de Strand,
wor de Möven schrieen hell in Stromgebrus,
dor is miene Heimat, dor bin ick to Hus.

Where the North Sea waves roll onto the shore
Where the yellow flowers bloom in the green land
Where the seagulls cry loudly in the roar of the storm
That is my homeland, that's where I'm at home

Where the seagulls cry loudly in the roar of the storm
That is my homeland, that's where I'm at home.

The wind and waves sang me my lullaby
That still often flows through my dreams today
They knew all I could see and all my longing
To fly out into the world, over land and sea
They knew all I could see and all my longing
To fly out into the world, over land and sea
Again and again I'm drawn to the green beach
Where the yellow broom blooms in the dune sand
Where the seagulls cry loudly in the roar of the storm
That is my homeland, that's where I'm at home
Where the seagulls cry loudly in the roar of the storm
That is my homeland, that's where I'm at home.

GLÜCKSTADT SCHOOL: JANN WILHELM FRIEDRICH SCHUMANN AND IDA MARIE SOPHIE GEVERS

Every heart with Christ is a missionary, every heart without Christ is a mission field - Vlad Savchuk.

THE MISSIONARY AND HUGUENOT FAMILIES MELD.

Jann Wilhelm Friedrich Schumann and Ida Gevers' wedding in Harburg.

Known by the local Zulu population as *uMasezela* ("The one that helps others"), Jann Wilhelm Friedrich Schumann loved people, and he loved the old Zulu history. Appendix C is a copy of an article on the Zulu villages written by Schumann that was published in *Die Huisgenoot* of 24 July 1936. Although he had inherited his no-nonsense character and humour from his father, his children adored him. Before taking over as headmaster at Glückstadt, he studied teaching in Pietermaritzburg. I suspect that he met my grandmother, Ida Marie Sophie Gevers, while he was in Pietermaritzburg and, it is at this point that the Gevers family joined that of the Schumann family. They got married in Harburg, just a little west from Pietermaritzburg, towards Greytown.

I have this lovely wedding photograph of them, but precious little information on their life together, other than what I remember from my mother's stories and from the Glückstadt Primary School Yearbook, 1910–1985.

Ida was the fifth child of Johann Jurgen Friedrich Gevers (born on 30 March 1861 and died on 4 January 1919 at the age of 58), and Marie Caroline Dorothea Meyer. They had nine children together. They did not stay in Harburg, but moved to Assegai/Hillcrest towards Durban, where they became prosperous farmers. After my great grandfather Gevers had passed away, Marie decided to donate the original farm homestead and surrounding property to the Lutheran church. A new church was constructed and some of my uncles were involved in the construction and building works. Prior to this, my mother remembers often visiting her grandmother there. Several huge pine trees stood in the yard, which, to my dismay, were chopped down just before my husband and I relocated to Australia. My grandmother, Ida, inherited a small property from her mother, Marie, at the foot of the hill, across the main road from the church. After Ida's husband, Friedrich, had passed away, she returned there with my mum and two of her brothers.

Hillcrest (Assegai)
Lutheran Church.
KwaZulu Natal.

Jann Wilhelm Friedrich and Ida went to live in a little house in Glückstadt not far from the school. They too had nine children of whom my mother is the youngest. Ida assisted her husband with his work at school, until the demands of a large family made it impossible for her to continue. The school was established to teach the children of the surrounding farming district. Although most of them were German, there were also Afrikaans children, and English was a required language.

During the Anglo-Boer War/Second Boer War (1899–1902), it became impossible for the farmers to send their children to Hermannsburg for education and therefore, the farmers' wives took over the education of their children. The Department of Education in Natal was approached for help in building a school and their application was successful. The new school was a wood and iron structure, which was hot as hell in summer and freezing cold in winter. Initially, the school had only two classrooms, which were increased as time went by.

Not only did Jann Wilhelm Friedrich become the local teacher and headmaster, but he was also a musician. He was the organist for the little congregation, choir leader and the director of the brass band. Being highly knowledgeable about the hydrotherapy (water cures) [46]of Dr Sebastian Kneipp (1821–1897), he also acted as counsellor and "doctor". For decades, he was the only one in the village with a typewriter, and he used to assist people with writing letters.

To expand his knowledge, Jann Wilhelm Friedrich continued his studies privately. He was also a member of the local debate society. Because it was extremely important for him to keep the German language going, he arranged an invitation to all German speaking teachers to meet at Harburg through the *Deutsch-Afrikaner*, a German magazine. In Harburg, the German Education

---

[46] Hydrotherapy, which is still used in Germany to this day, is based on Dr Kneipp's understanding of the healing power of water. These water treatments (water cures) rest on the following five pillars: lifestyle, water, exercise, nutrition and herbal medicine.

Society ("Duitse Onderwysers Vereeniging") was established on 6–7 July 1927. Jann Wilhelm Friedrich Schumann was appointed as the chairman – a position he did not desire, although he was re-elected every year, until 1932, and again in 1934.

Jann Wilhelm Friedrich's deepest wish was for every child to have the right to an education in their mother tongue. This is how it came about that, when there was German, Afrikaans and sometimes English children at the school, he created a complex teaching programme to accommodate all language preferences. School inspectors were astonished at what the new school principal had achieved in terms of teaching different grades in three languages and, therefore, they insisted that the Department of Education send the poor man an assistant. Prof. Alexander Reid, head of the Teaching Training College in Pietermaritzburg, made a day trip to Glückstadt to check out this achievement for himself. He spent entire day observing the lessons to understand what Mr Schumann was doing. In the end, he got his assistant!

During breaks, the teachers and the children played together. A game of marbles, called "doghies", was particularly popular. With his tongue stuck in the corner of his cheek, Mr. Schumann would often be seen, trying to encourage the "goen" in the right direction. He was an excellent chess player and taught his children the game; in particular, Onkel Kurt, Mama's brother, who went on to teach my brother, Eddie and ran the chess club at Pinetown High School, where Eddie became a member.

Back to Glückstadt: on Fridays' during breaks, Mr Schumann would play a game of chess with a Mr Krause. If the game was not won before the end of the day, they would continue after the weekend. On occasions, he would mount his bicycle and ride across the hills and valleys to Ceza – a journey of about 50 km – to meet with the Swiss Missionary, Sandstrom, with whom he would play chess for an entire weekend.

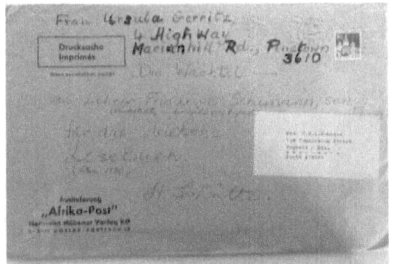 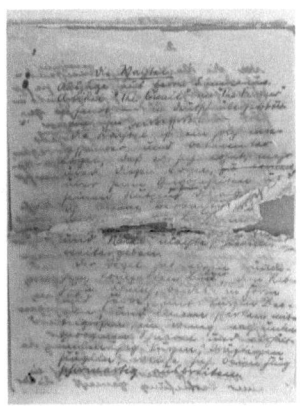

Found amongst my late mother's belongings. The contents are very fragile. The original manuscript was written in my grandfather's own hand, Headmaster Friedrich Schumann. A children's story book written in German 'Die Wagtel' now in the possession of the author.

His interests were wide-ranging, and his lessons were captivating. Students remember story time with *Jock of the Bushveld*. While he was reading, Mr Schumann would take a pinch of snuff with intense pleasure, while enjoying the story himself. In the afternoon, they always finished school with the following hymn, followed by The Lord's Prayer.

> Unser ausgang segne Gott
> Unsern Eingang gleichermassern;
> Segne unser täglich Brot,
> Segne unser Tun und Lassen,
> Segne uns zum sel'gen sterben
> Und mach uns zum Himmelserben

From Malmo in Sweden, Karl Steimer writes: "Our headmaster Mr Schumann was a strict but fair teacher. He used an old chair-leg called "Tomsack", to punish disobedient boys. One of his sons, Reinhold Schumann, and I were good friends. On our teacher's birthday, Reinhold and I decided to take a hen from the Schumann henhouse to make him a present. Stealthily it was transferred to school and put in a wastepaper basket near his desk. When Mr Schumann entered the classroom and seated himself, the hen started to cackle. Surprised, he asked what was going on. Since I was the bravest, I declared, "Sir, since it is your birthday, we decided to give you the hen as a present." Our charming teacher took the hen home, not knowing that it was his own hen!"

Their house in Glückstadt had four bedrooms and the five boys occupiedd one. They were sleeping dormitory style on iron divan beds. In order to accommodate all the children, even the lounge was converted into a bedroom. As if all the boys were not enough, the Schumann's also took on weekly boarders. This was before the proper boarding facilities became available. According to my mother, my grandmother, Ida (affectionately called "Dear" or "Gormuting", by her grandchildren), reigned supreme in the kitchen and prepared all the meals herself. "She would've killed the whole lot us if we were all in the kitchen at the same time". This soft, kind-hearted woman also played the role of disciplinarian, so as to keep all the children and three dogs in check for meals around the large dining room table. Since my mother was a poor eater, I suspect the dogs congregated around her chair. My mother told me: "Nero, in particular, used to lie and smile at me. How on earth this dog got named after the Roman Emperor Nero, is beyond me. He was a real *gedoy* (street dog) and looked like a greyhound but had the most gentle and placid nature with a permanent smile on his face". Well, if mama had Wednesday legs, Nero was a well-fed pooch! "Can you imagine, Ingrid, what our dear mother went through. Just imagine mopping floors only to find that the whole hoard of us kids has trooped right through again with wet and muddy feet. Lugging the wet red clay like earth all the way through the house followed with seconds to spare by three panting dogs. I might have packed my bags. She must have had the patience and love of a saint".

Baths were a weekly ritual in those days. Unlike the luxury of beautiful bathrooms with hot running water, baths were taken outside. Water was carried by hand in buckets and boiled in a big cast iron pot. Three to four people used the same bath water. The oldest always had the first chance to take a bath, after which it went down the pecking order, with my mother bringing in the rear. When she was very young, the maids would bath her, pulling her ears to make sure they were clean.

During the week, the maids had to wash all the children's feet, as none of them had shoes. It was very important to Dear, who washed all the sheets by hand, that the children's feet were spotlessly clean before they went to bed. "God, the woman would've had to break her back cleaning"! I can imagine the kids, all lined up in a row to have their daily feet wash and Dear checking each one to make sure that they had done a proper job. Walking barefoot over the icy frost in winter, they constantly suffered from frostbite, which caused the skin on their heels and soles to burst open. "It was so painful to have your feet scrubbed with a scrubbing brush", my mother would remember. Dear would have a tin of balm – consisting of candle wax, mixed with camphor and liquid paraffin – ready to rub into the feet. My mother-in-law would talk about the top and tail sponge bath, but Gan[47] had another name for it: "face, feet and fanny", with much giggling.

Gan continues as follows: "Before my father died, he often saw a strange light. Especially at night when he was walking home. Apparently, there was an old wife's tale that was well known in those days, that if you saw such a light, it meant that you were going to die soon. He told Dear often about this light, and she would try her best to calm him down and to re-assure him that it was nothing. One day they all went away on a little holiday to a farm. This farmer was known for propagating fruit trees and grafting especially citrus fruit. However,

---

[47] Gan Gan is the name that my children gave my mother.

this particular year the fruit trees were flowering strangely, and he mentioned to Dear "that it meant there was going to be a death in the family soon".

Ida never had the chance to tell her husband about this, as he had left early to return home, taking my mother with him. Soon after this, my grandfather died unexpectedly.

There are several of these lovely stories from the past published in a yearbook too. Paging through the celebration photos, I noticed my mother in the front row of a photograph of the students from 1920 to 1930. However, she was so busy chatting that she did not even notice the camera.

Back to the Anglo-Boer War (1899–1902): apparently, the Schumann's (Pastor Friedrich and Johanne and some of their children) were captured and taken to a concentration camp in or near Eshowe. The English thought that this missionary family would be accomplices to the burghers. They were put into bell tents and given refugee rations – mostly *mielie meal*,[48] which came in cotton or muslin bags. Numerous prisoners in the concentration camp died of dysentery. Eventually, they discovered finely ground glass in the meal, forcing them to sift it with great care. Johanne collected the glass and went to see the British Commissioner, asking why they were putting glass in the prisoners' food. He just shrugged, replying, "Well madam, for every corpse I receive a commission". One of their own children died in the concentration camp of dysentery. My grandmother told this story to my mother when she was a little girl. She never forgot it.

From Carine's books, we glean the following in terms of World War II (1939–1945). At the end of November 1941, Tobruk had fallen, and the South African soldiers were captured as prisoners of war. In order to placate the South Africans back home, the government began to round up as many German people and

---

[48] *Mielie meal*, which is essentially maize meal, is a rather coarse flour, made from maize (*mielies*) and used to cook porridge *(pap)* in South Africa.

descendants of Germans as they could, placing them in intern camps. With his son only a few months old at the time, Onkel Konrad, mama's youngest uncle, was interned from 13 October 1941 to 23 December 1942. He was sent to a camp in Koffiefontein. After 15 months, Konrad was released and placed under house arrest with his elderly parents. Even so, he was prevented from attending his brother's funeral. He became very close to his niece, Brunnie. Onkel Konrad is the author of the book *Aus dem Lebens eines Süd-Afrikanischen Taugenichts*, a compendium of stories and poems about Africa. The book reflects the keen insight he had of the Zulu people and their culture.

A newsletter in Carine's books captures the following: On 20 January 1943, Jann Wilhelm Friedrich Schumann passed away, after becoming a happy and proud grandfather a few months earlier. His eldest daughter, Irmgard, gave birth to a lovely little girl, Erica.

Right up to the end of his life, he appeared well and healthy. A few hours before his death, he was still leading the choir. He was happy and surrounded by friends. It was the evening of a *Polterabend* – a beautiful German tradition of having a party the night before the wedding. Mama, who was only nine years old at the time, was there with him, never far from her beloved father. She saw him laughing before he collapsed to the ground right in front of her. She never entirely got over the loss of her father.

Wanderlust

Ein Wand'rer sein, ein herrlich Leben,
So recht in Gottes weite Welt!
Die Sorgen kurz hinweggeworfen
Und frei, frei ziehn durch Wald und Feld!

Kaum graut das Licht in fernen Osten,
Schon zieht der Wand'rer seinen Weg

O Frühlingszeit! O frohe Welten!
Durch's Grüne fuhrt hinan der Steg.

Die Vögel lustig Marsche singen;
Es rauscht so hell der Wasserfall,
Und purpurn farbt mit seinen Schwingen,
Ein Wolkchen hoch, der erste Strahl.

Vom hohen Berge schaut man nieder,
Dort wo die Heimatswiege stand,
Und winkt und ruft: Ich komme wieder,
Jetzt zieh ich fort in's fremde Land!

Konrad Schumann

The Schumann Children and Generational Blessings

Headmaster Schumann and family with my mother Ursula Schumann middle front.

Below is a list of the names of the children of Jann Wilhelm Friedrich and Ida Schumann as well as their children. Pastor Friedrich Schumann and Johanne Schumann were their grandparents and the great grandparents of these children and grandchildren respectively.

Irmgard Maria Johanna Magdalena Schumann

Irmgard Maria Johanna Magdalena Schumann was born on 22 May 1917 in Glückstadt and died on 26 December 1971. She was married to Herbert Victor Freese, a descendant of the Cotton Germans. Like her father, Tante Irms, as I knew her, became a teacher in Pinetown, where she taught at both the junior and the primary school, later becoming the Vice Principal at the Primary School.

They had the following three children:

Erica Eileen Freese: born on 12 August 1942; died on 30 April 2024. Erica, who never married, became a teacher like her mother, but she specialized in Home Economics. Before her retirement, she became the Head of Department at the Edgewood Teachers Training College in Pinetown. She was an artist with a needle and won several prizes for her work, right up to before her death and posthumously. With her amazing spirit, Erica was a lifelong friend and niece of my mother whom she helped. Mama died in 2023.

Arnold Richard Freese: born on 21 May 1944; died 13 April 2024. Arnold married Marion Richards with whom he had four children. Apart from him being a pilot in the SANDF early in his life, I remember very little about him.

Brother and sister. Arnold and Erika Freese. Celebrating her 80th birthday. They passed away 17 days apart in April 2024. Photo supplied by Marion Freese Jnr.

Konrad Freese: born 11 April 1947; died ca. 2011. Known as Doy, Konrad married Marion Steel, and they had two children – Sandra, who became an Advocate (Barrister) and Hugh, who is a teacher in the United Kingdom (UK). Doy was a gentle soul who loved cars and mechanics. He had a profound influence on me in that regard.

BRUNHILDE SOPHIE ERNA SCHUMANN

Brunhilde Sophie Erna Schumann (known as Brunnie) was born 14 October 1918 and died ca. 20 January 1990. She married Arthur Friedrich Dinkelmann of the Cotton Germans, and she also became a teacher. Her husband, who was a farmer in Gingindlovo, died early, and they had the following four children:

Phyllis Ruth Dinkelmann, who married Maurice Greiff, an industrialist, with whom she lived most of her live in the French Canton in Vevey, Switzerland. They had two children of whom Robby passed when he was in his early twenties. Although he studied law, his heart's desire was to be a paramedic, which he did during vacations. At his funeral, the ambulances lined the streets. Both Phyllis and Maurice have passed and leave behind their lovely daughter, Natalie whom I think is still in Switzerland.

Elfi Marianne Dinkelmann, who lives in Cape Town, and was working for the University of Cape Town.

Hilda Solveig Dinkelmann, whom we know as Bambi, lives in Johannesburg.

Linda Olga Dinkelmann, who was one of my favourite cousins when I was a little girl and made a name for herself as a Springbok trampolinist and a multi award winner as a trainer for Olivetti.

Linda Dinkelmann Springbok trampolinist. Durban beach in the background. Image from Eddie Herrmann.

FRIEDRICH HERMANN SCHUMANN (CALLED FRITZ)

Friedrich Hermann Schumann was born on 9 February 1920 and died on 15 August 2016, married Tante Mine (Wilhelmine) Volker. Onkel Fritz became a teacher and later principal at the high school in Greytown and, I think, Durban Boys High. They had six children:

Ilse Mona Schumann, who became a librarian and married Edgar Hillermann before relocating to Sydney, Australia. They have three children.

Helmuth Friedrich Schumann, who won top marks for South Africa in academics in his final year at school. He went onto study Physics in Durban and Astrophysics at Cambridge University in the UK. He continued his studies in Operations Research in Toronto and became Policy Advisor to the Ontario Government. He married Elizabeth Ramsay and they have three children of whom one has become a barrister in Canada.

Rona Monika Schumann, who became a computer analyst/programmer with a BSc in Computer Science from Stellenbosch University. She married a mining engineer, Andrew Richmond, with whom she relocated to Australia after their wedding. They have three children of whom I know that two became teachers.

Erwin Wilhelm Schumann: with a PhD in Electronic Engineering. He used to be the Managing Director of Grintek. He married Candy Hay and they have four children. They live in Cape Town.

Martin Anton Schumann, also an Electronic Engineer with a BSc Electronic Engineering, married Irmgard Wentzel and they have two children. They relocated to Canada.

Arnold Walter Schumann: With a PhD in Agriculture (Plant Nutrition). Arnold became Prof. Schumann at one of the universities in Florida, where he married Rhonda Arnold. They had no children of their own. Of all Onkel Fritz's children, he is the one whom I remember. We attended Greytown Junior School together and he was very kind to me while I was a boarder.

Reinhold Friedrich Detlef Bernhard Schumann

He was born 6 March 1923 at Glückstadt and died on 16 June 1978 in Durban. He married Alma Emily Marion Watt. They had two children:

Gillian (Gilly) Schumann: Gilly, who was a teacher librarian, married Derek Schafer with whom she had two children. After intensely suffering from multiple sclerosis (MS), Gilly died on 21 September 2015.

Richard John Friedrich Schumann, one of my favourite cousins whom I seldom see. He started his own fishing business in Durban, later becoming internationally known as a fishing expert, taking wealthy people all over the world in their yachts to the best fishing destinations. He was a type of marine conservationist and published several articles. He is currently retired and living in the Eastern Cape, shooting the breeze and doing organic gardening as a hobby.

Waldemar Oswald Schumann

Born on 25 April 1924 in Glückstadt and died 11 October 1974 in Durban. He was married to Aunty Nan, who returned to Australia with her son (from a previous marriage) after his death.

Friedeborg Katrina Therese Schumann

Known as Friedel, she was born on 26 February 1926 in Glückstadt. She was trained and worked as a nursing sister until her marriage to Solomon Maritz of the famous Voortrekker Gert Maritz genealogy. He was a farmer in Zululand and owner of the farm Tussen Bay in the Babanango District, where we spent many wonderful holidays. They had three children:

Yvonne Maritz, married Keith Sidwell Downs. Yvonne, who was involved in cooking and baking, started "Something Special" – a home industry in Overport (Durban), mainly catering to wealthy housewives. Yvonne eventually sold the business. However, both Tante Friedel and my mother worked there later, when my mother was living with Solly and Friedel in Overport. They had three children: Kerry, Jacky and Jennifer, who live in Johannesburg. These sisters are best friends, and I am glad to be in contact with them. After many years, I met Kerry again at my mother's funeral in January 2023. She is in public health. Jacky is a nurse, and I am not sure what Jennifer is doing.

Johannes Friedrich Arthur Maritz (known as Johnny): He married Roule Klopper. He died in circa 2000 from cancer. He also became an electrical engineer and had a compelling career at Armscor – particularly in the era of the border wars and the sanctions against South Africa – an interesting period in South African history. He had a wonderfully generous and outgoing nature that endeared him to everyone. A big lad, with a love for the outdoors, camping and fishing, he took the whole lot of us to Kosi Bay for a holiday – the most spectacular holiday of my life! I absolutely adored this man. Willem assisted him with research into the Maritz family tree, which I have just found. They had three children of whom some are now living in Perth, Australia.

Walter Harold Maritz: born 29 April1952 and died on 16 September 1973 in a car accident near Eshowe. He was just a little older than my brother and the two of them hit it off big time. "Kiffie", as he was known, was to take over the running of the farm from my uncle, Solly. His death affected his father particularly hard. My mother adored her sister, Friedel, and they remained close and lifelong friends, until her death not too long before my own mama passed away. Tante Friedel outlived all her children and her husband, which must have been extremely difficult for her.

KURT GOTTFRIED GEORG SCHUMANN

Born on 24 November 1928 in Glückstadt and died on 2 September 2004 in Johannesburg. He was a carpenter who became a teacher and departmental head at Pinetown High School and Pinetown Boys High School. He was highly involved in the construction of the Lutheran Church in Hillcrest on my great grandmother's property from the Gevers/Meyer side. He was married to Maria Magdalena Elisabeth (Miemie) Van der Merwe born 27/12/1934 and died on 22/02/2025, and they had two children:

Linda Maria Cloete (Schumann) born May 21, 1964. She is my co-editor! We spent a lot of time together while we were growing up; particularly in our younger years. With a doctorate in Library and Information Science, Linda is a former librarian and part-time lecturer. She loves animals; particularly all her cats and dogs and champions animal rescue. She is married to Johannes Joachim (Duggie) Cloete born 29/11/1962. Married 7/7/1987 Kempton Park. They do not have children.

Eckhard Friedrich Schumann, born 2/11/1966 who is married to Madeleine Janse van Rensburg born 2/7/1974. Married 21/11/1998, Pretoria. They have relocated to Toronto in Canada, where Eckhard is an Associate Professor in Teaching Stream (Accounting) at the University of Toronto. They do not have children.

Eduard Robert Berthold Schumann

Born on 18 July 1930 in Glückstadt and died 6 May 1982 in Durban. As a young man, Onkel Edu was involved in a hit and run accident on the Durban beach front. The driver was never found. Due to an infection resulting from the accident, gangrene set in, and he lost his leg. Mum got on well with her brother and, when things were tough for both of them, they supported each other. He left mama some money, which she used for further study later on – something she always wanted to do. He also made sure that we got a telephone, and he often called to check up on us. To this day, I still remember the number. He also had that special Schumann humour. Onkel Edu, who never married, later died of cancer.

Ursula Martha Luise Schumann

Known as Ulla, she was born 9 August 1933 in Vryheid and, at the age of 89, she died on 6 January 2023 in Benoni, Johannesburg.

She married Ludwig Wilhelm Friedrich Herrmann on 9 October 1954 in Durban. He was the grandson of Gottlob Friedrich Wilhelm Herrmann, colonist and founding member of the Glückstadt Lutheran Church in Natal.

They had three children:

Eduard Friedrich Herrmann, Barbara Frieda Herrmann and me, *Ingrid Solveig Herrmann*. More details about our lives and children follow further on in the book.

This brings an end to the pioneering Hermannsburg Mission in my story, although the story of faith continued, in part, in the generations that followed.

As the families expanded, they gradually distanced themselves from their German heritage and the truth and teaching introduced by the missionaries.

Enter the Big Easy

The big easy: easy life, easy work, easy relationships, easy sex, easy entertainment. Let's get sucked into easy money; easy purchasing power; easy disposable things. Disposable food; disposable faith; disposable countries; disposable babies; disposable children; disposable spouse; disposable aged; disposable pain; disposable life; disposable unwanted people groups. The list goes on and on.

However, the most disposable and unwanted group of people in the modern world is **Christians – *actu*al** Christians: not the pseudo kind. You know, those flaky fake ones.

PART IV

THE PUZZLE PIECES COMING TOGETHER

DEEPEST DARKEST AFRICA AND CHRISTIANITY

"The evil committed by human beings is nevermore carefully and thoroughly done than from religious conviction".

– Blaise Pascal (1623–1662), French
theologian and philosopher

Ever since the illuminato, Mordechai Marx Levy, alias Karl Marx (1883–1881), at the behest of and with the financial support of the House of Rothschild,[49] turned socialism into an ideology with his books *Das Kapital and the Communist Manifesto*, the Christian religion has been under attack by evil forces seeking its destruction.

---

[49] Rothschild is a German name that means "Red Shield".

True to the precepts of Weishaupt, the followers of Karl Marx and later Vladimir Lenin (1870–1924), who wrote *The Communist Manifesto*, set about putting into effect their brutal assault on all religion, so as as to force it out of people's minds. It was more easily said than done, though. Believers – particularly Christians – proved to be an unexpected obstacle on the road to atheist world revolution.

We are all familiar with the tragic beginnings of the communist rule. The churches were either silenced or destroyed. By 1940, only 4,000 churches of the original 46,000 were left in Russia, and in the first 30 years of Bolshevist rule, 48 million human beings were "liquidated"; 40,000 of them priests and leading members of religious groups. Despite the cruellest persecutions – from Joseph Stalin (1878–1953) and Sergei Khrushchev (1894–1671) and their successors, down to the present day – they discovered that Christianity could not be extinguished. On the contrary, the numbers of believers underground kept growing. The promise of Jesus, that the gates of hell should not prevail against his church, proved to be stronger.

The perseverance of Christianity forced the communists to change their tactics. In addition to the external direct attack from outside, they infiltrated churches and theological seminaries with students who were agents of the KGB.[50] Many, if not most of them) were Jesuits. They corrupted the clergy or took over their functions themselves.

Obstinate priests were terrorized, locked up in asylums, sentenced to long terms of imprisonment, or exposed to public disgrace. Parents who had their children baptized were accused of endangering the mental health of their children. Fathers lost their jobs, and the children were barred from higher education.

---

[50] KGB is the Russian abbreviation for State Security Committee (*Komitet Gosudarstvennoy Bezopasnosti*). The KGB was the main internal security agency for the USSR, from 1954 until 1991.

Does this not sound alarmingly familiar to what is currently occurring around us?

In the West, the communists used different tactics. Since they could not make a direct attack on the churches, the tried-and-true method of infiltration as the only one available to them. They knew that they had a vast potential in the unbelievers and the lukewarm Christians and liberals inside and outside the churches.

In 1938, Georgi Dimitrov, the leader of the Bulgarian communists, put it this way: "Let our friends do the work. We must always remember that one sympathizer is worth more than a dozen militant communists. One university professor who isn't a party member but stands up for the interests of the Soviet Union is worth more than a hundred party members. One well-known writer or one retired general is worth more than five hundred nonentities who have just enough sense not to get beaten up by the police. A writer who isn't a member of the Party but defends the Soviet Union and the trade union boss who isn't one of us but stands up for the soviet international policy is worth more than a thousand party workers. Those who aren't party members or known communists have greater freedom of action. Our friends must confuse the enemy for us. They must export our principles and mobilize campaigns in our support against people who don't think as we do and whom we can't get at. We must use most especially ambitious politicians who need help, men who know that we communists can smooth their path and give them publicity and help them in other ways. Men like that would sell their souls to the devil; and we buy souls." (Source unknown).

In this way, the communists used liberals – "useful idiots", as Lenin used to call them – to advance the goals of communism in the West. Universities and the mainstream media are the main instruments that they use to spread ideological poison. Where have we witnessed that before? However, their easiest prey are modern, liberal parsons and theologians – men who have lost their faith and their vocation for whom God is dead and the Bible far from infallible. These are the easiest victims of a new gospel whispered by the Marxists.

They are to be found everywhere in the world these days. Wittingly or unwittingly, they work for the destruction of Christianity, for they have been taken in by the Utopia of an ideology that promises man the **Kingdom of God on earth.**

The communists know only too well that the decay in belief in the churches can best be achieved by a top-down approach. It is liberal theologians of that kind who are currently in control of nearly every church organisation and the distribution of their members' money. Since they are supported and funded by secret forces, they advance to high positions of influence and esteem.

Their main task, as they see it, is the liberalisation and weakening of all dogmatic structures in the church. By recruiting and training mostly leftist ministers, they succeed in watering down the Christian message and interpret it in new ways. The emphasis is shifted from the vertical – pointing to God – to the horizontal, compassionate-humanist, plane. By the distortion and denial of cardinal precepts of the Bible and over-emphasis on social and ethical questions they gradually weaken and falsify the Christian doctrine; and the result is confusion among believers and emptying churches. Theologians who want to build their Kingdom of God on earth in concert with the Marxists cannot help mixing Marxist jargon with their religious pronouncements. In this way, the fundamental, irreconcilable opposition between Marxism and Christianity is blurred.

The over-emphasis on social – and political – aspects inevitably lead to a garbling of Biblical utterances and a perversion of the Bible into a revolutionary handbook. For example, Jesus's missionary command to spread the Gospel is interpreted as a call to "dialogue" with communism, while the spiritual salvation of mankind suddenly means political liberation, and justice (before God) means "reconciliation" with human beings. In this way, the Good News of the Gospel is gradually transformed into a social-humanist ideology that can be taken over by atheistic communists, pagan cults and any other religions in the world.

This universal heretical trend appears to have the blessing of the World Council of Churches (WCC) in Geneva, for the WCC – more a worldly than a spiritual body – has long been demanding joint sessions and prayer jamborees with Buddhists, Muslims, Jews, Animists, Hindus, Taoists and all other types of sects.

In the United States of America (USA), it was the member churches of the World Council of Churches (WCC) that helped to drive the Americans out of Vietnam,[51] so that the entire country fell into the hands of the communists. The liberal theologians and churchmen are currently using the same tactics in Africa. Instead of funding the dissemination of the saving message of the Gospel, the WCC spends most of the money collected in the West on aid and comfort to Marxist murder gangs in southern Africa and everywhere else in the world, thereby preparing the way of the Antichrist.

Indirectly, the attack on the "white" positions in Africa had started as early as 1961. (We have since learned that these attacks have happened much earlier: even before the Zulu wars began, those foundations were being laid). In that year, the Orthodox Church of Russia was accepted as a member of the WCC. It was in that same year that President Kennedy – as though accidentally – ended the "cold war" and began the new era of "peaceful co-existence". That meant that, from then on, the West recognized the communist dictatorship, including that of China, as a "democratic system" on a par with the Western parliamentary systems.

---

[51] The Vietnam War (1955–1975) was fought between the communist government of North Vietnam and its allies in South Vietnam, known as the Viet Cong, against the government of South Vietnam and its main ally, the USA. At the heart of the conflict was the desire of North Vietnam to unite the entire country under a single communist rule, modelled on the Chinese and Russian regimes. Hidden beneath this are sinister agendas by the military industrial complex of the West.

The Orthodox Church had been a member of the Oecumenical Council of Churches for barely ten years, when politicisation began to settle in. It soon became clear to all that the Christian brethren from the east were less interested in spreading the Gospel than in expanding the soviet hegemony. When they pushed through the Programme to Combat Racism of the WCC in 1970 and fumigated it with Christian incense, the KGB officers active in the Church Centre scored their first striking success.

It has been the goal of the Soviet planners for a long time to exchange the anti-communist bastions in southern Africa for regimes subordinate to Moscow, so as to gain control over the strategic Cape route and the mineral wealth of the subcontinent. Their direct drive of supporting terrorist cadres with arms and ideological propaganda had not produced the desired results.

However, with the aid of the Programme to Combat Racism of the WCC, their efforts were sealed with the blessing of the churches. The terrorists constantly working to overthrow white governments not only received an unexpected moral boost and sanctification of their bloody deeds; they were soon able to dip their hands into the stream of Western money raised by the churches in the form of "humanitarian aid".

In view of such active moral support on the part of a world organisation of churches, many "progressive" Western governments – and of course – the UNO were swift to follow suit, digging deep into their pockets to stump up their share for the noble cause.

The Swedish government, which had already been contributing an annual subsidy of 150,000 dollars, now raised it to 4 million dollars. The Lutheran World Federation went out of its way to support the decision of the WCC and, in the following year (1971), handed over a sum of 35,000 dollars to the "freedom fighters" of FRELIMO (Frente de Libertação de Moçambique/ Mozambique Liberation Front).[52]

That same year (1971), the British Council of Churches also associated itself with the decision of the WCC to support the "freedom struggle" in southern Africa, as did the Presbyterian Church of America, the National Church Council of America, the Reformed Churches of the Netherlands, the All Africa Church Conference and the Christian Peace Conference. The Evangelical Church of Germany (EKD) held the work of the WCC in high esteem, as demonstrated by its contributions exceeding those of the highest share of any other members by several million. However, that is understandable: the President of the External Office of the EKD, Dr Heinz-Joachim Held, was also the Chairman of the Central Committee of the WCC. (What a stab in the back to all those missionaries and their endless dedication!)

In *Diagnosen,* Norbert Homuth (1984:42) writes: "The EKD with 2,2 million DM is paying the highest share of all the members of the WCC. For years the church has been arguing that none of the church funds had been used for the support of terrorism in South Africa, and at a meeting of the Central Committee of the WCC in January 1979 it was stipulated that the support for terrorists should not come from general church funds, but only from donations for clearly identified projects.

The chairman of the External Office of the EKD gave his word of honour for that. Thus, the public was deceived for years, until in November 1982 it came out that in the year 1982 at least the Oecumenical Council had handed over money to the terrorists that had been earmarked for world missionary tasks and evangelization and had come from the Evangelische Missionswerk; thus, church funds and Free Church funds".

---

[52] FRELIMO was established in Tanzania in 1962, with the purpose of overthrowing the Portuguese colonial rule in Mozambique.

I should add that they were far from fussy in their choice of organisations on which to pour their golden shower. Those that received the most favourable consideration seemed to be those with an anti-Western slant that had distinguished themselves as enemies of the "capitalist" free-market economy and that were subservient to the advance of atheism. In short: the organisations regarded as most worthy of support were, and still are, those serving the interests of Moscow. The great success of the efforts of the USSR and the WCC is demonstrated by the fact that Southern Rhodesia (now Zimbabwe), Angola and Mozambique are currently under Marxist rule.

Reviewing a few facts that illustrate this development, Homuth (1984) writes: "From 1970 to 1979 alone the WCC gave away 3 063 545 dollars. Of that 65 per cent went exclusively to Marxist terrorists in southern Africa. In 1978 the 'Patriotic Front' in Rhodesia, which was trying to overthrow the white pro-Western government, was given a sum of 85,000 dollars by the WCC. At the same time this Patriotic Front is financed by Cuba and the Soviet Union. Even before the WCC announced its donation for 'humanitarian aid', the Patriotic Front had killed 207 white and 1712 black civilians, not counting the 296 civilians mangled by terrorist mines. The WCC rejected all criticism from all sides and announced with pride that it had given another handout of over 125,000 dollars to Marxist SWAPO (Namibia). Altogether, SWAPO had received 823,000 dollars from the WCC by 1982. In Angola, the Russian-supported MPLA received 78,000 dollars, and the Marxist FRELIMO in Mozambique received 120,000 dollars. In 1978, thirty-five foreign missionaries and their children were murdered in Rhodesia by the terrorists financed by the WCC. Soon afterwards they shot down an unarmed civilian aircraft and killed all those who had survived the crash; and two members of the Salvation Army were also killed by the terrorists. Because of that the Salvation Army left the WCC".

The last and strongest bastion against communist domination in southern Africa and the principal objective of the USSR is the Republic of South Africa and South West Africa (Namibia).[53] The joint attack of the forces planning and promoting neo-colonialism in Africa is concentrated on those two countries, using them as a springboard for advancing the agenda of a planned New World Order (NWO).

The fact that there is such an agreement of objectives between international communism, the United Nations Organization (UNO) and the WCC should not come as a surprise to anybody who is aware of the pronouncements of one of the leading theologians of the EKD and the WCC, Professor Jurgen Moltman: " ... The churches should therefore make special efforts to get rid of national sovereignty and promote the development of the United Nations and a world government" (Homuth 1984:42–43). A report by the WCC admits quite openly that the support of terrorists in South Africa is intended "apart from compassion to enable the WCC to have a say in the new distribution of power".

The donations of the WCC make it quite clear among whom the power is to be distributed, if all goes according to the wishes and plans of the WCC. Since 1970, mainly Marxist "liberation movements" have received 7,5 million dollars in annual instalments "for the fight against racial injustice" and to give assistance to the "racially oppressed". The objectives of the recipients "must not deviate from the general goals of the World Council of Churches", as the WCC stipulated. That can only mean that a Marxist-communist, atheist order of society is in general agreement with the goals and intentions of the WCC. Since the donations were made "with no control over the manner of their use", there is nothing to stop the money from being spent on weapons, bombs, or Mrs Mandela's famous tyres, petrol and matches.

The extraordinary activities of the Oecumenical Council of Churches become more comprehensible when we are familiar with the parties most interested in its

---

[53] In 1990, South West Africa, which had been a German colony, was granted independence as the Republic of Namibia.

foundation. It was the National Church Council of the USA (NCC) that served as a model for a World Council. Financed by large contributions, particularly from the Rockefeller and Carnegie foundations, this body had become so firmly established in the clutches of the American Illuminati that, by 1936, the Naval Intelligence Services of the USA had classified it as one of the most dangerous and subversive organisations in the country. The Readers' Digest wrote that it is still being seriously accused by state commissions of enquiry of having been infiltrated by Marxists.

A few years ago, the National Council of American Churches sparked great controversy by acting as a co-plaintiff in a court case in Rhode Island, opposing a public performance of the Christmas story. No, dear reader: you have not misread that. The National Council of Churches in the USA actually took out a formal, written order against a children's representation of the birth of Jesus.

In his book *Vorsicht, Ökumene!* ("Beware of the Oikouméne") Norbert Homuth (1983) writes: "Just as the illuminati served the National Council of Churches of the USA, the same took place on the world level by the foundation of the Oecumenical Council in Geneva. It is one of the tactics of the Freemasons to try out something on a regional level before putting it into practice worldwide. One of the most powerful wirepullers in that business was Rockefeller. He is a high-degree Freemason. Rockefeller not only funded the UN building [should read: UN site; author] in New York, he also financed the establishment of the World Council of Churches in Geneva. To the question as to what extent the Oecumenical Council was connected with Rockefeller's Council of Foreign Relations the reply came from Geneva: 'The Rockefeller Foundation contributed substantial sums to make possible the creation of our Oecumenical Council. Four foundations contributed altogether 1,2 million dollars for the building of the Oecumenical Centre'".

In 1954, still more money came from Rockefeller, over 125,000 dollars, and in 1958, Rockefeller gave another 2 million dollars for the establishment of a training fund for theologians in Geneva. As Homuth (1983) writes: "The same Rockefeller who financed an abortion centre for over ten thousand abortions a year in New York also financed the sex-guru, Bhagwan, the Club of Rome and the World Council of Churches in Geneva. They all serve the same ends".

It was certainly no accident that both the UNO and the WCC were founded shortly after the end of the World War II (1939–1945) and financed from the same sources. It was the legal adviser to the Rockefeller family and later US Secretary of State, John Foster Dulles, who was appointed Chairman of the Commission for International Relations of the WCC in Geneva. His job was to integrate and coordinate the work of the WCC with that of the UNO.

"Dulles also ensured that a WCC office was opened in New York. Through this office in New York pass all communications to the UNO-UNESCO, in which 'God-is-dead' and communist inclined theologians are mass-produced. This theological seminary stands under the aegis of Rockefeller and his hidden influence," says Homuth (1983).

"A few years ago, Frau Dorothee Sölle, of all people, was the only German theologian to be invited to report to the WCC conference in Vancouver; whereupon a storm of indignation broke out from the Christian press in Germany. Why? Since 1975 Frau Sölle had been a professor at Rockefeller's Union Theological Seminary".

In his *Geschichte der ökumenischen Bewegung, 1948–1968* ("History of the Oecumenical Movement, 1948–1968"), Fey and Rouse (1974), write the following about the 2 million dollars that Rockefeller donated to the training fund for theologians: "The financial means of this fund and the services of the collaborators were used so cleverly that they led to a radical change in theological training".

According to Homuth (1983), the creation of a fund for Christian literature and music in 1964 was a logical sequel to that. Millions of dollars of Illuminati money must have flowed into the creation of "Christian" rock music alone. The upper ranks of the oecumenical movement are entirely occupied by high-degree Freemasons, Homuth (1983) indicates. This is also true of the UNO and the other large world organisations.

The Catholic Church, which has always been deeply hostile to the Freemasons, officially approved them in its new Codex Juris Canonici of 1983. As Homuth (1984) writes, "Pope John XXIII introduced the oecumenical-charismatic process into the Catholic Church, so that now the Vatican is populated by a whole army of Freemasons".

The fact that it is not any different in the Protestant churches can be deduced from a paper issued by the EKD and quoted by Homuth (1984). The official responsible for sectarian questions wrote to him: "A general objection to the membership of Freemasonry by Evangelical Christians cannot be raised. The rumour that a Freemason cannot be a Christian or a Christian a Freemason is in the eyes of the Christian church a breach of the Eighth Commandment" (Homuth 1984).

In this way, one brick is added to another to build the pyramid of the Illuminati. While the UNO is the incarnation of the future world state, the Oecumenical Council in Geneva foreshadows the emerging anti-Christian world church.

With the significant title of *One World*, its magazine leaves no doubt that the interests of the WCC in Geneva are identical to the *Novus ordo saeculorum* ("New Order of the Ages") of the UNO. Both organisations are the political instruments of influential forces that are changing the world, intending to enslave humanity under a totalitarian Marxist world government and a pseudo world church.

The WCC long since made it clear that it was not concerned with an oikouméne of the Christian churches alone (Homuth 1983:44).

Since the World Conference of Churches in Geneva in 1966, it has has become evident that its ambitions extend beyond Christian unity, aiming for an *oikoumène* that includes all religions, sects and cults. The focus has shifted from the unity of Christians to the promotion of a broader unity of all human beings in the liberal freemasonry sense. At the fourth plenary session of the World Conference of Churches in Upsala (Sweden) in 1968, they were already talking about a widening of the notion of unity: "The church makes bold to speak of itself as the symbol of the future unity of all mankind".

The following examples may illustrate the planned future of mankind:

- In March 1970, an oecumenical congress, organised by the WCC, was held at Holiday Beach, where not only representatives of Christian churches were present, but also those of Islam, Buddhism and Hinduism.
- In 1974, the Catholic Cardinal, Suenens, acted as host to a world conference of religions in Louvain, Belgium. For that, he received a prize from the Templeton Foundation – a Freemason institution that consists of representatives of the six world religions.
- In the spring of 1982, an Islamic-Christian "dialogue" was held in Colombo, Sri Lanka. The result was a decision by the Islamic World Congress and the WCC to form a Standing Common Committee.
- At a meeting held in Bossey Castle in 1980, the former Secretary General of the WCC, the Marxist Philip Potter, made an introductory speech in which he said: "The Charismatic Movement is a connecting link. It can help the World Council of Churches to attain the goal that it has set itself, which is the integration of all human beings all over the earth".

We can conclude that the goal of the World Council of Churches is clear. Obedient to the old notion of the Freemasons of a world brotherhood, it is working towards an integrated world with an integrated church in which atheists, communists, Christians, Muslims, Buddhists, Hindus, Unificationists

(Moonies), Scientologists and swamis of all sorts and colours can frolic to their hearts' content.

If they cannot entirely root out the sense of religion that is innate in all human beings – in spite of numerous attempts – then they will at least contain it within the confines of a universal pseudo-church and use it for the purposes of power politics. So it appears (Homuth 1983:47).

In his book, *Die Protestantischen Kirchen im Sog des Kommunismus* ("The Protestant Churches in the wake of communism"), Dr Beat C. Bäschlin (1987) writes the following:

> "The destructive elements that were able to usurp control over Protestantism so extensively are pursuing a twofold strategy. Absurd demands are made in the name of Jesus Christ.
>
> The intention is, on the one hand, to discredit the churches and shake the faith of believers or otherwise put them off; on the other hand, they intend to take over the ecclesiastical apparatus and its funds for the ends of communist policy and the advance of atheism. These two strategies reinforce one another.
>
> The more the Protestant churches allow themselves to be used in the war of extermination against Christianity, the more untrustworthy they become. And the more untrustworthy they become, the more successful is the effort to weaken the Christian religion in the West also and hasten its demise".

In this way, the destruction of the repute and "credibility" of the churches is one of the long-term objectives of soviet policy in the Western countries. The flood of defections from the churches by members disgusted by the support of communist terrorist groups by the churches is noted with satisfaction by the

KGB men operating in Geneva. It is a victory in their war against religion in general and the Christian churches of the West in particular.[54]

Despite the departure of something like 2 million members of the Evangelical churches in West Germany since 1965, the upper ranks of the EKD (and the nearly 300 member churches of the WCC) saw no good cause to condemn the atheistic ethos and soviet policy of the Oecumenical Council, far less renounce their membership. "On the contrary," said Bishop Lohse, the Chairperson of The Council of the EKD in 1983, "there is no alternative to the oecumenical organization of the WCC; the EKD is determined rather to strengthen its solidarity with the WCC" (Bäschlin 1983:30–31).

The German-speaking Christians in South Africa and Namibia, who stood in a "partnership relation" with the EKD through their church got a good taste of that solidarity.[55] By means of financial subventions and the despatch of predominantly trendy-lefty parsons to South Africa and Namibia, the EKD exercised a decisive influence on the policy of the German churches there. Together with the Lutheran World Federation, they also had a substantial share of the costs of a theological training centre in Natal. That, of course, gave them a decisive say in the selection of the teachers into whose hands the young aspirants to holy orders were confided. In this way, it remained in the (EKD) family, and the German communities that had been hoping to dispense with the "imported" and EKD-trained ministers in future and train their own ministers bound to the Scriptures and the Creed had congratulated themselves too soon.

The fact that the German head of the Faculty of Theology had signed the notorious Kairos Document,[56] which was filled with the spirit of Marxism and

---

[54] These initiatives against religion are evidence of the efficiency of the old policy of "divide and rule", from the Latin *divide et impera*.
[55] In 1987, the existing agreements were replaced by a "provisional arrangement".
[56] *The South Africa Kairos Document, 1985* is a Christian theological statement issued by a group of (mainly) black South African theologians that offered alternative

called for the violent overthrow of the South African government, hardly helped to pour oil on the troubled waters of the resentful German Christians in South Africa.

The South Africa Lutherans still loyal to their church saw themselves exposed by this "partnership relation" to increasing political pressure from their church leaders who, in total contempt for their rights, required them to condemn the policies of their country, while forcing them into "greater Christian unity" with their black fellow-citizens in an integrated church in which the proportion of whites would be less than 5%.

The fact that this unity between black and white Christians has always been interpreted spiritually and in the biblical sense means little to the church politicians, who exert the pressure, for the unity in which they are interested is of a totally different kind: the unity of organised power-politics.

Although the EKD was unable to fuse together all seventeen of the autonomous regional churches in the Federal Republic of Germany into one single church, they nevertheless demand the structural integration of all the black and white Lutheran churches in southern Africa. They could not manage it in Germany, where, in contrast to the multiplicity of races in South Africa and Namibia, there is complete uniformity of race, nation, language and colour.

Predictably, most German-speaking Lutherans have (so far) declined to comply with these pious injunctions. They are well aware of the political intentions behind them and of the fact that, as a minority, they would be deprived of all rights to self-determination and their characteristic German culture as a religious community, which they had built up for over a century and nurtured with love, would be endangered.

The descendants of numerous German missionaries who, with great self-sacrifice and privations, carried the Gospel to black people and dedicated their lives

---

theological models to resolve the problems in the country.

to the task, are now expected to put up with being reviled as "racists", because they are not prepared to accept the political programme of the WCC championed by the EKD.

German-speaking communities are to be misled by their synodal representatives with religiously camouflaged statements and financial aid – as a sort of Fifth Column of the EKD – into cooperation in radical "changes in the structures of the private as well as the public domain" of the country (Kauffenstein in The Kairos document 1985:5).

This can only be understood in the context of the radical forces, both at home and abroad, working for the overthrow of the present system of government. In its overt support of the communist terrorist groups by the WCC, to which the EKD contributes a third of the annual running costs, the possibility of a successful "structural change" being brought about was plain for all to see. The ecclesiastical structure-changers made their stance clear to an astonished German church community in Pretoria, when the visiting specialist on South Africa in the External Office of the EKD told them that the church had many friends in South Africa, "but unfortunately many of them are in gaol".

At that moment, a light went on for Germans in Pretoria. With the uneasy feeling of having been left in the lurch by an opportunistic church leadership and being ministered to by EKD pastors whose vocation was regarded as politically suspect, many members of congregations had been fighting for years for a total dissolution of the link with the EKD.

They accuse the churches of the Federal Republic, both Catholic and Protestant, of the greatest guilt in the collapse of general morals, legal concepts, the destruction of the family, the horrible number of abortions, and all the other phenomena of degeneracy that are now the norm in Germany.

Therefore, numerous of the foreign Germans in South Africa, who number about 120,000, and the far greater number of South Africans of German descent, have developed a sound mistrust of the activities and intentions of the

Federal German church organisations, which, on the pretext of trying to help, interfere in South African affairs, although they cannot keep their own house in order.

Their officially tolerated homosexual ministers, their support of atheistic terrorist movements and the numerous anti-South African agitators in German pulpits give German speaking South Africans grave doubts as to whether the ecclesiastical influences emanating from Germany are actually in the interests of their congregations and their fellow Christians of colour and are likely to be conducive to peaceful development in South Africa.

The dangerous part played by the local churches in South Africa may be judged by anybody who has followed the train of events in the successful revolutions in Nicaragua and other troubled countries. Even in the communist seizures of power in Rhodesia, Mozambique and Angola, the churches did a good deal of the preliminary spadework.

A young black South African woman and a former member of the African National Congress (ANC), Salamina Borephe, recently shocked Americans by admitting that she had mainly been incited by South African church leaders to participate in acts of murder and arson in the townships. Salamina Borephe was one of several witnesses who testified before a study committee of the Republican Party in Washington. Miss Borephe, who had become a Christian since breaking with the ANC, spoke of the sleepless nights and nightmares that had tormented her ever since. She said that, in 1975, she had attended the Congress of South African Students (COSAS), at which she was told that it was a branch of the ANC.

> The student members of COSAS were taught how to make Molotov cocktails, and parsons told us how good communism was. They promised us a better education in other countries; and that's why I joined the organization.

The Anglican priests taught us that communists were black people from Central Africa. Leaders like Samora Machel, Robert Mugabe and Joshua Nkomo were spoken of as heroes who would liberate us ... We were imbued with a powerful hatred of the whites, particularly the Afrikaners.

An Anglican priest and another clergyman (whom she named) were the ringleaders of the "opposition movement". "They told us that the local councillors must die, because they paid no attention to the people. There was a lot of confusion, and some people who went to work were beaten up, others were killed, some burnt to death.

On Sunday, 2 September, they had a meeting in the Catholic Church of Evaton and Sharpeville: By half past five on Monday morning we were on our feet and throwing stones at cars and buses". She described how a black councillor was seized by "the boys" and burnt to death with a petrol bomb. Another was hacked to death with pangas[57] as he was coming out of his house.

They always referred to the Bible to explain why we should murder the local councillors", she said. "They said that Mandela was like Moses, and he had been sent to set us free. We were also urged to kill policemen, and some members of COSAS had got hold of firearms for that purpose". The organisations also used children and adolescents from the ages twelve to eighteen. "We were told to burn down the schools because the communists

---

[57] A panga is a heavy, traditional knife that is used in Africa and Central and South America to cutting through heavy vegetation, or as a weapon.

would come and build better schools for the blacks (*The Citizen*, 29 June 1987).

However, several other clergymen and churches fanned the flames in South Africa. In its publication *UCA News* 11/86, the United Christian Action (UCA), an umbrella organisation of several Christian associations, writes: "Catholic Bishops in South Africa Smooth the Path to Marxism".

On 16 May 1986, the General Secretary of the South African Bishops' Conference, Father Smangaliso Mkhatshwa, was arrested for illegal possession of arms and ammunition. This event demonstrates the tip of an iceberg only, for under the leadership of Archbishop Denis Hurley, the South African Bishops' Conference has become a tool of Marxist revolutionaries. The United Christian Action (UCA) substantiates this by the following examples:

- **The Episcopal Namibia Report**
  On 1 June 1982, the South African Catholic Bishops Conference (SACBC) published a situation report on Namibia in which the Christian intentions and overwhelming support among black people of the terror movement SWAPO were arrested. Even the official party programme openly proclaiming atheism, Marxism and Leninism did not offend the bishops, as they argued it was only intended to "keep the Warsaw Pact countries in the mood to continue supplying them with arms" (South African Catholic Bishops Conference 1982:27).
- **Propaganda for the Marxist ANC**
  In 1983, Archbishop Denis Hurley played a key role in the propaganda campaign against South Africa in Germany, which was financed by the Catholic charitable relief organisation Misereor.

Misereor, which is lavishly funded by unsuspecting Catholics in good faith, represented the ANC as "the natural expression of the African desire for liberation" (Hurley 1981:21).

- **Class struggle in Catholic schoolbooks**

    In 1983, the Education Section of the Bishops' Conference published a course for school children in which the leaders of the South African homelands[58] were depicted as puppets of the South African government, who were merely continuing the oppression of the masses. Black policemen, soldiers and councillors and Coloured and Indian parliamentary representatives were abused as "collaborators" who were betraying their people in exchange for power and prestige.

    The Catholic course is illustrated with pictures of black children raising their fists and expressing their hatred in the caption: "We won't work for the whites anymore! Europeans get out! We won't pay any more taxes! Schools are useless! The chiefs are oppressing us! Give us land! *We'll never allow the Christians to rule us"!* (Signposts, 1/83).

- **Publication of the pro-Marxist New Nation**

    With a grant of over DM 250,000 from the charity funds of Misereor and Missio, two German Catholic relief bodies for famine and sickness all over the world, the South African Catholic bishops started a newspaper in 1985 called *The New Nation*. In issue 10/86 of 22 June 1986, the paper glorified the Marxist "comrades", who, by that time, had murdered over 500 black people, who had no revolutionary inclinations with burning car tyres.

---

[58] Seeking separate development, the apartheid government introduced an administrative mechanism to establish ten homelands and assigned every black individual a "homeland" according to his/her ethnic identity. The idea was to move the black people to the homelands, where they could establish their own independent governments.

- **Hand in hand with the ANC against national defence**
  On 13 April 1986, Archbishop Hurley led a five-man delegation to the ANC headquarters in Lusaka, Zambia. An excerpt from the communique issued by the bishops and the ANC:
  "The black majority knows from experience that the South African Police and Army are instruments of oppression ... The Conference therefore acknowledges the importance of the campaign to end conscription in South Africa" (*The Citizen*, 17 April 1986).
- On 19 June 1986, the episcopal newspaper *The New Nation* also commented on the South African commando action against ANC bases. According to *The New Nation* 10(86), the 176 objective was not the ANC but the economic independence of South Africa's neighbours. The military want to cause as much chaos as possible. They are afraid that the successful development of a multiracial socialist state in Zimbabwe or Mozambique will show up the absurdity of apartheid capitalism.

OTHER ACTIVITIES

The Catholic Bishops' Conference in South Africa acknowledged its support for the Marxist Kairos document (Kairos Southern Africa 1985*)*. It repeatedly demanded the withdrawal of the police and army from the townships in South Africa, while ignoring the threat to peace-loving inhabitants by radicals.

On several occasions, Archbishop Hurley perverted the Holy Mass by offering petrol bombs and firearms as sacrificial objects, ostensibly to strengthen the oppressed in their struggle for liberation.

The Catholic bishops of South Africa are not interested in the opinions of the members of their flocks – according to surveys more than 95% of Catholics in the country are opposed to any kind of sanctions against South Africa – yet their shepherds call for punitive economic measures. The Catholic organisation

TFP (Tradition, Family, Private Property) collected over 10,000 signatures against them. Another group that calls itself Concerned Catholics submitted a note of protest against the "socialist activities" of the bishops to the Vatican. At a three-day conference in Durban on 20 November 1985, attended by eighty senior black church leaders, a motion of censure was carried against the activities of Archbishop Hurley.

In an interview with *The Sunday Times,* a leading black theologian said: "The general feeling at our conference was that we are fed up with the white Messiahs who set themselves up abroad as martyrs for the black cause" (*Sunday Times, 1 December 1985).* Black priests then withdrew their support for Bishop Hurley's newly founded organisation, Christians for Justice and Peace, and the project collapsed.

"Yet the Archbishop is obviously confident that the Bishops' Conference does not need the support of the ordinary member of the congregation anymore. Foreign donations for the revolutionary activities of the bishops more than make up for the growing abstention. In 1984 the Bishops' Conference received DM 750 000 from abroad, mostly from Germany. A year later donations from abroad passed the two-million mark, which does not include the DM 250,000 for The New Nation Pastoral Project from Misereor and Mission. The Vicar General of Cape Town, Father Reginald Cawcutt, commented on the jibbing at the Bishops' Conference: "The bishops are the leaders of the Catholic Church and need not necessarily ask the community which road to take" (Cawcutt 1986).

The South African Council of Churches (SACC) also played a rather curious part in these events. Like all the other national church councils worldwide, it supported the interests and aims of the WCC and, therefore, its activities were comparable to those of the WCC. When these activities appeared to become threatening, the government instructed a Judicial Commission of Inquiry

– known as the Eloff Commission – in 1981 to examine the development, activities, aims and finances of 177 SACC members.

On 15 February 1984, after nearly two-and-a-half years, the Eloff Commission submitted its 451-page report to Parliament in Cape Town. The report shocked the nation. It stated that the SACC was waging "a political war of liberation in fraternal association" with the Marxist terror organisation the African National Congress (ANC) and other militant organisations. The main feature of the activities of the SACC was the fact that it would opt for a revolutionary, rather than an evolutionary, process to bring about change in South Africa. In the planning of its activities, it therefore identified itself increasingly with the so-called liberation struggle. It had embarked on a programme of "reinterpretation" of the Christian faith, to be able to justify its active participation in politics. With its own version of "liberation theology", the SACC was attempting to indoctrinate and politicise the churches associated with it and the black people in the country, while the whites were to be subjected to a "change of consciousness" to prepare them for a revolutionary change in the existing structures.

According to the Eloff Report (1984), Bishop Tutu, the Secretary General of the SACC at the time, frankly admitted to waging "a massive psychological war against the country and to a strategy of resistance and the promotion of the political fight for liberation. That included such tactics as persuading international governments and organisations to bring political, economic and diplomatic pressure to bear on South Africa.

In the country itself the SACC associated itself with "a large-scale campaign of civil disobedience", a disinvestment campaign and vociferous support for young men who refused to do their national military service. He incessantly prophesied the impending violent uprising and declared his solidarity with all who came in conflict with the government, whether they were striking teachers, militant black power movements or radical black trade unions.

Although the SACC was unable to enlist the support of the churches in South Africa – only 1.2% of its total budget was received from member churches – it had no difficulty in obtaining plenty of money for its programmes from churches, governments and other organisations abroad.

According to the Eloff Report (1984), most of that money came from Germany and mainly from the EKD. The SACC proposed to use "underground groups" in its civil disobedience campaigns, for that had proved highly successful when used by the Marxist guerila fighters in Latin America. The leaders of the communist Sandinista government in Nicaragua now frankly admit that it would not have been possible for them to take over power in the country without the support of the Catholic "base communities", the church underground groups.

With regard to the links between the SACC and the ANC, the Eloff Commission found that, after consultations with the ANC and other "liberation movements" in Lusaka, the SACC had passed a resolution "to enhance its credibility with the liberation movements". The SACC justified the terrorists' use of violence with skilful theological formulations, thereby giving them its express approval.

There was nothing theological about the pronouncement of the former Secretary General of the SACC, Dr Beyers Naudé: "Stone-throwing and the burning of cars and houses and the killing of collaborators occasionally" could not unconditionally be regarded as "violence".

The Eloff Report (1984) also states that Bishop Tutu had personal contact with Oliver Tambo and other banned ANC leaders and, evidently, had accurate information about activities planned by the ANC. Mr John Rees, another former Secretary General of the SACC, also had personal meetings with them.

Most of the payments made from the Dependents' Conference Fund went to former members of the ANC and the Pan Africanist Congress of Azania (PAC), another underground communist organisation. Yet another Secretary General of the body that was to become the SACC, Reverend A.W. Blaxall, had earlier been convicted for participating in ANC activities.

According to the report of the Eloff Commission (1984), Bishop Tutu's official statements were calculated to improve the "image" of the ANC and to make it more "respectable". Therefore, Tutu described Oliver Tambo as "a person of Christian convictions and sincerity in his endeavours for peace, justice and democracy in South Africa" – the man who was responsible for the bomb explosion in Pretoria in 1983 that killed 19 people and inflicted crippling and disfiguring injuries on over 200 two hundred others, including black and white women and children.

Bishop Tutu also called Nelson Mandela, a communist who was sentenced to life imprisonment for high treason for his terrorist activities, his leader, and spoke warmly of him as the future South African head of state. Tutu, who was to become the Archbishop of Cape Town and winner of the Nobel Peace Prize in 1984, who nonetheless boasted of being "no pacifist", predicted that the use of force in the fight for liberation would be unavoidable. In that case he could see nothing wrong with actively supporting the fight himself. In fact, he hardly ever uttered a word to condemn revolutionary violence, because, in his eyes, the use of force was justified, if the South African government did not change its course soon.

The Red Bishop, who declared himself a socialist and a hater of capitalism (*Sunday Times* 29 December 1985), appeared to take a strange view of Scripture when he could make public pronouncements such as the following:

- "Some people think when justice prevails over injustice, as in [Marxist] Zimbabwe, that shows that the Kingdom has already arrived" (EcuNEWS 11 1980).
- "I thank God that I am black. At the Last Judgement the whites will have much to answer for" (*The Argus*, 19 March 1984).

- "A young fellow with a stone in his hand can do far more than I can with a dozen sermons" (*Daily Telegraph*, London, November 1984).
- "Every Christian must be a revolutionary. Jesus was a revolutionary. I am a revolutionary, if by that you mean somebody who wants to change things completely" (*Rapport*, 20 April 1986).
- "As far as I'm concerned the West can go to hell" (*Cape Times*, 23 July 1986).
- "Some people think there was something funny about the birth of Jesus – Maybe he was an illegitimate child." (Cape Times, 24 October 1980).

Many Christians in South Africa were afraid that His Grace himself was already headed in that direction, and so many people have deserted the Anglican church, which now finds itself in sore financial straits.

The Eloff Commission report indicates that the Asingeni Relief Fund of the SACC, which was originally established as an aid fund for those involved in the rioting in 1976, included the defence costs of persons charged before a court. The judge who conducted the investigation drew attention to the nature of the offences with which most of the accused were charged: possession of explosive substances, presence at prohibited gatherings, public violence, attempted arson, housebreaking, malicious damage to property, riotous assemblies, stone-throwing, robbery, assault, attacks on police stations and administrative buildings, and sabotage. After these disturbances had abated, Bishop Tutu, the then secretary general of the SACC, considered it opportune to use the fund in future for the purpose of "liberating the oppressed". Thus, the Asingeni fund now became an effective instrument to promote the political aims of the SACC.

The Eloff Commission (1984) identified a man who seemed to have been the real "mastermind" behind the programmes and campaigns of the SACC – Dr Wolfram Kistner, who was the son of a German pastor and former director of the Justice and Reconciliation section of the SACC.

One of the main stumbling-blocks in the way realising the programme of action for a radical change in South African society was the existence of a theology that distinguished between spiritual and worldly matters. Therefore, he made it his task to convince the leaders of the member churches of the SACC that theology was, indeed, concerned with worldly realities and phenomena and that the church should investigate socio-political problems.

In his opinion, "the theology of the member churches had to be adapted" to the so-called "social gospel" or "liberation theology" and to a new definition of Christian ethics in which the old notions of sin and guilt would be identified afresh.

The importance of the cooperation and support of the churches in South Africa to the aims of the communist terrorist movements are made clear from statements made by Oliver Tambo (1917–1991), President of the African National Congress (ANC), on various occasions, for example:

- "I hope ... the church in South Africa will really be in the front rank of the advance ..."
- "The church must play an active part in informing the Christian community of the necessity of the liberation struggle".
- We also hear similar strains from SWAPO: "The churches must declare themselves for the liberation movements or else they are taking sides with the oppressors ...".
- Likewise, the Pan-African Congress (PAC): "The churches have an essential role to play in consciousness-raising."
- There is also the plain statement by the ANC in its monthly *Sechaba: Official Organ of the ANC*: "The most important strategic goal in our struggle is the forcible take-over of power from the hands of the white minority régime by the joint revolutionary forces of the black majority and all the other democratic forces in the country".

If we were to assume that the SACC and the South African churches were aware of the true character and ungodly ends of these Marxist "liberation movements", we may think that there would be unbridgeable differences between them. Yet, the Eloff Commission pointed to the closest possible cooperation between the ANC, PAC and SWAPO, on the one hand, and the WCC and many other oecumenical bodies on the other.

For example, at a joint session of the WCC and representatives of the ANC, SWAPO, PAC and the SACC, the subject of the church and the liberation of Southern Africa was discussed. In its recommendations, the following proposal was adopted: "The conference fully approves the demands of these liberation movements and wishes to declare its unconditional support in their fight against imperialism, colonialism, racism and minority settler rule. Moreover, the conference declares its respect for the African liberation movements and those groups which are taking up the cause of the total liberation of the African continent.

We therefore call upon all the churches, particularly those in Southern Africa, to take practical steps to support the freedom struggle ..." [Don't take your eye off the ball, the goal has always been the whole African Continent.]

At another meeting held in May 1982, the PAC explicitly thanked the WCC and its various organs for their moral and financial support in previous years and expressed the hope that it would be continued. Since then, conferences between representatives of the churches and the communist "liberation movements" were held regularly. With regards to the civil disobedience campaign, Bishop Tutu expressed the following view in a BBC interview: "... laws that seem unjust to us ... should not be obeyed; and then a disobedience process is set in motion on a large scale in which nearly all the laws of the legislation are disregarded, until this country becomes practically ungovernable". [and there goes the Rule of Law].

The role that had been designed for sincere Christian believers may be gathered from the words of Dr Kistner: "In view of the diminishing tolerance level of the authorities an increase in pressure emphasis should be placed on assisting Christians in preparing in underground activity on non-violent resistance ...".

As indicated by the Eloff Commission report (1984), during its "massive psychological campaign" against the existing power structure of the country the SACC more and more realized the importance of effective propaganda. Programmes were therefore designed to alter the mental attitudes of the whites. Special efforts would be made to exploit opinion-forming institutions, such as the mass media, for those purposes. They realized that a well-directed propaganda effort would be absolutely necessary not only to "arouse and inform" the clergy but also on the level of the parishes and the local pastors to enlist the necessary support for the "programme of change".

Constant defamation of the South African government was regarded as a fundamental element of this strategy, and so was the refusal to recognize the positive improvements that had been undertaken in many areas.

Mendacious statements were distributed, such as the black people in South Africa being in a condition of "permanent slavery", and the South African system being comparable to the Nazi régime in Germany, etc.

It is true that many black people were placed into a state of slavery, particularly in the mining industry. However, the exact people who put them into a state of slavery were the ones now telling them that they were slaves! This could easily be established by following the money – irrespective of the currency being used, it can always be traced to those nefarious men.

To improve the somewhat damaged image of the SACC with its meddling in politics, the question was frequently raised as to the expediency of bringing some prominent church leaders (of the EKD) from Germany, so that they could testify to their sympathy and solidarity with the SACC. However, Dr. Kistner suggested that it would be better to wait for the right moment, e.g. if the Eloff Commission should reach conclusions that would compel the government to hamstring the SACC in its political activities.

The strategists of the SACC were always fully aware of the fact that they could count on the full support of the WCC, the UNO, the Lutheran World Federation and the EKD. That explains the arrogance and self-confidence with which they behaved – both at home and abroad. As for the finances of the SACC, the Eloff Commission (1984) established that, between 1975 and 1981, it had received over R17 million in donations from abroad. Nearly R9 million (or 52%) came from West Germany alone, followed by 10% from the WCC. By far the largest proportion of the money from Germany came from the EKD and the churches in communication with it – altogether about R8 million. The EKD not only supported the SACC as its principal contributor, thereby practically keeping it alive; it also paid the salaries and retirement pension contributions of its mastermind, Dr Wolfram Kistner, and the former Secretary General of the SACC, Dr Beyers Naudé – two gentlemen who "demand the removal of the South African government and the take-over of power by 'the people' under the leadership of the ANC".

In its search for more rich uncles to pay for its revolutionary activities in South Africa, the SACC had very precise notions, it would seem. In addition to secret transfers of money from the United Nations Trust Fund (UNTF), channelled through the WCC, they looked for even more copious fountains.

They not only canvassed foreign governments and church organisations, but also leftist bodies such as the International University Exchange Fund (IUEF). The IUEF gave direct financial assistance to the ANC, which they regarded as the leader of the national liberation movement in South Africa, also to the PAC and SWAPO, as "the only legitimate liberation movement in Namibia". The activities of the IUEF [59]included programmes for the training of specialists for "the future liberated countries of Zimbabwe, Namibia and South Africa". The

---

[59] In the author's view, the IUEF is a front organisation, financed by the CIA.

IUEF was particularly hostile to South Africa, with the clearly stated intention of destroying the existing order by a revolutionary coup.

The Secretary general of the SACC at the time, Bishop Tutu, was compelled to admit before the judicial commission of inquiry that he had personally addressed the organisation at its headquarters in Geneva twice, and that money had been sent to South Africa by a detour through the WCC to disguise its real origin and enable them to give out to the South African public that it was "church funds".

The foregoing are only a few points from the official report of the Eloff Commission, and they speak for themselves.

When one considers that, contrary to its own claims, the SACC, as an offshoot of its parent organisation the WCC in South Africa, represents only a small minority of the Christians. More than 97% of its budget of millions comes from abroad – more than half of it from the EKD – then it must be clear that a curious game is being played.

The increasingly blatant and constant pressure of the EKD to manoeuvre the German churches in South Africa into the fold of the SACC becomes apparent. Against the background described in the foregoing sections, such attempts by no means allay suspicions about the real intentions of the organisation.

These attempts actually raise the question as to whether South Africa and its German churches would not be wiser to withdraw completely from the sphere of influence of the organisation, send the imported pastors and teachers packing and rely entirely on their own financial resources and those of their adopted South African home.

The irreligious activities of the SACC are by no means an exceptional case, and neither are they confined to South Africa. For example, the government of Singapore ordered the dissolution of the Christian Conference of Asia, the regional headquarters of the WCC there. In a statement by the Foreign Minister, the Council was accused of using Singapore as a theatre for pro-communist "liberation movements" all over Asia. Five foreign leaders of the supposedly religious body were given two weeks to get out of the country.

It also came out that members of the Christian Conference of Asia were behind a "Christian Marxist" conspiracy to overthrow the government in 1987 and that they had close connections with the radical opposition in South Korea. The WCC and other organisations associated with it were also accused of having paid millions of dollars to the National Democratic Front in the Philippines – the political arm of the guerrillas of the New People's Army. A laudable exception was the National Church Council of Indonesia, which withdrew from the WCC "because it had supported the pro-Soviet liberation movement in the whole region".

These are ominous examples that should be noted by the people of South Africa. Known for its Christian character, the South African nation is particularly vulnerable, through its churches and clergymen. In the 1980s, South Africa was known as a country where the churches were full every Sunday; where government and parliament opened every session with prayer; where grace was still said at the table and evening devotional readings were not uncommon; and where the pastors still commanded the undisputed respect of their flocks. Hence, the vulnerability for influences from the church.

The enemies of South Africa have long been aware of the South African nation being vulnerable to the influence of churches and church leaders. By infiltrating the church leadership and subtly brainwashing the clergy and training at Christo-Marxist seminars, they have been attempting to undermine the churches, gradually converting them to a new, humanistic gospel, while subjecting the unsuspecting believers to a process of political "re-education", which is occurring almost unnoticed.

The following question may be asked: How it possible that so many clergymen and church leaders nowadays preach a political "gospel", while supporting militant atheist terrorists and having fallen into the pit of Marxist ideology so easily? The question is probably best answered from Scriptures, which give clear warning of the seduction of the faithful in our time. At this point, it may be wise to listen to the voice of a man who condemns Marxism and its adherents from his own excruciating experience, Alexander Solzhenitsyn:

> "Never before has the world seen a godlessness that has been so organized, militarized and evil through and through as that of Marxism. Within the philosophical system of Marx and Lenin hatred of God is the main driving force and the heart of their psychology, even more fundamental than their political and economic pretexts. This militant atheism is not a mere fringe phenomenon of communist policy, not a mere side-effect, but its central pivot. To achieve its diabolical aims communism needs control over a humanity that lives without religious faith and national consciousness. Both these intentions are openly admitted by the communists and no less openly put into practice."

Thus, said Alexander Solzhenitsyn (1918–2008), a man who had good cause to know what he was talking about. The attack on South Africa is not confined to its strategic minerals and control of the Cape route. – It is also a satanic, eschatological attack on one of the last bastions of Christianity still standing in the way of the Marxist New World Order and its universal pseudo-church (Vaque 1989).

Is it becoming clear that the nefarious little men never stopped? Although some say the Russian Revolution[60] was the pivot, it was not: the Cross was, as all

---

[60] The Russian Revolution (1917) occurred in two phases. – In the first phase, the imperial government of Tsar Nicholas II (1868–1917) was overthrown and, in the

the lessons learned from this by the nefarious men were masterfully fine-tuned for the next onslaught. The plan, which is old and fluid, can adapt to changing times and circumstances. "But how can we stop this?" you may be crying. The truth is, you cannot: you can only do as you have been asked to do, if you are a Christian. And what is that? – *Jesus said to him (a Pharisee, a lawyer):*

> You shall love the LORD your God with all your heart, with all your soul and with all your mind. This is the first and greatest commandment. And the second is like it: You shall love your neighbour as you love yourself. On these two commandments hang all the Law and the Prophets (Matthew 22:37).
>
> You have heard that it was said, 'You shall love your neighbour and hate your enemy.' But I [Jesus] say to you, love your enemies, bless those who curse you, do good to those who hate you, and pray for those who spitefully use you and persecute you, that you may be sons of your Father in heaven; for He makes His sun rise on the evil and the good, and sends rain on the just and on the unjust (Matthew 5:44–45).

It is particularly important for you to grasp this: God is allowing it!! The nefarious men can only do what God allows them to do. He [God] is still sovereign, and He is still God and God is good. He never abdicated. No, not ever. The evil one is under His rule. Satan *never* has the freedom to move without His permission. Satan is *not* opposite and equal to God and, therefore, my subtitle "The Battle of Two Kingdoms" may be slightly misleading. Because there is only

---

second phase, the Bolsheviks, under the leadership of Vladimir Lenin (1870–1924), were placed in power.

one Kingdom – now and for all eternity. The other is completely fake, and it has already been overcome. Therefore, we can take courage from these words:

> During a recent radio interview, I was asked to respond to those who fear what's happening in our culture. My response was simple: "Fear not! We have a good God at the helm." I know that answer doesn't whip up votes or pressure anyone to give or fight or defend. Yet, in it is the heartbeat of our Saviour who encouraged, *"Be of good cheer, I have overcome the world"* (John 16vs33). My friend, I don't pretend that everything in the world is good. But I know that He who made the mountains the world is His. From His peace may you live and move and be (Winkler 2024).

And where did Christ overcome the world? On the Cross. His death and resurrection sealed the deal.

I have had the good fortune of delving deep into the biographies of many missionaries – a worthwhile pursuit that I highly recommend. What strikes me is this: these missionaries relied on Scripture; they applied the Word to their lives; they loved and trusted the Lord, Jesus Christ. Above all else, they relied on the Holy Spirit to interpret the Word.

They were generally humble, kind and loving people; they practised the notion of loving your enemy and praying for them, even in the face of death. In this regard they were fearless; they freely forgave their enemies.

Do I still love the country of my forefathers? Yes, I do. I love it in the same way Christ still loves her. That does not mean that I do not mourn the wrong things. I do. In getting this far in the book, I have been exploring my inner Saxon in its full context and have not avoided or denied the truth of our origins. I would love to visit all the birth places of my family members and relatives.

And of course, I would like to visit Hermannsburg in Germany too; maybe even browse in their archives. There is so much I would like to investigate as to the Gevers family and the Meyers, but at the moment, my heart is set on Nesse near the North Sea. I have been listening to that song, which I quoted at the end of my great grandfather Schumann's story, *Wo de Nordseewellen trecken an den Strand (Friesenlied)*. I have Ronny's version, with his deep baritone on my German Spotify playlist. It starts with the sound of the waves and the seagulls, before launching into this beautiful melody.

When I studied the images available on Google, I saw how perfectly the song describes the scenery. God willing, I would love to spend some time there – perhaps on one of the islands – time to rest, reflect and to heal ...*do is miene heimat, do bin ik zu hus.*

MY COLONIST'S FAMILY AND THE WARS

THE KLINGENBERGS

The town Holdenstedt was first mentioned in documents in 1061 and is home to the Holdenstedt Castle built in the beginning of the 18 C. During World War II it served as military hospital and officers' quarters. The manor house was privately owned until 1977. It now belongs to the city of Uelzen and is undergoing renovations.

My family owe Hedwig Schutte a great deal for the amazing work she has done in her lifetime preserving so much of our heritage and family history. In this particular book on the Klingenberg family, *Die Klingenberg's in Süd Afrika, 1859–1997,* she is paired up with Edith Klingenberg who has taken over as family historian.

Not only does it narrate the wonderful stories of our forebears, but it is also laden with updated genealogy as the family has grown and changed. Much of the information that I have taken out of this book has been translated by myself and paraphrased. If there are any errors, I apologise in advance for them.

MY THREE TIMES GREAT GRANDPARENTS

Johann Heinrich Wilhelm Klingenberg, who was born on 12 August 1811 in Holdenstedt, married Catherina Dorothea Radeke, who was also from Holdenstedt. He was a weaver by trade and joined the Hermannsburg Mission Society as a colonist. Because his trade was severely affected by the downturn in the economy after the Industrial Revolution (1760–1840), he decided to migrate to Africa with his entire family. On 1 October 1868, Klingenberg, his wife, Dorothea, and their six children left for Africa on *The Candace* (*Kandatze*). They accompanied the Bishop Karl Hohls, who had taken over after the death of Fröhling. They arrived 105 days later in Durban.

A telegram was sent to Hermannsburg, indicating that the ship had sunk, but it was a false message, as they had, in fact, arrived safely. From Durban, they were transported by ox wagon to Hermannsburg, through Zululand and onto Lüneburg, to his son in-law, Christian Kohrs, who had arrived in South Africa in 1859 as a Hermannsburg Mission colonist with Johann's oldest daughter, Dorothea. The farm was called Dreiling, because three families had been living there from the start: Christian Kohrs, August Hinze and Heinrich Rabe. Johann stayed on the farm until his sons had established their own farm, after which he lived with his son on the farm La Bella Esperanze. In his declining years, he moved to his son, Heinrich, who had no children, and lived there until he passed away at the age of 86.

Catherina Dorothea Radeke was born on 15 June 1815. Although she was known as having a happy disposition, she had a very difficult time in Africa, where there was a continuous struggle to survive. The most difficult time was that during the Zulu Rebellion and the Zulu Wars. During that time, they had many sleepless nights, when she would often hear the Zulus blowing on human bones. That meant that they had to secure themselves and the house. On one such night, they had to flee into the night, and she fell into a sawmill pit. She was greatly praised and honoured by her family and friends.

When her eldest daughter got breast cancer, she moved in with them and assisted the family and helped to nurse her daughter, until she passed on 17 September 1888.

The Second Generation in South Africa

1. Catherine **Dorothea** Klingenberg: born on 18 September 1835 in Germany; died on 19 September 1888 at Bergen, Transvaal.
2. Johann **Heinrich** Friedrich Klingenberg: born on 31 August 1838 in Germany; died on 31 December 1914 at Lüneburg, Natal.
3. Johanne Sophie **Marie** Klingenberg: born on 21 November 1840 in Germany; died on 14 February 1895 at Bergen, Transvaal;
4. Catherine Marie **Luise** Klingenberg: born on 30 March 1844 in Germany; died on 21 June 1935 at Bergen, Transvaal (my two times great grandmother);
5. Johann Heinrich **Wilhelm** Klingenberg: born on 28 May 1849 in Germany; died on 17 August 1920 at Lüneburg, Natal;
6. Heinrich **Friedrich** Peter Klingenberg: born on 5 July 1851 in Germany; died on 11 May 1889 at Bergen, Transvaal; and
7. Johann Christian **August** Klingenberg: born on 9 June 1854 in Germany; died on 22 June 1939 at Verden, Natal.

The Martins

The Story of Catherine Marie Luise Martin née Klingenberg and Johann Karl Martin

Carl Martin and Louise Klingenberg

The name "Martin" is derived from the Latin "Martinus", which is a derivative of Mars, genitive Martis, the Roman god of war and agriculture whose name may ultimately derive from the root "gleam".[61]

Johann Carl Martin was born in Oppin in Wiedemar, Leipzig, Germany. Oppin was first mentioned in a document in 952, when King Otto I exchanged it with Billing for places near Göttingen. In 966, the place was given to the Moritzkloster, Magdeburg. Around 1237, it was the seat of a German ministerial family named after the place.

---

[61] Born to Juno and Jupiter, Mars was a significant god in the Roman pantheon. He was seen as the protector of Rome and the father of Romulus and Remus, the two brothers who founded Rome.

Pioneering

On 20 January 1869, Luise arrived in Durban with her parents, after spending the last few years in Hamburg, Germany.

The first few years, which she spent with her sister-in-law in the Pongolo bush sawing wood, were particularly hard. They sawed the six-to-seven-foot base off the trees and stood in the sawmill pit to pull the long saw. She also grounded corn (*mielies*) for the workers. If they were sawing at night, she often had to be at hand to look after the fire, to prevent wild animals from coming close and having enough light to work by. During the Zulu Wars, there were many times that she had to tie a bundle of necessities and flee into the night.

On 12 June 1869, about six months after her arrival in South Africa, she married Johann Karl/Carl (spelling varies) Martin. Karl, who was a military officer and a farmer in Germany, was one of the folks who helped build the church in Hermannsburg in Natal. As a very thorough worker, he was a perfectionist, and his gardening tools were "a place for everything and everything in its place": none were packed away without being thoroughly washed and dried. (I think he would have had a few words with me about that).

Their first son was born on 14 March 1870: Christian Wilhelm Carl Martin. During the Zulu Wars, Luise and Karl Martin were in Botshabelo, where their sixth child, Bernhard Wilhelm Martin, was born. Later, at Bergen, they bought the farm Driehoek, where they lived and farmed until their deaths.

Before the Second Boer War (1899–1902), Carl Martin married Catherine Marie Mathilde Prigge. He was on commando with the Boers for the duration of the war. His wife, Catherine fled to Harburg, where she stayed in a little cabin at the Schröders, where Carl joined her later. After the war, they returned to the farm Koppie-Alleen, near Lüneburg, where they stayed until their deaths.

Their second son, Carl August Martin, who was also a soldier during the Anglo Boer War, died of typhoid. He was found dead under a water pump, where he had tried to cool down his fever.

A LOVE STORY

Their third child and my great grandfather, Wilhelm Friedrich Martin, was born on 7 September 1873. He was also a soldier during the Anglo Boer War, having joined the Transvaal Boer Commando at Zungwini Mountain, near Vryheid.

Emma Louise Sophie Hein, the eldest daughter of the Hein family, who lived at the foot of the mountain near Vryheid, was about 16 years old at the time of the war.

(Her father Wilhelm Hein and his brother Franz Hein fought in the 'Caffrarian Vanguard Corps' in 1878 during the Zulu Wars to protect Lüneburg. I have established that they are of Prussian descent. I have also recently connected with a second or third cousin from the Hein's now living in New Zealand. Linda Lomberg neé Hein remembers Emma well as she often came to visit her brother at the family homestead. Linda and her parents also visited my parents on the farm in Scheepersnek.)

Emma often gave her family members and relatives visiting from the commando thickened milk to take back with them. One day at camp, they said to Friedrich that he should join them at their family farm and be introduced to Emma, who was a lovely girl. He declined politely, because he did not intend to visit any girls during the war. Because soldiers often did not survive the war, he did not regard it as fair to any girl.

However, one day he did allow himself to be persuaded. Along with others, he was invited to dinner, and Emma set the table and prepared the meal. She made a real impression on Fritz, who thought she was young, lovely and independent. He visited more often and, one day, he received a pearl necklace from her, which she had made for him as a keepsake from her. He looked into her eyes and told her that his heart was deeply touched. Later, the guests left the Hein farm and sought shelter in the small town of Vryheid, from where they travelled to the coast, near New Hannover and Wartburg.

Fritz was captured and sent to India as a prisoner of war (POW). Three years after the lovely dinner at the Hein family, he returned to the farm on horseback. Emma watched the rider approaching from a distance. She thought it looked like Fritz and, as he came closer, she jumped up and knew that it was him! At first, she could not believe her eyes, because she had heard that he had been shot.

Fritz was supposed to have been shot by a firing squad after a court martial in India, but he was a man of faith and prayed: God's will be done! All he ever had done was his duty as a soldier. He promised the Lord that, if He would let him live, he would give some of his income, for the rest of his life, for the work of the Lord and for the extension of His Kingdom. That is what he prayed.

And here he was, back at the farm of the Hein family, asking if he could stay overnight. He was on his way to his sister in Glencoe and needed shelter for the night.

Like all guests, he was warmly received, and his horse was also well attended to. This was New Year's Eve. All the young people on the farm had planned to hike up the mountain the next day, which was New Years Day and a Sunday. The guests consisted of the Hein family and their relatives from the Cape, one of whom was Hulda, a cousin a little older than Emma.

Emma took Hulda aside and asked what they were going to do about Fritz. It was decided that they could not leave him out, and so, he was invited to go with them. Suspecting he was there to meet up with Emma, Hulda told her cousin that Fritz was not there by accident. She leaned over and whispered to Emma, if he cut her a walking stick from one of the trees while they are hiking, then it meant that he was serious about her. Although not very long, the path they took was very steep. Fritz went to a tree, cut off a small branch, and cleaned it up into a walking stick. After fiddling with the stick for a while, he casually offered the stick for Emma.

Back at the farm, they had a devotional time together, because it was Sunday. They all gathered outside after lunch, in the shade of a black wattle tree. Gradually, everyone got up and left, leaving only Fritz and Emma. Because she could not find an excuse to leave as well, she remained sitting there with him.

He asked her whether she knew why he was there. Being slightly obtuse, she answered that it was because he was trading in maize and had come to Vryheid to buy maize. Gently, he said that she was wrong and that he was, in fact, there to visit her, at which he enquired if she was going out with anyone in particular. She responded that she went in a crowd and that she was free.

After reminding her of the last thing he said to her three years ago, indicating that he had never forgotten her since that evening, he asked her if she would go out with him. He was not quite prepared for her response. She told him that she did not believe that he loved her, because he had returned from India some time ago and could have contacted her much earlier, but he did not even send a letter.

He explained that the war had robbed him of everything. He simply would not have been able to offer her any sort of life. It took time to rebuild the farm and the farmhouse, which had all been destroyed in the war.

They had lost everything because of the scorched earth policy.[62] He had to rebuild it all from scratch and he had only just completed the buildings.

He asked her if she would be prepared to marry him and share a life and a future with him. He declared his love for her by remaining true to her all these years while they were separated. When he was taken prisoner, the pearl necklace was broken, and the pearls scattered. When he returned from India, he went

---

[62] Scorched earth was a policy implemented by Lord Kitchener, which involved burning the farms and homesteads, in order to prevent supplies from the farms reaching the Boer soldiers.

back to the exact spot where that happened, where he was able to retrieve some of the scattered pearls. He opened his hand and placed the pearls in her open palm as proof of his love for her.

Before this, Emma had shown him respect because he was quite a bit older than her, but now she saw him in a different light and other feelings began to emerge. Before she could answer, he told her that she did not need to respond to his proposal immediately, offering her time to think things through. He would be back after ten days to get her answer. However, there was something else she needed to consider – his elderly parents would be living with them and she had to be sure that she could accept that arrangement. After speaking to her father, he rode out to meet with his sister.

After ten days, she was waiting for him to return, as promised, but he did not arrive. She began to doubt his sincerity and wondered if he was playing with her and had left her in the lurch. However, the following day, he arrived from Vryheid. His excuse was that he met an old friend from the war in Vryheid, who had been taken prisoner with him in India. He felt he had to spend some time with him and, as it happened, they never saw each other again.

Emma declared that she was ready to marry him. She was so impressed with the way he treated his parents and her respect for him grew. She was quite happy to live with them in the same house and to take care of them. She valued unity and did not want any division in the household.

Furthermore, she was prepared to adapt to the way his parents had been living and willing to fit in with their lifestyle. She intended to be a kind and loving daughter to them.

Emma's father gave her the right to decide for herself if she wanted to go ahead with the marriage. She could not have been more than 20 years old. Yet, the maturity she displayed was beyond her years. The wedding took place at the Hein farm.

Emma had not yet met her in-laws, but his parents were delighted that he was finally getting married, as he was already over 30 years old. Louise Martin (Klingenberg), who had been a cook/chef in various hotels in Hamburg, took over the cooking. Emma was quite happy to do everything else, including all the sewing. Her submissive humility gained her great respect from her in-laws of whom she took great care, right up to the time they needed nursing and passed away. To Fritz, she was worth more than pearls.

Fritz Martin with Emma Martin née Hein. Photo from Eddie Herrmann.

Emma tells that, right up to the end, Fritz would sit down and play a tune or two on the harmonica after a hard day's work, and they would sing together, songs such as *Wo findet die Seele die Heimat der Ruh* or *Es gibt ein Reich da Jesus wohnt* ("Where does the soul find rest" or "There is a kingdom where Jesus dwells").

She had never seen anyone die so peacefully before, like a small child, he just closed his eyes and went to sleep. He was 85 years old. Although she was heart-broken and living without him proved to be very difficult, she did not deny his rest and considered herself blessed. Emma passed away at the age of 86.

THE ANGLO-BOER WAR THROUGH THE EYES OF FRITZ MARTIN

The following pages are excerpts from Fritz Martin's war memoirs of a German-Afrikaner in the Boer War of 1899 to 1902, capturing the experiences involved in 15 months as a POW in India, the rebellion of 1914,[63] and peace and farm life up to 30 November 1937.[64]

The Searchlight

When the searchlight from the gunboat
Throws its rays upon my tent
Then I think of home and comrades
And the happy days I spent
In the country where I come from
And where all I love are yet
Then I think of things and places
And of scenes I'll ne'er forget
Then a face comes up before me
Which will haunt me to the last
And I think of things that have been
And happiness that's past
And only then I realise
How much my freedom meant

---

[63] The Rebellion of 1914–1915, also known as the Maritz Rebellion and the Boer Revolt, was a pro-German uprising in South Africa, at the start of World War I (1914–1918).

[64] Translation and paraphrasing by the author.

> When the searchlight from the gunboat
> Cast its rays upon my tent
>
> Joubert Reitz

AND SO IT BEGINS ...

"War was declared. War against England. Everything that our government did to negotiate peace was in vain. The truth is that England wanted to have the rich gold fields, and this is what the old States President Paul Kruger realised. For he didn't want to have war, but nothing satisfied England. And so, we had to decide whether we were going to fight for our rights and our independence or bow beneath England's dominance and we chose to fight and were called up to join the Commando. They called it 'Fight for your freedom and independence and for your rights'. Yes, we had the right to defend ourselves but what did we as "Burghers" know about war and cannons? What did we know about world power or about England? Most of us had never seen a canon in our lives.

We were just free 'Burghers' and independent. Our Commando was District 2, Piet Retief, under Colonel Friedrich *Meyer*, the son of the old missionary Meyer who had founded the missionary station at Entombe.

This commando was made up of 200 men. Out of those, 72 were German-Afrikaaners. Colonel Meyer was the brother-in-law of Oberst [Colonel] A. Schiel that was later wounded at Elandslaagte and taken prisoner. He was then sent as a POW to St Helena [concentration camp]. Oberst Schiel was married to Colonel Meyer's oldest sister. After peace was declared. Oberst Schiel was sent to Germany where he died very soon afterwards.

Our commando camped for two weeks in tents on Colonel Meyers farm at Zaaihoek, next to the Titane River. From there we rode to Bosrand, which is also known as Doringberg. That is in the vicinity of the Buffalo River. There we stayed for another two weeks. One afternoon we were all gathered together, and General Lucas Meyer from Vryheid addressed us. 'Today we are going to go into Natal. It is enemy territory. Tomorrow early we will attack the English camp at Dundee'".

Lucas Johannes Meyer

A Boer War General, a Voortrekker leader and member of the Volksraad of the Natalia Republic. As a young man he went to Natal and lived in Ladysmith and Newcastle, but in 1865 he settled in Utrecht district in the South African Republic. In 1872 he was elected field cornet.

He strongly opposed the British annexation of the Transvaal. At the Battle of Ingogo, during the First Anglo Boer War he was badly wounded and unable to fight at the Battle of Majuba Hill

(Wikipedia 2024)

"Each officer addressed us as well, including our own colonel. He ended his address with 'I expect and know that each one of you will do your duty. We have the right to fight against England. We fight for justice and independence. Also, no enemy should underestimate us, even if they are stronger and better equipped than we are.

For many of us this may be the last days of our lives. But remember, God is with us!' It was a serious speech, and I really took it to heart.

I just want to point out something. For us as Germans it went without saying to be faithful to our duties, because that is how we were raised by our faithful God-fearing parents at home and by our teachers and pastors at school and in the church".

Talana Set the Tone

At the outbreak of the Ango-Boer War on October 11, 1899, Britain had 27,054 troops of all ranks, both imperial and colonial, deployed over a wide area of Southern Africa.

The major concentration of forces was in Natal, with Ladysmith as their base a detachment of between 4 000 and 4 500 men, under the command of Major-General Sir William Penn Symons, had been sent forward to Dundee, arriving in the latter part of September.

British military consensus held that the northern Natal triangle, vulnerable to attack from several points from across the Buffalo River and over the Drakensberg, should not be defended and the principal town evacuated.

However, a strong lobby, swayed by colonial mining interests, demanded the defence of Dundee and Elandslaagte – their mines were vital to the shipping companies.

The British government was relying on the shipping companies to transport men and materials from Britain and the Empire. However, rebellion by dissident Boers in the Biggarsberg and by disaffected Africans was a real threat.

The decision was taken to defend Dundee.

By first light on the morning of October 20, the Boer forces has taken up their positions. On Talana Hill the commandos from Utrecht, Wakkerstroom, Krugersdorp and a portion of the Ermelo commando together with three guns were ready and waiting.

On Lennons Hill the commandos from Vryheid, Middleburg, Piet Retief and a few men from Bethal had taken up their position.

When the fighting was over, the British troops had driven Lucas Meyer and his men off both Talana and Lennox – but the Boers were by no means a defeated army.

Although at first glance it appears as if the British won the battle, within 30 hours they were forced to abandon the town and retreat to Ladysmith.

Talana may not rank as a major battle in terms of the total numbers engaged but it had a significant moral effect.

It was the first battle of the war and it seemed that the impact of the Boer victory over the British at Majuba in 1881 had been reversed.

The Boer forces formed an entirely different impression of the British soldier. He was far braver and more determined than they had been led to believe.

The British soldier also realised that the Boers, although an irregular army, would prove to be a formidable foe. – The Mercury Anglo Boer War Commemoration 1999 – 2002

Bella Siege of Ladysmith

General White, Woolls Sampson, Major Crosby, Mr Nourse Varty, Mr Arnott and many others all came to tea this afternoon and we were kept very busy.

The rumours have been confirmed that General Joubert was injured, and popular feeling is that General Louis Botha is to take over command in Natal.

Arthur Crosby said after he left the goldmines and went to Vryheid, he was interested in coal, and met with Lucas Meyer, the Emmetts and Louis Botha.

He is of the opinion that Botha will be a formidable opponent.

Woolls Sampson confirmed this.

The General was concerned and sent up the balloon man.

He confirmed that the boers have moved their big gun to Lombards Kop and that there is considerable activity towards Colenso way.

Uncle Fred came in and said they received despatches by heliograph that the Boers are digging in their heels on the Tugela and building up their forces (Fouche 2020).

THE FIRST BATTLE

"In order to attack Dundee, we had to cross the border into Natal. Later, I thought that this was a mistake. Only a very disciplined and experienced army would be able to attempt that. We were the biggest unorganised lot that I have ever seen on the day we attacked the English.

From Talana Mountain, our canons should have fired at the English camp towards Ebene just before Dundee, very early in the morning. The gunners responsible for the canons had to transport them up the mountain themselves, because the ground was too uneven for the transport animals. None of the canons were entrenched as they were supposed to be. General Lucas Meyer simply gave the command, 'Go! And greet the English!' The gunners tried to reason with him, 'But General we must first entrench the canons!' His response was rash and simply not thought through: 'Ek sê vir julle; Groet hulle! [I'm telling you; go greet them!]. The canons were on Talana in the open, exposed without any cover or protection. We let loose into the English camp. The result was terrible as the canon fire was unexpected. Apparently Major-General Symons had been warned not approach the Afrikaners on horseback. They retaliated with canons but missed us by a long shot. However, it didn't take long and our unentrenched canons were hit. The English soldiers under cover of canon fire stormed the mountain from all sides. We held on until midday and then we had to retreat. With no real leadership or discipline in our warfare we were left to our own devices. Each had to see to themselves and decide how best to attack the enemy. If we had been well organised, we might have won the day.

I was separated from the rest of the troop and only had my friend and comrade August Reinstorf with me and another boer from the Wakkerstroom commando. We tackled the enemy. We hid behind a stone wall as the soldiers tried to storm us but came under canon fire. Below us was a gully, between Eucalyptus trees and so we were reasonably well protected.

The canon fire below continued uninterrupted and therefore never noticed that our canons had stopped firing. The soldiers stormed and we shot. At such close range each shot was a hit.

Later, after my capture at the POW camp, soldiers that were also at the battle of Talana, reported that at that precise spot where I was, 75 English soldiers lay dead.

Our rifles became so hot that we had to be careful when loading not to burn our hands. A stone or granite splinter hit my neighbour on the side of his head ripping open a small vein.

Soon his whole face was full of blood, and I asked him, 'Hoe lyk dit maat, kan ek jou help?' He answered, 'Nee man, dis alles reg, skiet jy maar'. [Can I help you, my friend? He answered, No, man, all well, you can shoot.] I will never forget his face as he continued shooting.

An English stretcher bearer approached from the other side of the gully. I had him in my sights and would have sent him into eternity, if Reinstorf had not called out, 'Don't shoot! The man is wounded'. I yelled out to him to put his hands up and he immediately stood still. He was about 20 ft way from me. He gave himself up and asked us why we were still fighting. Had we not noticed that all the Boers had retreated? At first, we did not believe him but then we noticed the silence. It was very quiet, but the English continued to storm up the mountain. We took this officer with us and firmly believe that is why we were saved that day, otherwise we would either have been shot or taken prisoner. Unfortunately, that is what happened to Gustave Flygare. He was a little bit further along the same wall about 500 ft from us. His body lay near the wall".

Retreat

"We got down to our horses, which we had left early at dawn at the bottom of the east side of the mountain with our *agterryers*.[65] They came running up to us with worried faces urging us to mount up quickly, as the English were approaching. No sooner were we in the saddle and shots began being fired at us. Not one shot hit us.

A little further away, we came across a small house with a Red Cross on it. That was where the fallen and wounded were brought. We dismounted to go and see our wounded perhaps for the last time. Many helpers of the Red Cross came running up towards us. They were German! They gave us news about various wounded and fallen and that is how we found out that our dear friend Anton Prigge was badly wounded. Three splinters of shrapnel had hit him in his abdomen. Eventually, I found him in a side room. He still recognised me, and we said our final farewell. We had to depart in a hurry and as we got to our horses, bullets began to rain down on us again. We managed to get away unscathed.

---

[65] *Agterryers* were men – often Zulu men – with spare horses.

I had a little adventure with my *agterryer* (groomsman) here. His name was Nyama. His horse was spooked by the bullets and wouldn't stand still for him to mount.

Nyama took a running leap to land on the saddle but landed on the other side of the horse instead. I had to dismount and help him. The animal really became out of hand. Bullets were flying at us from all directions. As soon as Nyama was in the saddle he sat bolt upright like an American cowboy, everything forgotten and ready to gallop. Right after that a few grenades exploded next to us and we took off to join our commando at Ebene – what a terrible disorganised chaos! What a dreadful disappointment: Lucas Meyer had asked for a ceasefire and that was accepted, otherwise we would have been wiped out. Opposite us, in Gregory's Neck, stood six to eight canons. But not one fired.

My old friend, the Hollander, Van Oordt, a gamekeeper who worked for the South African government at the Lebombo boarder never saw his agterryer and three horses again. He plodded by foot between the soldiers. No one gave him a horse, even though many had spare horses available. I immediately got Nyama to give me his horse and I gave my horse to my friend, a pure bred. Nyama soon managed to get two more horses one for himself and a spare.

We retreated to Bosrand and arrived there exhausted. At 3pm, it began to rain very heavily. It rained as though buckets of water being emptied over us from heaven. It carried on raining heavily deep into the night. Van Ordt an Nyama arrived early enough to get into camp but many including me, had to make camp outside as by then no track or road was visible anymore and the animals were exhausted. With my horse, Van Oordt received, my saddle, a brand-new raincoat and a double thick blanket – and guess what? I had nothing! This was one of the worst nights of the war. We made camp at daybreak and Van Oordt offered me a swig of gin which took care of any cold or flu lurking".

The Retreat of the English

"The English fled the next day from Dundee to Ladysmith. It was the perfect opportunity to chase them down. It would not have been difficult to overtake, surround and capture them, but we were not allowed to. Instead, we let them get away to Ladysmith and where General White entrenched himself with approximately 1000 men. We were then supposed to surround them and starve them out.

This is how our generals, including Piet Joubert, did warfare. That was the beginning of the end of the war. We sat around and did nothing. Nothing happened. Eventually, the men came up with the idea to take leave. They went home to check up on their wives and children.

Leave of absence was duly granted, and that is how it came about that many of the Boers were missing when the action started. It also gave opportunity to much shameful betrayal".

Talana Museum on the retreat of the British forces from Dundee

121 years ago yesterday the British forces in Dundee retired from the town to Ladysmith. Please note British forces never retreat or withdraw – they retire.

I am currently re-reading Commando by Deneys Reitz as it is many years since I read it and there are some wonderful descriptions.

On the evening of the 21st October he was part of a group of men detailed to remain in the town to prevent further looting by members of the Boer commandos – one of the first things they wanted were the rubber macintosh raincoats as protection against the cold wind and rain, and he writes" After they

(British) were gone we searched around for one of the less damaged houses, as we had no idea how long we might be marooned here and decided to be comfortable. Towards evening I rode up again to the English camp to have another look at it and, wandering about, I came on the field hospital, flying the Geneva Cross. One of the tents, was a large marquee for wounded officers, and here I saw General Penn-Symons, the Commander of the British troops. He was mortally wounded, and the nurses told me that he could not last the night. The next morning, as I was again on my way up to the camp, I met a bearer-party carrying his body, wrapped in a blanket, and I accompanied them to where they buried him behind the little English chapel.

.... but that afternoon a dishevelled horseman rode into the town with tidings of the disaster that had overtaken the Johannesburg men at Elandslaagte. He was in a state of such excitement and gave us a much-exaggerated account of the fight, probably to excuse his presence so far to the rear, I decided to go off in search of our commando, as I could see there would be other fighting.

The temporary Corporal in charge of us forbade me to leave, as instructions were to remain in Dundee until further notice, but I rode away within the hour.

As it was late when I started, darkness came on before I got very far, and I spent the night at Glencoe Junction where I found other fugitives from the Elandslaagte Battle, from whom I gathered we had lost 2 guns and many men killed and wounded ... At the station, too, I saw the wife of Gen Koch, who commanded the Johannesburg commando.

He had been badly wounded and taken into Ladysmith by the British, and the poor women was hoping to get through their lines to see him ... but I do not know if she ever succeeded in reaching her husband, who died a few days later.

I rode on before daylight the next morning, the memory of her tear-stained face giving me the first hint of what women suffer in time of war. I went down the Wasbank Pass all by myself, and although I was new to the country, I had no difficulty in finding my way, as the road was all trampled and churned by the hundreds of horsemen who had gone before.

Although not totally accurate as the British forces retired down Van Tonders Pass (further to the south east) and it was the civilians from Dundee under the leadership of the Town Clerk, Francis Birkett, who withdrew down the Wasbank pass.

The Siege of Ladysmith and the two battles in the Rietfontein area

...So on to modern-day Rietfontein. The dining room of the main farmhouse used to be the old Boer operating theatre. Instead of blood, guts and gore spattered around, it is now furnished with a beautiful dining room table salvaged from the Colenso Hotel. The walls are festooned with photographs, Regimental crests of those units that fought in the area, and a rather crusty-looking lot of ancient Generals. Oregon Pine floors, bay windows, an old Victorian tiled fireplace and high ceilings complete the look. Rather gruesomely, outside the back door is the blue-stone building that was used as a mortuary. Occupants were assured of a comfortable, although permanent, night's sleep. A ghost, known only as "Harry" is an infrequent but persistent visitor (Rundgren 2020).

THE ATTACK AND PATIENCE OF THE ENGLISH

"General White was an excellent officer who made the best of every opportunity. He managed to get through several attacks and heavy battle fire, until he was rescued by General Buller.

General Buller eventually managed to break through various skirmishes and heavy losses, e.g. at the Tugela Bridge, where he was almost captured by General Louis Botha, and later at Spionkop, where he tried to break through to Ladysmith to rescue General White".

SPIONKOP

"At Spionkop, us Germans experienced hell on earth. For days, we came under unending cannon fire. We only had our Mausers with which we were expected to storm the enemy. During this grip of incessant cannon fire but even here General Buller had to retreat with heavy losses. And now I would like to tell you about the bravery, diligence and trustworthiness of our German comrades.

At Spionkop, the Boers of Piet Retief Commando Number 1 under the command of K. Engelbrecht left us. It became too hot for them. As we looked around us one morning, this 'hero' had vanished in the night with his commando, and we had to fight it out alone. We would press on day and night until the enemy weakened. It was really a superhuman effort with bravery courage and endurance. Yes, we were very good. We also could have 'vanished' and saved our own hides, but that was not how we were raised. General Buller could not break through but we could not hold out much longer either. It would take immense strength from everyone while our troops became less and less, and the enemy became stronger and spread themselves out across the land. Buller retreated to Colenso and there he received reinforcements and ships canon".

The turn of the war

"Then the English began to shoot the area up for days on end, and especially on the Bosrand Hill not far from the Tugela River. This place was no longer strongly occupied as before, and it gave General Buller the opportunity to capture Bosrand after four days and it was finally over. With his big cannons positioned on top of the hill he could shoot all the places where we were stationed.

We had no option but had to retreat. General Cronje was then captured at Mafeking and taken prisoner. Buller broke through to Ladysmith and the very brave General White was freed. We retreated as best we could".

Guerilla warfare

"We began using guerilla warfare and practised various tactics: how to attack and how to retreat and attack from behind. When we knew that our enemy did not have the support of cannons to defend them, we managed to inflict heavy losses. The English were not used our small calibre fire when we had no cannons. We also received better Generals like Louis Botha and Christian Oppermann among others.

General Oppermann took over the leadership of our commando, and although much better, it was still not perfect. There was no unity among the officers".

The Battle of Vryheid Berg

"Early one morning, we were supposed to attack the British camp at Vryheid Berg. Everything went well. The enemy did not notice us. We had virtually captured the whole mountain and were very close to the English cannons, which were peppering us. We targeted the gunners and did away with them. Two comrades and I crept up to a small *koppie* (hillock) from where we could shoot down at the enemy from behind a wall close to the cannons. From that position, we had a hit from every shot. Soon the cannons were left useless. I soon had to take off my felt hat with a feather emblem of our unit, after two bullets ripped through its wide rim.[66] The hat was a good target for the enemy. Now in haste I covered my head with grass and weeds that were growing next to me. I lay on my stomach under the beating hot African sun and rain of bullets for four hours.

At about 2 pm that afternoon we were supposed to have stormed the mountain, and the cannons were quiet, came the unbelievable command to retreat! The first thought that shot through my head was that this must be a mistake or perhaps treason? As it transpired, two commandos on the other side of the mountain had run out of ammunition.

Later, we heard that others had received similar commands but were told that the Piet Retief Commando had no munitions and that we had to retreat. I was flabbergasted. What a disappointment, since we had already captured some of the blockhouses. No cannons were shooting at us anymore – we had virtually won! And now we must retreat?

After several days the skin peeled off my face like a snake in the summer when they shed their skin. I often liked to watch them shed their skins.

It may be good for the snake to shed its skin but it was not very nice for me at all. Afterwards it came out that no one wanted to take responsibility for the retreat – and that is how we fought for justice and freedom! Deception and treason were the order of the day.

Much later, the English soldiers that were there at that battle, told me that they were stunned to see the Boers retreat. They literally could not hold out any

---

[66] This hat was later donated to the museum in Vryheid.

longer, it was a matter of minutes, and they would have given themselves up had we stormed them. Their commander had fallen that morning and as the cannons were rendered useless, they were ready to give themselves up".

A short history of Vryheid

The aftermath of the Anglo Zulu War of 1879 left the remnants of the Zulu Kingdom in the hands of Uzibhebhu, Dinizulu's uncle. Dinizulu, the rightful heir, enlisted military support from the Boers in restoring him as king. After a successful campaign Dinuzulu was sworn in and in return the Boers were granted a large tract of land.

On August 16, 1884, this land was proclaimed as the Nieuwe Republiek with Vryheid as the capital and Lucas Meijer as the president. A *raadsaal* for the town fathers, a presidency for Lucas Meijer and a goal for miscreants were built. The fate of the tiny republic followed that of many others and by 1888 it had been absorbed by its neighbour, the Zuid Afrikaansche Republiek. The *moederkerk*, which occupies pride of place in the centre of town, was completed in 1894.

At the outbreak of the Anglo Boer War on October 20, 1899, the Vryheid Commando swung into action and, led by General Lucas Meijer, fought at the Battle of Thalana. They went on to take part in the siege of Ladysmith and had the honour of capturing the British guns at Colenso.

Vryheid itself was left relatively unscathed by the big battles fought against the British forces to the west, but smaller skirmishes with the Imperial forces did occur at Scheepersnek, as well as a major Boer attack on the British garrison stationed on Lancaster Hill just north of Vryheid. During this battle Lt Col Gawne was mortally wounded and a cairn demarcating the place where he fell, as well as the British fortifications, can be viewed on the hill. General Louis Botha, one of five famous generals from Vryheid, tested the British lines the next year and led a successful invasion into Natal via Bloemfontein, drawing thousands of imperial troops from the Transvaal and the Free State in a desperate attempt to trap him.

The incursion finally ended at Italeni and Fort Prospect where the Boers were defeated, however General Botha managed to elude the pursuing British as he led his men back to the Transvaal.

At the culmination of the Anglo Boer war, chief uSkhobobo Sibiya, encouraged by the British civil authorities, attacked a Boer camp on the eastern slopes of Holkrans Mountain (KwaMthashana), killing 56 burgers of Commandant Jan 'Mes' Potgieter's commando. After the Anglo Boer War the town was incorporated into the colony of Natal.

The Carnegie library (presently the Information Bureau) was built with funds from the Carnegie Foundation and houses started springing up along Bree, Kerk and Hoog Streets, as well as above the railway line at the base of the hill. 1910 saw the Natal Colony join the Union of South Africa and in 1912 the town was granted municipal status. It gradually grew into an agricultural marketplace for maize, sheep and cattle. The Empire Theatre in Hoog Street, the site of many musicals and revues, was completed in 1927.

Coal, which had been used by the early residents of the area east of Vryheid, became commercially viable from 1908 onwards, with the construction of a rail link to the coalfields.

Two mines, Coronation and Hlobane, in time grew to provide thousands of jobs for the inhabitants of the area. With the increase in population so the need for water led to the construction of the Grootgewacht, Bloemveld and Klipfontein dams" (Vryheid Tourism Association 2014).

Many lose hope

"As the English troops went through Piet Retief and destroyed everything, many of our commanders gave themselves up. Our commander, Engelbrecht, was one of them. However, we of the second Piet Retief commando took possession of the Hlangampiesberg. Here the enemy did not dare to come. From here we fired at them whenever the opportunity arose".

Plunder and destruction

"I was on patrol with many of my brave comrades as we saw an English convoy approaching. They were coming from the direction of Bergen on their way towards Annyspruit to collect coal for the English camp that was in the command of General Dartnell. The convoy was made up of six cannons and approximately 200 men. Some of the cavalry left the convoy and rode towards the mission station Goedehoop. It was the mission station of Heinrich Prigge. A few days before, he was taken prisoner with his wife, four daughters and a young son and taken to an English concentration camp. General Dartnell had promised him to protect his home from plundering. However, the cavalry with one officer rode out to the mission station not to protect it but to pillage and plunder. Chickens and geese were killed and taken back to the convoy.

I reported this to our Colonel, Friedrich Meyer, and immediately asked if I could have six men to go and teach this band of robbers a lesson the next morning. "Because I know they will come again." I said, "They have tasted goose flesh, and an English soldier would give his life up for a goose". My request was rejected. It was apparently too much of a risk and too big a responsibility etc.

So, I gathered three men together and we took off on our own. We left the horses behind at camp as they would have been a hindrance. At 3 am we stopped; it had been a tough hike in the mountains at night, over rocks and stones and all manner of obstacles and we could have broken our legs or even our necks. But it went well, we weren't sissies at all. *Wir waren doch keiner Weichlinger*. We had no fear, and we were well prepared.

We had an action plan that helped us to overcome any difficulties along the way. Our aim was to be there at the break of day. We were now very close to the mission station Goedehoop, Johannes Krieger, as son of the missionary H. Krieger[67] wanted to find out from some of the Zulus if the enemy had arrived in the night and if they were still there. If that were so, we would have had some difficulties and gave him permission to go and told him that we would not be waiting for him. We had to press on because we had quite a distance to go. He then had to ensure that he was at the prearranged rendezvous. If by chance he could not make it, he was to go back to camp very carefully.

Soon, we saw two wagons with 20 English cavalry on horseback approaching the mission station. I knew it! They wanted to rob despite the promises made

---

[67] I did not manage to find a record of Missionary H. Krieger.

by General Dartnell. On this day an officer was also there. Our spy, Krieger, was not in time to join us. It was just three of us left and we still had to go another 400 yards to get to the appointed meeting place. We crouched down low on our stomachs to allow them to pass so that we could attack them on their return. The officer set two guards outside, they were sitting high up on their horses, and I found it really funny that they didn't see us. We crept on hands and knees to the spot from where we wanted to surprise them and left them to steal the remaining chickens and geese.

They were brazen to say the least and very sure of themselves because they had the two guards to warn them of any attack. And so, the hunt was on. Doors were hacked off with axes. They stole everything they could lay their hands on and left it desolate and open. Two wagons can carry a lot of stuff. Even the church was broken open and the beautiful altar cloth with an embroidered cross was ripped off. We later found it in one of the soldier's saddle bags. Chickens and geese were throttled, and the two guards watched and waited.

Soon, the wagons were packed, and they were ready to return to camp with their loot. We had planned it in such a way that they would be caught in the crossfire, and I turned and said to my comrades, "here we fight or fall but there is no such thing as retreat! Are we all in agreement with me? I will let off the first shot and you are to wait for that signal. Their convoy ought to come right up to the wagon gate and the dip, which is about 80 feet.

The wagons rolled forward and came exactly as predicted. One sergeant was helping the wagons through the dip and when they reached just the right spot, I shouted: "Hands Up!" However, the sergeant did not listen until I fired the first shot. The bullet hit him square on his munition belt. His whole shoulder shattered from his own bullets that went off.

Lt. Mutter rode off at haste with eight men up to about approximately 200 yards away and then jumped off their horses and opened fire in all directions. Some of them took shelter behind an anthill and were wondering why they were still being hit. The soldier leading the wagon now tied a white hanky to the end of his whip and held it high. That is how the officer came towards us. Their guns they had left just where they were. At about 20ft I thundered at him to hand himself over and put his hands up. The arms went up like eagles' wings. I could hardly stop myself from laughing when he said, We English are damn fools to be captured by three Boers'. To his men he said, 'Did I not tell you keep a look out, that they will get us?' We freed the oxen very quickly because we knew that there was still the main convoy with cannons. Gun fire was already raining in on us and several oxen had been hit. I ordered my comrades to pull back into their positions otherwise we were going to be shot. 'Tell the others also'! But of course, there were no 'others. In the riverbed above the dip, I saw two men who had fired at us. I crouched down low on my stomach and let off two shots. Both fell where they were.

Another came charging towards us and nearly got taken down by a head shot from one of my comrades. The bullet grazed his cheek and he immediately fell with his hat in his hands. This was our spy! He was unable to go back as decided because the wagons had already appeared. He had hidden himself in the riverbed until two of our patrols came along and he joined them. They thought we were surrounded and wanted to free us. I could not understand such stupidity from a soldier. How could they just begin to shoot without giving us a warning? The other two were later brought to me by one of my comrades. Fortunately, they were not badly wounded. It was Johannes Reinstorf and E. Posselt. Now we could finish off and move out with the loot we reclaimed. The officer, Lt. Mutter, asked me for a horse so that he can return to camp and General Dartnell by the church in Bergen. He wanted to get an ambulance to collect the fallen. Only after he solemnly swore that he would only use the horse for this reason, I gave him it to him.

However, when he got back to the General, he lied and said that he had been attacked by 50 Boers and after he had bravely withstood the attack, he gave himself up and the Boers shot most of his contingent. His scandalous lie was found out a few days later and he was discharged and returned to the Cape and later sent back to England.

Bergen Church

The congregation of Bergen was formed in 1884. This came about because of expansion of the German population and the acquisition of farms in the area. The Church and school opened in 1893. Today the church has been abandoned and only ruins are remaining. Both structures were destroyed during the Anglo Boer War. After the war some church members asked that the church be moved closer to Piet Retief where many of them lived. When they did not get the full support from everyone, a group of 12 split off and moved away to establish the church at Wittenberg, which is still standing today.

The Bergen Church and School were rebuilt. I am not sure when the building was abandoned however, one feature which is still intact and being well looked after is the cemetery".[68] (Muller 2017).

THE AMBUSH

"Two days later, our colonel wanted to send out some spies, but he made the mistake of relying too much on the locals who later betrayed us. A strong English contingent lay close the mission station at Entombe. It was the mission station of Missionary Wagner. From where we were, we wanted to go out at night to

---

[68] Some of our relatives are buried in this cemetery.

see what we could do to damage the enemy. We were eight men in total. From the English camp at Entombe to the English camp at *Bergen* was a distance of 2.5 hours by horse. We had noticed that officers with not enough guards often rode between these two camps. That is why we wanted to capture them and thought that it was quite possible. We knew this area like the back of our hands and had enough courage to do it. But the local natives betrayed us to the enemy. A patrol of 12 men were positioned on a hill where we would hide ourselves. I set out guards, two men on three different points to ensure that we would not be surrounded.

Just to make sure I asked the Colonel again if he was absolutely sure that there would not be an English patrol at the *koppie* to which we were riding. He was absolutely sure. We would not be able to see the English camp before we got the *koppie,* I said, "It is unbelievable that there should be no guard if the camp was right there'!

This time, there was one! For the first time, they set up a patrol there because of the information and betrayal of the local natives. Unaware, we rode in single file through very rough and uneven territory to the *koppie* and were already a few feet past it when suddenly two men jumped out from behind big rocks and shrubs. Standing behind their raised guns, they commanded us to halt and put our hands up.

Our colonel, who was very hard of hearing and on some days was really bothered with rheumatism, didn't hear a thing. He thought we were already at the camp and that it soon would be his. I shouted that they are shooting and had already jumped off my horse with speed seeking shelter behind some rocks. He had done the same. Two shots went passed us but did not find a target. Only the air got two holes. We were unharmed. But the two 'victorious' enemy soldiers were killed. Another one was shot in the neck but not fatally, it was an open flesh wound with much blood loss. The wounded soldier became really animated because another nine men were hidden behind the rocks and our bullets had not been able to hit them.

They must have thought to themselves; "We have seen them riding towards us about 300ft from us. We wanted to capture them. At such a short distance it would be impossible for them to fight back." However, we had no intention of giving ourselves up and would have been successful if they had not received reinforcements of a platoon of 50 men. However, in the meantime I called out twice for them to give themselves up or die. But it was too late as the reinforcements arrived and we had to give ourselves up. The rock behind which I hid had four bullet marks on it, but none had hit. Our other 6 comrades were unable to free us as we were between them and the enemy. They were afraid that they might shoot us. Fortunately, they escaped capture even though a search party had gone out after them. Then the English Colonel snapped at us. Asking us why we did not give up right away, fighting at close distance and did we not know that it was surely murderous.

And then he asked me a question that I will never forget. 'What are you fighting for? Don't you know that you are fighting against a great and civilised nation?' and I answered him saying, 'We belong to our government, and we are their soldiers, to fight, to be obedient and true'. He then wanted to know where our government was and under which general we are fighting. And I answered, 'Under all'!

When he noticed that we were German, he swore and declared that he would destroy our homes and everything we have will be left in ruins.[69] We were stripped of all our amour and taken down the mountain into the big English camp to General Dartnell. On the way the soldiers found more of my armour, a spare magazine belt and a bayonet. They were absolutely horrified and anxiously

---

[69] The Martin homestead was completely destroyed, as was the entire farm. The Bergen Church, where Dartnell was camping, was also destroyed.

asking what I was doing with these. Later even my pocketknife was taken away from me. I was considered a dangerous murderer".[70]

From my research on Facebook - The Anglo Boer War and Bambatha Rebellion 30.08.2019, I received the following information:

> "Maj - Gen. Sir John Dartnell. His column, primarily Natal Police, operated from their regional HQ in Piet Retief into Swaziland in early 1901. So, your Lt Mutter was most likely under his command" – Paul Alexander.
>
> And:
>
> "Lt Mutter" - the only Lt Mutter on the rolls is Lt FAC Mutter Commander-in-Chief's Bodyguard (formerly Pte 3468 Cape MR). He served with the CinCBgd from November 1900 to April 1901 when he resigned. His resignation date has the note "AO 367 06-07-1901" - this indicates Army Order 367 - something was published relative to his resignation. This seems unusual and worth following up - you will need a good military library in UK - try The National Army Museum, London. [unfortunately, I was not able to take this investigation further due to personal circumstances].
>
> From a record on National Archives of SA. FAC Mutter is "Frank Andrew Christopher" – Meurig Jones (Studied Commonwealth Studies at the Institute of Commonwealth Studies at University of London)

---

[70] Fritz was only 26 years old at the time of his capture as a POW.

The Court Marshall

I found it difficult to translate the text in this section and to understand the course of events. Additionally, I found it difficult to connect the events coherently. According to Emma, Fritz was supposed to have been court martialled in India, but according to his testimony, it was before being sent to India. It is possible that misinformation had been given to her. Also, the letters that he wrote from the POW camp in Ladysmith never reached her.

"I was to be court martialled before General Dartnell. My heart sank as I had no confidence in him and his lack of integrity. How am I supposed to greet this 'gentleman' that gave his word to the missionary Krieger and then broke it? He was supposed to protect the mission station but instead he allowed Lt. Mutter to plunder it with two wagon loads. Not surprising the general had been given a false report about the events.

It was said that we had captured two scouts earlier; shot another two and wounded another. In astonishment, I exclaimed, that we were riding in the open with no knowledge of the guards until we were 13 ft away and two soldiers jumped out in front of us. I explained that we did not want to give ourselves up and instead wanted to fight our way out of the situation and we would have managed it if it had not been for their reinforcements that came. They shot first but missed. We retaliated and shot both soldiers and wounded another. We were the ones who were attacked at close range. We only tried to defend ourselves. It was no use; the general would hear nothing of it. He insisted that we should not have continued to fight. To him it looked like murder. At this point they brought out my magazine belt as evidence, containing three dum-dum bullets. I had carried these bullets with me for four months in my belt, in a separate pouch, so that they would not be used by mistake in the heat of battle. These bullets were used for game hunting only. The general stood his ground, the evidence spoke for itself. Then to my amazement further bullets were taken out of my pouch and I was asked if these bullets were mine. I had never seen those bullets before. The tips had been filed into sharp points right up to the casings and were brand new and shiny. We had had rain the whole night and I was asked again whether I had any files. Of course I had files which were used for my horse hooves. A rasp, knife, a small hoof hammer and hoof nails etc. I had put new shoes on my horse just a few days ago.

The verdict according to the general was clear. I must be court marshalled. Apparently 'someone' had pleaded under oath, just a few days before that the sergeant under Lt Mutters' command was shot by a dum-dum bullet and was dead. His shoulder was ripped off and that I was the culprit who shot him with that bullet. In my defence, I explained to them how the bullet had struck the sergeant's magazine belt which caused the brutal damage.

Surely, Lt. Mutter would have seen this for himself, as he was standing right next to me as I was removing the damaged magazine belt from the fallen sergeant. I would have shown them the belt, but it was with my platoon at camp. However, with regards to the dum-dum bullets, I have had those since the battle of Dundee. I have seen thousands upon thousands of such bullets and again also a few days earlier when we captured the loot and wagons, I collected 40 such shells out of the magazine belts of Lt. Mutter's troop and showed them to my superior officer.

At this point a smaller, younger lieutenant jumped up and swore at me, "You're a damn liar! Standing in front of the general and telling nothing but lies! I turned around and gave him a filthy look and told him that he could not prove that I was liar, but that I am NOT a damn liar I would prove very well. They just needed to ask my colonel who would testify to the truth. The colonel was duly brought in and questioned. He testified to the whole thing and was even able to give them the number of bullets involved.

As I was led outside, I saw Lt. Mutter who greeted me with a big smile on his face. 'Hallo! Today you're in our hands'. I nodded my head and agreed 'You are right. Today I am in your hands. But you remember a few days ago you were in my hands. The big difference between you and me is this: you asked me for a horse, and I gave it to you so that you could fetch help for your wounded. I personally went and fetched water from the river and gave it to your wounded to drink. You witnessed that all yourself. You also witnessed the shooting of your sergeant and me taking off the damaged magazine belt. You know all this. However, here I am being charged with a court martial as a murderer, and thereafter I am to be shot'. At this, he said that my case does not look good at all, but that he hoped I would get off".

Condemned to death but saved by God

"My hearing lasted three days. Then it was decided that I should face the firing squad in the morning at 9 am. Even the guards knew. When the change of guard happened at 2 am, they were discussing the trial and the verdict between themselves. I could hear every word. Perhaps they thought I was sleeping. I was in shock and in turmoil. It was very difficult to accept what was happening to me. To be shot innocently. I bowed before the Lord, and pleaded my case with Him, just like David did as he had to flee from his son Absalom. 'Lord, please confuse the council of the enemy'!

My prayer was heard. On the third day around 3 pm, I was brought out again and they explained to me that I had been pardoned. General French had re-investigated and proved that everything I had said was true and wished me well. I had conducted myself with honour and Lt. Mutter was stood down. Yes, that what comes from the wisdom of the great".

Under Strict Guard

Fun in the camp

"We were very strictly guarded day and night. After 16 days we were transported to 'Tin Town' in Ladysmith. [On page 6 of the photo section at the back of the book "Die Klingenbergs in Südafrika", is a photograph of Fritz Martin with Bernhard Böhmer and Col. Friedrich Meyer as prisoners of war 1901.] One day, a herd of goats came into the camp and the 'Tommies', our nickname for the English, wanted to milk them so that they could eat it with their bowl of Phutu, a Zulu dish of cooked maize meal. The English hated it, and thought it was not fit human consumption. However, the lambs had already been drinking from their mothers and taken all the milk. In desperation they tried to milk each one but there was nothing left. Then one guard pipes up, 'Look here Charlie, this one is a large one with a huge udder'. She was caught by her legs and held by her big horns. A bucket was placed beneath her, and the enthusiastic milking process began. Nothing! Then John leans over to Charlie and says, 'Leave him, he might be a 'he' goat.' They were trying to milk a ram! The tears of laughter – I was just about doubled over. And so, the Phutu had to be eaten without milk again.

A few days later, I had a bit of fun with the sergeant. This bloke really hated my guts. Anyway, he used to come marching past our tent, proud and puffed up. However, one day he came into our tent as friendly as a cat *ganz Katzenfreundlich* and asked if one of us was able to repair saddles.

Oh, it must've hurt him to ask us. He had a brand-new saddle which was rubbing the horse. I volunteered to make his discomfort even greater and told him to provide the horsehair. While he was off to fetch the saddle and the horsehair, I leaned over and told my colonel, 'If one day this 'hero' should be shot off his horse, then perhaps one of our Boers will inherit a good saddle'! The saddle was brought to me with horsehair enough for ten saddles. After about 8 hours, the sergeant came around to see if the saddle was finished. I had already finished it long ago. It pained him immensely to say thank you. I said to him smiling, 'I really only did it so that my own friends will get a really good saddle should they be so lucky to shoot you off your horse, and hopefully that will be soon'.

Two days later, the sergeant was sent out on patrol with 50 men. They had seen some Boers in the vicinity of J. Freyer's farm. After about two hours we saw this big dust cloud rise up in that direction that cavalry had disappeared into.

Later through this thick dust we could see the riders who came back with great speed, and I said to my colonel, "the saddle!" It was almost as I had predicted. The heroes fled for their lives. Two horses were shot but the riders were not hit.

My brother, Carl Friedrich *August* Martin (born on 6 December 1871 and died 17 December 1901), died while I was still in a concentration camp. He was part of my commando. He died in the district of Ermelo on the farm of W. Buhrmann and that is also where he is buried. He was 30 and 11 days old when he died".

Censored letters

"While we were still at Ladysmith, they allowed us to write letters to our families, but we were not allowed to mention anything of political significance. Most of our families, women and children, were taken captive and held in a very big concentration camp at Volksrust.

In my first letter, I wrote about the treasonous behaviour in the camp. Some of the Boers became turncoats. It meant that we were fighting our own people. The work they got in the camp earned them 10 shillings per day and half of the bounty from the house raids. I found this absolutely shocking and sickening and couldn't wait to leave the place. We had heard that we were going to be deported to India. Anyway, the letter was sent and a week went past and I wrote a second letter in similar style with similar content.

The following day, a sergeant came to collect me from my tent. 'The major wants to see you outside the gate'. This was Major Foster of Camp Tin Town. I was taken towards his big tent, where he sat at a round table with both my letters in front of him. 'Are you F. Martin'? I said yes. 'Did you write both these letters'? I needed to check if both the letters had my signature at the bottom, so I bent right over the table, almost with my head up against his face. 'Yes, this is my signature and I have written these letters'. He then asked me if I knew that we were not allowed to make any political comments. When I acknowledged that I knew he demanded, 'Then why did you do it'? I then told him that I was not aware that I had done it. Then he began to read the letters back to me in German.

Every important place had been underlined in red ink. So I told him that I had not written these things for political gain. I just wrote the truth. At this he tore both letters in two and threw them into the wastepaper basket and threatened to throw me into a very deep dark hole, if I tried one more time. [I love this man to bits. I think I inherited some of his spunk.] My response was: 'I'm really sorry to have lost both my stamps in such a way. As for you throwing me into a deep dark hole, I couldn't care less'"!

> The first 500 burghers had already landed at Bombay in India in April 1901. About 9 000 prisoners of war were ultimately housed in the seventeen camps between Abbotabad in West Pakistan and Trichinopoly in the South of India.
>
> The prisoners of war were housed in camps which were more or less set out as follows: The camp was enclosed by two fences of barbed wire, the outside fence being higher than the fence on the inside. The space between the fences was known as 'Dead Space' where the guards could shoot any intruder without

warning. During the night the camp was brightly illuminated. According to local circumstances, the prisoners of war were housed in either tents, corrugated iron huts, or bamboo and grass huts.

Not only burghers of the two Republics, namely the Zuid-Afrikaansche Republiek and the Orange Free State, were interned in the camps, but also foreigners who took part in the war as volunteers, among others George Caralampides from Greece, Angelo Monteli from Italy, Eppo Castingh from the Netherlands and Alois Ortner from Austria. Many young boys and aged men were also sent to the camps as prisoners of war, among others Johannes van Heerden, aged 7, and Gideon Van Zyl, aged 78.

Inactivity, loneliness, nostalgia and boredom were fundamental problems these prisoners who were thrown together from various places, had to contend with. To combat these problems all available talent was utilised in order to fill the empty hours productively.

From May 1902 rumours about peace negotiations were spread in the camps. Although they were overjoyed when they heard that peace was negotiated, they were sceptical and dismayed when they were informed what the conditions of the peace treaty were. A considerable time would elapse before the majority of the prisoners would be willing to take the oath of allegiance to the British crown. From July 1902 ships e.g. the Aurania, with POWs on board started the voyage back to South Africa. Many irreconcilables refused to take the oath of allegiance. In 1903 there were still diehards 'Bitter Einders' who refused to sign the oath. Of the 577 prisoners who died, 62 were buried at sea (War Museum of the Boer Republics)

INDIA

"Very soon after that, we were sent to India. A few days before that a bribed Burgher came to spy on us in our tent. It was his job to spy. He came in as though he was a part of talking about the war and this, that and another thing but I knew this traitor! I jumped up and commanded him to "get out and to disappear before my eyes or else die! Even if I only had my pocketknife with me, I would use it. You Satan, you snake!" He cleared off with great speed through the door. It was a very good thing he did, because I don't know for how much longer I would be able to control myself. Such characters ought not to be allowed to live, especially during the war.

According to records Fritz Martin was captured on 01 March 1901. His POW No. 18010. He was 26 years old and sent to Ahmednagar.

18010   Martin   Fritz   Swaziland   1901-03-01   Ahmednagar   26   Driehoek
(Record from Angloboerwar.com)

Colonel Lucas Meyer stayed behind in Tin Town, and I visited him in hospital the day before our departure. He was very sick. When he had recovered from his illness, he was transported to a ship berthed in Durban harbour and that is where he stayed until the end of the war".

THE *VIERKLEUR* OVER INDIA

"Hawks and vultures and other such birds are protected by law in India, which is why there are so many of them. Many times, when the cooked meat for our meals came out from the kitchen to the dining room, the hawks would swoop down and steal the meat out of the dish. We would end up with nothing.

A few of us decided to get together and catch one of these birds when the opportunity arises. We planned to tie the Transvaal flag to its legs. India should also get to see this flag! Anyway, one day we were lucky to catch a bird at our table. It was a lovely grand specimen of a hawk and kept him hidden under a breadbasket and then smuggled him to our officer who had some string. This we used to tie the flag on our "messenger pigeon's" left leg – the beautiful *Vierkleur*.[71] With grand majestic swoops our *Vierkleur* circled over Fort Ahmednagar three times and then flew away.

Photo of a fort in or near Ahmedabad. This would have been where Fritz was held captive during the Boer War. He describes the stone walls in his memoirs. (Source: https://commons.wikimedia.org/wiki/File:Ahmednagar_fort_inside_of_the_fort_gate.jpg).

The Ahmednagar Fort (Ahmadnagar Qilaa) is a fort located close to the Bhingar Nala near Ahmednagar in Maharashtra state western India. It was the headquarters of the Ahmednagar

---

[71] The *Vierkleur* is the Afrikaans word for the flag of the South African Republic.

Sultanate. In 1803, it was taken by the British during the Second Anglo-Maratha War. It was used as a prison during the British Raj. Currently, the fort is under the administration of the Armoured Corps of the Indian Army.

In 1803, the Ahmednagar Fort was round in appearance, with twenty-four bastions, one large gate, and three small sally ports. It had a glacis, no covered way; a ditch, riveted with stone on both sides, about 18 feet (5.5 m) wide, with 9 feet (2.7 m) water all around, which only reached within 6 or 7 feet (2.1 m) of the top of the scarp; long reeds grew in it all around. The berm was only about one yard wide. The rampart was of black hewn stone; the parapet of brick in chunam, and both together appeared from the crest of the glacis to be only as high as the pole of a field-officer's tent. The bastions were all about 4½ feet higher; they were round. One of them mounted eight guns en barbet, pointing eastward; all the rest had jingies, four in each. In 1803 two guns were visible in each bastion, and 200 were said to be ready in the fort to be mounted.

A gunshot to the west of the fort was the Pettah of Ahmednagar. The main gate of the fort faced the pettah, and was defended by a small half-circular work, with one traverse and several little towers for men. There was a wooden bridge over the ditch, which could be taken away in time of war, but it was not a drawbridge. It was reported that an iron trough as large as the bridge, could be placed upon it, or on the supporters of it, and fill with charcoal or other combustibles, to which could be ignited as an enemy approached.

The fort is also called as Bhuikot Killa, which means it is a land fort and is not constructed on any hill. It should not be confused with other Bhuikot Killas in Maharashtra like Solapur Bhuikot Killa.

A small river came from the northward, round the west side of the pettah, and passed to the southward of the fort. A nullah also passed from the northward, between the fort and a town called Bhingar, about a gunshot to the eastward, and joined the river. A potential defensive weakness was a little hill or rising ground close to and east of Bhingar, from which shot from siege guns could reach the fort.

Two nills or covered aqueducts came from the hills, a mile or more to the north, passed through and supplied the pettah and the town, and then went into the fort, either under or through the ditch, into which the wastewater fell.

There were no passages across the ditch from the sally ports, and no part of the aqueducts appeared above the ditch. The nullah mentioned above had steep banks and passed within 60 yards of the fort; the aqueduct from Bhingar passed under it. There was no bridge or even a prominent crossing point at the nullah and hence no clearly defined route between the fort and the town of Bhingar.

There were many small pagodas and mosques around the pettah and the fort, but none exactly between, or between the fort and Bhingar, or nearer to the fort than those towns.

"The fort was built by Malik Ahmad Nizam Shah I (after whom the city of Ahmednagar is named) in 1427. He was the first sultan of the Nizam Shahi dynasty and he built the fort to defend the city against invaders from neighbouring Idar. Initially it was made of mud but major fortification began in 1559 under Hussain Nizam Shah. It took four years and was finally finished in 1562. In February 1596, Chand Bibi the queen regent successfully repulsed the Mughal invasion but when Akbar attacked again in 1600 the fort went to the Mughals.

Aurangzeb died at Ahmednagar fort at the age of 88 on 20 February 1707. After Aurangzeb's death, the fort passed to the Nizams in 1724, to Marathas in 1759 and later the Scindias in 1790. During the period of instability in the Maratha Empire following the death of Madhavrao II, Daulat Scindia had the fort and its surrounding region ceded to him. In 1797, he imprisoned Nana Phadanvis the Peshwa diplomat at Ahmednagar fort.

In 1803, during the Second Anglo-Maratha War, Arthur Wellesley defeated the Maratha forces and the East India Company came into possession of the fort.

The fort was known as Ahmednagar Fort and was used by the British Raj as a prison and this was where Jawaharlal Nehru, Abul Kalam Azad, Sardar Patel and nine other members of the Indian National Congress were detained for almost three years after they passed the Quit India Resolution. Jawaharlal Nehru wrote his popular book – *The Discovery of India* – while he was imprisoned at the fort. During the same time, Congress leader, Maulana Abul Kalam Azad, also compiled his acclaimed *Ghubar-e-Khatir* ("Sallies of mind") (Urdu: غبار خاطر) which is considered as the best example of "Epistolary Essays" in Urdu literature.

During the same time, Odisha's first Chief-Minister and ex-Governor of undivided Bombay State, Harekrushna Mahatab also compiled three volumes of the History of Odisha in Odia. This has later been translated and published in English and Hindi.

Currently, the fort is under the administration of the Armoured Corps of the Indian Army (Wikipedia 2024).

BRITISH RULE (1817–1947)

When the British Government took possession of Ahmednagar much of it was almost ruined. Many former rich areas were depopulated because of famine and continuous fighting between the British soldiers and the freedom fighters. They continued to rise in arms taking resort to villages and the hills and mountains-mostly Parner, Jamgao and Akola areas. The Kolies and the Bhils harassed the British troops intermittently. Raghoji Bhangria headed this mutiny. At last he was caught at Pandharpur in 1847 and was immediately hanged.

During the great freedom Struggle of 1857 (which the British call Sepoys' Mutiny) Ahmednagar was a scene of considerable disturbance. The active freedom fighters were about 7000 Bhils under the leadership of Bhagoji Naik. They were active in the hilly t5racks and especially in the Parner, Jamgao, Rahuri, Kopargaon and Nasik areas. But at last, all these attempts to rise against the British failed and the slavery came to stay. By about 1880 it was almost quiet everywhere.

Lokmanya Tilak organized political movement in the whole of India and was put behind bars by the British Government. But he passes away in 1920 Mahatma Gandhi took up the leadership in 1920 and carried on the responsibility of organizing Civil Disobedience Movements. Thousands offered Satyagraha and courted arrest. The Satyagraha Movements were launched many times between 1920 to 1941. The last unarmed Movement was spontaneously started by all the Indians throughout the length and breadth of the country from 9th of August 1942 up to 1944.

All the leaders of India including Mahatma Gandhi, Sardar Patel, Rajendra Prasad, Maulana Azad, Subhash Chandara Bose, DR. Syed Mahmood, Shankarrao Deo, were arrested Most of the leaders excepting Gandhi were kept in the Ahmednagar Fort.

I have confirmed through the Anglo Boer War Website that Fritz was indeed taken to Ahmednagar. None of the research I did on the camp above include information that it was used as a POW camp for the Anglo Boer War. Although that information was available years ago, it appears to have been removed from certain websites. However, Fritz's description of the camp from his memoirs fit that of the pictures available on the Internet. I did find a You Tube video of photographs that mentions it. 'Ahmednagar Fort: Boer and German POW'S held by the British.' (https://www.youtube.com/watch?v=p-x1q3J2Mm4&t=34s)

EXCITEMENT IN THE CAMP

"We could not have wished for a better response. It appeared the English were in a crisis. They assumed that they were coming under attack being arranged from the outside. Very hastily, canons were placed on the walls. There were six in total, and they pointed in all directions because the attack was expected soon. Yes, my friends and I were delighted. We were more than 400 men and began to whoop and make a huge noise as well as subversive movements towards the guards, who sincerely believed that today something was going to happen. Even in India we were able to create a little fear and trepidation in the 'Mighty Force' and the outside world got a good look at the Transvaal *Vierkleur*".

THE TERROR OF BEING IN PRISON

"To be imprisoned in such a place, separated from the world, with only the heavens above you and the high walls around you, is enough to make anyone go mad. We noticed this happening to 11 other POWs who had written the Major pleading to join the English.

They now wanted to fight against their own people in Africa so that the war could end quicker. And they did this for 10 shillings a day and a free horse and saddle. However, the Major did not respond to their request and instead gave the letters over to our officers. Everyone was called together, which was odd since it was not mail day, so we were wondering what was going on. Commander Colman read the letters out loud to us and the 11 traitors were sentenced to 35 lashes from a thick leather belt.

This happened just after we had had a good drenching rain, and the ground was still wet and full of puddles *because there was no proper drainage*. We laid into them with our belts. Two guards decided to come their rescue, but without prior permission from their superiors. They came in with their rifles and pistols, but these chaps made a terrible mistake because they did not know us Afrikaners.

In a blink of an eye, we had them lying down with their rifles and bayonets under our feet in mud and water. Their helmets had been removed and we started to play football with them. 'Kick it up', one would yell, and the helmet flew through the air. It had hardly touched ground before we called again to kick it up into the air. The guards had to crawl on their hands and knees to get away from us to retreat through the gate. This is what they learned from the Afrikaner school of hard knocks: first think and then do! After about 10 minutes the Major sent a corporal and another Tommy to ask us very nicely if they could have both guns and helmets back, please. But all that remained of the helmets were a few shredded pieces of cloth. The guns too were in a terrible condition.

They were badly trampled in the mud and damaged. We enjoyed this little bit of light relief from our usual routine".

Boer Prisoners – Internment in India

Mr William Redmond: I beg to ask the secretary of State for India whether his attention has been directed to the statements in the official gazetteers of India respecting the position and sanitary conditions of the town and fort of Ahmednagar, now being used as a Boer prison; whether he is aware that Major Gambier, R.E., reported in 1873, after the drainage operations, that all who lived in the fort, both Europeans and natives, suffered from fever; and that, in consequence, all troops were withdrawn from inside the fort and quartered in barracks outside it; and seeing that the mortality of Ahmednagar town was 79.75 in 1899, 55.04 in 1896, and 61.63 in 1897, and the mortality of children under one year of age was 524.89 in 1899, against an average in that year of 196.97 for the whole Bombay Province, whether he will consider the advisability of the removal of the Boer prisoners to some other station.

This request was rebutted by the then Secretary of State for India Lord G. Hamilton, with an argument about statistics.

Satara

"After nine months, we were let out on parole to Satara, which had previously been used as a British military camp and was situated in a healthy mountainous region. There, I got very ill. The doctor was a good man. He took a lot of trouble with me and did everything he could to help me, but it appeared nothing was helping. Later on, after my discharge from hospital, I thanked him, and he said to me that it was only my strength of character that saved my life. He said his ability and medicines alone did not do this, but that fate had stepped in for me to get better. We all know what 'fate' that was – praise God".[72]

THE END OF THE WAR AT LAST: BUT HOW?

"At last, the war came to an end in May 1902, and we were free to travel home. We were going back to our beloved country for which we had been very homesick. On our arrival, we were greeted with terrible scenes of destruction.

Our homes had been burned down and the farms destroyed. Even our church, the minister's house and the school in Bergen were burned to the ground. Our beautiful church bell from Germany had been thrown to the ground and broken. I was absolutely horrified and disgusted when I saw the destruction of the church. Is this how we conduct war? And is God quiet throughout all of this? But His ways are not our ways. He is the judge over all injustice and treason"!

A NOSTALGIC TRIP AFTER THE WAR

"The two English soldiers who had died before my capture that day on the *koppie* were buried that same afternoon in a mass grave near the wagon dip at the Entombe River. This mass grave was created during the Zulu Wars in 1879 for slain English soldiers and was surrounded by a stone wall. I remember that one of the dead soldiers was wrapped in my double sewn commando blanket and was buried in it. After 15 months as a POW, I returned from India and had to ride with my horse through this same wagon dip. I got off the horse to see if I could find their graves. I found them and the wooden crosses with their names,

---

[72] Fritz supported the Red Cross for the rest of his life.

dates and how they fell. It was all correct. Now they have a memorial outside the walls of the graveyard as a memorial to those who had been killed in the Zulu Wars in 1879.

From there, I rode on to the sight where I was captured that eventful morning. I found the scattered pearls and six bullet casings behind the rock that I used as a hiding place. You could still clearly see the four ridges made by the bullets that hit it. I still have four of these casings in my possession as a reminder of God's grace and protection. I knelt with a grateful heart, and thanked God for His goodness and mercy to me".

ANGLO BOER WAR TEACHES SOME HARD LESSONS

The Anglo Boer War, declared by the Boers on October 11, 1899, gave the British, in the famous phrase of Rudyard Kipling, "No end of a lesson".

The British public expected it to be over by Christmas. It proved to be the longest, most costly, bloodiest, and most humiliating war for Britain between the Battle of Waterloo and the First World War, which broke out in 1914.

The Anglo Boer War lasted two and a half years, cost more than 200 million pounds, and exacted 22,000 British, 25,000 Boer and 12,000 African lives.

The war left a legacy of recrimination and bitterness that has lasted to this day.

Although up to 26,000 Boer women and children are said to have perished in the British concentration camps, military historians have estimated that at least 14,000 black people died in separate concentration camps. The number of blacks who died could be as high as 20,000, according to new research by the War Museum of the Boer Republics in Bloemfontein.

Britain's uncompromising response to the guerilla tactics of the Boers was the construction of concentration camps – it was the first time in modern history that such a concept had been devised. Not only did tens of thousands of Boer women and children die but the survivors returned to devastated homesteads.

In addition to the large number of black people who lost their lives in the field – runners, messengers, farm workers and servants – 107,000 were imprisoned in the concentration camps because the British feared they might side with their masters.

NEW BEGINNINGS

Painting of the Martin Farm, Drie Hoek, rebuilt after the Boer War. Painting done by an Italian prisoner of war during WWII. My grandmother, Frieda Martin, is depicted on her horse. Full painting in the possession of my brother Eddie Herrmann.

"We had to start farming from scratch. There was no living animal left; only deserted farms. I bought a span of oxen in Natal for 20 pounds. A new wagon from Merryweather cost me 140 pounds. Along with these, I bought yokes. Everything was very expensive.

Two years later, those with cattle and oxen faced another disaster. – the terrible cattle plague, *rinderpest*.[73] It affected everyone even on Drei Kop. Altogether, it affected 60 head of cattle. Two oxen and a small bull could not breed. The entire district was placed under quarantine for two years. I was forced to sell that expensive wagon for 40 pounds and buy a smaller one. I bought donkeys, so that we could plough the land and even the donkeys cost 20 pound a head.

In the first year, we also had a horse plague. Yes, we faced many challenges and adversities, but we were able to overcome them all. Today, the cattle industry is doing very well again, and we get a good return on them.

We have even been able to get a train to the district of Piet Retief to help transport our products. By God's grace, we remain healthy, and we have been able to build ourselves up again".

Fritz and Emma Martin had three children:

- *Frieda Christine Hermine Martin* (my grandmother): born on 30 April 1905 in Driehoek, Bergen Transvaal; died on 18 Nov 1996 at the age of 91 in New Germany and was buried in Vryheid Cemetery, next to her husband and son. She outlived both her husband and son as well as her two younger brothers.
- *Emil Wilhelm Carl Martin*: born on 14 July 1906 in Driehoek, Bergen Transvaal; died on 27 January 1972; and buried in the Wittenberg Lutheran Cemetery (near Bergen) Transvaal.
- *Rudolf Wilhelm Heinrich Martin*: born on 31 October 1907 in Driehoek, Bergen Transvaal; died on 13 March 1984.

---

[73] *Rinderpest* is a highly infectious viral disease that mainly affects cattle. The virus can be transmitted rapidly and results in a 100% death rate.

The Martin's and Herrmann's

Martin Family: Back row: Friedrich Herrmann with Frieda Herrmann (née Martin) in the middle flanked by her two brothers and their wives. Middle row: my father, Ludwig Herrmann, Emma Martin and Fritz Martin, then Lily Herrmann. Front row: The grandchildren of the Martin's.

THE BROODING DARKNESS WE WOULD LIKE TO FORGET

For years the public all over the world has been systematically fed thousands of snippets of information, some true, some false, some relevant, some irrelevant, some contradictory, some incomprehensible. To the average citizen, it seems a meaningless mosaic of unrelated bits and pieces.

He shrugs and gives up trying to understand the world situation. He turns instead to the sports broadcasts or reads the juiciest gossip about some divorce or devotes his attention to the photographic representation of female anatomy. His mental withdrawal and failure to understand the present state of the world of course make it infinitely easier for the international wirepullers to steer governments and peoples in the desired direction (Vaque 1989).

It is unbelievable how rapidly things have escalated after the Anglo Boer War and at the start of the 20th Century – not only in South Africa but in countries all over the world, as demonstrated by the Russian Revolution (1917), World War I (1914–1918) and World War II (1939–1945). All information is based on ideology and there are those who believe that all wars are based on a system of faith. I tend to agree with Klaus Vaqué that ideologies and systems are used to manipulate the masses. However, where he blames the little nefarious men, I would go even further to say that they themselves are being manipulated.

For example, as we dig a little deeper into the origins of the international banking cartels, we can see that these were birthed in very old, established dynasties that can be traced back to Venice and then to the Amalfi Coast (Italy), while being riddled with ancient Gnostic mysticism, e.g. on the Isle of Capri.

> The Knights of Malta, whose membership continues today, claims continuity with the Knights of Hospitaller, a chivalric order that was founded about 1099 by the blessed Gerard in the Kingdom of Jerusalem. Blessed Gerard was a Benedictine Priest who came from the city of Amalfi.
>
> Amalfi, located along the West Coast of Italy, was also a cult centre and had gained control over the Isle of Capri – hotbed of Mithraic and Cybelian cults built by the Emperor Tiberius and maintained as a mystery cult headquarters to this day. The official emblem for the City of Amalfi became the emblem for the Hospitaller Order of St. John of Jerusalem – commonly known as Rhodes and Malta aka Knights of Malta.
>
> The Knights of Malta were given permanent headquarters on Malta in 1530 by the King of Spain. In return, it is said that they had to send a single Maltese falcon to the King of Spain each year on All Saints Day (aka Halloween) as 'payment'.
>
> The Maltese Coat of Arms, the sickle with the Ouroboros symbol of the snake devouring it's own tail representing the

eternal cycle of destruction and rebirth with a depiction of a skeleton knight stopping or breaking time. This gives a direct or very significant relationship between the King of Spain (from the House of Habsburg who ruled as a dynasty from 1516–1700), who supplied them with their official headquarters, and the Knights of Malta.

The relationship between the Knights of Malta and the emergence of the Malta Freemasons, who were largely made up of Knights of St John of Jerusalem (aka Knights of Malta) and Catholic priests. The Malta Freemasons used the freemasonic "French Rite" at the origination, later making the shift to British Freemasonry. The Knights of Malta had taken over the institutions of the French Templars (Source to remain anonymous).

Pope Francis (1936–2025) was the Pope of the Roman Catholic Church. He holds the title of Pope as *ex officio* as Bishop of Rome and sovereign of the Vatican City, as well as current *de facto* Prince and Grand Master of the Sovereign Military Order of Malta (aka the Knights of Malta).

Most, if not all, the mystery religions, including Gnosticism, have their origin in Babylon. There is a clear trace of how these were introduced to the Jews when they were held captive there during the Babylonian exile. I do not intend to go into more detail on Gnosticism here. There are several historians, who have obtained far more information on the Gnostic beliefs that have permeated throughout the world.

I want to fast forward to the birth of Christ, who called those practicing these beliefs "a brood of vipers", and then to the cross to demonstrate the extent to which some of these beliefs had already infiltrated into the Jewish religion. We are told that Christ arrived at exactly the right time. Trading routes between the known world and the East, were well established and the banking systems had been created.

Rome was already an open door to most of these ideologies. Numerous Jewish diaspora never went back to Israel and established themselves in Asia and the known parts of Europe.[74]

Within about 300 years, the established church had also been infiltrated and, since then, it has been used as a means of expanding their ideologies and hidden financial and political agenda across the world – similar to a front business. When things got terribly dark during the Middle Ages (ca. 500–1500 AD), which were followed by the Reformation (1517–1648), the counter-attack was initiated – a counter-attack that has been destroying the witness of the church to this day.

One of the pivotal characters in this attack was Sabbatai Sevi (1626–1676) – an exceptionally charismatic Rabbi and Kabbalist from Anatolia (Turkey), who published the *Lurianic Kabbalah*, named after Rabbi Isaac Luria (1534–1572).

As Jews around the world gained access to occult literature on the deeper meaning of their faith, the popularity of Jewish mysticism soared. This occult literature resulted in a mystical synthesis between pagan teachings, which preceded the Torah, and the Gnostic elements of Judaism. Many texts pertaining to the Kabbalah,[75] including *The Zohar*,[76] state that the task is not to destroy evil, but to return to its source. The theme of a secret hidden occult identity became part of this religious philosophy.

---

[74] See the book of Esther and the book of Acts in the New Testament for more information.
[75] Originating in the 12th century, the Kabbalah is a mystical and esoteric tradition in Judaism that seeks to understand the nature of God, the universe and the soul.
[76] As the foundational text of Kabbalah, *The Zohar* is written as a commentary on the Torah that explores hidden meanings and deeper spiritual insights in the scriptures.

Sabbateanism is the matrix of every significant movement to have emerged in the eighteenth and nineteenth century, from Hasidism to Reform Judaism, to the earliest Masonic circles and revolutionary idealism. The Sabbatean believers felt that they were champions of a new world which was to be established by overthrowing the values of all positive religions (Sepehr 2015).

The nihilistic tendency of Sabbateanism[77] was still mild compared to the movement that followed. The followers of the new Polish-Jewish religious leader, Jacob Frank (1726–1791) were known to seek redemption regularly through infamous orgies on solstices and equinoxes. Frank himself summarises his own philosophy as follows: "It is one thing to worship God and quite another to follow the path that I have taken". Among the Frankists, a clear-cut ideology of Jewish territorialism developed.

Rabbi Antelman (2002) explains the source Jacob Frank's financing as follows:

> Frankfurt at the time was the headquarters of the Jesuit, Adam Weishaupt [also a Jew], founder of the Illuminati, as well as Rothschild Brother's financial empire. This is worth repeating: Frankfurt was the birthplace of both the Illuminati and the Rothschild Empire. When Jacob Frank entered into the city, the alliance between the two had already begun. Weishaupt provided the conspiratorial resources of the Jesuit Order, while the Rothschilds contributed the money. What was missing was the means to spread the agenda of the Illuminati and the

---

[77] Sabbateanism was a 17th century Jewish movement centred around Sabbatai Zevi, a mystic who claimed to be the long-awaited Jewish Messiah. When faced with persecution by the authorities of the Ottoman (Turkish Empire), Zevi deeply shocked his followers by converting to Islam.

Frankists added with their network of agents throughout the Christian and Islamic worlds. Jacob Frank became instantly wealthy because he was given a nice handout by Mayer Amshel Rothschild of Frankfurt.

Adam Weishaupt founded the Order of Perfectibilists[78] – better known as the Illuminati of Bavaria – but he was educated by the Jesuits, who converted him to Catholicism after the death of his father when he was five years old. He became a priest, but defected when he joined Rothschild, who financed the Illuminati agenda.

The long-term political goals of their occult secret society called for the execution of the following plan:

1. The abolition of all monarchies and all ordered governments
2. Abolition of private property and inheritances
3. Abolition of patriotism and nationalism
4. Abolition of family life and the institution of marriage
5. The establishment of communal education for all children
6. Abolition of all religion

The Jewish author, Barry Chamish (2005), remarks as follows:

> The Rothschilds goal was to control the wealth of the planet. And the Frankists vision was the destruction of Jewish ethics to be replaced by a religion based on the exact opposite of God's intentions. When these factions blended, a bloody war against

---

[78] The Order of Perfectibilists (Illuminati) is a secret society that as founded in May 1776 by Adam Weishaupt (1748–1830), a professor of law in Bavaria. The society aimed at promoting Enlightenment ideals, such as reason and moral self-improvement, while opposing religious and political oppression.

humanity, with the Jews on the front lines, erupted and it is reaching its very pinnacle at this moment.

In 1777, the Illuminati began to cooperate with the Masonic Lodges, in order to infiltrate them. Even the Duke of Brunswick, the Masonic Grand Master of Germany, said in 1794 that the Illuminati controlled the Masonic Lodges. Rothschild convinced Weishaupt to adopt the Frankist doctrine. He aimed at fulfilling the Frankist plot of subverting the world's religions and the Zionist objective of instituting a global government that would be ruled by a King from Jerusalem.[79]

In Latin, Lucifer literally means "Light bearer". Therefore, members of the Illuminati possess the" light of Lucifer" (i.e.the counterfeit light). Ultimate world government through corporate monopolies was the goal, to ensure that even the largest fortunes of the *goyim* (non-Jews) will depend on them. Being utterly ruthless and using the police as domestic soldiers, they are applying numerous strategies to maintain total mind control and to create internationalism. In an attempt to establish an "universal human brotherhood", we are currently witnessing nations co-mingling with other nations and the promotion of homosexuality and promiscuity.

Most Jews are unaware of the Illuminati agenda: like everyone else, they are being manipulated and compromised. Judaism has been hijacked and is now based on the Talmud, which consists of the interpretation of sages (Pharisees) during the Babylonian exile (586 BC–1040 AD).

Divide and conquer. Divide and rule. Divide and reign.

---

[79] In these times, much is happening in Jerusalem, where they are attempting to return to a theocracy. There is also talk of Netanyahu being the chosen King.

The Testimony of a Witch

I had many privileges as a high priestess and I greatly benefited from these in my day-to-day life, but I continued to thirst for ever greater power. A few years after becoming a high priestess I reached my goal of becoming a bride of Satan. Many high priestesses call themselves bride of Satan, and in a sense, they are, but Satan also has few chosen women that become his brides in a more exclusive manner. Only five to ten, and usually only five exist in the United States at a time. This position is the most 'honourable' position to which a woman can attain within Satanism. One woman is picked by Satan from a large region of the country. That woman is considered the most powerful and respected and loved in the whole area. These women also sit on the national council which runs all the Satanists in the country and has also much power internationally because of the great wealth in the United States.

Satan himself came to me to tell me that he had selected me for this great honour. He presented himself to me in the physical form of a man, very handsome, in fact, the exact image of what I held in my mind as being the 'perfect' man. He told me that he had selected me because he loved me above all the others, and that he both liked and respected my courage and abilities. He behaved in a very loving and romantic manner, telling me of his love and of the wonderful times we would have together. He also promised to give me much greater power and many special privileges.

I was honoured and excited, mostly excited because I hoped that at last, I was truly loved. I thought that I was the most powerful and honoured of all women. I thought Satan had picked me because of my abilities and my love for him which had grown stronger year after year. I did not at that time see that Satan was merely using my love for him to benefit himself. He used me to get other people to do what he wanted and used my love for him for my own destruction. All his declarations of his love for me were lies.

The ceremony was held in a large city nearby. One of the city's largest and most beautiful churches was rented by the cult for the occasion. I am sure that the owners of the church had no idea what their church was being rented for. I had arranged to have a three-day weekend off from work.

The ceremony took place on a Friday night, the first night of the full moon. I was carefully guarded, and my every wish attended to.

I was so very excited and elated. As my companions and I approached the church I was briefly impressed with a feeling of heavy darkness hanging over the church, but I shrugged the feeling aside, turning my thoughts to the love and admiration I held for Satan.

As I stood just outside the sanctuary peeping in, I was surprised and greatly honoured to see that not only were there many people there from the surrounding states and California, but also a number of older members of the cult from the Eastern world. This was indeed a great honour. The signal to start was Satan's sudden appearance in physical appearance on the throne.

He appeared as a man, dressed in white, wearing a crown of gold with many jewels in it. The whole congregation stood with a shout and much worship was given to Satan, all heads turned to the back and started forward down the aisle. I was escorted by the High Priest, followed by the Sisters of Light. When I reached the end of the aisle I stopped before Satan's throne and bowed down before him and paid homage to him. Then he gave me the command to rise. As I did so he arose from his throne and came down to stand beside me. The high priest performed the wedding ceremony. Most of the wedding ceremony was singing, chanting and proclaiming the praises of Satan.

The ceremony took almost two hours and signed a contract with my own blood. Then I was given a liquid to drink from a golden goblet, I suppose there were some drugs in it, as I felt rather light-headed after drinking it. I was told that the contract was binding. There was absolutely no way to get out of it. Satan doesn't believe in divorce.

He treated me with great respect, told me how I looked to him and that I could become what he had always hoped for the mother of his son, 'The Christ' the redeemer of the world. I was completely taken in by his deception.

Satan gave me a beautiful broad gold wedding band with an inscription inside it which said: "Behold the bride of the Prince of the World".

I received many advantages with my new position. I held absolute power over all the witches and warlocks and even the high priest. I was untouchable. I gained more power and more demons.

Only one witch was foolish enough to take me on. With merely one look, I pushed her into the wall itself so that she had to be cut out. She sustained many broken bones and other injuries as a result. She never again tried to harm me and neither did any other human.

I rapidly rose to the position of top bride and my responsibilities grew also. I became one of Satan's representatives. I made many trips within the USA and other countries. My trips were more for the purpose of helping to co-ordinate Satan's programs with Satanists in other lands. I saw very large sums of money change hands and the involvement of many government officials. All my trips were 'off the records' in private jets. Most powerful and wealthy organisations serve Satan. The 'little' people of those organisations do not know this, but those at the top know.

I was completely deceived by Satan. He lies to all his servants. I thought I was the most powerful and knew everything about his organisation. After I got out, I realised that Satan doesn't tell any of his servants the truth about his activities or his organisations. Everyone of any position in Satan's kingdom is told that he or she is the greatest and most powerful. All of it is lies.

It is during this time that I met many rock stars. They all signed contracts with Satan in return for fame and fortune. The evolution of rock music in the USA was carefully planned by Satan.

I lived in constant fear and to live a completely double life. I was careful that my family and friends had no idea what I was doing. I wanted to enjoy the benefits of lots of money but was too afraid to do so. I had no peace and I felt very trapped. My greatest problem was with the incredible evil perpetuated within the cult. The brutal discipline and human sacrifice.

Sex for others in the cult was free and easy and just about all the time. Also sex with children. A very high percentage of all children within the cult are regularly sexually molested from a very young age. The cult members mostly pair off with others from the same power level. Almost every ceremony or meeting ends with a sex orgy.

There was sexual intercourse with demons also. Demons that could be seen and heard and felt in a physical manifestation. This would occur usually at meetings and Sabbaths where a lot of drugs were used.

Demons also had sex with unwilling people. People who were being punished for not doing what the demons wanted to have done.

Often a man was forced to watch while more than one demon had brutal sexual intercourse with his wife. That was a very effective way of discipline.

Fear is a tactic that is used more often than anything else. Fear of death, fear of having your family tortured in front of your eyes. Both humans and demons were tortured. Many times demons were forced to physically manifest, then they were tortured and torn into pieces by other stronger demons because of some minor disobedience. The sights and sounds of these hideous episodes were burned into the minds of everyone present. The group was then told that this was an example of what would happen to them if they dared disobey Satan or the demons.

Torture of loved ones especially children, is also a favourite tactic to ensure absolute obedience. Parents are forced to stand and watch as their children are beaten to death, brutally sexually molested, or stripped of their skin. If the child survives, the parents cannot take him/her to hospital because they would be thrown into jail for child abuse. They could never prove that they had not done the torture to the child. There would always be other Satanists who would step forward to testify that they had seen the parents abusing the child.

Discipline of sacrifice – always there is a time of breathless horror and fear just before each human sacrifice as every member waits to see just who will be sacrificed. Many of the sacrifices are people who have been disobedient or who have tried to pull out of the cult.

Demonically inflicted illness, accidents, loss of jobs etc. Children dedicated to Satan = opposite of Christian child dedications or baptisms. Baptism by blood, sacrificial blood. This goes on for generations creating demonic bloodlines with generational curses, unless some parents are willing to let Jesus become their Lord, Saviour and Master of their lives and let his blood wash away all that sin.

The blood of Jesus is so powerful, and his work on the cross so complete, that even the werewolves can be saved if they want to be. Jesus can raise the dead today just as He did when He walked on earth in a human body. People under Satan's control are dead.

Large numbers of young people become Satanists through Rock music, occult role playing, fantasy games, and of course by individual recruitment.

These groups are usually heavily involved with drugs – these are the groups careless enough to get caught in their various crimes of ritualistic child abuse, human sacrifice, etc. Satan doesn't care how many of these ends up in jail for the crimes they commit"[80] (Brown 1992).

You may wonder why I am writing this. Satan knows that there is not much time left and he is wrecking as much bloodshed, death and destruction on earth as he possibly can. If you look around you, you can see all the evidence. Who do you think owns the drug trade, the music industry, the politicians and the armies? Who is responsible for the constant wars and the thousands and upon thousands of children who are sold into slavery? Who do you think owns the abortion trade? Who do you think owns the pharmaceutical industry, which produced the drugs that legally kill its victims, the universities and all of education. You should remember those nefarious little men – the Jesuits. Who do you think they really belong to? First, they owned the education systems and now they own churches too. Why do you think there are churches being declared bankrupt, running on empty, being closed down and converted into chic little shops?

I have tried to demonstrate the regression and the deception of how things have developed through the ages in a real way and through the eyes of my family. I have tried to handle the information delicately up until this point. Now, it is time to rip the plasters off your eyes and say look! Why do we not have an abundance of good news that are real and truthful? Why do we feel that that there is nothing but lies and deception in our world and no one we can trust? Why are we being hounded for our personal information and have every marketing ploy in the book dumping their greedy little claws into our bank accounts?

I should not get started on the banking industry, the media and investment companies. The list goes on. I urge you to refer to the referenced list at the back

---

[80] Prisons all over the world are over full of them.

of the book for a comprehensive list of material that you can consult to conduct your own research.

Satan's hatred for God has always been transferred to mankind. His lust for power knows no end and he has mapped out lethal strategies to deceive us into thinking he is the real God – to the point of mimicking the birth of a saviour!

The bigger an army of humans he can gather to perform his dastardly evil plans, the better. There is truly nothing new under the sun. He has been at this game for a very long time, and he wants to kill you!

We are the reason God has not put an end to this yet. Because I hear a crowd of you shouting, "Well, if God is a loving God, then he would put an end to this endless suffering, death and destruction"! Yes, He could instantly do so; no trouble at all. But that would close the door to the period of grace. You see, grace entered the world with Jesus and grace will have completed its course when Jesus returns to collect His people.

The question is: are you a part of His people? Have you accepted the invitation by grace to be a part of His Kingdom – the true Kingdom? He has sent you invitation after invitation, but you have refused. So, He tried again and again, patiently and lovingly. It is costing God all the love that He has to wait for you. Come and step over the crimson thread and enter into the banqueting hall, the marriage feast for the bride of Christ. The sinner at the cross on his death received grace. Look at Jesus today, while there is still time, and ask Him to take you too. You only have today …

THE CROSS NULLIFIES WITCHCRAFT. PART 2

A. Central to the Gospel
   a) Only basis of everything good we receive from God (Heb. 10:4–14)
   a) Through the cross, Jesus administered total, eternal, irrevocable defeat to Satan and his kingdom

    a) Satan attempts to obscure work of the cross (Gal. 3:1)
- B. Witchcraft obscures the cross
  Work of the flesh (Gal. 5:20): (i) Manipulate (ii) Intimidate (iii) Dominate
  Evil spiritual power
  Illegitimate power that supplants legitimate authority
  Allied with rebellion (1 Sam. 5:23)
- C. From this present evil age (Gal. 1:3–4)B. From the law (Gal. 2:19) ??
  From self (Gal. 2:20)
  - Pride, egotism, personal ambition, sectarianism, nationalism, racism
  - Remedy: Esteem others better than ourselves (Phil. 2:3)
  - Against personal ambition and competitiveness
  - Against love of self, money, pleasure (2 Tim. 3:1–5)
  - Result of deliverance from self: (i) freedom to serve ((Mark 10:35–45); (ii) freedom from self-effort and self-promotion (2 Cor. 4:5)
  - No need to prove yourself right (1 Cor. 4:3–4 [compare 2 Tim. 2:24–25])
- D. From the flesh (old Adamic nature) (Gal. 5:24 [compare 1 Cor. 15:23]
      a) Crucify the flesh (Gal. 5:24)
    - Flesh/Spirit in conflict (Gal. 5:17)
    - Cannot please God in the flesh (Rom. 8:8)
    - Put to death deeds of the flesh (Rom. 8:12–13)
    - Aspects of the flesh: fear, resentment, anger, greed, covetousness, sexual lust and fluctuating moods result from the flesh
    - Freedom from sin; freedom to do God's will (1 Pet. 4:1–2; 2:21)
    - Expect to suffer in the flesh
    - Deny self—take up cross (Matt. 16:24)

    b) Release from curse of trusting in the flesh (compare Jer. 17:5)
    c) Freedom to worship in the Spirit (Phil. 3:3–4)
E. From the world (Gal. 6:14)
    a) World is society not subject to God
    b) Be totally committed to government of Jesus
    c) Released from Satan's dominion of the world (1 John 5:19; Rev. 12:9)—including:
- Opinions
- Values
- Judgements
- Pressures
- Enticements
- Deceptions

    d) Spirit of God and world are opposed (1 Cor. 2:12–13)
    e) Spirit of God in believer more powerful (1 John 4:4–6)

On Satan's day of judgement, he will fall, and the armies of heaven will be unleashed upon the earth.

> In the beginning was the Word, and the Word was with God, and the Word was God. He was in the beginning with God. All things were made through Him, and without Him nothing was made that was made. In Him was life, and the life was the light of men. And the light shines in the darkness, and the darkness did not comprehend it.
>
> There was a man sent from God, whose name was John. This man came for a witness to bear witness of the Light, that all through him might believe. He was not that Light but was

sent to bear witness of that Light. That was the *true* Light which gives light to every man coming into the world.

He was in the world, and the world was made through Him, and the world did not know Him. He came to His own, and His own did not receive Him. But as many as received Him, to them He gave the right to become children of God, to those who believe in His Name: who were born not of blood, not of the will of the flesh, nor the will of man, but of God.

And the Word became flesh and dwelt amongst us, and we beheld His glory, the glory as of the only begotten of the Father, full of grace and truth. John bore witness of Him saying, "This was He of whom I said, He who comes after me is preferred before me, for He was before me." And of His fullness we have all received, *and grace for grace*. For the law was given through Moses, but grace and truth came through Jesus Christ. No one has seen God at any time. The only begotten Son, who is in the bosom of the Father. He has declared Him" (John 1:1–18 NKJV).

THE HERRMANN FAMILY

The German Herrmann is a patronymic surname which means "soldier, army man, or warrior" derived from the Germanic elements *Heri*, meaning "army," and *Mann*, meaning "man." Harmon and Hermon are common English variants of this surname.

Alternate Surname Spellings: Herrman, Hermann, Herman

Famous People with the Herrmann Surname

Bernard Herrmann – American composer best known as the author of scores for Orson Welles and Alfred Hitchcock films including Citizen Kane and Psycho

Alexander Herrmann – French magician known as "Herrmann the Great"

Hans Herrmann – Former Formula One driver from Stuttgart, Germany

Edward Herrmann – American actor, best known for his role as the patriarch, Richard, on "Gilmore Girls"

Jakob Hermann –Swiss mathematician

Walter Herrmann – German nuclear physicist

I am sad to say that I know very little about my Herrmann family. Returning to the beginning of the book, I would love to think that my ancestors are, in some way, connected to Hermann Billing in Harms *Oude Dorp*. Wouldn't that be grand! However, since I cannot prove or disprove it, I shall leave it as wishful thinking on my part. However, before digging into the history of the Herrmanns, I should introduce the Fortmann family first.

EMMA ELISA ANNA FORTMANN

Emma is the direct descendant of the original pioneer family that arrived with the Cotton Germans of Natal. According to research, the surname Fortmann originated from Forth near Nurenberg. Alternatively, it could come from the occupational origins of "helping someone over a 'furt'".

Her grandfather, Heinrich Ernst Wilhelm Fortmann, was a bachelor when he arrived with The Bertha in Durban. He was born in Hesepe, Hanover on 25 June 1822 and died on 3 May 1892 in New Hanover, Natal, on the farm

Hopewell. He married Amalia Maria Anna *Meyer* in New Germany, Natal, on 10 December 1849. She was also from the Cotton Germans of Natal. She was born 26 January 1832 in Schleptrub, Kirchspiel Engter, and died on 27 July 1893 in New Hanover, Natal.

Her parents were Casper Christian Wilhelm Fortmann and Maria Regina Erfmann. Casper Christian Wilhelm Fortmann was born in New Germany on 3 September 1856 and died on 14 July 1921 in Uitkyk, Noodsberg, New Hanover, Natal. He is buried in Lilienthal. He married Maria Regina Erfmann, who was also a descendant of the Cotton Germans of Natal. She was born on 28 August 1859 in New Germany, Natal. At the age of 41, she died of pneumonia and exhaustion during the Anglo Boer War on 7 July 1901. She is buried in Harburg, New Hanover. I was gifted a copy of the Dalton & District Area Annals written by the Dalton Woman's Institute. It gives a lovely account of who the original landowners were, which, apart from prominent Cotton German families, also include the Martiz family as well as many English settlers.

> Three families had purchased land near the Sterkspruit on the farm Mooiplaats and formed the nucleus of a congregation there. In about 1880 German settler families moved, mostly from New Hannover to what was then known as the Noodsberg. In 1886 seven of the men of these families formed themselves into a congregation which they called Neuenkirchen. The names of the seven were Heinrich, Friedrich and Casper *Fortmann*, W. Thöle, F. *Gevers*, J Thies and C. Küsel. The name Neuenkirchen being the name of the place Mrs C. Küsel had come from in Germany. This small congregation was an affiliation of the Kirchdorf congregation at New Hannover. About four years later the present site of Harburg church was chosen and named

after the village the pastors wife came from in Germany (Dalton Woman's Institute, 1972/3).

Emma, who was my great grandmother, was born on 27 December 1884 in rural Kwa-Zulu Natal and died on 17 February 1967. At the age of 82, she died of terminal bronchopneumonia and Hodgkin's lymphoma in Greys Hospital in Pietermaritzburg, where she was buried. We have some lovely photos of her holding Eddie as a child. She married my great grandfather, Gottlob Friedrich Wilhelm Herrmann, and moved with him to Vryheid.

The Fortmann family members were very good to our family and Emma remained close to her daughter in law. Tante Bertha Fortmann was particularly helpful to my grandmother when my father passed away.

Gottlob Friedrich Wilhelm Herrmann

The name Domnitz is of Slavic origin, 600–750 AD. A Benedictine monastery, built in 985 AD, underwent various dukedoms, ending with the Duke of Wettin towards the beginning of the 1300 AD. Domnitz was Christianised through Otto I in 660 AD.

Halle, Saxony-Anhalt

Halle is the largest city in the German State of Saxony-Anhalt. In order to distinguish it from Halle in Westphalia It is also called Halle an der Saale (literally "Halle on the Saale River"), and in some historic references simply Saale, after the river). The current official name of the city is Halle (Saale).

It is situated in the southern part of the state, along the Saale River, which drains the surrounding plains and the greater part of the neighbouring Free State of Thuringia located just to its south, and the Thuringian basin, northwards from the Thuringian Forest.

Leipzig, one of the other major cities of eastern Germany, is only 40 km away.

Burg Giebichenstein is a castle in Halle (Saale) in Saxony-Anhalt. It is part of the Strasse der Romanik (Romanesque Street)

My great grandfather, who was a farmer from Domnitz, near Halle, arrived as a colonist in Natal in 1890. He was born 29 October 1870 in Domnitz, Wettin-Loebejuen, Saalekreis, Saxe-Anhalt, Germany as the son of Friedrich Wilhelm Gottlob Herrmann and Henriette Grosse. He died on 28 May 1937 at the age of 66 in Scheepersnek, Natal. While she was in Germany, my cousin, Veronika Herrmann McGee, did some research, but she was unable to find a marriage certificate in the region, although they may have been married elsewhere.

Friedrich was away fighting in the Franco Prussian War[81] when Gottlob (known as Wilhelm) was born. Henriette must have had a very tough life, having a soldier as a partner and giving birth to twins and triplets and losing all but one. Veronika goes on to say that she suspects that the family moved to Halle an der Saale before Bertha was born and Wilhelm left for South Africa in 1890.

She remembers her father mentioning that the family was from Halle, which is close to Domnitz. Their ship's papers indicate their residence at the time as

---

[81] The Franco-German War (1870–1871) was an armed conflict between France and a coalition of German States, led by Prussia. The war ended with the defeat of France and the establishment of a unified Germany.

Giebichenstein, which is an area in Halle an der Saale. Bertha must have been born in Halle, as there is no record of her being born in Domnitz.

Gottlob Snr., Henriette and Bertha also emigrated to South Africa in 1902. This just leaves one surviving triplet, Friedrich Albert Herrmann, born in 1875 for whom we have no immigration papers. According to Meisie, a brother went to Lüderitz (South West Africa/Namibia), which is also where Bertha ended up. The only trace we can find of him is in 1907, when Albert Herrmann was a sponsor at Hartwig Albert Gustav's Christening (i.e. my grandfather's brother).

Name:	Gottlob Herrmann
Departure Date:	3 Dez 1902 (3 Dec 1902)
Destination:	Durban
Estimated birth year:	abt 1846
Age Year:	56
Gender:	männlich (Male)
Marital Status:	verheiratet (Married)
Family:	Household members (See below)
Residence:	Giebichenstein
Occupation:	Landarbeiter
Ship Name:	Kanzler
Shipping Line:	Deutsche Ost-Afrika-Linie, Hamburg
Ship Type:	Dampfschiff
Emigration:	Reise
Accommodation:	3. Klasse
Ship Flag:	Deutschland
Port of Departure:	Hamburg
Port of Arrival:	Amsterdam; Lissabon; Südafrika (South Africa)
Volume:	373-7 I, VIII A 1 Band 138
Page:	2862
Microfilm Roll Number:	K_1777

Name:	Henriette Herrmann
Departure Date:	3 Dez 1902 (3 Dec 1902)
Destination:	Durban
Estimated birth year:	abt 1845
Age Year:	57
Gender:	weiblich (Female)
Family:	Household members
Relationship:	Mutter (Mother)
Residence:	Giebichenstein
Ship Name:	Kanzler
Shipping Line:	Deutsche Ost-Afrika-Linie, Hamburg
Ship Type:	Dampfschiff
Emigration:	Reise
Accommodation:	3. Klasse
Ship Flag:	Deutschland
Port of Departure:	Hamburg
Port of Arrival:	Amsterdam; Lissabon; Südafrika (South Africa)
Volume:	373-7 I, VIII A 1 Band 138
Page:	2862
Microfilm Roll Number:	K_1777

Name:	Bertha Herrmann
Departure Date:	3 Dez 1902 (3 Dec 1902)
Destination:	Durban
Estimated birth year:	abt 1887
Age Year:	15
Gender:	weiblich (Female)
Family:	Household members
Relationship:	Tochter (Daughter)
Residence:	Giebichenstein
Ship Name:	Kanzler
Shipping Line:	Deutsche Ost-Afrika-Linie, Hamburg
Ship Type:	Dampfschiff
Emigration:	Reise
Accommodation:	3. Klasse
Ship Flag:	Deutschland
Port of Departure:	Hamburg
Port of Arrival:	Amsterdam; Lissabon; Südafrika (South Africa)
Volume:	373-7 I, VIII A 1 Band 138
Page:	2862
Microfilm Roll Number:	K_1777

Another cousin, Remo Herrmann, mentions that Gottlob/Wilhelm was brought out by a Mr. Sander. Bertha was later married to a Sander, which leaves a mystery as to the exact connection.

Wilhelm and Emma Herrmann had seven children:

1. Friedrich Casper Herrmann (my grandfather), born in Dalton
2. Hartwig Albert Gustav Herrmann, born in Dalton
3. Erna Herrmann, born in Dalton

4. Walter Friedrich Ernst Herrmann, born in Dalton
5. Ewald Johann Heinrich Herrmann, born in Dalton
6. Helene Johanna Weber (Herrmann), born in Scheepers Nek and baptised by Pastor Schumann
7. Wilhelm Heinrich Herrmann (known as Bill), born in Scheepers Nek and baptised by Pastor Schumann

In the *Vryheid Gazette* of 28 May 1937, the following is recorded:

Scheepers Nek; Prominent Resident of Scheepers Nek. Funeral of Mr. G.F.W. Herrmann

"Mr G.F.W. Herrmann of "Stolberg Farm" who died at the age of 56, was buried on Sunday in the Graveyard of the German Church at Scheepers Nek. Mr Herrmann had a severe illness about a year ago and had been ailing ever since.

More than 200 people from Vryheid, Glückstadt, Piet Retief, Kambula and Lilienthal attended the funeral as well as almost all the local community. The Rev. R. Drews conducted the service. Mr Herrmann was a well-read man and interesting to talk to. He was born in Germany in 1870 and came out here in 1891 and worked at his trade as a blacksmith first at New Hanover, at Escourt and at Lüneburg.

> Was your grandfather a Blacksmith my father did point out to me where the black smith Hermann had his Smithery. A friend of my dad was Hartwig Hermann he had a shop in Vryheid(if I am correct a hardware outlet).It is correct Pastor Schumann would on foot walk to Vryheid to hold his monthly Service in the houses of his church members at Scheepersnek and Vryhied. Today by road it is about 50km from Glückstad to Schepersnek.
> 17:31

Observations by André van Ellinckhuyzen and Gert Meyer of Vryheid after enquiries from the author, 2023.

In 1894 he went to Ermelo and to Johannesburg. In 1895 he started a business of his own at Tabankulu, Vryheid district, moved to Denny Dalton at the time when the mine was doing well, and later to Glückstadt. (where he was involved in the establishment of the church).

In September 1899 he went on Commando and was at the Talana fight. In 1901 he was captured in the Vryheid District. (Although I have made enquiries of his involvement in the Boer War, I have not had much luck. Eddie says he had never heard that he was involved in the Boer War. We are assuming that this was something he did not like to mention or talk about.)

Subsequently he went to work at Harburg and there met and married Miss. E. Fortmann in 1904. In 1914 he bought the farm 'Stolberg' here and again took up his trade as a blacksmith. Mrs Herrmann who helped him on the farm, survives as well as six children. They are Friedrich, Hartwig, Walter, Mrs Weber, Ewald, and Willie. (No mention of Erna as she had passed away at the age of three months). There are also five grandchildren.

Mr Herrmann was a member of the local farmers association and was its president at one time. He was also vice-president and a member of the executive committee and was a regular attendant at the associations meetings as long as his health allowed. He took a leading part in the affairs of the local German Church.

The farmers association sent a wreath, and others were sent by his loving wife, Ewald & Willie; Friedrich, Frieda and family; Mr & Mrs G. Fortmann; Mr & Mrs Von Varendorff; Mr W.

Fortmann; Eddie & Natalie *Meyer*; Mr & Mrs Wittmann; Mr & Mrs E. Muhl.[82]

My brother, Eddie, inherited a home-made garden clipper made by our great grandfather at his smithy in Kambula. A hundred years later, it still works perfectly.

The garden clipper made by our great grandfather at his smithy in Kambula. In the photo with Eddie Herrmann, January 2024.

Friedrich Casper Herrmann and Frieda Christine Hermine Martin

My grandparents established the farm called Oakford in Scheepers Nek, which *Grossmama* (Grandmother) inherited from her father, Fritz Martin. According to information I received from my brother, our grandfather was more an entrepreneur/businessman than a farmer, and the major tasks in the day-to-day running of the farm were performed by *Grossmama*.

Having learned farming from her father and being an accomplished rider, she managed to grow crops and vegetables. She did particularly well with

---

[82] The original clipping is in the possession of my aunt, Lilly Russeau (Herrmann).

long-stem roses, which they sold at the market. She won several prizes for her roses. *Grossmama* loved all flowers – Dahlias in particular – and she grew them at my aunt's home in Vryheid and at our home in Mosely.

Not only did *Grossmama* learn how to farm, but also how to cook from her mother, who had been a chef in Hamburg. I have very fond memories of her tasty dinners. When we returned from school, we would always be served a hot meal. These were simple meals, meant to to tide us over until dinner. I would watch her bake lemon muffins, (lemon scones, as she would call them). Eddie's favourite was her *Butterkuchen,* something I have not baked in a while. Mama loved her pickled fish, which she could whip up at a fishing trip. A family favourite was her *Melis Brot* ("corn bread"). She had a special fluted mould in which she steamed the bread like a pudding. This would be served with roast meat and gravy or fresh butter soaking into the delicious hot bread. I can still see her standing at a table outside our kitchen in New Germany. Papa had harvested a good crop of maize. This she cleaned and minced through the mincer by hand before preparing the dough.

According to my father, his dad was a grumpy man and a harsh disciplinarian at times. For example, as a young boy, my father had to get up at three in the morning to help with the cattle and the plantation and to chop wood for the household. Only then could he leave for school. There was not much of a relationship between the two. Later, *Grosspapa* and my father owned all the butcheries in Vryheid. The Herrmann family, who was known as very hard workers, did very well for themselves. Not only did they work hard, but they also enjoyed camping trips, fishing trips and holidays.

Ludwig Herrmann (in the middle) with friends and family on a fishing trip. Photo from Eddie Herrmann.

Later, when my parents got married, the farm was handed over to my father as his inheritance. He himself built his parents' retirement home on their plot himself, Eensgevonden in the Vryheid district. This is where my grandfather passed away at the age of 60 years and eight months. I think I only met him once at the plot (as we called it). It had a beautiful apple orchard and gardens, as my grandmother would have laid them out, and a pool. There are photos of me and Karin, my cousin, skinny dipping in the hot sun with the sprinklers going. We could not have been more than four years old.

Tante Lily inherited a property in Vryheid, probably from the sale of the plot, and *Grossmama* moved in with them. She lived there for many years and occasionally she would spend a month or two with us in Pinetown. Later, she moved into an aged facility of the Lutheran Church, Port Natal Altersheim, in New Germany. It did not take her long to get going in the gardens there. She was already very old when she fell and broke her hip.

Standing: Werner Egly, Ursula Herrmann, Eddie Herrmann. Seated: Lily Herrmann, at Frieda Herrmann's 90th birthday, with Sua Herrmann and Ingrid Herrmann. Photo from Eddie Herrmann.

As it often happens when the frail and elderly fall, they do not make a full recovery from such a trauma. I remember visiting her in Addington Hospital. I was absolutely horrified by the roaches in the wards. To think this was once one of the leading teaching hospitals in South Africa. I tried to visit her every week at the home and often took the children with me.

I will never forget the day she passed away. Willem and I had paid her a visit without the kids. When I heard her heavy, laboured breathing as she was sitting in a chair, I knew something was wrong. However, the nurse on duty assured me that she had been in contact with my aunt in Ballito. I read her some Scriptures from her Bible, which she enjoyed, but she did not talk much. In my spirit, I knew she was passing. When Willem wanted to leave, I asked if I could stay, but he insisted that I go home. By this time, she was wheeled into the dining room for dinner. I did not want to leave her. I spoke to the nurse again, who assured me she would be in contact with my aunt.

Grossmama passed away in the night. The nurses had *not* called my aunt.

My life was in a turmoil at the time; it was 18 November 1996. A memorial service was held at the Lutheran Church in New Germany. I am not sure, but I think it was Pastor Molke who led the funeral service. In her testimony, which she had written for the funeral service, she narrates how the death of her son, my father, had been a very hard blow for her to bear and a pivotal time with her faith journey. I believe this is when she personally met the Lord Jesus, and she developed a beautiful and strong faith.

She would often come to visit us at our home, when we would have long chats. The most important thing on her mind was that her grandchildren and great grandchildren should come to know the Lord, Jesus Christ, as she had done.

This is the one thing she prayed for every day until her death.

Friedrich and Frieda Herrmann had two children:

A. *Ludwig Wilhelm Friedrich Herrmann*: born on 13 March 1929 in Vryheid and died on 30 May 1975 in Wentworth Hospital on the Bluff, after major surgery on his throat due to throat cancer or cancer of the oesophagus. After the memorial service at the chapel of the funeral parlour, he was cremated and his remains interred with his father in Vryheid. I was 13 years and ten months old at the time, and my father was 46 years old. The South African Defence Force flew Eddie home to attend our father's funeral. Eddie was fighting in the Border War.[83]

B. *Lily Helena Emma Hilda Herrmann*: born on 15 July 1936 in Vryheid and currently living on the Dolphin Coast of Kwa-Zulu Natal. She married Heinz Egly in Vryheid, and they had two children:
   i) *Karin Egly*, who is about three months younger than me. Although we grew up as good friends, we drifted apart for many years. We only reconnected recently, at my mother's funeral in January 2023. It was wonderful to get together again after such a long time. We spent quite some time together and had much to reminisce and

---

[83] The South African Border War, also known as the Namibian War of Independence, was a conflict that occurred in Namibia, Zambia and Angola, from 1966 to 1990.

laugh about. Karin was married but has since got divorced. They do not have any children. Having started her career in the aviation industry as an air hostess in Vryheid, she is currently the Marketing Director of one of the leading aviation companies in South Africa. As an air hostess, she was involved in an airplane crash and, although she sustained spinal injuries, she continued with her career. She was also an excellent swimmer and an up-and-coming water skier. However, a skiing accident during training broke her confidence.

i) *Werner Egly*, Karin's younger brother, followed his mother into dental health and studied in Pretoria. He ran his own business in South Africa on the North Coast of Natal for many years, before he was head hunted and relocated to the Sunshine Coast of Australia. He is married to the lovely Natasha, also previously an air hostess, and they have two sons, of whom one has recently passed his board examinations as an attorney in South Africa. I recently met up with Werner on the Sunny Coast. We had not seen each other for over 30 years. It was a complete delight to meet up with him again.

Because wealth (say raw materials) in the hands of its possessor means power and freedom and independence; especially if that wealth is easily exchangeable for money. The sovereignty and independence of a nation, therefore, is a matter of its state of power and financial resources. Therefore, all the strenuous efforts during this century to turn the world into a socialist dictatorship (or "new world order", as the UNO prefers to call it) have been concentrated on undermining the sovereignty of *all nations* to deprive them of all power to resist their future absorption into the "new world order". [84]

---

[84] Klaus Vaqué wrote his book in the late 1980s. I believe that there is currently not a single nation that has not capitulated to some degree, if not entirely, to "them".

The whole eastern part of Europe has already fallen victim to the plot; and all the communist countries, including the USSR and China, are therefore mere vassals of high finance; exploited colonies which, because of a utopian collectivist economic system, have no chance of ever attaining economic independence and are thus condemned to eternal bondage to their capitalist creditors.

Andrew Young, a former American delegate to the UN, paid a visit to Windhoek in South West Africa a few years ago, where he frankly admitted to the journalists present that the USA had no intention of interfering with a communistic Angola or Namibia; on the contrary, he said; the communist countries had always been the easiest markets for American goods ...

Payments are of course mainly in the form of minerals or other natural products extorted from the enslaved peoples. That is what happened with the much-lauded "decolonization" of Africa and other continents. Never had those countries been so exploited by the colonial powers as they are now by international high finance. The former colonial territories and practically all the Third World are now in the pockets of international money powers, which lend them billions of worthless paper dollars that they have to repay with the wealth of their minerals. Thus, the whole business of decolonization was simply a deliberate ploy on the part of international finance groups to enable them to get their hands on those countries.

The old colonial empires were emasculated and their control over their colonies was wrenched from their hands; so that now they must pay for their raw materials and natural products from the "decolonized" countries – now recolonized by the banks – in expensive US dollars. So, two birds are killed with one stone and at the same time the way is paved to the assimilation of the countries into the New World Order.

A strong, white, independent government in South Africa in possession of the biggest gold deposits in the world and next to those in the USSR the richest reserves of strategic minerals is therefore necessarily a serious obstacle in the road to the projected socialist world order. On the other hand, a corrupt black communist government in the guise of the "liberation" movements that are so zealously supported by the One-Worlders in the Western governments would very soon find itself obliged to repay its credits to the financial powers of Wall Street in the form of the mineral wealth of South Africa.

From that angle we can now understand the apparently irrational handouts, the multimillion-dollar credits given to almost every country in the world; often positively forced on them and in many cases – and this is intentional – with no prospect of ever being repaid. It might not seem the soundest way of doing business; but it becomes intelligible when we realize that these vast sums are guaranteed to the banks by the Western taxpayers through their governments.

The international bankers have no scruples; and they are certainly not simple or stupid. For repayment or security all they require is the assignment of the minerals, future crop yields or other economic assets of the countries concerned. Thus, they are the real masters of the countries whose governments they control.

The undeclared worldwide war against South Africa can only be understood against this background. How it will end will affect not only the black and white people of this country but also all the other peoples of the – so far – free world. And now we go to the post pandemic period where huge amounts of loans were made to countries to afford the vaccines. These all must be repaid. Where countries refused the extended benevolent arm of the bankers, they were forced. See South American and African nations as an example (Vaqué, 1989).

Memories of Oakford
by Tante Lily Herrmann

Frieda Herrmann, Friedrich Herrmann, Lily Egly née Herrmann, with Karin Egly and Heinz Egly.

Frieda Herrman sitting and Lily Herrmann at Oakford farm Scheepers Nek.

Photos from Lily Herrmann.

It is such a blessing that my cousin, Karin Egly, had sent me the voice messages of Tante Lily's memories of life on the farm. Tante Lily is still alive as I am writing this, but her memory is beginning to fail, and she often gets slightly confused with the timeline. However, Karin patiently led her through the process of remembering. I listened to 12 voice messages and translated them directly from German into English before paraphrasing and collating the information. Tante Lily, who is in her late eighties, currently lives in Umhlanga Rocks. In order to give a slightly different perspective of certain events, I add some of Eddie's memories into the narrative, as he heard them first-hand from our father, Ludwig.

After her mother had been in labour for three or four days, Tante Lily was born in Vryheid. In those days, medical science was not as advanced as it is today to ease a difficult labour; particularly in the case of a big baby. Tante Lily entered the world with a head of black curls and weighing 10 lbs. Her father was overjoyed that he finally had a beautiful baby girl. His daughter had arrived! Because he loved lilies, he named her Lily. Her other names came from her grandmother (Emma) and her aunt (Hilda). Hilda was her mother's sister-in-law.

Ludwig was seven years older than Lily. There were mainly boys in the Herrmann family and, along with her aunt, Lily was the only girl. This is a trend that seems to be repeating itself with my own grandchildren. Her father built the sheds and garages on Oakford to house the farming equipment, cars and tractors. Ludwig was taught to drive the vehicles and tractors and how to manage the farm. By the time he was 15 or 16, he already shouldered much of the farm work.

Lily was taught to help her mother. She had to help with the chickens and collect the eggs for packaging, so that they be taken to market, along with the cut flowers which was *Grossmama's* pride and joy. She also had to plant vegetables and flowers of various varieties and then pack them in bunches for Ludwig to take to market. Eggs were packed in boxes and delivered to the station at Scheepers Nek, where they were collected to be taken to Durban.

Ludwig, who was in charge of the cattle, had to learn how to milk the cows. Later, he was made responsible for the supervision of the milking operation, as well as the care of the pigs and the sheep, the *mielie* (maize) fields, potatoes and the wattle plantations. He was also responsible for the farm workers and their wages.

Milk was collected in large milking cans and taken to the shed, where the cream was separated from the milk. The cream was used to make their own butter and cream cheese. They also made their own soap, either from herbs or from animal fats boiled in large pots that were continuously stirred, until it had settled, after which it was poured into moulds and cut into long slabs.

One day, Lily was taken to watch the cows being milked by her father. She did not like drinking milk at the best of times, but this day, her father encouraged her to try the fresh milk that had just come out of the udder. After taking one sip, she could not drink anymore. Since that day, she did not drink fresh milk again on its own.

They supplied fruit and vegetables for the markets too – citrus, guavas and plumbs, as well as various varieties of apples and avocado pears. Huge avocado trees were laden with fruit that would fall to the ground. Vegetables included cabbages, Swiss chard, spinach, brinjals (eggplants/aubergines), spring onions and garlic.

At first, Tante Lily was home-schooled by a neighbour, but she attended high school in Vryheid. Ludwig went to school in Scheepers Nek. In Vryheid, she was taken in as a boarder with a local family. After breakfast, which started with devotion and prayer, they had to do their chores, before leaving for school.

They had a wonderful youth on the farm and made their own toys from mud and clay. Making oxen and cows from clay is part of the African culture that we learned from the Zulu children, who were our friends on the farm.

There was no such thing as going to the shops quickly. They were lucky to go to town once a month and get a Fanta or another cold drink, which was an occasion that felt like Christmas. None of the luxuries that we know and take for granted today were unavailable to them. They made ginger beer, beer from potato skins and pineapple beer, which would all be kept cold, and that was their cold drink. Ludwig was highly skilled in making those beers, and later he also made potato wine.

Holidays involved camping expeditions either to False Bay or St Lucia, where they would hire boats for fishing. Ludwig loved fishing with his father and caught lots of fish. The Egly family would often join them and, as a teenager, Heinz would start flirting with Tante Lily.

There was no electricity, and all perishables were stored in a coal ice cupboard. At night, they used lamps and candles. In the winter, they would light the fire in the lounge, where they would hold the evening devotions as a family. Later, they got a generator and had electric lights. Her father had a little radio that they used to listen to the news. In those days, the main news was of World War II (1939–1945). They would listen how ships got bombed, planes shot down, or houses bombed. After the devotions and the evening news, it was bedtime, as they all had to be up very early the following morning.

On Sundays, everyone went to church in their Sunday best, whether it was raining or not. Church was always priority, and you simply went to church, whether you liked it or not, or whether you were sick or not. Our father wore an overcoat to protect his suit. Oma wore a corset to look slightly slimmer, and always stockings. A picnic basket was packed with coffee, tea and the homemade cold drinks. After church, there was an hour break for lunch, after which it was time for Sunday school and confirmation classes with Pastor Drews. These activities, including the obligatory visit to the cemetery where all the Herrmanns were buried, took the entire day.

The Eglys came to visit every Sunday, sometimes their watchmakers as well. Tante Lily, who was about 15 or 16 years old at the time, loved dancing. Her father taught her to dance around the dining room table. When a watchmaker tried to kiss her on the cheek once, he was given a thorough talking to. Her father was highly possessive of her, but not so much about Ludwig. Ludwig, who often got into trouble, had many hidings with a *sjambok*, if he was insolent.

We had three farms that kept Ludwig very busy, and he was often away from home. He also did a year in the army as the first intake after the war and a road trip with his best friends around South Africa. It was after his return he met Ulla. He was allowed to go to parties. The Germans always had parties over weekends either on a Friday night or Saturday night.

Ludwig was an upbeat guy who loved dancing and music. Although he was very popular and all the girls loved him, he fell in love with Ulla Schumann, whom he wanted to marry.

The engagement party took place at Scheepers Nek. The wedding was postponed, until Ludwig had built the new house for his parents on the plot. The work on the house took him away from the daily running of the farm, but his father never laid a brick to help with the building of their retirement home. All the building expenses were paid from the running capital of the farm and from their pension, which was calculated from a percentage of the gross profits – not the net profits – which is why the farms began to run at a loss. The farms were never signed off to Ludwig and remained the property of his parents. Ludwig bought an extra wattle plantation in the hope of making a slightly bigger profit for the upkeep of his new family. He wanted to leave the farm to make his own way, but that plan was refused. When the new plantations burned down, the insurance did not pay out, because the fire breaks had not been up to standard. With building the home and outbuildings on the plot and running the farm, Ludwig was spread too thin.

When returning from their honeymoon in the Cape, they were given the large guest bedroom at the end of the house. His parents only moved to their new home about a year later. Not long after that, Eddie was born – the first little Herrmann. *Grossmama* wanted the farms to go to Eddie, but it was never formalised in writing. It was only years later, after my father's death, that she heard that Eddie really would have loved to take over the farms. She burst into tears. My parents left Oakford after the new plots went into liquidation, freeing Oakford for his parents to sell and having a nest egg for their old age.

Ulla liked her own ideas of gardening. *Grossmama* was more traditional, but Ulla liked landscaping, and she did it beautifully. Because plants were expensive, Ludwig had to run around, finding plants for her. Ulla was more a home person.

Christmas was wonderful and very exciting. We had a small Christmas tree, and we received presents. Her aunts would give her a large apple with a one Rand coin hidden inside. Other Christmas gifts were a little chocolate and dolls.

She says that she spent her teen years alone, since Ludwig was much older and already out of the house, so to speak. She does remember that her parents adopted Ute Huck, a child from the old Germans in Halle, Germany. During the war, they were poor and could not care for all their children. They asked Tante Lily's parents whether they would like to help and if Ute could come and live with them in South Africa. They agreed and Ute came on her own on board the Union Castle Line, when she was about 14 years old. We travelled two days by car to Durban to collect her. She was so small with her little suitcase. She came as a refugee, very poor. She moved in with them as an adopted daughter. Tante Lily and Ute got along very well and she was known as Uschi. Ute later married Dr. Halwachs. Karin still has contact with her.

Lily was seven months pregnant with Werner, when her father died, who was a heavy smoker and drinker. She had to help on the plot to harvest or gather the *mielies* for transportation to the market. *Grossmam*a could not drive and, if she wanted to go anywhere, she would get her driver to take her. Quite a few years later, her brother died. The deaths of her father and her brother hit her very hard. Our family disintegrated due to illness.

Tante Lily currently lives in Umhlanga Rocks and is in her late eighties.[85]

Werner Egly, Karin Egly and Tante Lily Herrmann (my godmother) 2024. Photo supplied by Karin Egly.

Ludwig Wilhelm Friedrich Herrmann and Ursula Martha Luise Schumann

The mission and colonists unite

Wedding photo of Ludwig Herrmann with Ursula Schumann – my parents. Photo from Eddie Herrmann.

---

[85] I listened to 12 voice messages and translated them directly from German into English before paraphrasing and collating the information. Not all the information has been captured in the book.

I am not quite sure where my parents met, for at that time, my father was living in Scheepers Nek and my mother had moved south with "Dear" to the Pinetown, Hillcrest area. However, I do know that they got engaged in Pinetown. My father took my mother for a drive from Pinetown, where she was staying with her oldest sister, Tante Irms at Fields Hill, through Kloof to Hillcrest and then ducked down one of the quaint little lanes off Old Main Road to the left.

These lanes were boarded by huge old trees, making a leafy green canopy across the road leading towards Highbury School. The homes here were mansions. In this beautiful spot, he proposed. Photographs were taken of their engagement in Pinetown.

Ursula Schumann engagement photo.

None of this occurred very easily. Papa's parents, who did not wholly approve of the engagement, let the couple know in subtle ways. My mother thought it was because she did not come from a wealthy farming background and, according to my brother, she was probably correct. *Grossmama* wanted to have someone with a strong background in and knowledge of farming to continue the legacy they had built. She was ostracised and my father was embarrassed by his parents' behaviour. They were not given permission to get married, until he had built their retirement home on the new plot they had bought. Instead of letting them have a separate engagement party, they made it coincide with their own lavish silver wedding anniversary.

The wedding took place on 9 October 1954 in the Lutheran Church in Durban. Mama's brother-in-law, Arthur Dinkelmann, paid for her wedding. By all accounts, it was a beautiful wedding, and the bridal couple was captured in wonderful photographs. Onkel Fritz, her oldest brother, walked her down the aisle. My father thoroughly enjoyed the reception and, much to my mother's delight [no], invited half his friends to join them on their honeymoon!

Ida Schumann née Gevers with Emma and Fritz Martin at my parents' wedding.

Heinz Egly's father, Ludwig Egly, who was the master of ceremonies at the wedding, wrote a beautiful poem for the bridal couple. The poem, several pages long and written in German, is entitled *Wedding Newspaper*. My mother kept the poem with all her memorabilia all these years and is now in my possession. Ludwig Egly was a very kind mentor to my father.

> ... Es ist bei allen Hochzeitsfesten
> Die Braut doch stets der Mittelpunkt,
> Bestaunt, bewondert von den Gasten
> (dazu hat man ja wohl auch Grund)
> doch was von unsern Brautigam
> der heut' im hochsten Himmel schwebt,

er hat gezeigt, dass er ein Mann
und trotzdem ihm die Hose bebt.
Schon lange ist er da am Uben
dass ihm die Rede heut' gelingt,
drumm last uns seine Freud' nicht truben,
wir wollen hören was er bringt
doch 'ne Rede halten Frisch vom Leder
ist nichts für 'nen Farmersmann
und stecken bleibt dabei wohl jeder
bosonders ein junger brautigam.
Unglücklich sitzt er und bekommen
Jetzt noch hinter seinem Tisch
Darum soll er gleich dran kommen,
Den, dann hat er's hinter sich etc ...
(Excerpt from *Wedding Newspaper*, written by Ludwig Egly)

Ludwig (Luddy) Wilhelm Friedrich Herrmann

We already know that my father's youth was tough. In his teens, he asked to learn to be a mechanic, which was only allowed because it would benefit the farm – i.e. to fix the vehicles on the farm – and as soon as he was proficient enough, that trade was brought to an end. He did not want to be a farmer. He had his sights set on the hospitality industry and his dream was to have a German delicatessen, similar to that of the one in South Africa called "Schwaben – Home of traditional German Foods." My brother and sister-in-law, Helena, took me there in January 2023 to this delicatessen and it is magnificent. We had a wonderful German breakfast and brought home loads of cold meats and pre-cooked meals to enjoy. I could just see my father behind the counter: it would have suited him perfectly.

He did his national service in the infantry the year, after World War II had ended. Although he was disappointed that he could not take part in the war, he did well in his training, and he became a "sharpshooter" – what is currently known as a "sniper".

He took over the farm as soon as his parents moved into their new home. However, they kept a tight reign on the farm and did weekly inspections with much criticism. They also required a monthly stipend from the farm, which left the young couple cash poor and next to nothing for working capital.

My father Ludwig Herrmann at the Vryheid show c1955.

The Show
1955 · Vryheid
With Ludwig Wilhelm Friedrich Herrmann

He was a very hard worker and having been raised on the farm, he was fluent in Zulu. In fact, he had mastered the Zulu language so well that Zulu people could not distinguish between him and their own people.

They trusted him completely and he was often called in to negotiate on their behalf between two fighting families or factions. He also earned their respect because of his incredible strength. Having spent his youth chopping wood and doing much other strenuous physical work, he developed a particularly strong core strength.

Negotiations with either farm workers or trying to sort out a problem on a fishing trip. Ludwig Herrmann with his back to the camera, left. Image from Eddie Herrmann.

He enjoyed wrestling and became the private sparring partner of one of his good friends, the South African boxing champion, Ewart Potgieter. I managed to get hold of Ewart's nephew in New Zealand, who managed to give me some information. It is said that Ewart had a very soft, kind heart and that he was primarily a farmer. He should not have been a boxer. Yet, thanks to his size, he did very well and even went to box in the UK.

Through his immense core strength, my father led by example on the farm. He was able to lift weights that none of the farm workers could do. His skill in wielding an axe would have made his Saxon ancestry proud, and it made him something of a legend among the workers. He understood their language, traditions and their culture, thereby earning their respect.

When my father was offered to buy a sugar cane farm in Pongola, he wanted to leave Scheepers Nek to make a fresh start. As one of the most lucrative crops in Natal, sugar would have been ideal for him and mama, while giving them a little space, away from his parents. However, his plans were quashed by his parents, yet again. He became despondent and lost interest in the farm altogether, often going away on extended fishing trips with his friends, leaving my mother to cope with the daily running of the farm. It was not easy at all.

In a bid to make really good money, he planted a large plantation of wattle for the paper industry. It was a good venture. The trees are fairly quick growing, and the profits were good. However, before he could harvest his first crop, the entire plantation burned to the ground, completely ruined. For hours, he tried to fight the blaze himself with as many men as he could muster, but it was in vain. They did not have enough manpower to quench the blaze.

Apparently, the fire was caused by a neighbouring farmer, who was burning scrub, and his workers allowed the fire to get out of control. The farm insurance did not pay out and the farm went into bankruptcy. As a broken man, my father began drowning his sorrows.

Ursula (Ulla) Martha Luise Schumann

Born to an academic family and gentle parents, Ulla had a good life in Glückstadt. The home was filled with love and laughter. She was a strong learner at school and looked forward to furthering her studies. In her younger years, she struggled with her tonsils, until the local district nurse advised her one day to eat lemons. So, mum was let loose in her grandfather's orchard, where she would eat the lemons straight from the tree. The following year, when the district nurse visited the school, there was nothing wrong with her tonsils. She never had her tonsils removed and for the rest of her life, she continued drinking lemon juice first thing in the morning, on an empty stomach, with a little celery salt or a dash of Maggi sauce. She was the only one of her family not to get cancer and she died peacefully, just before her ninetieth birthday.

She loved her parents, and from her mother she inherited the Gevers' gentle spirit. From her father's side, she inherited the quick wit and sense of humour that is such a part of the Schumann family. She was no stranger to getting up to mischief, but it was all good clean fun. She got along well with all her brothers and sisters, but when her brothers decided to dismember all her dolls and hang them up with string in the nearest tree, she was heartbroken. Oh, the tears!

She loved visiting her grandparents, but she was slightly weary of her grandfather, who was known to be bit grumpy. She thought he was a little unkind with her beloved grandmother, when he made a snide remark about the flower beds she planted – "You can't eat flowers". My husband was fond of saying that to me, in order to get away from buying flowers. Now that they are both in heaven, they are probably getting on famously.

Her world was rocked to the core by the death of her father. The entire Schumann family felt it's impact on their lives. The home they lived in belonged to the Education Department and Dear would have to move. In desperation, Dear sent her daughter to boarding school in Hermannsburg, which she absolutely hated. The teachers on duty would find her sobbing herself to sleep every night. One of the teachers was very kind and would bring her a sweet to eat and comfort her.

Since this was during the war (WWII), food was rationed, and the morning porridge was often full of weevils. If you were really hungry, you soon learned to pick them out and continue eating. She just missed Glückstadt and their carefree life, watching her grandfather catch snakes and tending to the orchards.

Fortunately, this little interlude at Hermannsburg came to an end and she was sent to live with her Uncle Otto Gevers at Blood River. She got on very well with her cousins, Rita and Waldemar, even though they were older than she was. Nurtured by their kindness and love, she started to heal. One day, when I was no more than ten or eleven years old, she took us out to see Onkel Otto on their farm. It was a big sprawling place with beautiful gardens and clay tennis courts. I spent most of the afternoon playing outside, until I jumped off a little stone wall and sprained my angle, cracking the heel. X-rays and crutches followed our return to Pinetown.

Later, Mama joined her mother in Hillcrest, who by then, had moved into the home at Assegai, which she had inherited from her mother. Mama loved it there. She took long walks, and, during school holidays, she often went swimming in the pool at the Highbury School. She would catch the train to Durban, where she was completing a secretarial course at college. She was hauled out of school to learn something useful, so that she could start working and supporting her mother. Dear had adopted the old ways of doing things: the youngest daughter of the family was expected to remain a spinster and to take care of her mother. However, after World War II (1939–1945), times were changing and, when her brother, Kurt, intervened, he managed to persuade his mother to change her mind. However, it was too late for Mama to finish school and go to university. That opportunity would never come again. Therefore, she moved in with her sister, Irms, and started working at Barclays Bank in Pinetown when it was still the beautiful old colonial-style sandstone building on Crompton Street.

She joined the Pinetown Bachelor Girls and participated in the annual production of plays and pantomimes held in the Airfield Hall. Because of her German heritage, the war years (1939–1945) in Pinetown were difficult, although I cannot remember her complaining much. Her sister was teaching at Pinetown Junior School at the time and Mama was sent there for a year. She still remembers the old bucket system in the toilets. Later, when Eddie attended school there too, his class teacher was Tante Irms (Irmgard Freese).

Life at Oakford through my mother's eyes

Once my parents had returned from their honeymoon on board one of the Castle Liners and spent a week or so exploring Cape Town, she was brought home to the farm and introduced to all the farm workers. Because her Zulu was virtually non-existent, she had to master the language, while learning how to be mistress of a farm. Another setback was that she could not cook. Oh, the shame!

Where was she supposed to have learned to cook, since she was sent from pillar to post since her father's death? When she was sent to the kitchen to prepare the first meal for her in-laws, she had no clue where to start. My father felt sorry for her and helped her prepare the meal. From then on, he taught her how to cook. The "intellectual-meet-farmer" did not sit well with his parents.

She took all her heartbreak into the vegetable gardens, where she learned to grow vegetables and later flowers of all kinds. Her first Christmas present was a pair of gum boots! She knuckled down and raised chickens, which she drove to Durban markets herself in the Bedford truck. Driving was another skill she had learned and, therefore, she was able to drive the truck and even double D clutch. When Eddie was born a year later, there was much rejoicing and celebrating at the farm. It was a boy!

My parents had three children:

1. *Eduard Friedrich Herrmann (known as Eddie):* born on 5 November 1955 in Vryheid. He married Susarah (Sua) Pretorius in Newcastle on the 10 December 1983, and they had one child, *Eckhard Friedrich Herrmann.* Sua was born on 21 December 1962 and passed away at home after a lengthy battle with cancer on 13 October 2016. Two years later Eddie married Helena Maria Swanepoel (née Neethling) on 1 December 2018. She was born on 11 December 1957 (just a few days after my sister Barbara).

Eddie Herrmann with Sua Herrmann, his late wife.

Ulla Schumann with Eddie Herrmann and Helena Herrmann (second wife)

Eddie's son from his first wife Sua. Eckhart Friedrich Herrmann and his beautiful bride Jaydene. Image used with permission.

2. *Barbara Frieda Herrmann*: born on 30 November 1957 in Vryheid and died nine months later, on 1 September 1958. This was a devastating blow from which both parents never recovered.

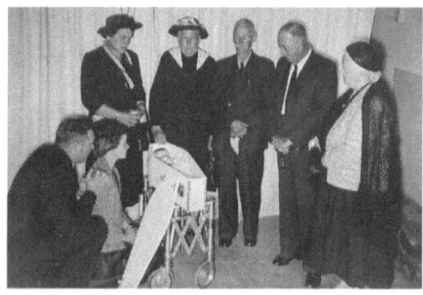

Barbara Herrmann's funeral with parents, grandparents and great grandparents.

3. *Ingrid Solveig Herrmann*: born on 26 July 1961 in Vryheid: aka me! When naming me, Mama decided to go all Scandi, and she named me after her best friend at school.[86]

Ingrid Herrmann looking across the valley of the farm Tussen Bay in Zululand.

---

[86] The name Ingrid originates from the Old Norse name Ingríðr, which translates to "charming goddess" or "elegant lady". It is a name that radiates power, loveliness and elegance, rendering it an ideal selection for any infant girl" (Wikipedia 2024).

PART V

INGRID SOLVEIG HERRMANN

GROWING UP

My mother raised us in the faith in which she was brought up – German Lutheran. My father came from the same religious background, but after his confirmation, he seldom set foot inside a church, except for weddings, baptisms or funerals. I do not know what happened to shake his faith this way. His sister, Lily, who is my Godmother, is a devout Christian, even to this day. Eddie, my brother, was his pride and joy and he took him everywhere with him, mostly carrying him on his shoulders – something that Eddie did with Candice when she was born, leading to great chuckles from ear-to-ear. However, my father was also very strict with Eddie, and it nearly broke my mother's heart to watch Eddie getting up again to follow his father. Eddie adored the ground on which my father walked.

Eddie and Papa at Oakford Farm, Scheepersnek, KwaZulu Natal. Photo from Eddie Herrmann.

Mama had a pagoda built out of sandstone rocks and laid out beautiful gardens on the farm for which she earned herself several prizes. She took this newly found talent with her into her old age, and she was always surrounded with flowers.

She was the only one who could stand up to my father when he was in a bad mood or about to lose his temper, which was quite often. Although she was tiny in comparison to him, he would always soften with her and listen. Lord, help the person if he should lose his temper and my mother was not around. The farm workers understood him very well.

When Barbara, my sister, was born, Mama had to attend to both the farm and the baby. She depended heavily on her maids to help her. Barbara was the sweetest little thing, with a very placid nature, and her death broke my parents. Someone in the family had the audacity to blame my mother for her death. That obviously did not sit well with either of my parents. They barely lived; they were merely existing. The initial shock and the deep sadness did not last forever, but it was buried deep inside. Alcohol took its toll on my father, just as it had with his father, and eventually my mother too, many many years later.

Then came Ingrid, born with all the cheek in the world. Nothing could set my father off more than a little bit of backchat. The battle lines were drawn: me versus Goliath and his mate. My mother was caught somewhere in the middle.

This is the fundamental difference between me and my brother. – As the eternal strategist, Eddie would think and then act. Ingrid is quite the complete opposite: she would act without thinking and then instantly regret it, wondering why she has just done this or that? So, between opening my mouth to change my feet, my creative, impulsive nature was born. These became the roots of non-conformism, which in retrospect had both a positive and a negative effect. Edith Schaefer in one of her books writes that you can never be a non-conformist in reality. If you are going against a particular grain, you are swapping it for another. Eddie just kept to the middle of the road and did things nobody else could see. His 'non-conformism' only revealed itself later. My parents could not have had three more different children, even if they wanted to.

When the wattle plantation burned down, they left the farm so that his parents could sell the farm. My father was helped by wealthy and influential family friends, the Steenkamps, who gave him a job in Empangeni as a butcher in one of their butcheries, including accommodation in a house down the road. All those years at the butcheries in Vryheid with his father had set him up for a career change. Our Mama got a half day job at Loftheims and I was looked after by a nanny they brought with them from the farm.

Empangeni

Empangeni is a town in KwaZulu-Natal, South Africa. It is approximately 157 kilometres north of Durban, in hilly countryside, overlooking a flat coastal plain and the major harbour town of Richards Bay 16 kilometres away.

Located in one of the important cattle-raising areas in South Africa, the town is the centre of the sugar industry in Zululand and also a market centre for cotton, dairy products, fruits, timber and vegetables. It is a junction on the main railway line from Durban to Swaziland and has an airfield.

According to folklore, the name Empangeni comes from the Zulu word "Pangaed" which means "grabbed" and is thought to refer to the number of crocodile attacks on water bearers in the nearby Empangeni stream. But it more likely comes from the Mpange trees that grow along the banks of the river.

Empangeni was like a breath of fresh air for everyone, and we had really good times there. The weather was very hot and humid in summer and temperate in winter. I do not think we had a single winter in Empangeni. There were family fishing trips to different locations, including Richards Bay and Fanies Island.

Both my parents enjoyed fishing and soon Eddie was hooked too. I was left to do my own thing, which was generally to scare away the fish. This was particularly easy when they went river fishing. At the White Umfolozi, I was found hopping from one rock to another and paddling in the water, singing songs and making up friends. Tubing down the river over the rapids was also great family fun.

On occasion, we would drive up to Durban, where Eddie would be on the go carts and boat rides. I would be found in the paddling pond trying to drown. I remember burning sand and black rubber body boards that Eddie was very fond of and that could be hired on the beach. Large umbrellas and Ingrid trying to paddle into the deep sea without a care in the world and a hysterical mother bringing up the rear. On the way back to Empangeni, we would stop at a sugar cane plantation and Papa would cut a stalk of juicy sugar cane that he peeled for us. Chewing on the sugar cane and sucking up the sweet juice kept us happily occupied all the way home. Who needs candy!

Empangeni also had its own pool and paddling pond. Mama worked half day and, on hot afternoons in summer, we would often walk up to the pool to cool down. The water would be slightly warm because of the heat, but we enjoyed it anyway. One weekend, my parents decided to take a family outing to the pool. Being four sheets to the wind, my father decided to go for a dip. The only problem was that he had never learned to swim. In his enthusiasm, he picked me up and plunged into the deep end. I remember my mother yelling for my father to stop, but it was too late. Before I knew what was going on, I was swallowing copious amounts of water in a sheer panic. Some of the bystanders, who were watching the scene in utter horror, plucked us both from the water.

Eddie had made some great friends at school in Empangeni. Up to this point neither of us had learned any other language other than German and Zulu. Now we were being introduced to Afrikaans and English. Having lived on the farm for six years, Eddie's Zulu was excellent. His only mates were the children of the farm workers. When he was ready to go to school, he was sent to boarding school in Glückstadt, but he hated it. In Empangeni, he was sent to an Afrikaans-medium government school. His knowledge of German gave him a head start and soon he was speaking Afrikaans fluently, after which he completed his schooling in Afrikaans.

Eddie always spent the afternoons with his pals. They often came to our home, where they pretended to be Tarzan, climbing trees and swinging down from the branches. It looked like so much fun, and it used to irritate me immensely that I could not join them. So, when he was at school, I would practice climbing trees and, one day, I decided to swing from the branches, the way they did. I was overly enthusiastic and lost my grip, crashing down and breaking my fall with my right elbow. Oh, the pain! Mama had a lady visitor, and I had been warned not to bother them. In those years, children were supposed to be seen and not heard. However, eventually, Mama could no longer ignore the cries. When her guest went home, I was taken to old Doc Van Rooyen. X-rays and a plaster cast later; we could all go home.

Those were the days when children were safe and given free rein, provided you were home before dark. I tagged along with the guys, until they made it very clear that I was not welcome. So, I got stuck into Eddie's prized collection of Dinky cars, removing all the rubber tires. That really endeared me to him!

When we were not in the trees in summer, eating mangoes, we were building racing tracks with cement freshly mixed by Mama, who was building more garden beds. One day, my father decided to build Eddie and company a foofy slide (cable slide). Like all others, our cable slide had a home-made design, made of good cable and a metal tube. The braking system was your feet. There were strict instructions, that the boys were allowed to use the slide under adult supervision only. Eddie thought about it and, one afternoon, he decided that he was clever enough to do this on his own. He fell from a dizzy height, onto his face and his teeth went through his lip – blood everywhere. This was followed by a trip to the emergency room and stitches. Needless to say, the cable slide was dismantled before worse injuries could take place.

During my childhood, I mostly played on my own, footloose and fancy free. I cannot remember ever wearing shoes, unless we were going somewhere that did not include a beach. I did have an English friend, who lived a few doors up from Eddie's buddies. However, visiting them meant that you face a feisty little terrier that seemed to delight in sinking its teeth into me. During that time, there was a particularly bad outbreak of rabies. We lived very near the sugar plantations that were filled with cane rats, which carried the virus to the domesticated pets.

The dog of Eddie's pal, Skalky, had been diagnosed with rabies and the family was placed in quarantine. True to form, the noisy little pest next door to Skalky bit me. Mama kept a very careful eye on me and, exactly ten days later, I came down with a terrible fever. I was hauled into the car and driven at breakneck speed to Doc Van Rooyen. Tests were taken and it turned out that I just had a very bad dose of tonsillitis. Crises avoided.

My mother decided that I needed some feminine education (to be more feminine rather than the tomboy I was fast becoming) and sent me to the kindergarten of the local convent. I was introduced to my teacher, who was wearing a wimple and who spoke to me in a strange language. She frightened the life out of me. At the age of two, I was already speaking three languages: German, Afrikaans and Zulu, and now I was learning English as a fourth language. My little English friend had not taught me much English. Apparently, I had an ear for languages, and I was made to recite my skills to everyone who cared to listen. This also included singing and reciting poems. The control regime did not temper the wild spirit in me.

Eddie, who suffered badly from asthma, regularly went blue in the face. This often occurred in the middle of the night and my parents would be rushing around with hot steam baths, towels and pumps. I got used to seeing Eddie's head covered in towels, bent halfway into a basin of scalding steaming Vicks. One day, Eddie got an asthma attack at school and my father got an emergency call at the butchery. Although I suspect that he might have been a bit "under the weather", if you get my drift, but he got Eddie to the medical emergency just in time. Eddie claims he should have been dead a few times, and I think this was one of those occasions. Back at the farm, the Zulus would give him a puff of *dagga*,[87] which would immediately settle his lungs. They knew the traditional remedies worked long before anybody else became familiar with them. Of course, my mother put a stop to it the moment she found out. I can still hear her

---

[87] The word 'Dagga' originates from an old Khoi word 'dacha' which was originally their name for leonotis leonurus, so called Rooi dagga, Wilde dagga or Klipdagga which was smoked by the Khoikhoi in the same way as tobacco - word for cannabis or marijuana. The Zulus used the wild dagga as the Khoi did. The extended notes is a better explanation as rural Zulus in those days would not have had access to imported drugs. https://www.fieldsofgreenforall.org.za

saying, "Imagine that he's just a little boy and they are teaching him to smoke *dagga*"!

When Papa's drinking got worse, he was sent to Durban by our mother to dry out at the Lulama Rehabilitation Centre. Although it was quite an expensive centre, its security was not up to scratch, and the patients soon learned how to get out and smuggle in some drink. Papa lasted about a month there and returned, not much better than when he had left. Unfortunately, it also cost him his job.

Pinetown

It was about 1966 when we packed up and moved to Pinetown, Mama's old stomping ground. This was probably a smart move that would give her better support. Papa got a good job at the Pinetown Butchery in Station Road. He was good at his job and he worked hard, having been read the riot act by my mother. Mama soon got a job at Nedbank in Park Lane. We were temporarily housed in St Johns Court, opposite the Dutch-Reformed Church. I think it was No. 5, right next to the main entrance. Eddie was placed in Pinetown Junior school, with his Tante Irms as his teacher. Here he made some friends for life. In 2023, they all met up again for a 50th reunion at the Shark Tank, Kingsmead in Durban.

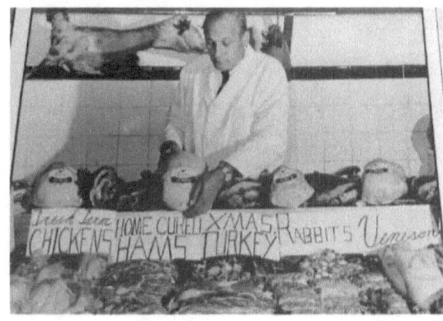

Ludwig Herrmann in the butchery.

From 1966 to 2012, Pinetown becomes the centre of our family history. I therefore include the following, brief history of the town that was thriving in the post-war boom.

> The earliest settlers established themselves in the Pinetown area about 1820. Pinetown was actually founded in 1849, the first Local Administration and Health Board being established in July 1926. It attained the status of a borough in 1948. The town was named after Sir Benjamin Pine, a one-time Lt. Governor of Natal. The advantages of Pinetown's climate were early recognised, as it was renowned as a health resort during the latter part of the last century. Recuperative camps were established in the area for soldiers engaged in the Zulu Wars. Pinetown was described as the healthiest spot in the British Empire!
>
> The first railway to Pinetown was opened in 1876, and greatly facilitated the movement of troops to the town which was used as a military centre. Among regiments stationed at Pinetown were the 6th Inniskilling Dragoons, 7th and 13th Hussars, 60th Rifles, and Bengal Lancers. Associated with these regiments were famous soldiers, Sir Baker Russell, Lord Allenby, Lord Baden-Powell, Col. Pennefather, Co. Rymington, Bromhead of the 24th Regiment who defended Rorkes's Drift, and Capt. J. Malone, V.C., a hero of Balaclava and who is now buried at St. Andrews Churchyard. Many regiments were stationed at Pinetown during the Anglo Boer War, and a local hotel [the Fairydene Hotel] was used as a military hospital.
>
> Descendants of the early pioneers still live in Pinetown, and the names of others are recalled as Street and Site names, etc.

A century ago, the first pioneers from Port Natal and the Voortrekkers sighted the valley in which the present Pinetown forms a part, was granted to Marthinus *Laas* in 1847.

Archibald Keir Murray in 1849 also acquired a portion of this farm, 1,361 acres. On this he laid out a township named Pinetown. In 1871 Canon Crompton took transfer from A.K. Murray of the remainder of his Estate, 801 acres, which forms the central portion of the town.

The Pinetown Public Committee took transfer of the Market Square from Crompton Estate in 1910 when the present Town Hall was erected. From a Health Committee in 1924 Pinetown rose to a Borough Status.

Thereafter, Pinetown witnessed a phenomenal industrial expansion which has in no way detracted from the scenic beauty and natural amenities of the borough (Pinetown Gala Committee 1952).

Although we did the odd excursion to other locations, Pinetown remained the hub; the place to which we always returned; the place we called home. Looking through the old brochure of the Pinetown Gala Committee (1952), with all the advertising of the businesses of that era, I can still remember most of those names. George Laas, a descendant of Mathinus Laas, became one of my brother's best friends. George Van Rooyen was another very good friend whose father was the Police Commander for Durban West, which included Pinetown. Of course, there were others who formed part of this core group of friends, but I cannot remember all their names.

Apart from a few ups and downs, which occur in the best of families, this became a stabilising and generally happy period in our lives. Our parents worked hard to build themselves up again. As a flourishing town, Pinetown was an ideal place to live and work in and the perfect environment for raising children. The inhabitants were generally God-fearing people and there was very little trouble.

Not long after we had established ourselves in St, Johns Court, our parents bought a new house in New Germany, which bordered on Pinetown to the north. My father immediately started a large vegetable garden and rebuilt an old pick-up truck, which he used to sell the veggies for a little extra cash. When she had time, my mother established the gardens. It was not a big property, but it had everything we needed. Mum drove an old grey Opel sedan through which floorboards we could see the road.

Most Pinetownians considered New Germany a suburb of Pinetown, but it had its own borough and municipal buildings. It was the original place of the Cotton Germans of Natal, which means that we had come full circle. The little church that the original pioneers had built became our home church and my mother started teaching Sunday school classes there. Pinetown and district was very British colonial, and this kept us connected to our German roots and faith.

Three generations. Ida Schumann née Gevers with Ursula Herrmann née Schumann and Ingrid Herrmann.

I was soon sent to kindergarten, which was run by Mrs McCarten, who used to be a nun, but had got married. The house that she used for teaching was set in a large garden with big hydrangea bushes. These bushes housed large chocolate Easter eggs once a year. The house was located off a road, just on the other side of Pinetown Station, but has since been demolished to make way for expanding infrastructure of the railways and goods yards, as well the new highway that bypasses central Pinetown up Fields Hill and Kloof.

The driveway to Mrs Mac's house was lined with tall palm trees and she was a good friend of old Mr Pine, who annually dressed up as Father Christmas and rode up the drive in a horse and buggy to dispense loads of gifts to all the screaming and squealing children. Every now and again, she would still dress up as a nun, which never failed to do me in. However, she endeavoured to tame this little independent wild child with marginal success. I lived my life in my head and, therefore, I had the concentration span of an ant. Consequently, I never listened to a thing she had to say and was incapable of following instructions. I got the reputation of being a bit of a dunce, with whom the rest of the children had much fun.

Goliath and his mate had quite a bit of fun with it too. I have no idea how Eddie got to school, but I was picked up by a lady from Pinetown Taxis, first thing in the mornings, and again unceremoniously deposited back home in the afternoon. Eddie was brought home by my father, I think. One day, Eddie had to drive my father to the emergency rooms after chopping off one of his fingers or a portion thereof. Mama was highly unimpressed. Goliath and company thought it was grand. The rest of the time before mama came home, they enjoyed making fun of me.

My spirit, which is what I call my "wild side", protected me, defended me and helped me survive, for underneath the bravado, existed a highly sensitive child. Mama soon cottoned on to what was going on and stepped in to defend me. However, that just made matters worse and split our family in two. Mama faced a great deal of criticism for it.

As a result of breaking my left arm at a very young age, I believe my brain decided to become partially right-handed. There was this period of discombobulation between my right hand and left hand, and I would often get confused as to which hand to use for certain tasks. Until my brain worked it all out, it was a bit of a bother. Currently, I think I am bi-dexterous, rather than ambidextrous. In other words, I cannot perform the same tasks with both hands. Instead, there are tasks that only the left hand can do and other tasks that only the right hand can do. For example, I play hockey with my right hand, but I play tennis with my left hand. I write with my left hand, but cut bread with my right hand, etc. Being different is not easy – particularly not in those days.

Eddie was the eternal academic and flew through school with flying colours, followed by his sister, who was still living her life in her head and barely scraping by. It was a great concern to the entire family. By the time I was sent to Pinetown Infant School, things were looking dire for Ingrid. Mama was called into the principal's office and told that I had some intelligence issues. I was simply incapable of listening and did whatever I wanted to do and to hell with the rest. 'It was obvious that she failed to understand certain things', which did not mean that I was rude or badly behaved or even insolent: I was simply not interested in the least in whatever they were doing. Every single report card reflected the same dirge: Ingrid does not pay attention in class; Ingrid is lackadaisical; Ingrid spends her time daydreaming and staring out the window; Ingrid does not participate in group activities. Blah, blah, blah. None of the teachers bothered to determine that, if I was capable of speaking four languages before attending school, then surely there had to be more than one grey cell between my ears. And so, the psychological and emotional warfare continued for many, many years.

These issues were interspersed with wonderful times, such as going to the *Berg*, (colloquial South African name for the Drakensberg mountains) on holidays with our mother. Eddie commandeered every horse and soon was galloping over hill and dale.

He also suffered from a condition which my mother called "pythons", it meant that his hollow legs and stomach never got enough food. He would start at one end of the buffet table, grazing right through to several deserts. My mother wished the floor would open and swallow her, but Eddie could not help it. He was a growing lad and would soon overtake my father's 6 ft something. By the time he reached Std. 5 (Grade 7), he was the tallest in his class. Anyway, we would take long walks and drink the cool clean waters of the rivers directly from the melting snow.

Mosely and Kloof

> Kloof is a town that includes a smaller area called Everton, located approximately 26 km north-west of Durban in KwaZulu-Natal, South Africa. Once an independent municipality, it now forms part of greater Durban area of the eThekwini Metropolitan Municipality.
>
> The word *kloof* (cf. cleft) means "gorge" in Afrikaans and the area is named after the deep ravine formed by the Molweni stream (stream of high cliffs).[88]
>
> Destinations near Kloof Include: Assagay, Bothas Hill, Camperdown, Crestholme, Drummond, Gillitts, Hillcrest, Inchanga, New Germany, Queensburgh and Waterfall.

---

[88] I have many happy memories of hikes along the cliffs and even climbing up the waterfall in the winter. These days, you are not permitted to do that. We would have lovely Sunday afternoon picnics here. A little further up the road is a most beautiful look out point over the gorge. Even in our childhood years, there were still leopards to be found there.

By the time I reached Std. 1, my parents were ready to leave New Germany for greener pastures in Mosely, which was just outside Pinetown, on the other side on the way to Queensborough. We lived on a steep road. The house they bought had been standing empty for some time and vandals had entered the property, making a fire in the middle of the beautiful parquet flooring in the lounge. It was a solid, Spanish styled house with thick walls and large supporting beams. According to the seller, the house was used as a "safe house" during the war – something that endlessly thrilled my brother, who was into *skop, skiet and donder*[89] ("kick, shoot and thunder"). We each had our own bedrooms, with French doors leading to a manicured garden with a huge Jacaranda tree in the far-left corner, which the local monkey population had claimed for themselves.

Our house in Mosely.

In summer, it was absolute bliss to let in some cool breezes. The floors got sanded and everything spruced up with fresh paint, which we all did ourselves. Everyone chipped in and helped. The double garage had a large spacious apartment/cottage attached to the back, where dad's cousin, Remo, and his pal, Linton, would stay when they came to Pinetown to do their apprenticeship with Barlow's South Africa, which had a massive factory on the right, just as you

---

[89] *Skop, skiet and donder* is an informal Afrikaans expression for violent action and dramatic adventure in a film.

drove into New Germany. They had started an electronic division and brought out their own Hi Fi system. Influenced by Remo, that was what we got. Mama loved it.

Both Eddie and I made friends with the neighbours, and we would visit one another from time to time. Suzie, the cat my father brought me when we were still in New Germany, had a litter of kittens and entertained me royally. Eddie's cat, Mietzie, was a little wild and liked the outdoor life. Trees were her speciality. The monkeys were not in a sharing mood and, when they smashed her to the ground, she shattered her back leg. The local veterinarian in Pinetown did a fantastic job of putting her back together with steel pins. She lasted like that for many more years, eventually dying of old age.

I am not entirely sure when Fuchs joined our household. He was a magnificent canine specimen – cross Doberman Pincher and Alsatian – black from snout to tail, with all the brown spots at the right places and the body and fur of a good German Shepherd. He was an amazing family pet and we adored him; as did the cats. However, you did not want to be an uninvited guest. He listened to one voice and that was my father's who had him well trained. We felt safe with Fuchs around.

Mum decided to continue her quest of educating me and decided to send me to the private convent school in Pinetown, which had a stellar reputation. So, I was sent off with my new uniform and white hat with a badge in the middle. Each nun decided to give it their best shot to tame this wild child in their midst. Only two came close, and that was the music teacher and the art teacher. Sister Davide, who was trained in London and used the Oxford curriculum, ran the music department like clockwork. Soon, she discovered that I had a little talent and gave me much encouragement. The art teacher had the coolest classroom. She did not just teach us how to draw, but also to observe, as well as many crafty things like batik, melting candle wax and dipping whole bits of cloth into various coloured dyes.

However, it was Sister's Davide's annual operettas that got my full attention. The hall had a fantastic stage and a back choir. To me it was huge. I never attended mass there, because Protestants do not do that. So, I did not go, no matter how hard they tried. We had professional stage sets built for each show. *Iolanthe* and *The Pirates of Penzance* were performed: Sister was passionate about Gilbert and Sullivan. The shows would run for about two weeks, with both matinees and evening performances fully booked. From behind the curtains, we loved watching the people arriving and taking their seats, until it was our turn to have our make-up done. All the major roles went to the high school girls, but I managed to get into the chorus. This delighted my mother endlessly: at long last, Ingrid was getting cultured!

After making a complete mess of Std. 2 (Grade 4) and having to repeat, Ingrid began to shift gear. As my confidence grew and the childhood traumas were being addressed through art and music therapy, I began to pay attention to some academics. Okay, so I am a slow starter. Pinetown Convent School did my mother proud and performed a turnabout that she had not quite expected. People have been telling me all my life, "I never knew you had it in you" – simply because I was living in my head they assumed that I was not listening. The truth is, I did listen, and I learned and shelved the information, until I decided to retrieve it.

Home was a lesson in intense observation. Every night after dinner, we remained behind at the table, before clearing the dishes, to talk. I think this was my mother's favourite time of the day and Eddie was right there with her. Every subject was discussed – socio-economic and political history and military history in particular. My father enjoyed space travel; so that became a discussion point too. Eddie absorbed it all like a sponge and began to take part in the dinner time debates. Ingrid would mostly keep quiet, munching on her chicken bones until every shred of meat and cartilage had been devoured. The nuance of the arguments and the analytical thinking to which I was being exposed never went to waste. Every shred of information was being mulled over and filed away.

After dinner, Eddie and I had to clear the table and wash the dishes. Mama and Papa would generally make themselves comfortable in the lounge and listen to classical music.

I was raised on classical music. When the programme *U Eie Keuse*[90] ("Your own choice") came on once a week, you were expected to be as quiet as a mouse. God forbid if you made a noise. The same applied to the news. Just before bedtime, after we had had our baths, we gathered under Mama's wings to read from the Bible in German, after which she would tuck us in, and pray with us before we went to sleep.

Sport became an obsession for both Eddie and me. We had been raised in the great outdoors most of our lives and sport was a natural extension of it. From Std. 5 onwards, Eddie was involved with rugby – not only on a junior level, but also at high school. Since the high school that year did not have enough players for that age group, they recruited players from junior school. Eddie and all his mates joined in. A year or so later at high school he was selected for the second team, followed by the first team of Pinetown High School. Pinetown High was a dual medium co-ed school in those days. They had made it to that magnificent team that beat Westville Boys and, if I am correct, they only lost two games. They became legends among their peers. Thereafter, the army took over and rugby became a beautiful memory, a part of history.

Early in high school, Eddie's asthma was still a problem, interspersed with hay fever and sinus. He still turned blue periodically and was sent to a specialist in Durban, a doctor Segorin, whose speciality was asthma in young children. Apart from treatment, he advised Eddie to continue with rugby. He had to run it out; exercise it out. It worked.

---

[90] I always thought *eie* was eggs, as in the German *Eier*. The joys of being multi-lingual.

Ingrid ran, just never fast enough for the sprints, no matter how hard I tried. Tennis came and went, and so did netball. Then along came hockey. It had that little bit of violence that suited my slightly angry disposition well. I played a mediocre game in Pinetown before I got myself sent off to boarding school in Greytown. There, I received excellent training, which was followed by first team hockey and inter-school hockey champs. However, in athletics, I discovered that my distance was 200, 400 and 800 m and broke the record. My record stood for many years, but ought to be delegated to history by now. Swimming became a breeze and soon I was racing with the best.

I should have carried on with my schooling at Greytown High School after junior school, because back in Pinetown, the training was not as good, and I soon lost interest. In the afternoons after school, I started cross country running, all over Pinetown. This is where pent-up, bleeding emotions were spent. The other place I visited almost every day in summer was the Pinetown public swimming pool at Lahee Park. I swam until my limbs ached. They had an Olympic sized pool and plenty of room for all the kids who met there.

Sometime between all this growing up, my parents sold the house in Mosely, trading up for a lovely house at No. 9 Old Main Road in Kloof. Buying and restoring old homes was their way of re-building themselves financially. Mama represented the creative side and my father the builder, who made everything happen. There was very little that he could not put his hand to. The house initially belonged to old doctor Wallman and, when we went to view the property, he had this beautiful old baby grand piano in the lounge. The main part of the house was the huge rondavel and thatched roof. The front entrance from the slasto (slate) patio was through French doors into this spacious lounge with Van Dyke carpets and a crystal chandelier hanging from the centre of the ceiling. There was an alcove for the dining room, with a breakfast bar into the kitchen shaped in a bow around the original round walls of the rondavel. Opposite the dining room was larger alcove with a guest room and bathroom. A large rectangular extension was down a few steps, leading off the side of the kitchen. A long passage to the left led to two bedrooms to the right: first my parents' bedroom, following by mine, with the main family bathroom opposite. Through my bedroom, up a step, was Eddie's huge room with doors going outside on either side.

Three generations: Frieda Herrmann, Eddie and Ludwig Hermann at Eddie's confirmation. Lutheran Church, New Germany, KwaZulu Natal.

Everything appeared slightly run-down when we moved in, but that did not last long: new thatch, electrical wiring, paint and décor soon made a vast difference. The bathrooms were redone and, with the exception of some of the bedrooms, the entire house was done in beautiful parquet flooring with Rhodesian Red Wood. I think these floors got sanded and re-varnished and then lovingly polished once a week.

Once the house had been redone, mama began on the gardens. The sunken garden received new plants collected from all over, particularly from forests on our Sunday afternoon drives. All the plants received much tender loving care.

Eddie Herrmann at 9 Old Main Road, Kloof. The front porch with Petria in full bloom.

Kloof was set on the west side of the Pinetown valley, on the plateau after the dangerous Fields Hill drive. Things were a little more expensive up here. It was a lovely property situated right at the edge of the highway that travelled all the way from Durban through Pinetown, leading to Pietermaritzburg and onward to Johannesburg in the Transvaal. The fence line was planted with trees as a noise break. The house itself was one of the original homes owned by the pioneers from yesteryear and as we later found out came with its own ghost. The driveway, which went all around the house, was lined to the left with magnificent azalea bushes and Jacaranda Trees. By October, the ground beneath would be a carpet of violet blooms.

This lovely old heritage house has since been demolished to make way for upmarket office space and architects.

Back to Pinetown Convent. They were the ones who initially got me to learn how to swim. No fear whatsoever, Ingrid jumps into the deep end, trying to drown. My father was roped in to collect me from private swimming lessons at the Pinetown pool. Mr Johnson's method was to drop you in the deep end and see what happens next. Just at that moment, Papa arrived to see how I was doing. I was hauled out by the scruff of my neck, spluttering after swallowing half the pool. It did not go that well with Mr Johnson and that was the end of my private swimming lessons. All my life, my mother had a horror of me drowning.

Apparently, she used to have nightmares about it. This explains why she was this hysterical woman, herding me away from the water edge. Later, when I had my own children, she nearly had full-on heart failure when we bought a house with a pool. Every conversation I had with her either started or ended with strict pool safety instructions. However, the magnificent two were taught to swim before they could breathe and were at home in the water as much as they were on dry land.

Another activity to which I was introduced, was ballet. Although you can hardly imagine this wild child doing ballet, I took to it like a duck to water. Ballet became everything and Margot Fontaine was my greatest heroine. Mama and I attended the ballet performance of Swan Lake in Durban, but Goliath and mate did not accompany us. We did manage to get them to the ice shows in Durban every now and again.

At that time, Eddie was a little obsessed with Houdini, which meant that I was tied up to the washing line and had to try and escape, or I was arm-locked and frog-marched around. Eddie found it highly amusing, me not so much.

His frustration grew when he could not hurt my shoulder, no matter how high he forced my arm up behind my back. In the end, a supple body and ballet got the better of him.

My capacity to absorb trauma and anger was exceptionally high, which does not mean that Eddie and I did not get into spats: we did daily. It would have been extremely unusual for a day to pass, if we had not been in each other's hair. To say that we did not get along that well would be an understatement. However, there are only two times that I can ever remember losing my temper. For years, I did not remember this incident, but Eddie reminded me of it when I was already married to Willem. He must have been pushing my buttons one time too many, when I snapped, grabbed my hockey stick and chased him all through the house, until we got outside, where he was able to outpace me. When he told me about it, he confessed that he was genuinely afraid that I was going to bash him good and proper. The second time I lost my temper was much worse, but more about this incident later.

We made friends with the neighbours' children and adopted Kloof as our backyard. Erica was given permission to swim in a pool belonging to an elderly lady living on her own on the other side of the highway. The pool was puke green with algae, and the Lord alone only knows what else was lurking underneath. However, we survived and came home dripping with green stuff and green hair.

The Kloof Cottage Tearoom was located on the same side as the pool. It was our go-to spot for everything sweet and savoury. They made the very best pies, and I am sure this is where my love for all things savoury comes from. One day, my cousin, Karin, from Vryheid came to visit us for a week or so during the school holidays. I simply had to treat her to a glorious chicken and mushroom pie. She had barely taken a bite when I casually mentioned that they were made from boiled cat's eyes, pointing to the little button mushroom within. That was it for her: she could not finish her pie and would gag every time she tried to. Of course, this meant that I had two pies in the end. Not too shabby. She never returned for a visit, except for my wedding day and, to this day, she cannot eat pies.

From an early age, I had to learn to ignore my father and brother when they started to put me off my food. I assumed Karin had been weaned on similar tactics and thought it was hilarious. I will never forget the day my father told me milk was made from blood. With the exception of chocolate flavoured milk from the corner shop near Pinetown High, milk from the bottle was not for me. I only started eating yoghurt when Creamline Dairies and Clover started stocking flavoured yoghurt, such as apple and cinnamon.

Fuchs and the cats settled down to life in Kloof very well. Every afternoon, when Papa came home from the butchery, he would park the car at the side of the house, where all of them would be waiting for him on the driver's side, barely able to contain their excitement. They would all be sitting in a row salivating.

Out would come a piece of steak for Fuchs and a handful of mince for each cat. Imagine trying to do that now, with the price of meat being as high as it is. In the evenings, the cats would find Fuchs lying on his side in the lounge. One of them would curl up next to his belly, another between his paws, waiting for him to nuzzle the scruff of their necks before they all settled in for the night, warmed by his body.

Things were not going particularly well with my father. I understand now that he was suffering from deep depression, but as children, we were not told about this. It was only later that we worked it out for ourselves and, when I got together with Eddie after my mother's death, he gave me the reason why. Barbara's death and the loss of the farm still tormented him. It was on one of our Sunday afternoon drives that my father put his foot down on the accelerator and headed straight for the concrete pylons at the foot of a bridge. I was sitting in front with my mother and Eddie was at the back. To this day, I can hear my mother screaming for him to stop. Our mother saved our lives that day.

One day, my father saved my life. We were still living in Mosely at the time and, on the way home from work and school pick-ups, we often stopped on the left side of the road, so that Papa could run across the street and get milk and bread from the local corner shop. I was firmly told to wait for him in the car, but as usual, Ingrid acted first and left the thinking for later. Fortunately, my father looked back to see that I had stepped out the car to follow him. I had never seen his body move so fast. He lunged into me, almost in a rugby tackle from across the road, just in time to avert the screeching tyres of the fast-oncoming car with the hooter blaring. The burnt rubber tyre tracks remained there for months as a reminder. It had rattled everyone's cage.

In Mosely, Eddie had built a really good go-cart (go-kart) with wheels from a pram. We used to ride down the hill on Eddie's go-cart, scraping our knees if we came short. I think I still have a piece of asphalt in one of my knees. In Kloof, Eddie tied it to the back of the Ford pick-up truck and we all had a go being pulled around the driveway while Eddie drove. Dangerous? Absolutely. But it was so much fun! Growing up in the late 1960s and 1970s was a completely different experience from childhood today.

Ingrid was the sickly one in the family, until Dr. Turner removed my tonsils and a large mole on my back just for good measure. I was still struggling with sore throats and ear infections at the time.[91] Prior to that, I was anaemic with some bug I had picked up. I was taken to Mariannhill Hospital, where the sisters regularly took blood with a pipette from my finger to check whether the iron levels were normal. One day, when we were with our aunt and uncle on their farm, *Tussen Bay*, in Zululand, Eddie and Kiffie left me alone in the field on top of a haystack. An insect must have bitten me, because I came down with a terrible fever. Fortunately, Tante Friedel was a nurse, and she phoned Mama to come and collect us. By the time we got back to Pinetown, the fever had progressed to cold shakes. The following morning, at the doctor's rooms, I was shaking so badly that they had to turn the heaters on. After the diagnosis, I was transferred to Marian hill Hospital with encephalitis. My neck was as stiff as a board and my head throbbed terribly. The little boy next me, who also suffered from encephalitis, had to have a lumber puncture. There was a slight debate as to whether I would need one too. However, I responded to the medication quickly and the spinal lumbar puncture was disappointingly avoided (I was a bit jealous that I did not have spinal lumber puncture to brag about). The headaches lasted until long after my children were born. If there was a grade for headache intensity, I would grade them as Mach 5.

Storms were one of the greatest experiences in Kloof. We would sit on the steps on the front patio, watching the clouds roll in with magnificent lightning

---

[91] My mother was aware that our family from the Frohling/ Schumann side were high risk for cancer. It was one of her big worries for herself and Eddie and me.

bolts that lit up the entire sky, followed seconds later by deafening thunder. The wilder the thunder, the better it was for me.

However, these storms were entering the house, where lightening was being replaced with a war of words. Salvos of spears and daggers were being thrust in the bedroom next door. Ingrid would huddle under the sheets and have nightmares. To get up at night and go to the toilet meant facing the danger of all the snakes under the bed.

You never ever wake up Papa in the middle of the night. Thunder and lightning may strike. So, you jump as far as you could to avoid the snakes and creep very quietly into their bedroom and sneak in with Mama – my safe zone.

Back in Pinetown

One morning, after an incident, I was bundled up with the luggage in the car. Eddie opted to stay with Papa, who was outside the kitchen door screaming with pain. For a few nights, Mama and I stayed with Tante Irms in Pinetown and then in a dismal flat, just up the road from St John's Court, with no furniture and no food. The days were grey. By this time, Mama had left the bank and was working as a Secretary at Pinetown High School. Onkel Kurt was a teacher there too, with Erica, Tante Irm's daughter and my cousin, who was teaching Home Economics. Home from home.

When Ekka – as I used to call Erika – left to teach at the college in Pietermaritzburg, we went to live in Ekka's room at Tante Irm's house. I would catch the bus to school and back. I had retreated into my head and mostly forgot to get off the bus, until bus conductor came over at the bus depot and helped me off the bus. The walk home from the depot was a little distance, but not too bad.

I lost the ability to read and write, but Tante Irms tenderly began to put all the pieces back together again. I made best friends with my cousin, Doy (Conrad). When he took the dogs for a walk in the late afternoon, I was allowed to tag along. We would walk along the railway line as it started to ascend Fields Hill, right up to a little waterfall, then back down towards Lahee Park, where Doy would look out for mushrooms – the big ones, called *Makowas* and favoured by the Zulu people.

One day, Tante Irms brought a big box of Noddy books – the entire set. In those days, we were still allowed to read them. She let me read them before she wrapped the box for her grandchildren's Christmas present. She started her Christmas preparations quite early. Ekka often came home for the weekends, and she taught me to sew and knit. I was not too clever with the knitting needles, and a little distracted with the sewing, but I managed it in the end. It was a nurturing and friendly environment. The best was watching Ekka cook or bake; particularly her lovely Christmas cakes, which she also baked well in advance of Christmas, soaking them in plenty of brandy.

Eddie was not doing too well. Papa was losing the plot altogether. Remo and Linton had to flee a mighty raging bull, one out the window and another out the door, fleeing for their lives. Mama was summoned and, after a small suitcase was packed for him, Papa was taken to Fort Napier in Pietermaritzburg, where he was accepted and found the help that he so desperately needed. He stayed there for almost a year.

Just before Christmas, Tante Irms became very sick. By this time, I had read all Ekka's childhood books of Huckleberry Fin and the whole set of Malory Towers. Then I discovered her recipe books by *Time Life*, with the cuisines from countries all over the world. My favourite was the one on Italy. Tante Irms had a tumour on her spine and passed away just after Christmas.

Papa had been released and was visiting Mama from time-to-time. He was also attending weekly AA meetings in Durban. One night, he came over, very excited: the pastor at the meeting told him all about the *Gospel of the Kingdom*, and Papa was glowing, smiling from ear-to-ear. Mama and I moved back to the house in Kloof with Eddie. Papa got a flat in New Germany that had been built by the Frame Group. There, he made all sorts of lovely things with leather – craft work that he was taught in Pietermaritzburg.

Back in Kloof, we were trying our best to get by. Eddie was studying for his matric examination by reading every western novel he could lay his hands on. And during breaks, Marcus and Eddie would take turns taking potshots with a pellet gun at Erica[92] and me, while we were playing outside. Maybe I should mention that the pellets were made of lead. This is where I learned how to leopard crawl along the driveway, hiding behind the hydrangea bushes. All in a day's fun. Needless to say, Eddie did not do so well in his finals. Although he passed, it was not nearly as good as everyone had hoped for. So, Mama made him rewrite a couple of subjects after she had read him the riot act. With that good dose of encouragement, he did much better.

I asked to be sent away to boarding school, mainly because I was influenced by Erica, who was doing the same, but at a different location. At the time, Mama's older brother was headmaster in Greytown; so she sent me there to the Junior School.

In Greytown, my confidence returned, and the daily discipline did me the world of good. Apart from sport and generally getting up to mischief, I quietly, without anyone really taking notice of me, spent most of my breaks in the library. I got into all the medical journals, books on anatomy and other interesting things. The librarian at the time scoffed at me, but I did not pay her any attention. I enjoyed my world.

The following year I was returned to reality. Mathematics was the worst subject ever!!! It made no sense to me, and I could not for the life of me see why I needed it. I began to be a pain in the classroom, peppering the teachers with questions and unusual observations.

---

[92] Erica was Marcus's sister, and they were our next-door neighbours.

Back home, Mama had started to accumulate books on esoteric knowledge, and I would dive into the books of Lobsang Rampa.[93] When I got bored with those, I would walk down to the local library and begin reading everything I could lay my hands on. From novels to non-fiction; nothing escaped me. This trend continued all through school. Writers like Tom Sharpe, the entire range of Flash Man books. Very risqué! Let us not forget P.G. Wodehouse and his Jeeves and Wooster stories. Hilarious stuff. Mrs Sherratt, my class teacher at the time, could not get over the fact that this low-life Schumann, who never lived up to her cousins' achievements in Westville, was reading Wodehouse!! Although I missed C.S. Lewis somehow, I got stuck into another of the Inklings[94] – J.R. Tolkien. I demolished the entire Trilogy in time for my finals. Sometimes, I would get so engrossed with my book that I would read through the night, getting ready for school the next morning without any sleep.

Much to everyone's surprise, Ingrid began to get grades beyond expectation, Ingrid proved that she was not all that stupid after all. I had taken the route of least resistance and had only one science subject, Biology, which was great. A little bit of blood and gore never did anybody any harm. The rest were languages, Art and History. Out of all of those History was the most interesting. In my final assignment, I read up on Hitler's esoteric ways and shocked the school by revealing his Satanic involvement in "The Golden Dawn" and similar groups.

---

[93] Lobsang Rampa was the pen name of Cyril Henry Hoskin, a British author who became famous in the mid-20th century for books claiming to recount his experiences as a Tibetan lama. His books describe mystical experiences, including astral projection and spiritual practices.

[94] The Inklings were a gathering of friends in Britain, most of them working at Oxford University and many of them creative writers, who used to meet on Thursday evenings for readings and criticism of their own work. Years later I went to the pub they used to frequent in Oxford, where they had most of their meetings.

By this time my mother's beautiful blond hair was almost snow white. She heaved a huge sigh of relief: Ingrid passed with university exemption. However, I was tired. I was barely living. The past six years had been hell.

After the house in Kloof was sold, Mama and I moved into a lovely flat near the Pinetown pool: Lunlor on Kings Road. It was a lovely neighbourhood in those days and the pool was my saviour. When Papa got sick, he came to live with us. Eddie had already left for the army, where he became a signal man and sharpshooter (sniper). He was recruited for undercover work, which was right up his alley. The Border Wars suited him well and he volunteered for an extra year or two.

> "We members of the Communist Party are the most advanced revolutionaries in modem history ... The enemy must be completely smashed and rooted out of the earth before the communist world can be made a reality." Nelson Mandela, former leader of the African National Congress (ANC)
>
> "As I write these words the 22nd "Church Day" has been drawing to a close in Frankfurt, Germany. According to the newspaper reports an entire day was devoted to "discussing the situation in South Africa". A hundred thousand people, including the Federal Chancellor Helmut Kohl, filled the Wald-Stadion in Frankfurt to hear Dr Allan Boesak, the South African president of the World Federation of Reformed Churches, conduct the closing service, "constantly interrupted by thunderous applause", in which he pleaded for a "new world" (order?) filled with freedom and justice. Ten thousand "demonstrators against apartheid" later marched through the streets of Frankfurt, riotously at times.

It is significant that a man like Dr Boesak should have been chosen as chief speaker for this so-called Church Day, a man who is known in South Africa more for his inciting speeches under the red hammer and sickle flag than as a faithful shepherd bringing the Gospel message to his troubled flock" (Vaqué, 1989).

The Congo fell. Mozambique fell. Angola fell. Rhodesia was falling, and South Africa and South West Africa a heartbeat behind.

Young girls would line the streets of Durban, as the next intake of young soldiers, who were on their way to the Border War, marched along the Parade to the trains waiting for them. Mothers were crying. They were just boys, but they were to become men very soon. With the world uniting against South Africa, we did not really stand a chance, but we gave it everything we had.

The day Papa died, I was on a school excursion near Howick Falls. It had been a very wet weekend and I was sitting in the bus, covered with mud from head to toe. My uncle arrived to pick me up as my mother was at the hospital. On the bus, I already had a bad feeling: I knew something was amiss. We just got past Murray Square on Old Main Road, when my uncle blurted it out. I sat stunned for the rest of the drive. He dropped me off at home and drove off. I was left standing outside with no way of getting into the unit, and I knocked on Mrs Rusch's door. The kind Dutch lady took me into her arms and let me stay with her, until Mama came home.

This was the final straw for Mama. Her weakened faith got snuffed out and she embraced all the esoteric religions of her sisters. Tante Irms, Tante Brunni and Tante Friedel, had, after their own traumas, fallen away. Mama joined their ranks, and I was hauled along for the ride. Before the house in Kloof was sold, we had a range of tenants, but they never stayed very long and we could never figure out why, until one day, when one of them blurted out that the place was haunted. The ghost, who was very happy with us, did not seem to like the tenants! Mama got a Catholic priest to do an exorcism.

However, this did not stop us from getting involved with yoga, visiting strange healers, spiritualism and singles parties. On occasion, Mum would take me along to those, only to experience dirty old men trying to grope me. It was as if Mum had got off on another planet. She went out every weekend and stayed out with Roy, until the early hours of the morning. Sometimes, during the week, we would visit the Landers, her best friends from Rhodesia, whom she had met at Nedbank. There, she would stay until two or three in the morning and, occasionally, until dawn. I would have to steer her home and change the gears. The other nights, she would get into a bottle of wine, sitting up, until she passed out on the bed, at which point, I would get up and tuck her in, putting out the cigarette that was burning into the mattress.

We barely managed to get on by mum's income. By this time, Eddie had returned from the Border Wars but he departed just as quickly to New Castle, where he did his apprenticeship as an electrical engineer in the coal mines. He sent money every month and, once a year, he sent me money for my birthday in July to buy clothes. The rest of my clothes came from Bev Lander. On occasions we did not have soap to bath with or toothpaste to brush our teeth.

Eddie would come to visit a couple of times, but he did not quite get the full picture of what was going on, no matter how much I asked him to do something. To be fair what could he do?

So, I started running. I ran and ran and ran, until my calves cramped badly from lack of sodium and potassium. I read and read and read. And then, one day I snapped. If you cannot beat them, you join them. I began to smoke and drink too. Every weekend was a party. Mum often supplied the wine and made sure I had enough cigarettes. Imagine that.

I had some good friends of whom the best was Spook. I will never forget the way he introduced himself to Mum. She opened the door, and he said, "Hi, my name is Spook. I glow in the dark". I thought Mum was going to keel over from laughter, for she had a brilliant sense of humour. Spook had his issues too and we discovered that we were at school together from Grade 1. We mostly hung out in a group, Spook and the girls, and together, we got up to all sorts of mischief. I guess it was all blowing off steam. Margit, Spook and I had the same problems. Although not as bad, Helene had her own control issues, but she did not hang out with us that much. We still met after school, but that faded out and now, we have not seen one another for years. As far as I know, Margit returned to Austria, before moving to Germany.

Once Spook went to the army, he changed quite a bit, and then he was involved in a terrible accident with a bus on his way back from university. A lovely, brilliant mind and an amazingly fun-natured human being. He did well as an architect and, as far as I understand, he is back from the UK and working in South Africa as the founder of Dean Jay Architects.

I had just broken up with a boyfriend and found myself at loose ends for our matric farewell. All the school secretaries decided to help me find a date. Peter was a teller at the bank across the road, and I was to meet him. We began dating and, the following year, I joined the bank before leaving for university in Pietermaritzburg to study fine art.

I did not do very well at university. I experienced a breakdown of sorts, a deep depression. In the meantime, Mum broke up with Roy and married Willie. The joke was "willie or won't he"! Willie drank heavily as well, and he used to buy far too much wine for Mum.

One weekend, we came home, I found Mum, her neck appeared broken like that of a chicken, her head lolling lifelessly on her chest. All the blood drained from my face, and I went into a rage like you cannot imagine. I flew down the stairs, threw the kitchen table over, opening drawers to find my father's butcher knives. Peter stood to one side, absolutely horrified. He knew what was coming next and spoke to me very quietly. I was halfway up the stairs before I stopped, my body starting to shake, and I dropped the knife.

I was pregnant when we got married the following year, after which things went south quite quickly, mostly, if not all, my fault. By the time we got divorced, things had become acrimonious and loveless. I broke his heart and the children suffered too. Although we were church-goers, I did not have a personal faith to hold onto. Mum and I had stopped going to church long ago, except when I was forced to get confirmed. From there on, things only got even worse.

When Peter's ageing father passed away, we went to spend the afternoon with his mum and brother. Granny Grey Hair, as the kids used to call her, needed someone to go through the sympathy cards with her, and Peter was comforting his brother. The kids were playing in one of the bedrooms, when our little boy, who could not have been older than two or three, came out and began to behave strangely. He hit his head on the dining room table and was falling over, almost as if he was drunk, but his grandparents did not have any alcohol in the house. We decided to go home.

At home, it got much worse, and he fell off the bed. The telephone rang and a very distraught Granny Grey Hair reported that she had found that her prescription tranquillizers had been tampered with and some were missing. We bundled the children into the panel van and drove at breakneck speed to Addington Hospital in Durban, where a nurse was waiting for us. We were ushered straight into emergency and various tests were done to ascertain how serious his dosage was. If he had eaten one more of those tablets, he would have died from heart failure. He was given black charcoal to eat and then bottles of water to make him vomit it all back up again. By the end of this ordeal, we were both black and wet from head-to-toe. Eventually, he was placed in the children's ward, where we stood guard until he fell asleep.

We returned very early the next morning, with hardly any sleep. Our little man was much better but still firing on over drive. It was full speed running everywhere. My mother and Willie came to help us, and poor Granny was terribly distraught. We were all so grateful, but unfortunately our marriage was still ailing. I began to reach out to orphans and folks in hospital, particularly the children's wards, to show some love and attention in a bid to show how grateful I was to have my child still alive. Some people have it much worse. However, my heart was empty and aching. My lifelong quest for love and acceptance, for loving kindness, was going to get me into the worst possible trouble ever. The marriage ended. Emotional hardship is seldom seen.

I had met a guy living in Westville, who turned out to be very wrong for me. *Meine Sehnsucht* – my longing for love and to be loved – clouded my thinking. He was seriously bad news and there were times that I feared for my life. We often went fishing at one of the inland dams near Pietermaritzburg. On one weekend, when the kids did not accompany us, he started "turning" and I knew I had to get out of there fast. Very quietly, I smuggled the car keys into my pocket and kept my handbag near the exit of the tent awning. When he went into the caravan, I ran, started the car and drove forward, without turning the headlights on. The next thing, a heavy wooden piece of furniture was smashed through the windscreen on the driver's side, narrowly missing me. Somehow, I got away in pouring rain. I drove to the nearest police station and made a statement without laying a charge. On another occasion, came the fist, a black eye and the knife. That was enough for me.

There were other terrible incidents, but here is the thing: somehow, through my downward spiral, I was trying to find goodness, which came in a highly unusual package. Her name was Mam 'Khize. She lived with us as a housekeeper, but she was a highly trained ICU nurse and matron. She is one of the most remarkable women I have ever met, and I owe her my life. I found myself in a deep darkness, and Mam 'Khize began to minister to me daily and over weekends, fasting and praying. She told me her amazing story and was instrumental in helping me escape from the darkness.

I Danced with Samora Machel

Mam 'Khize was the first-born child to a Zulu chief in the Valley of the Thousand Hills in Natal. When she was only six years old, her uncle, who was a teacher, came to pick her up, as arranged by her parents, and took her with him to Paris, where she was to receive a European education. In Paris, she was left in the care of a Catholic orphanage, not far from the Notre Dame De Paris. She was taught French, and she did her nurses training there too. She made a few friends; particularly two orphaned boys who were twins, as was discovered later. The three of them became inseparable. One of the twins became a doctor and the other a priest. After working in several hospitals in Europe, she became well-known in the nobility and wealthy set. If anyone needed nursing, they would get her to be their private nurse. She began keeping a journal, which she wrote long hand in French. She travelled to Rome, where she learned a little Italian, and later to Holland.

At some point, the French doctor, who was her friend, decided that he was in love with her and tried to court her, but she wanted nothing of it. She would transfer from one hospital to another, until he found out where she was and followed her there. Therefore, she moved through Europe, until, in desperation, she decided to return to Africa.

Mam 'Khize was an amazingly brave woman. She had heard about the atrocities done to pregnant women by Idi Amin,[95] and had devised a plan to assassinate him by plunging a poisonous needle into him. Amin's bodyguards were everywhere, and it was an exceptionally dangerous thing that she planned to do. While she kept helping women to give birth to their babies, measuring and weighing them, this abominable man was ripping them alive from their

---

[95] Idi Amin was a military officer and politician in Uganda. From 1971 to 1979, Amin served as the third president of Uganda, which he ruled as a military dictator.

mothers' wombs, killing both mother and child. Someone had to put an end to this horror. However, she could not get anywhere near him.

She moved to Lourenço Marques (LM), which was to become Maputo, the capital of Mozambique, where she joined the hospital as a theatre sister/matron. She was very happy there, and she began wonderful mission work among the poor – particularly among the women and children.

Mozambique was still a Portuguese colony at the time, and she learned Portuguese. She had already learned a fair bit of Portuguese while in Europe, for she had nursed there at some time. LM was known for having its own bull ring for bullfights, beautiful cathedrals and the warm Indian ocean. The country is extremely hot in the summer and temperate in winter. The sea is so shallow that you can walk for about a mile into the ocean, and it will still only come halfway up your calf. The Herrmann family loved to have their annual holidays in the beach cottages there, surrounded by apes and birds – a tradition started by our grandparents. I nearly got burned to a cinder one year. The Portuguese food – particularly the LM prawns – was to die for.

Back to Mam M'Khize. It did not take that long for "him" to trace her, and he applied for a position at the same hospital. Eventually, she gave in. They bought a lovely double-story house and, being very proper, they kept separate apartments, until they got married. An old Portuguese lady took care of the house for them. With her parents' permission, they got engaged.

The Congo was already in the grip of a revolution, and they were often flown there in a small plane, as a part of the Red Cross, to take care of the wounded. They would always take these trips together. However, this time, "he" instructed her not to accompany him, almost as if he had a premonition. He made some excuse that she needed to take care of some important administrative work in his absence. She did as she was told, but she did not really listen either, as she got onto the next plane to the Congo. Although it was probably only the next day, it was too late. He had been killed when a mortar shell or bullets exploded near him. (I cannot remember exactly where he was). She took his body home with her. Mam 'Khize was well acquainted with grief and suffering.

The Congo

Let us recapitulate briefly: In the course of the so-called decolonization of Africa the Belgian Congo was to be given its independence in 1960. At once two power blocs were formed in the new nation. On one side there was Patrice Lumumba, "a gin-drinking, pot-smoking communist rowdy whom Khrushchev called a great African leader." Opposite him was the Moïse Tshombe group, firmly anti-communist and an ardent champion of the free market economy.

When Belgian officers were forced to leave the army and the country under pressure from Lumumba, the army went on a spree of looting, rape and murder. The European inhabitants fled in sheer terror, leaving behind everything that they had worked for over the years. Tshombe asked America for help to keep Lumumba's red hordes in check. But Washington refused to help and told him to apply to the UNO for a solution to the problem. On 14 July 1960 the Security Council of the United Nations resolved to send some troops – with the assent of America and Russia – in support of ... Lumumba!

In his book *Die Herrscher* (p. 1 69) (English title: *The Fourth Reich of the Rich*), Des Griffin writes:

"In less than a week thousands of UNO soldiers streamed into Central Africa. Belgium withdrew its troops immediately and thus handed over the Congo to the dubious mercies of Lumumba's plundering mob and the 'peace troops' of the UN.

These last did little or nothing to help those who really needed help and to restore tranquillity and order. Most of the time they looked on inertly as the country was devastated and got more and more under communist control".

That was no doubt also the intention of the UNO strategists, as is clear from what followed. In this situation of chaos and naked anarchy Moïse Tshombe could see no other way than to break away from the communist-controlled central government and declare the independence of Katanga Province. With Belgian help he restored peace and order, and normality returned to life in Katanga.

In the words of his Minister of the Interior, Katanga should become "a bastion of anticommunism in Africa." His fateful words: "I detest communism, and I shall never change my attitude" must have so enraged the "peace-loving" UN Supreme Command that soon afterwards they attacked Katanga with UN forces.

As Des Griffin writes (p. 170):

"After initial reverses the Katangese troops struck back and foiled greater successes by the 'peace troops'. Frustrated by their failures, the UNO soldiers started a terror campaign against the Katangese civilian population. Murder, arson, rape and looting were the order of the day. Ninety per cent of the houses destroyed by UNO bombs were civilian buildings. Astonishingly, the Katangese held the UNO barbarians in check and staved off capitulation from their new homeland".

Griffin continues: "A year later a 'top secret' memorandum of UNO got into the hands of the American Committee for the Support of the Katanga Freedom Fighters. It contained a detailed plan for a second decisive blow against the anti-communist province. It also said 'As in the past the United States will consider itself bound by UN resolutions to make available the necessary transport aircraft, and later helicopters ... The State Department bases its policies on the UN and will by no means neglect its commitments to the UN'".

On p. 171 he tells us that "on 29 December 1962 the 'peace' barbarians of the UN, fully equipped with American dollars and war material, attacked freedom-loving Katanga for the second time. A month later, when the invaders stormed its last bulwark, Moïse Tshombe said to his brave troops: 'For the last two-and-a-half years you have twice fought heroically against the enemy. Now their superiority has become overwhelming.' Soon after the last flickering hope of independence and freedom in the Congo died".

A few more examples of what the use of UN "peace forces" meant in practice should suffice to illustrate the wickedness and hypocrisy of this organization, which had been sold to the world as "the last hope of humanity" and which Pope Paul VI had declared to be the reflection of the Kingdom of God on earth.

When Katanga was attacked in 1961 and American Globemaster transports landed UN troops complete with armoured vehicles and artillery in the heart of Elizabethville, they immediately began to shoot up everything that appeared in front of their muzzles, such as the Lubumbashi Hospital (including doctors, nurses and patients), churches, shops, offices, schools and private houses.

On 12 December 1961, Smith Hempstone, African correspondent to the Chicago News, reported from Elizabethville:

"A man pulled up in front of the Grand Hotel Leopold II, where we were staying. 'Look at the work of the American criminals,' sobbed the Belgian driver, 'take a picture, and send it back to Kennedy.' In the back seat, his eyes glazed with shock, sat a wounded African man cradling in his arms the body of his ten-year-old son. The child's face and belly had been smashed to a jelly by United Nations' mortar fragments".

In his book The Fearful Master G. Edward Griffin writes that 46 civilian doctors of Elizabethville issued a joint report of the United Nations' actions against Katanga, which included the following account of the December 12, 1961 UN bombing of the Shinkolobwe Hospital.

The doctors wrote: "The Shinkolobwe Hospital is *visibly marked with an enormous red cross on the roof* of the administrative pavilion. At about 8 a.m. two aeroplanes of the United Nations flew over the hospital twice at very low altitude. At about 9.30 a.m. the aeroplanes started machine-gunning the market square, then the school, and then the hospital, in which there were about 300 patients and their families. In the maternity section the roof, ceilings, walls, beds, tables and chairs were riddled with bullets".

"A bomb exploded in another pavilion ... the roof, the ceiling, half of the walls and half of the furniture had been blasted and shattered. The blood from the wounded makes the building look like a battlefield. In the maternity ward, four Katangan women who had just given birth, one newly born and a child four years of age, were killed".

One Professor Ernest van den Hague made a personal visit to the Congo to witness at first hand the events and conditions there. Commenting on the United Nations' statement that the only civilians wounded in Katanga were combatants in the resistance, he said: "It is hard to speak, as I did, with a mother whose husband was killed at home, in her presence, with bayonets by UN soldiers. She was in the hospital to help take care of other six-year-old, who was also severely wounded by United Nations' bayonets. A child's bayonet wounds are hardly due to having been suspected of being a mercenary combatant" (*South African Opinion*, September. 1978, p. 67).

If we were to list all the horror-stories about the UN forces in the Congo, Korea and other places they would fill hundreds of pages. The Western mass-media, which in the ordinary way of things gladly seize every opportunity to gratify the sensational appetites of their readers, scarcely breathed a word about such things.[96]

The reasons why the communists enthusiastically supported the UNO from its inception can be found in a brochure printed in September 1945 under the title The United Nations and circulated by the communists. It clearly shows what the purpose of the organization was. To anticipate somewhat: its purpose was certainly not the maintenance of peace! The brochure states: "It (the UNO) purports to put an end to wars; but ... as everybody knows, it will be possible to end wars only when the capitalist system is got rid of".

It then goes on to say that there are three main reasons why communists should support the United Nations:

---

[96] I encounter this all the time in conversations – people telling me, "Oh, but the media never told us that". Go figure!

1. The right of veto would protect the USSR against the rest of the world.
2. The UNO would be able to frustrate any co-ordinated foreign policy of the principal Western powers.
3. The UNO is a particularly useful instrument for the breaking-up of non-communist colonial empires.
4. The UNO would gradually bring about the fusion of all the countries in the world into one single soviet system.

It would hardly be possible to be more explicit.

Since it is indisputable that it was the Rockefeller clan that donated the plot of ground by the Hudson River for the administrative palace of the "Red World Parliament", and America has been bearing most of its costs ever since the organization has been in existence, we must deduce from that that the goals of international communism and those of high finance and the American governments since 1945 have been identical. In their joint drive for control of the world they both make use of the UNO as an instrument for their covert plans (Vaque 1989).

Mam M'Khize remained in Mozambique and got involved with the growing political storm there. "Ingi, I danced with Samora Machel"! As the revolution hit Lourenço Marques, it became extremely dangerous to remain in the country, and the South African Airways (SAA) sent several flights to collect the last South Africans still living there, and to bring them to safety. They literally had to pry her away from the operating theatres. She only managed to grab her toothbrush and passport before boarding the plane.

After leaving Mozambique, she became a private nurse to French Mauritians in Westville (Natal). She had to relearn Zulu, her mother tongue, as well as the Zulu culture and customs. She had become far too European for her own people, and it was a difficult time for her. When she went home to the Valley of the Thousand Hills to visit her ageing parents, she had to take taxis.[97] From her stop, she still had to walk a few kilometres before she reached home.

The election period was very dangerous time for all African travellers. There were strikes and people were killed for trying to get to work. Mam 'Khize would leave her home about 2 am in the morning, walking all the back pathways through the tall grass to avoid being seen, until reaching relative safety, where she was able to catch a rogue taxi. She often did not arrive in Westville before mid-morning. Sometimes, she would be binding up the wounded along the way. I suspect that this saved her life more than once.

> So, let us be wary of swallowing the specious reasons for the present campaign against South Africa: they are entirely bogus. South Africa is only one of the battlefields of this century in a war that all the Western nations are engaged in. The forces of the world revolution are sapping away surreptitiously from both sides of the Iron Curtain, which is why their activities are so effective and so dangerous.
>
> That is also why Joe Slovo, a Colonel in the Russian KGB and leader of the proscribed South African Communist Party (SACP), has such complete freedom of movement in the West; why the terrorists of the African National Congress (ANC) are trained and armed by communist states while being allowed openly to have offices and accommodation in the Western capitals; and why the red carpet is unrolled for Oliver Tambo, leader

---

[97] South African taxis are a law unto themselves: a Toyota Hi-Ace that is packed to the rafters.

of the ANC, when he is received with honour by high government officials.

That is why the savage punishment of the fiery "necklace" inflicted by the ANC on innocent blacks in South Africa does not deter the leading newspapers in the Western world from honouring Winnie Mandela (the wife of the imprisoned communist leader Nelson Mandela) as a heroine, although she has publicly expressed her whole-hearted approval of that incredibly atrocious form of murder. ("With our matches and our necklaces, we shall liberate this country"!)

That is why Archbishop Desmond Tutu, Dr Allan Boesak, Dr, Beyers Naudé and other South African clergymen, who make no bones about displaying their sympathies with Marxist terrorist "liberation movements" and preaching sermons under red hammer-and-sickle flags, are hero-worshipped in the West and even honoured (like Tutu) with the Nobel Peace Prize.

These heroes, the darlings of the liberals and the Western press, command little respect within South Africa itself; opinion polls show that they are entirely unknown to most black South Africans. Yet abroad they set themselves up as spokesmen for the "oppressed black masses.

That is why the SWAPO and ANC bombers and mass-murderers are not instantly arrested and extradited in the West, as they would have been in earlier "normal" days, so that they could receive just punishment for their abominable deeds. Instead, they are now made welcome at the UNO and courted by Western governments, receiving instead of the gallows millions of public money, and the taxpayer who pays for all this is bamboozled into believing that these people actually do represent genuine liberation movements in Southern Africa, and as such are worthy of the sympathy and honour and esteem granted them. On top of this absurdity, the "liberators" are still consulted about the problems of the countries that they profess to represent, although they know them only at second hand, since they have mostly been in voluntary exile for decades.

By contrast, the genuinely liberal and moderate (now retired) President P.W. Botha, who introduced more costly reforms and measures in favour of the blacks than all his predecessors put together (and at the cost of much resentment by his white electorate and loss of their support) is snubbed, denounced and declared *persona non grata* by most of the Western governments; yet he was so popular among the blacks that he could walk about their townships with only a token escort and address them to thunderous applause and singing and dancing (Vaque 1989).

Mam M'Khize would tell me, "Ah, Ingi, I can tell you many things. I have them all written down in my diary. Do you know Ingi, people can just disappear without any apparent reason if they cross the wrong people. The world is like that". She remained in contact with the other twin, who hung up his priestly robes and became a doctor and lived in Canada, possibly in Quebec. One day, he pitched up out of the blue and wanted to know if she still had all her diaries. He sang her a song of getting them published overseas. She never saw hide or hair from him again and the diaries vanished. Some may say they never have existed. No: I am a witness. I saw them with my own eyes.

She spent months trying to locate him through contacts she still had overseas, but he seemed to have disappeared into the ether, never to be heard from again.

We had to plan my escape meticulously. I had been to the local magistrate's office in Pinetown and petitioned for a peace order to be granted against "him", after which the packing and moving had to happen all in one day. With Peter's permission, the children moved back into the house with the pool and our belongings were stored in the garage. I moved in with my mother, who had sold their beautiful five-bedroomed home in Dundee and moved into a two-bedroom apartment on Mariannhill Rd, next to my old school, Pinetown Convent, now known as St Dominic's. I managed to squeeze in a bed in one corner of the plethora of stuff filling the rooms. It was not an ideal situation, but it was all I had.

In order to make a little money, I took up house painting. One of my first jobs was to paint a fancy garden cottage in Kloof. The lady said the previous tenant was a heavy weed user, and she was preparing for a new tenant to move in. It was a lot of work, but in the end, I managed to do a pretty good job. At least the smell of weed was finally gone.

Mam M'Khize had insisted that I return to church, which was very difficult for me, because I had to return to the church where my in-laws and my ex-husband knew everybody. Peter's father was not only the retired main branch bank manager, but also the church treasurer and occasionally the organist. I had to eat a lot of humble pie. Mam M'Khize had insisted I go back to church. It was one of the church elders who eventually offered me a job in Durban. Once I had a stable income, Mama and company decided to move to a unit on the Bluff. At this point, I was able to move all my belongings and take over the lease of the unit in Pinetown. The block belonged to one of Mama's old friends from her youth, Dicky Baasch, who was very kind to me.

Dicky had been a very successful builder in Pinetown. While Mama was still a secretary at the school, Dicky's son, Richard, who had a brilliant mind, got hit by a car at full speed one day, as he was crossing the street. Mama, who heard the accident from her office, rushed to the scene. Richard had been flung high over the car and was lying lifeless on the tarmac. He was still alive, but unconscious. Mama managed to stabilise him before the paramedics arrived on the scene.

Richard remained in a coma for about six months. It devastated the family. His mother was a lovely, spirit-filled Christian and she prayed for her son. He survived and, after much rehabilitation, he was eventually able to walk again, with a walker or walking sticks. The brave man joined me in my matric year to study for his German examinations, and we became quite good friends.

Richard passed away in 2012, the year Willem and I migrated to Australia. He is buried along with his brother and parents in The Lutheran cemetery Hillcrest, which is a part of the church where my Gevers family built the church.

In the meantime, Peter was healing and moving on with his life too. I spent many nights babysitting the kids while he went on dates. His mother passed away, which must have been very hard for him. However, I knew something was brewing in the background and that I would never get the children back again. It terrified the life out of me. I was still struggling to survive financially, barely able to pay the rent, let alone food. I often went without food for days, just to make sure that the kids would have enough food over the weekends. I was looking down a dark abyss and could not see a way out. It would be better if I were dead.

I walked into the bedroom that fateful evening, so long ago, but I remember every detail as if it were yesterday – the fear, the desperate cries to God, begging Him to either take my life or take control of it. The Bible on my nightstand, its words burning into my mind: *Thou shalt not kill.*

This is where my BC days end, but the best is still to follow.

> "For whatever is born of God overcomes the world. And this is the victory that has overcome the world – our faith. Who is he who overcomes the world, but he who believes that Jesus is the Son of God". – I John 5 vs 4-5 NKJV

PART VI

HER NAME IS GRACE

A New Life and a New Purpose

I had already moved on and remarried, when I got a phone call from Greggie aka Mam 'Mkhize. "Ingi, Mother Teresa is coming to Pinetown. Please could you fetch me from Westville and take me to meet her"? It was something I gladly did for her. We stood in the long queue in the blazing hot sun for several hours, and sure enough, Mother Teresa, already frail and stooped, shook each hand as she moved down the line. Greggie, could not contain her excitement. I stood behind her holding her forward from the jostling crowd. Then Mother Teresa stopped, took my hand and held it with her leathery, wrinkly ones and, just for a moment, she looked deeply into my eyes. She did not say a word, seconds passed as if time had stood still, and then she moved on.

Rev. Willem Herbst and Mam M'Khize.

Eddie and Sua came to visit a week after my conversion. There was literally no food in the fridge or in the cupboards. They went to the nearest supermarket and came back laden with food. At last, I was able to tell them my story. They just smiled, looked at each other and said, "We've been praying for you"! They offered to help me to relocate to Johannesburg, where I would be able to find a good job. The salaries were also better in Johannesburg. However, I did not want to leave without the children, and I did not want to take them with me and separate them from their father. So, I stayed.

THE LEARNING DAYS

The Holy Spirit filled me with an insatiable hunger for the Word of God. Where the words used to be lifeless, they sprang to life with full meaning and understanding now. I could still feel the afterglow of the morning after that fateful night; to new light and the deep peace in my soul. I joined the Bible Study classes that the church offered on Wednesday evenings. I was like a sponge and could not get enough. There was someone else at the Bible Study who began to take notice, but I chose to ignore it.

People were ostracising me, which I could not understand. If God has forgiven you, accepted you as His own, surely it is something to rejoice! He had given me His unconditional love, but His people struggled to do so themselves.

Sometimes I got visions and prophetic dreams, which I thought everyone did. So, I did not keep quiet about it. When the word got round to the rector, I received a warning letter from the church: such epiphanies were not tolerated there; it was far too charismatic for them. As usual, I retreated into my head.

It was 1991, when I got the call to write my story. It was not an audible voice, but rather a "silent" voice in my spirit. I only started writing the book in 2024, which means that it has taken me 33 years to pen this book. I started and stopped so many times, unsure of myself and clueless of where to begin, where to get the information and what exactly to include in the manuscript.

I recall a little incident that occurred when I was at high school. I had made friends with a couple of lads, who might have been slightly too old for me, who wanted to take me out. Quite understandably, Mama would not allow me to go. Before they left, one of them turned back and said: "You are going to talk". I wondered what he meant, then he said, "You are going to be a speaker, but not in the normal sense – perhaps something religious. Wait and see".

Willem was not one for understanding the meaning of the word "No". In fact, it made him even more persistent. Eventually, I agreed go for coffee with him after Bible Study – as friends. That was all: just friends. Nothing more. Ingrid was in no mood for romance. Besides, he was far too old for me. He began to call me his *Apfelstrudelchen*,[98] because we would go to the Black Forest Restaurant, where we would order coffee and *Apfelstrudel*. What followed, can only be described as "The War of the Roses".

---

[98] *Apfelstrudel* is a traditional sweet, Viennese pastry (with an apple filling) that is particularly popular in Austria, Germany and Croatia. *Apfelstrudelchen* is the diminutive form of *Apfelstrudel*.

Another old friend, but closer to my age, began to take a little more notice. He would send me a huge bouquet of red roses to my work every Friday. Willem would counter react with proteas from the Cape and the tiniest little bouquet of red roses personally delivered. It was simply too much. So, I made a rational decision. One was a Christian and other not. One was still married and the other not. The decision was simple. Or so I thought. However, as it turned out it was the right choice. Love did not come right away for me. Instead, it grew from respect, rather than from romantic emotions.

Willem was good to me. He took the children and me to Benoni for Christmas, and we got engaged on Christmas eve. Barely a month later, on 18 January we got married.

Willem was a one-woman man and, like most men, I think he always loved his first wife. I was fine with that. We were comfortable with each other's silences. Although we had disagreements, we generally had a good time together. He supported me and steered me in the right direction. He could be an absolute pain and a comic at the same time. He loved to embarrass us in public, just to see our reactions. He was a consummate traveller, and it was not long before he arranged a family road trip, with a German family he had met through his stamp collecting hobby, through South Africa which lasted about three weeks. Not long after that, we built our home in Mariannhill Park. He designed it himself with a few hints from Ingrid. Nothing special or fancy, but comfortable. He did it, so that I could be closer to the kids.

We discovered some odd coincidences in our past. – We had lived in St. John's Court at the same time and, later also at Lunlor. His first wife's family lived next door to us in Mosely and the cottage I repainted in Kloof was meant for him.

When Peter got remarried to an Australian girl, things changed dramatically. Everything became a negotiation with barbed wire and razor blades. Willem and

I took the children for a trip to Mauritius to meet up with Willem's son there. It was such a good time.

Later, in the Spring of 1995, Willem took me on a five-week road trip through Europe. He had worked it out meticulously and called it "Tour de Herbst": a magnificent holiday, but exhausting. We arrived in München, from where we drove down to Austria, into Italy and then back up into parts of Germany – Lichtenstein and Lake Constance – and into Switzerland, exploring bits of Italy and the Swiss side of Zermatt. Down the Val d'Aosta into Italy and *Ivrea* through to the Napoleon route into France, with poppy fields making way for miles of lavender and the French Riviera.

Silently and without fanfare, spiritual things began to happen, and we got to experience the power of prayer. At Antibes, near Monaco, we had a car accident on a wet and rainy day. A French lady, who was driving way too fast for the wet roads, collided with us around a bend, and very nearly took out the guests at a street café on the opposite corner.

Willem's face got blown by the steering crash bag. His glasses broken over his nose. An ambulance was called. I scrambled to recover our documents and valuables. The rest of the luggage remained in the car.

What now? We did not know what to do and we started praying, right there in the back of the ambulance. When we arrived at the hospital, Willem was taken for X-rays. Fortunately, nothing was broken on his face or nose. The police arrived to try and ascertain what had happened, but they did not speak much English. They took down our details, including Willem's mother's maiden name Fouché, both policemen broke into huge smiles and a stream of French which we could not understand. In the end, they said we would have to report to the police station in the morning to make an official statement. Just as they were about to leave, we asked them what had happened to our luggage and where we could find the car. They pointed us to the road and told us to turn right at the "Tricolour", which we assumed was the French Flag. Willem marched off to find a phone booth and there, on the floor, he found a wad of French Francs. He was unable to get through to the South African consulate, so we started to walk down the road. Finding no flag, we turned back, realizing that the policemen were referring to a traffic light – not the French flag. About 100m up that road, we found our car in a panel shop. We were just in time to rescue our luggage.

Picture the scene. It had been a long day travelling, we were tired, dishevelled and Willem still had traces of blood on his face and clothes from the collision. Where were we to find somewhere to stay for the night? Right across the road, there was a camping site! We looked a mess, and the very chic owner looked us up and down and was not quite convinced if she should let us in. Fortunately, she relented, and we were able to pitch our tent. There we met two young South Africans, who were working on some billionaire's yacht. They gave us the directions to the police station and the EuropCar Rental company. That was not the end of the blessings, though. We met another lovely South African living in France who just happened to be at the police station too when we arrived. She spoke fluent French and helped us with the translation of our accident statement. What could have taken a long time took no more than ten minutes and we were freed of any responsibility for the accident. At the hire company, we were given an upgrade diesel Golf with a sunroof, which was far more spacious than the Fiat Punto we had been driving before the accident. And would you believe it, they needed someone to take the vehicle back to München! God is good all the time!

The next half of the tour took us all the way through Monaco, where we drove on the Grand Prix track with all the paraphernalia still out. The race had been the day before and Willem was in seventh heaven. From there, it was into Italy, as far as Rome, where we viewed one cathedral after the other, only to realise that none of them had much to do with Christ. We found candles lit for Mary but nothing for Christ. Those alcoves were empty and dark. My heart began to ache, and I knew we would have to return there one day.

We had the same experience for the rest of our tour. Looking, searching and hoping to find a glimpse of true faith, only to find there was nothing. They had everything the world could offer – antiquity, history, beauty and wealth: the lands of philosophers and academia. And yet it was all an empty shell. Nothing.

Pick Up your cross and follow Me

It happened exactly as I feared it would. The children left with Peter and his new wife to live in Australia. I fought. I fought like a raging lion. I fought at the meeting with the church and then I fought through the justice system. When the advocate (barrister) warned me not to continue for the sake of the children, the bottom fell out of my life, and I let go. Defeated.

These children were my life. It was the hardest thing I have ever had to do. It completely crushed me. My children left for the airport first thing in the morning. Thereafter on the same day, I went to attend the funeral of my grandmother who had passed away about ten days before.

It was November 1996. And the Lord asks, "Ingrid, how much do you love me?" and I answered, "Lord' with all my heart", tears of grief streaming down my face, to which He replied, "Come, follow Me"!

I have given an abbreviated version of these events – not because of dramatic effect, but because even after all this time, it is still intensely painful. And the Lord says, "Ingrid, pick up your cross and follow Me". Something went wrong with Ingrid, though. She was angry. She was bitter and filled to the gills with resentment. Layer-on-layer-on-layer of unforgiveness.

At this time, Willem was the Chief Health Inspector for the Borough of the City of Pinetown. We were navigating our way through the most turbulent time in South African political history. After the elections of 1994, Willem had to face constant and severe tension every day, as his job was in serious jeopardy. Having grown up with politics right from his fathers' knee, Willem was a highly astute political man. He became friends with many of the politicians and knew what was going on.

Willem in his office as Chief Health Inspector.

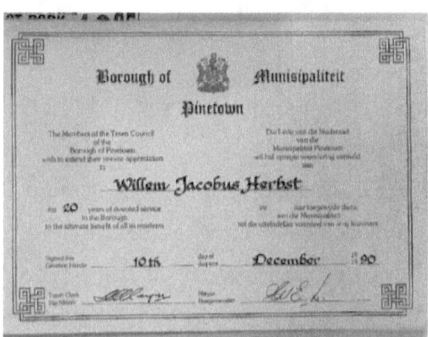

Willem's certificate of long service – 20 years at the Borough of Pinetown.

When he saw we were being 'sold down the river', as he called it, he sat up straight and squared his shoulders and wrote letters to the South African President at the time. He received a response with half-hearted promises to the first letter, which he wrote before the 1994 elections. When he wrote again after the elections, he was not quite so polite, virtually wagging his finger in their faces. "Why? What have you done"?? He did not get a response to that letter.

Few people still know that, as long ago as 1965, a plan of campaign, complete in all details, for an invasion of South

Africa was devised. Under the title *Apartheid and United Nations Collective Measures*, the Carnegie Endowment for International Peace, a tax-free American foundation, issued a 170-page document describing in explicit detail the military measures by land, sea and air necessary for an attack on South Africa, after which the country would be placed in black hands and come under the "international trustee system" of the **United Nations**.

It went into such great detail that even calculations of the probable numbers of dead and wounded on both sides were set forth. According to the *Chicago Tribune* of 24 July 1965 in its review of the report, "altogether 93,000 ground troops with air and sea support would cost 94 537 000 dollars for a thirty-day blitzkrieg".

The Carnegie Foundation report had the entire approval of the then Marxist Secretary General of the UN, U Thant. We cannot be certain whether the plan was dropped because it went too far for some of the Western delegates or whether the military planners of the UN suddenly became wary of the fighting strength of the South African forces. At any rate, the fact remains that the possibility of a direct military attack on a sovereign Western state was seriously contemplated. And it must now be obvious to even the most complacent citizen of the West how the UN proposes to "preserve" world peace.

We should also know that the disarmament programme for the super-powers – and subsequently for *all the other nations* – so assiduously advertised, has as its objective nothing less than the transfer of all the armaments systems in the world to the UN (Vaqué, 1989).

South Africa endured – one country standing alone against neighbouring countries that had been completely taken over and were ready to support whatever measures necessary. We had the Border Wars; developed our own weapons; manufactured oil from coal; and discovered large deposits of offshore gas.

However, the pincers of sanctions and boycotts crippled our economy and demoralised the population. At this point, the internal terrorist activities began with bombs, tyre necklacing, terrible intimidation campaigns – particularly in the townships. We became a country under world siege. Nothing in, nothing out.

The terror campaign in the suburbs is continuing uninterruptedly to this day. Homes have been turned into fortresses with electrified fences, razor wire fences, burglar alarms, and 24-hour armed response units patrolling the neighbourhoods. Farmers are being tortured and murdered with regular monotony. In most municipalities, the infrastructure has virtually collapsed. South Africans are still streaming into Canada, Australia, New Zealand, the UK and the USA.

In Article 43, Chapter VII of the Charter of the United Nations we read the basic "treaty law" for the establishment of an "Armed United Nations":

"All members of the United Nations, in order to contribute to the maintenance of international peace and security, undertake to make available to the Security Council, on its call and in accordance with a special agreement, or agreements, armed forces, assistance, and facilities, including rights of passage, necessary for the purpose of maintaining international peace and security".

The unavoidable logical conclusion to be drawn from Article 43 can only be that the United Nations intends to equip itself with unlimited powers to wage war.

The American Major Arch E. Roberts, in his book *Victory Denied* (p. 76) writes: "Article 43 will wipe national boundaries off the map. It will create an irresistible international army. And it will chain the peoples of the world to the wheel of a military juggernaut".

He continues: "We have now arrived at the concealed objective of the United Nations Charter. Absolute, monolithic world military power ...".

COME FOLLOW ME

One night, Willem and I were reading in bed. I had been reading the Bible and Willem was reading a commentary on the book of Hebrews by Arthur Pink. He turned around and said: "God has given me a Scripture and I think that you are right. We are being called into missions.

These are the verses from Isaiah 6:8 that God used to soften Willem's heart:

> Also I heard the voice of the Lord, saying:
> "Whom shall I send, and who will go for Us?"
> Then I said. "Here am I! Send me". – Isaiah 6:8 NKJV[99]

I turned around and showed him where I had marked the exact same verses in my own NIV,[100] several weeks before.

Once Willem makes up his mind about something, he pretty much mobilises immediately. This time his mind was made up for him. The only question was: where to? My heart already knew the answer to that question, but it took

---

[99] NKJV is the abbreviation for New King James Version
[100] NIV is the abbreviation for New International Version

Willem a few more weeks to come around. The following day, after he had been enlightened, he had me registered with a teacher in Pinetown for Italian language lessons. That was when I discovered how close Italian was to Zulu phonetically.

The Lord had been showing me much more than missions. He was opening my eyes to the "Brooding Darkness". Even before the children left, I was teaching the Std. 5 (Grade 7) learners about this brooding darkness at our Sunday School and getting them to memorise certain Scriptures. I taught them to think about and analyse everything they hear and see in the media; to recognise what is of God and what is not of God. In this way, I was trying to help them to become rooted in truth, because deception was all around. The Lord was exposing false world views and showing me how they had infiltrated almost every sphere of society.

I studied every book on Roman Catholicism I could lay my hands on. What I found, drained the blood from me. Willem was introduced to a mission's biography by Edith Schaeffer, entitled *L'Abri*,[101] which was a game changer for him. After reading that book, I went on to read almost all of Dr Francis Schaeffer's works. His writing introduced me to the world of apologetics and worldviews, and I eagerly embraced these concepts.

We began investigating various mission societies. We were fortunate that our church was missions-orientated, and Willem and I had been involved in setting up the missions week exhibition for that year. We were given much exposure to various organisations.

Our Bible Study group supported one of our own missionaries, the late Francoise Le Juge de Segrais (Anderson), who was in Paris at the time with CEF (Child Evangelism Fellowship), and Arndt and Dindy Strube from our church in

---

[101] Schaeffer, E. 1992. *L'Abri*. Crossway.

the Cape, who had gone to Burma/Myanma with the Wycliff Bible Translators. We were also a part of the missions' weekly prayer group.

For about a year, Willem served as the cook for the weekly Men's Breakfast and prayer meeting, where around 50 men gathered every Friday morning. I was involved in our care group of approximately 50 carers serving the needy in our congregation with prayer, comfort, food parcels, and visiting the sick and the bereaved, ensuring help was given in every possible situation. The lady who ran it was called Enid, but we called her Lovey. It was actually meant as a joke, because Enid could never remember anyone's name and would call everybody "Lovey". She arranged a weekly food bank for the poor in our city, a mammoth undertaking, sponsored by congregation members. It would take a large team of carers to sort and package everything ready for collection.

Another couple bought a house in Pinetown and converted it into an HIV Aids Hospice. A place where the sick and the desperate could spend their last days, while receiving loving care. It was called the Rose of Sharon House. Soon, they bought a farm to create a sanctuary for Aids babies and orphans and called it The Lily of the Valley.

Lily of the Valley – Our Story

When Lily of the Valley was established in 1993, the focus of the organisation was on palliative care for dying children. As the children were given proper medical care, nutrition and love, many recovered from their AIDS-related illnesses and their life expectancy dramatically increased.

Over the years, Lily has evolved from an organisation that was preparing children for death to one that is now preparing them for life.[102]

Later, the church denomination took over the task. Through one of my old teachers at Junior High, I got an interview on one of the local radio stations to appeal for wool donations. The result was my son's bedroom being filled to the rafters with boxes of wool donated to make blankets for the children and the babies.

In my spare time, I delivered wool all over Pinetown and the greater Durban area to ladies who had volunteered to knit or crochet squares, which were sent to another team, who used the squares to make blankets.

Even the doctors' rooms received a box of wool and needles, so that patients could knit while they were waiting for the doctor. Through the Sunday School, we made toys for the orphanage in Durban, and these were delivered to each child. We also made up a large box of gifts with a Bible verse for homeless men, who were gathering near Durban harbour at a place called "The Arc".

Remember the Old Willem Herbst? By Robyn Scott Highway Mail 4 Apr 1997

Anyone seeing Pinetown's chief health inspector, Willem Herbst, after some time would say he doesn't look the same man. He's not.

The trademark bow tie has gone, and the body is leaner and trimmer. But it is not just external appearances that have

---

[102] Consult the following website for more information on Lily of the Valley: Lily of the Valley. 2024. *Hope for 120 children.* https://childrensvillage.org.za/

changed – Willem Herbst has had a change of heart. Last week he quit his job to become a missionary in Italy.

The new Willem said he accepted the Lord in "quietness of my home one night" and now he and his wife Ingrid – both members of Christ Church Pinetown – are taking lessons in Italian and are committed to spreading the Word…

One regret about leaving Pinetown is that the couple will miss their parents and their cats.

"We haven't sold our house. We have given it to the church for their use until we need to retire. The young minister who be living in the house has promised to look after the cats and we hope they will be fine."

Although we were essentially deeply involved in missions already, we were called to do the same work somewhere else. We were accepted by OM (Operation Mobilisation) – a large dynamic international mission. At the time, OM was run by George Verwer, the founder of the mission. You had to supply your own financial support when joining. While most missionaries received donations from their home congregations, we relied on Willem's pension for support. During our absence, we provided our home to the youth pastor and our car to the OM leader in Durban.

OM – It's not about becoming a missionary. If you love Jesus, You're already His missionary.

It's about exploring new places and ways to serve the mission you are already a part of. For over 60 years, OM has been working around the world to motivate and equip Christians to share God's love. In 1957, George Verwer and two friends took a mission trip to Mexico. What began with three men who deeply desired to share God's love with those around the world who did not know it multiplied into a global movement of believers with the same passion.

Today, more than 5,000 OM workers representing 134 nationalities are serving or in partnership in over 147 countries, in addition to on board OM's ships.

We pray for people. We talk to people. We share God's love with people. We believe that you can do these things too. Our heart is to inspire you to discover and embrace God's heart for the world and to equip you with tools to help you grow, share God's love with people who don't know it and to inspire others to do the same (OM International 2024).

OM Boskop Training Centre in the Old Days

Our three-months' OM training began at Boskop, outside Pretoria. It was a converted abandoned camping ground. We were exposed to harsh living conditions to prepare us for all eventualities in the mission field – even freezing showers in the middle of winter, when the gas was "supposedly" not working. Willem's introduction on arrival was to unblock the toilets for the females training staff; so much for being the Chief Health Inspector. I was roped into a group with pickaxes to dig trenches for piping. Our responses were carefully monitored at all times: were we able to humble ourselves; to dig deep into our faith and endure all things?

We were divided into groups to do the cooking on large gas rings on the concrete floor, and the fridge was a walk-in cold room. Food, which was essentially grocery items that had gone past their sell by date, was supplied by the local Pick 'n Pay. Every now and then, we found a few surprises hidden in the bags of oats. None of us got sick or died from eating "stale food".

I am reminded of the film "Wasted! The story of food waste" made by the late American celebrity chef, Anthony Bourdain, in which he exposed the lie of the sell-by date and the enormous wastage of fresh produce. It is strange that, 30–40 years ago, we all survived on crooked carrots, malformed tomatoes and no sell-by dates. We relied on good, old-fashioned common sense and honest trade. All over the world, there are people starving in First World countries, while truckloads of food never reach the markets, because it is malformed. We are wasting food while people are starving.

The dining room was completely exposed to the elements, and we were there in winter, with heavy frost and temperatures dropping to below zero. The dining area was not enclosed properly and freezing cold winds whipped through. Dishes were washed outside in large tubs. If you were fast enough, you got your dishes washed before the water went cold and slimy. We all brought our own mug, plate and cutlery from home in a tie up bag made from a dishcloth. With the exception of salads, which were made in plastic basins, food was served directly from the pots. As the training progressed complaints became less as we were exposed to missiology, dying to self, humility, long suffering and a big dose of gratitude for the food we did receive.

Early morning devotions, which were literally that – *early,* were followed by praise and worship and breakfast. The remainder of the day was devoted to lectures, which included Bible studies, prayer, missions, evangelism, cross-cultural evangelism, introduction into spiritual warfare, Muslim and Hindu evangelism, doctrine, theology, public speaking, preaching and much more. We were taught to write newsletters to our prayer support networks and churches at home, which made me wonder why so much of this content was not taught in the churches, because evangelism begins at home. We have allowed our churches to become holy huddles, shrinking year after year until they vanish entirely – one less beacon of light in the darkness.

On the practical side, we were sent on mission trips to Gazankulu and Laudium, a Muslim enclave near Johannesburg, and speaking engagements at local churches and at home. In Gazankulu, we lived in tents with the bare minimum of water and no bathroom facilities. Showers were taken in the openair, with a makeshift screen for privacy and just a mug of water. You brushed your teeth first and washed in whatever water was left over. We took turns to preach every day in a rudimentary, makeshift building. The services lasted several hours. At night, we were confronted with the drums and local witchcraft. We ministered to people who had fled war-torn Mozambique through the Kruger National Park to this vast, dry wilderness of Gazankulu. Many refugees were eaten by lions in the Kruger National Park.

On our way back to Pretoria, we stopped at a hidden army camp in a national park, where we preached to war-hardened African soldiers and mercenaries, who had been fighting in various parts of Africa and in the Border Wars. I find it hard to forget the hardness etched on their faces and their loss of hope. Yet, this was the life they had embraced. Many years later, I would see that same look on the faces and in the eyes of men incarcerated in maximum prisons. The light of their souls barely visible behind their eyes.

Christine, our leader's wife, was our counsellor. As a psyche she made sure any emotional issues and past traumas got attended to and resolved. I went to see Christine several times and I received much help from her and her husband, Marius. We were warned what could happen to us on the mission field; particularly the spiritual warfare we would encounter. *The enemy always strikes where you are weakest.*

We soon started our preparation for the long trip to Europe. When the Italian Consulate in Pretoria heard about our intention to minister in Italy, we were invited to meet with him in his home in Pretoria. When you step out in faith, God truly provides and opens doors. We were unprepared for the large crowd that had gathered in his home. It turned out that he and his family were converted in South Africa from Catholicism and joined a large, vibrant church here. They were excited that there were people willing to go to Italy. He personally ensured our documents and visas were sorted out without any hiccups.

On another occasion, we discovered a small church 'Christ Church' in Benoni, not too far from where my brother lived, where we were welcomed and prayed for. Rev. Potgieter was so friendly and invited us up to give our testimony. We were immediately embraced by this lovely church. One of the congregation members, who was thrilled to assist us financially, also gave us the name for our newsletter – *Willing*. Created by joining the first half of our names together, the newsletter title demonstrated that we were ready and "willing" to follow and lay down our lives if necessary.

Before returning to Pinetown to say our goodbyes, our family in Johannesburg gathered many of our cousins at Phyl and Maurice's house for a BBQ. It is so sad to think that six of my cousins, including Eddie's first wife Sua and now Willem, are no longer with us. It was the last time we all met together like that. A very special farewell.

Back in Pinetown, Willem and I made final medical appointments to ensure nothing would stand in our way. Willem was given sufficient medication for his diabetes, and I went to see my gynaecologist in Westville. For the last few years, I had been struggling with pre-cancer symptoms of the cervix. Laser treatment against those cells did not help and the condition was being closely monitored. I told the doctor that I was leaving for Europe in a couple of weeks and was there for a final check-up.

He wanted to book me in for a full hysterectomy immediately, but there was no way I could allow that. I would not be able to travel so soon after major surgery. No, no, no. no! That was simply not an option. Right then, I felt a wave of heat from the top of my head, right down to the soles of my feet. I was enveloped in the Lord's peace, and I knew immediately that I had made the right decision.

The doctor agreed reluctantly to let me go only on the provisor to do a final pap smear, he would only give me the go-ahead if the results were clear. Praise God they were! The results came back completely clear. No trace of cancerous cells – all gone!! Our God reigns!! I have kept this story to myself for many, many years and only recently began to share it. With many of my family having suffered from cancer, I did not think it was appropriate. Now let it be known, Jesus heals today, just as he did while He was on earth, more than two thousand years ago. All glory, honour and praise belong to Him. That is my King!

> And the whole multitude sought to touch Him, for power went out from Him and healed *them all.* (Luke 6:19 NKJV)

OM ITALY VIA HOLLAND

OM South Africa made a block booking with Turkish Airways and, after a celebratory farewell dinner at a fancy restaurant serving wonderful food, the whole team boarded the aircraft in Johannesburg. However, the flight remained grounded due to a technical fault, which took ages to sort out, but eventually we were airborne. Due to the delay, we missed our connecting flight from Istanbul to Schiphol Airport in Amsterdam.

We were on our way to the annual OM missions conference, which was held at the De Bronn Conference Centre just north of Zwolle. We were ferried in small groups, some via Frankfurt and others directly to Amsterdam, as they found empty seats. In Amsterdam, we had to wait for everyone to arrive and for the bus to return from Zwolle to collect us. By the time we arrived at the conference, my feet had swollen like balloons. I was rushed to the camp doctor, where I was checked for an aneurysm, before he prescribed medication to drain the excess fluid from my legs and feet.

After meeting missionaries from all over the world, it was time to meet up with the Italian leaders and to undergo a final assessment. What a joy it was to hear nearly a thousand voices singing at full throttle, no holding back. I imagine that is what heaven will be like – a multitude lifting their voices in praise.

The conference lasted an entire week. OM is also a famous book distributor via the missions' ships – their own floating libraries – and when we were not attending talks, we were looking for books at the large OM book exhibition.

Willem and I realised that we were not going to have free access to English literature where we were going. We found a much-advertised book by George Verwer, written by Charles Colson. Charles Colson was the founder of *Prison Fellowship* in the United States and came to know the Lord through the work and ministry of RC Sproul, another of my favourite authors. Charles was the USA Attorney General and found himself in prison after the Watergate debacle. We loaded ourselves up with books and discovered later at the airport that we had too much. Again, the Lord intervened, and we were able to take the whole lot with us without paying a cent for extra luggage.

There are two dates which almost everyone remembers: Princess Diana's death (31 August 1997) and the attack on the Twin Towers (11 September 2011). Willem and I were listening to the radio in our room when we heard the bad news. The conference was abuzz with it – Princess Diana was dead.

We arrived at the Torino Airport on 6 September 1997. It was my daughter's birthday. We phoned her from Schipol airport first thing in the morning after sleeping overnight on the airport benches. We made it our business to phone our families regularly. We did not have long conversations; the idea was just to let them know that we cared and that we loved them. Anna and Sergio took us directly to their home in the little village of Chiaverano, where we were given a good lunch. Later, Sergio dropped us off at our new residence on Via Torino, conveniently located just across the road from the Italian OM National Office.

A little further down the road stood the small *Waldensian Church* of Ivrea, which was part of the Protestant denomination that, like the Huguenots, had endured persecution in medieval times. Ivrea is in Piemonte, the southern Alpine region where this little protestant community was brutally persecuted so very long ago; and the same village we drove through on our way to France and the Riviera in 1995. In fact, Catholic persecution of the Protestants in the area continued sporadically for some time; it is said for up 50 years ago. Anna's father, who was in his early nineties when we met him, had a deep indentation in his skull from where he had been physically assaulted with a blunt object.

In 1933, 32-year-old Adriano Olivetti took over as general manager of the typewriter factory his father had founded outside of the picturesque Italian town of Ivrea, in the foothills of the Alps.

> At the time, it was a small family business. But, in the next 30 years under Adriano, the Olivetti company would become a global phenomenon, and Ivrea the focus of ambitious experiments in how to build what he called a more "human" industrial city.
>
> "The street, the factory, the house are the most substantial and visible elements of a civilisation in evolution," Olivetti argued in his book *Citta dell'Uomo (City of Man)*. He complained that Italy's cities had been expanding "incoherently for uniquely selfish goals, materialistic, speculative, without a real plan coming from a general vision of life".
>
> Published in January 1960, just weeks before he died, it called for urban development "on a human scale", with the goal being "harmony between private life and public life, between

work and the home, between centres of consumption and centres of production".

By then Olivetti had become a massive company, with factories in five countries and distribution in more than 100. Best known for its stylish, portable typewriters, beloved by writers from John Updike to Cormac McCarthy, its machines were already considered icons of postwar Italian design.

And Ivrea had been transformed. From a small provincial town, it became a major hub of Italian manufacturing, attracting engineers, designers and factory workers from across the country. By the late 1950s, there were more than 14,000 people working for Olivetti in Italy, most of whom were in Ivrea. Between the 1930s and 1960s, the town's population roughly doubled, from around 15,000 to 30,000, with many more in the surrounding areas.

Olivetti hired Italy's leading architects to design blocks of flats with no more than four storeys.

(Source: https://www.theguardian.com/cities/2016/apr/13/story-cities-21-adriano-olivetti-ivrea-italy-typewriter-factory-human-city)

Ivrea was filled with bright, avant-garde architecture. Hiring some of the country's leading architects, Olivetti built new neighbourhoods for its workers, carefully planned with abundant green space and small blocks of flats with just three or four storeys.

New factory buildings were erected almost entirely of glass, because workers inside "had to be able to see the mountains, the valleys, where they come from ... and also so that people outside the factory could see what was happening inside," explains Beniamino de Liguori, Olivetti's grandson.

"All the factories and the places of private production were absolutely integrated into the urban fabric of the city," De Liguori says. He described his grandfather's goal as nothing less than finding a way "to combine and to harmonise man and machine ... to use technology in a human way, because it was really at the service of man".

Inside the factories, workers were paid more and conditions were better than at other companies at the time, says Federico Bellono, a representative at the Fiom Metalworkers Trade Union. "Then there was this system of services that was more structured than elsewhere".

Olivetti's new factories were designed with in-built space for cafeterias, playgrounds, rooms for debates and film screenings, and libraries with tens of thousands of books and magazines. Outside, an extended network of social services was constructed including nursery schools, Ivrea's first hospital, and mountaintop retreats for workers' children.

Olivetti also helped finance the first masterplans for the city and surrounding area. In 1959 a new plan for Ivrea was approved, organising it into a network of integrated residential areas and proposing a ring road, a new bridge over the river

Dora, extensive and decentralised industrial expansion, and the renewal of the historic centre.

"From the 1930s until he died in the 1960s ... [Olivetti] said that to organise the city you have to plan it," says Patrizia Bonifazio, professor of urban planning at the Politecnico di Milano. "The factory economically supported the studies and the urban planning proposals, but these were never confined exclusively to the interests of the factory; they always concerned the city in general".

In the late 19th and early 20th centuries, thousands of small towns and cities across Europe and North America were transformed by industrialisation. Along with the archetypal, exploitative "company town", there were also a number of experiments in more benevolent developments such as Bournville in the UK, near Birmingham, built by the Cadbury family of Quakers as a "model village".

For Olivetti, urban planning was part of a broader political project. In the late 1940s he founded a new party called Movimento Comunità (Community Movement) and was elected mayor of Ivrea in 1956. Two years later he became a member of parliament in the national government.

He argued that Italian politics should be fundamentally restructured around a federation of relatively autonomous municipalities, or "communities". The ideal community, he said, would have between 75,000 and 150,000 inhabitants.

"The giant factories, the overcrowded metropolises, the centralised and monolithic states, the mass parties ... are without a doubt the leviathans of our time, also destined to disappear to leave room for forms of life that are more agile, more harmonious and, in one word, more human," Olivetti concluded in *Citta dell'Uomo* (*The Story of cities*): Olivetti tries to build the ideal 'human city' for its workers" (*The Guardian* – Europe.

This is the company for which my cousin, Linda Dinkelmann, worked. She was flown to the USA and collected by limousine from the airport to the awards functions.

When he first started in Ivrea after the war, Olivetti built apartment blocks for his factory workers. We rented one of these, a very comfortable one-bedroom unit for which we paid extra every month. The little Brethren Church, which was tucked away in the medieval part of town, supplied everything we needed and filled the little bar fridge to overflowing. This South African had to learn to use a gas stove, gas oven and to clean white ceramic floor tiles throughout. To this day, I cannot understand the attraction to white floors.

Nini and Paulo came to visit us at the office. They lived in Chiaverano too. They were a beautiful couple, who came to encourage us and to teach us the rudimentary bits of Italian before starting our proper language lessons with another teacher at the local school. They shared their remarkable story with us.

Paulo lost his eyesight while he was still quite young. Apart from reading brail, he also had special computer programs that helped him. He found a job as a switchboard operator at Olivetti in Ivrea. Through his day-to-day work, he got to know a lady, Nini, on the other end of the line working for Olivetti in Naples. Nini was a remarkable woman and the two of them really began to hit it off. Soon they made arrangements to meet up in Rome. This was no problem for Paulo, as he had researched the timetables and the change of trains at various stations along the way. He caught the bus to the station in Ivrea from Chiaverano and off he went.

Since neither of them knew what the other one looked like, they arranged to wear a red rose each, which is actually rather funny, given that Paulo is blind.

It is therefore no surprise that Nini found him first and, when she discovered that he was blind, she did not skip a beat; she just carried on. This beautiful and brave couple got married and Nini came to live with Paolo in Chiaverano.

Before anyone could protest, they decided to tour Italy by motorbike with a side car. And they had the time of their lives. Nini drove and explained every detail that she saw to Paulo. She was his eyes. He literally saw the world through her eyes.

Nini took me, Willem and Rada, another team member, to Cervino on the Italian side of the Matterhorn. She would stop and take his hand and trace the skyline of the Alps, giving the name and a description of each peak. They must have done this a few times before, because he could tell us where we were and what mountains we were passing.

Instead of going all the way to Cervino, we ducked down a little side road to a tiny alpine village called Bramsc. From there, we walked to a restaurant, tucked away behind huge boulders. We enjoyed an excellent polenta and dessert before taking a long walk into the hills. After about 500m, we came across a group of friends engaged in an outdoor game, the kind of which we had never seen before. Something that is made up in a remote area that only the locals know.

Life reveals the most extraordinary people, if we open our eyes and our hearts to connect with them.

Another Introduction into Prison Ministry

Willem was given his own office and put in charge of distributing tracts nationwide to participating Italian prisons and evangelists. OM Italy printed the tracts in Torino after translating them from German to Italian. They originated from Switzerland. When Willem received a response from the prisoners, he would send them a Bible and a book on the Gospel that had been translated from English into Italian. I was supposed to assist Anna with the day-to-day office work, but there was one problem – Anna was doing everything herself. She could not let go.

This lovely couple suffered so intensely from perfectionism that they could not see how their obsession was destroying the team spirit. The evangelism team in Chiaverano took much strain too. I think our leaders wanted to impress their peers in the village, thereby putting enormous stress on themselves.

Today, I can see things in a more objective light, but at the time, it was difficult for me. It felt as if we were walking on eggshells. I am sad to say that the spirit of disharmony and growing tension were creating obstacles to our unity. These challenges were complicated even further by conflicting spiritual beliefs and practices, and spiritual warfare. The enemy always strikes where we are weakest.

One of our highlights was the Italian lessons for foreigners at the local school in the evenings, where we met people from all over the world, including a Chinese doctor. This was where we could discuss the Gospel in a relaxed and friendly atmosphere, and we made many friends along the way.

Every year, villages all around Italy celebrate their patron saint's day. Ivrea exploded into a light display that lasted hours. A procession of various floats paraded around the streets, including effigies of their saint and floats with esoteric symbolism. I stood in the crowd and started to pray earnestly. Music was blaring and many young men were getting drunk. Suddenly, a beautiful lady in front of me turned around and looked straight into my eyes. Her face was hard and her eyes dark and cold. Without opening her mouth, she spoke into my mind: "Stop what you are doing. We know who you are, and we will destroy you". The menacing message, which revealed abilities that I had underestimated, chilled me to the bone, leaving me shaken. I started paying more attention to my surroundings and I saw all the trappings of witchcraft being sold in the market squares and in the New Age stores. Satanism thrives behind Roman Catholicism. Although we had some training, it was woefully inept to fight what we were facing. I only realised later that our team – and particularly our leaders – were under severe spiritual attack. They were trying to destroy the team, like they did a few years before. I had to let go of all the pent-up offence. Torino is or was one of the main centers of Satanism in Southern Europe.

Two young girls from Pretoria, who were friends of the Consulate, came to visit us. When they saw what was happening, they covered us for a brief period in prayer. Prayer is particularly important in situations like this. This is why the newsletters are so important to get as many people as possible to pray.

Sundays were always mapped out for us to encourage the local church. The church we were assigned to was very small, with no more than ten or fifteen families and about three children. Willem and I would walk to church, about 4 km, in rain hail or snow. Ladies were required to wear dresses to church.

These South Africans were poorly equipped for the European winters on the foothills of the Alps. Everyone in the congregation chipped in and donated winter clothing for us. They were such a wonderful people.

Anna's father could take it no longer that I did not have any stockings and bought me a handful of exquisite French black stockings for my freezing legs!

We were always – *always* being the keyword – invited to lunch with the Bertocci family, right after church. We got to call them Mama and Papa Bertocco. We became their family and, even if they were invited to lunch somewhere else, we were always included in the invitation. They often invited Mark and Litizia too. They lived in a three-story villa on the outskirts of Ivrea in a village called Borgofranco. Mama and Papa lived on the ground floor. Franca, their daughter in the apartment on the second floor. The third floor was rented out to a family from Iran, who sold Persian carpets.

Gino Bertocco drove as though he was being chased, hurtling through the ancient, cobbled stone lanes, taking tight corners at the speed of light. We always arrived at their beautiful home somewhat relieved to be alive. Gino was well known by the local Carabinieri after several accidents. Lunch was a lavish affair, served in the salon. Their loving kindness radiated as naturally as their hospitality. Lunch lasted all afternoon and, if it was getting late, more wine came from the cellar, followed by a light snack for dinner.

It was here that I picked up most of the language, as well as an insatiable love for true Italian cuisine. Antoinetta's food was amazing. She made all her own liquors and pasta, as well as all baked goods, including confectionery. Antoinetta was truly an excellent cook!

We were driven into the mountains, where we set off with baskets to collect fungi. Unfortunately, we did not find any porcini mushrooms that day, but we had an absolute feast with the mushrooms the following day for lunch. Papa picked through them with a well-seasoned eye to remove all those that might be poisonous.

Antoinetta preserved the mushrooms that were left over in jars of olive oil *(sott' olio)*, placing them in the large chest freezer in the cellar. The locals are very protective of their porcini patch. Any invader was dealt with *pronto* (promptly), and having your tyres slashed was the least of your worries: it could be much worse!

In the Spring we had days of collecting *Frutti di Bosco*, which are tiny, wild strawberries that pack a flavour punch like no other, and wild arugula.[103]

On another occasion, we were taken out for lunch on a little farm near Andrate, where there were lovely vineyards and a villa from the Middle Ages undergoing much needed restoration. There must have been a plumbing issue, as all the men were gathered around, giving advice without doing much other than gesticulating wildly with both arms. Very typically Italian.

Because of whipping cold winds that day, lunch was served in the cellar underneath beautiful Gothic arches at a large table so heavy that ten men would

---

[103] Wild arugula, which grows freely across the Italian countryside, is a herb that resembles rocket.

be required to lift it. The table was laid with a blue gingham cloth and laden with olives, country sour dough bread, freshly sliced *salme* (salami/cold meats) and bottles of their finest red wines, which were brought out of an alcove tucked away in a corner. This was followed by the pasta, which the lady of the manor was preparing by hand when we first arrived. Parmesan cheese was grated at the table. Once the Primo was dispatched, the grilled meats were served with salads. We were at least ten altogether that day, and it was a true feast. After copious glasses of red wine and a magnificent lunch, their son then took us for a drive to Andrate, at high speed through the narrowest of spaces and hairpin bends. While the others climbed up the radio tower to get a better look at the view, Antoinetta and I collected *castagne* (chestnuts) for our lovely hosts. On our return, I watched the couple making a risotto with fresh porcini, which was to die for, while they were giving explicit instructions as to what makes the very best risotto.

Over time, I began to recognise the relentless pursuit of perfection of the Italian culture. The main difference between perfectionism and excellence is that their roots are in two different kingdoms. Perfectionism in the hands of Marxist or Socialist ideology can be very cold and judgmental whereas excellence as practiced through 1 Corinthians 12 & 13 is tempered by kindness and goodness. In Africa, we did not struggle with perfectionism so much.

In South Africa, we were not fighting one another, but rather a Marxist ideology to which many had been duped since the early days of colonisation. Basic survival was at stake, there was no time and little energy for judging others against your own standards.

Our faith was deepened by adversity and prayer – particularly corporate prayer – revived in increasing numbers. Our trust in the "vertical life" intensified, and we called on the Most High God to come to our rescue. As time went by, you can see things from a bird's eye view, but while you are in ground zero it is often difficult to distinguish. Although I had done a considerable amount of research before we arrived, I heard only a little of Babylon and the Mystery Religions and the influence they had and were still holding in the world. A good reference here is a book by Johnathan Kahn 'The Return of the God's'. We are living at a time where younger generations no longer have a cultural Christian worldview. We are living in a post Christian era.

In Italy, numerous people in the church were voting for communism, given the fact that the opposition parties were not offering them anything better. They were strongly influenced by unions and socialism, which was evident through the work and life of Benito Mussolini (1883–1945), the leader of the Fascist Party and dictator in Italy during the course of World War II.

Around us, entire regions were still in bitter conflict with one another. They did not understand, or fully understand, the spiritual implications attached to it. As in most western countries, Christian parliamentarians and parties were small and without influence. They did not have the financial backing of other parties. And we all know where that came from. In this way, many across the world are caught in the Valley of Indecision. Many can see the Brooding Darkness, but they have not associated it with the Beast Kingdom as yet.

I was in a prayer meeting with a dear prayer partner yesterday. She referred me to the film *The Matrix* and the red pill and the blue pill from which you have to choose. I had seen that film a long time ago. As she revealed what she had learned, I was reminded of the Garden of Eden and the Tree of Life and the Tree of the Knowledge of Good and Evil. Since the beginning of time, we have been given a choice: choose Life or choose Death. Choosing one tree leads to eternal life and choosing the other leads to the promise of eternal death, disguised in riches and power untold, while you are on the physical plane.

> Gnostics follow the eastern pagan idea of *perfection* [author's emphasis], which is the <u>undifferentiated</u> unity of all things. Many Gnostic myths speak of an original androgynous human

being. This is the ideal because the original catastrophe was not human sin producing the fall, but it was the beginning of differentiation. This differentiation manifested itself firstly in the separation of male and female. [can you see where mankind is going]. Gnostic influence reduced faith to the interior, the personal and the subjective. The rejection of the external and fixed sound doctrinal formulations and the authority of the church resulted in believers floating in a sea of relativity.

When the subjective is elevated to the level of the absolute and the external God-ordained authority of the church cast off or denigrated, the Bible can easily be misused and misappropriated and those who are most forceful can manipulate others on the basis of personal "revelations".

In the true Biblical perspective, *we* are not the meaning of the story. The creation story begins with the transcendent creator who brings creation and time into being. Our existence, our beginning is part of a far larger story, and we need to find the meaning of our existence outside of ourselves" [In Him]. (Doveton 2010).

Jesus said to him, "I am the way, and the truth, and the life. No one comes to the Father except through me …"(John 14:6: NKJV).

The Illuminists and, in turn, all Free Masonry and, therefore Marxist ideology, have adopted all the mysteries into their agenda. Deceived themselves they too are only puppets on a string. In the meantime, they scatter death and destruction before them, thereby contributing to the ruin of mankind, the results of which we are experiencing right now.

Willem and I were fortunate enough to lead a small group of Italian teenagers to Teen Street[104] in Wolfsburg Germany. We were basically there to support the group, all of whom were from Mirano, north of the Veneto, towards the Austrian border, where both Italian and German are spoken.

Three other adults accompanied us and arranged the transport – the parents of a teenager and a missionary from TEAM, originally from Canada. Willem and I travelled by train across Italy, arriving in Mirano in the late afternoon.

That night we were given accommodation with a participating family, before setting off to Germany early in the following morning, picking up teens as we went. Wolfsburg is the capitol of Volkswagen and located in the North-east of Germany.

It was a long drive, particularly with hyperactive teens. One in particular grabbed my attention. I shall call him the "crown", as he had spiked his hair to look like a crown. He was a real character – tall and slender, with blond hair and blue eyes. Those blue eyes held the haunted look of pain and, as we went along, I established that he had his issues.

The conference was directed at teenagers all over the world, but mainly from Europe, giving them exposure to Kingdom Living on a large scale. All the teenagers roughed it on hard floors or tents, while Willem and I were given a classroom with no mattresses. By the end of the week, every bone in our bodies was aching. Willem was a big "hit" with the boys and he even began teaching rugby – a sport with which he had been involved since his school days. He also played on college level and semi-provincial level in the Northern Cape, and later he played club rugby in Pinetown. There was also a soccer tournament, and our little Italian team did very well. All and all, Teen Street was a great experience for us.

---

[104] Teen Street is a week-long, international conference for Christian teenagers, organised and presented by Operation Mobilisation (OM).

As Willem and I did not have our own transport in Italy, shopping involved a bus trip to the supermarket situated slightly out of town. If we missed the last bus back to Ivrea, we would have to walk the entire way with packages of groceries. A lovely young couple from church took pity on us and collected us every second week. Antonio worked as a prison guard at the local goal. We had numerous long conversations with him, encouraging him to put his faith in action with evangelism. Eventually, I wrote to Prison Fellowship in the USA, requesting assistance. However, at that point, none was available for Italy.

Not long after returning from Teen Street in Germany, our leaders were asked to arrange the Italian delegation of young adults and students to an international mission conference in Zuidlaren in Holland, right up near the North Sea. This was a far larger undertaking than Teen Street, and Sergio and Anna were slightly stressed. The scope of this conference was enormous and the advertising extensive throughout all the churches and universities in Italy, from Sicily to Aosta. The aim of the conference was to give these students exposure to international missions.

I was roped in to answer the telephone and to make all the bookings, coordinating the collection of fees and reconciling the payments. Sergio organised buses to collect the delegates from various pick-up points across Italy.

We drove with Sergio and Anna to Zuidlaren in a day and arrived before the buses. The conference organisers had arranged accommodation with a local Dutch lady for us. It was winter, just after Christmas, and the air was cold and crisp.

Willem was in charge of the Italian male delegate students, and I was in charge of the ladies. The accommodation halls teemed with people, pressed tightly together on thin mats.

The conference was attended by close to 9000 delegates, from all over the world, with a large number of mission societies exhibiting in the exhibition halls. Prominent international Christian authors and speakers were invited to present talks between services and praise and worship, which almost took the roof off. The ladies from our OM team were suffering and much tender loving care was required. Things were coming to a head. As a team, we had not realised the battle we faced spiritually, and we fell apart, emotionally exhausted. We were all at fault. We were not rooted in love and truth and we had allowed offences to get a hold of us.

Pinetown Church group visits us in Ivrea Italy. Enid van Niekerk, aka Lovey, in the orange jacket. Collected by us from Interlaken Switzerland 1998.

Willem and I resigned from OM Italy. He could no longer take the tongue lashings – a stoic man, who could normally roll with the punches, he had enough. I was devastated, because I had taken on the language and the culture and felt at home. I left a piece of my heart in Italy. It was not long before the evangelism team dismantled too. Later Mark, and Litizia relocated to Manchester England.

A NEW DIRECTION

We left Ivrea in January and returned to South Africa via London. We needed a little down-time for a few days before getting settled in Pinetown. We had no idea where we were going or what we were going to do. The missions committee from church took us under their wing. By that time our house was being leased to a church couple whom we were helping; so we did not have accommodation. We stayed with Lovey in her cottage in Kloof.

Our belongings, which we shipped over from Italy, arrived and we decided to go and see our local general practitioner (GP) for a full check-up. When he heard our story, he said, "But surely, you could open the newspaper and find another mission who would be willing to take you"? This jolted Willem into action, and he marched right across the road to the church admin offices to see our Curate at the time. Willem's thinking was: "If God can talk through the jawbone of an ass, He can surely speak through Grant". As it happened, Grant was perplexed too and suggested that we go to college in Muizenberg. He did not think for a moment that Willem was up for the challenge, but Willem was already on the phone to Cape Town. He spoke to Doc Seccombe, who also did not take him seriously, although he indicated that he would be happy to have us, if we wanted to come to Muizenberg. Doc Seccombe went back into his meeting, laughing and joking that we might be coming. He left it at that.

Muizenberg and Lavender Hill

We arrived in Muizenberg on Willem's 60th birthday. It was a Sunday afternoon, and nobody was expecting us. There was no student accommodation ready, and the house coordinator was jumping in all directions to try to get something ready for us. Eventually, everything got sorted out. After Willem had passed away, I received this letter from David Seccombe:

> Dear Ingrid,
>
> I was saddened to hear that Willem had gone to God – not that he'd gone to God, but that he had left you. Thanks for getting the news to the College.

You must be in the aftermath stage now – wondering what to do with yourself. I had not known that he was sick. I don't know how long that had been going on, but he sure managed to pack a lot into his life from the time he came to college. I don't know much about what went before – except that he married you, which wasn't bad!

He was always full of joy and positiveness; I will always have good memories of him (and a funny story). It was brave of you both to come to GWC and we did have such a good time together then. And Lavender Hill was a bold undertaking...

He closes his letter with this lovely benediction: 'May the Lord watch over you, Ingrid, as you continue your journey with Him.'

Willem was enrolled in a three-year course and, as his wife, I could do the first year for free. We both did reasonably well. Just to make things a little bit more difficult I added on an extra challenge. During the July break, I had arranged to take a group of underprivileged South African children for a first-hand experience of Teen Street 1999 in Germany. I was enthralled by the power of the Kingdom of God in the lives of young teens.

Each teen was to be nominated by their church minister, and expected to help raise funds towards their own airfare. We were a motley bunch of about eleven from all population groups and, we got along very well. Willem was not coming along this time. Instead, Rev. Dug Wannenburgh would be accompanying us as the pastoral carer of the team. ABSA Bank sponsored us with T-shirts with the view of financial backing for the following year. None of these youngsters had been overseas before, or was hoping that they would ever get there, for that matter. It was beautiful to observe the courage and joy with which they were embracing this experience.

When we arrived in Germany, we were picked up at the Stuttgart Airport by a Pastor and his son living near Mossbach, where the Operation Mobilisation (OM) headquarters were also situated. On our first night, we camped out in the church office. The following morning, we made our way to the train station to catch the train to Heidelberg, where we allowed the teenagers some time to do sightseeing and to climb up to the famous Heidelberg Castle. Later, we boarded the train onto Offenbach, which was packed with teenagers from all over Germany, to where Teen Street was being held that year.

Teen Street 2000. Group photo taken in Heidelberg Germany. Author wearing sunglasses and Rev. Dug Wannenburgh the photographer.

It was the first year that a South African team attended the conference, and the OM International leaders were particularly kind to us. Dug and I were housed in our own tents with the other leaders, while the teenagers were split into boys' and girls' accommodation, with Donnè from Pinetown and Rodney from Lavender Hill as their leaders. Both were experienced youth group leaders at their own churches.

What joy it was to see our group carry the South African flag in the opening ceremony on the first day. They threw themselves into all the activities, and Rev. Dug conducted excellent Bible Studies.

I had a chance to meet up with some of the Italian teenagers from the previous year – particularly "the crown", who was volunteering this year, with his hair now dark (no longer blonde) and well cut. We had some great talks. He was such a lovely young man, and I still hope that he would go far in life.

An entire day was set aside for fund-raising for a school in India. Since we did not have any sponsors, the international leaders sponsored our team members. The fund-raising initiative, which was held on the shores of a lake, included activities like obstacle courses and rowing. One of our young team members outdid himself and raised a significant amount for India.

The following year, Dug introduced something similar to the Crossroads CESA (Church of England in South Africa – now known as REACH) youth camp. A South African missionary took Willem's place in the rugby training, and all our boys participated. Soccer was back on the agenda as well, as were several other activities that facilitated team building and unity.

One afternoon, I took the team for a treat of German *Eis,* which is an ice cream parfait, served in huge, ornate glasses. The week passed far too fast, and soon it was time for the return trip to Mossbach, where we were given lovely rooms in the mission house. We spent the afternoon at the local park, where we discovered wading through Dr Kneipp's water therapy with the locals. I remember my grandfather promoting this in Glückstadt and my great grandmother taking ice cold baths to improve her health. The following day, we made our way back to Stuttgart and then back to South Africa.

A few weeks later, our residence coordinator at the college arranged a reunion for all the Teen Street delegates at the Newlands Rugby Stadium. What an awesome treat it was for us to walk on this hallowed field, followed by a proper South African braai.

BAD NEWS

It was the end of the first year and time for my graduation. Willem would carry on and complete the full three-year course. Then the bombshell was delivered by kind courtesy of my ex-husband. – Candice had run away from home. She made life hell for everyone at home and was given an ultimatum by her stepmother. I was shocked to the core. He could not have painted a more horrible picture. How could this beautiful, talented child have undergone such a character change? The year before they left home from South Africa, my child was the Dux learner at her school and had been offered to apply for a bursary to attend Treverton College near Mooiriver in the Natal Midlands – a prestigious school. Kloof High School also had offered her a full bursary. I found the entire situation extremely hard to believe. I was completely dazed and given no hint this storm was brewing. In the time that they had been away, they never complained.

The rug had been pulled out from under my feet, but there was no time for self-pity. Ingrid had to scramble to get to Australia as fast as humanly possible. Doc Seccombe helped by arranging funding for our girl's final year. The family pulled together. Gan decided to come along to support her grandchild, and I managed to get the funds from a trust account that was set aside for such an eventuality. Willem paid for himself. December and January flights were far too expensive, and we only managed to get to Australia in early March.

Hold Onto Me – Lauren Daigle

When the best of me is barely breathing
When I'm not somebody I believe in
Hold on to me

When I miss the light the night has stolen
When I'm slamming the doors You've opened
Hold on to me
Hold on to me

Hold on me when it's too dark to see You
When I am sure I have reached the end.
Hold on me when I forget I need You
When I let go hold me again

When I don't feel like I'm worth defending
When I'm tired of all my pretending
Hold on to me

When I start to break in desperation
Underneath the weight of expectation
Hold on to me
Hold onto me

Hold on to me when it's too dark to see You (I'll hold on)
When I am sure I have reached the end
Hold on to me when I forget I need You (I'll hold on)
When I let go, hold me again

I could rest here in Your arms forever
'Cause I know nobody loves me better
Hold on to me
Hold on to me

On arrival, we hired a car. Our amazing girl had secured a holiday rental in Redcliff for us, and we managed to negotiate some time with our son too. It was only when we started attending meetings with the headmaster, teachers and social workers at school that the whole, full story came out.

We had been told nothing but lies. In fact, the school claimed to have high hopes for her getting prestigious marks for the school, but she had been kicked in the teeth, and they could not understand how that was possible. We tried to convince her to return to South Africa with us, but she declined. We went to the immigration department to arrange this, should she agree, but it was no use. Instead, we did everything we could to help support her. We helped to get a unit of her own, with furniture and all the things she would need, praying that she would survive this. Oh, Lord, why did she not come with us?

My answer came a year later, when almost the exact same thing happened to my son. This time, we had no funds to assist, and his amazing sister took him in and they supported each other. He managed to finish school, while she worked. I have so much love, admiration and respect for these two children. I carried them through this the only way I knew how – on my knees!

Rev. Willem Herbst after his ordination in Cape Town for the Church of England in South Africa. Now known as the Reformed Evangelical Church of South Africa. Photo belongs to the author.

Even before Willem graduated, he was ordained by the Bishop Retief as the Minister of Lavender Hill Church, where we had been assigned to assist with ministry as students. The church in Lavender Hill was very poor and located on the dismal sand dunes travelling far inland from False Bay. There was no lavender in Lavender Hill – a grey community housing estate for the poorest of the poor on the Cape flats.

I had to become the breadwinner, as our little church was not able to support the pastor. By 2002, I had started working again, first as a credit controller for a company supplying fresh fruit and vegetables to shipping and the local supermarkets. Later, I worked at a large manufacturing concern near the airport in Cape Town, where they manufactured clothing for Addidas, Tommy Hilfiger, Woolworths, Edgars, etc. A modest monthly amount from our fixed investments helped pay for the rent.

We moved out of the student residence and into a beautiful apartment on Beach Road. It was an old Herbert Baker house. We lived on the top floor of this magnificent house that was owned by a lovely Jewish family now residing in Canada. We had our own grand entrance, and the view was to die for – the entire False Bay and the whales romping in the water outside our dining room window. The top floor was divided into two flats. We occupied the one-bedroom flat, with exquisite bespoke cupboards and a bathroom the size of a lounge, with a large porcelain bath in which you could drown. A spacious kitchen sealed the deal for Ingrid.

The Herbert Baker House in Muizenberg Cape Town.

Candice managed to save for her own airfare, and we paid for Chris to come over. Gan flew down from Johannesburg and we were all reunited in our tiny one-bedroom flat.

Gan and her lovely grand children in Muizenberg Cape Town.

Old Rusty was put through its paces on a road trip of the Cape – the winelands, Ceres and up the West Coast, across the Swartberg Pass with much screaming and hilarity. Then when the day came to say goodbye; it was tears all over again.

I did ministry at night, driving into Lavender Hill, which was riddled with drug lords and regular shootings. I assisted Rodney our youth leader, and helped to gather the young people, collecting them from their homes in Old Rusty and dropping them off after youth group on a Friday. I never felt unsafe except for one day when after youth, I locked up the church and had delivered the cups and juice from the evening back with Rodneys mum. Just as I was ready to start the car, (this time it was the Opel Monza), the police screeched to halt behind me, blocking me in. Our car, which had rusted down to the bones in the Durban beach air while we were in Italy, rattled in sympathy. Two policemen hemmed me in on either side and demanded to know what I was doing there. My heart was pounding through my chest as I explained that I was the pastor's wife. What a horrible experience.

We were given the use of Old Rusty, the church *Kombi*.[105] Every Sunday, Willem did the early run around the surrounding neighbourhood to pick up the oldies, who had no transport to get to church. They all called him "my Pastor" and would greet him with a bear hug and a kiss. After this group had been delivered to church, someone else would take over and collect others on a different route. At this point, I would arrive at church with the Opel Monza.

One day, as I reached the traffic lights near the church, the passenger window was smashed, and a thief grabbed my handbag off the passenger seat. I instinctively grabbed hold of the strap and held on for dear life, one foot on the brake and the other on the accelerator. Billows of smoke rose from the tyres and, as soon as the lights changed, I sped off towards the church with the thief hanging onto the bag, until he finally let go in defeat.

The kindergarten that hired our hall during the week regularly flushed the disposable diapers down the toilet, blocking the system. Willem often had to strip half naked to unblock the sewers before cleaning up and getting ready to preach. All in a day's work for the ex-chief health inspector.

We made wonderful friends here, who will always remain close to our hearts. We were given the assignment from the outgoing minister to host Crossroads International, who would be ministering the Gospel in Lavender Hill for a week to ten days. I was put in charge of logistics and Willem gathered his trusted friends to help him repaint the entire church and to convert the hall into a mini-hospital, complete with a portable dispensary.

---

[105] Although it referred to a Volkswagen Kombi initially, in South Africa, a Kombi is any minibus that is used to transport passengers.

In February 2002, the *Southern Mail* reported the following:

Doctors spread the message through healing

St Paul's Church in Lavender Hill was briefly transformed into a mini day hospital by a team of 10 foreign and South African medical doctors and nurses who, for five days last week, dispensed free medical check-ups and medication to residents of the area.

The transformation was part of a campaign that was labelled: "Bringing Christ to Lavender Hill, through free doctor treatment and medicine and evangelical crusades."

The campaign involved evangelism, women's and children outreach programmes, a youth rally, a musical team that performed at schools and churches and soccer clinics as well as a soccer tournament.

The church's pastor, Willem Herbst, showed the Southern Mail registration tables, church benches filled with patients, nurses taking pulse rates and sugar diabetes levels, and doctors examining patients in cubicles inside the church hall.

He said the doctors were hoping to see between 170 to 200 patients a day, over the five-day period. He went onto to explain that the patients first register, and then a nurse or doctor takes their pulse, checks their blood pressure and blood sugar levels.

A second doctor examines the patient and prescribes medication which is given free of charge at the temporary pharmacy. While they wait, they get tea and sandwiches served for free. They are then counselled on Christian religion before leaving.

Mr Herbst said that the doctors – most of whom were from America and some from Kwa-Zulu Natal, had paid their own transport and accommodation costs, while they were in South Africa. He said they were all connected to Crossroads International: Durban and Chicago, (USA) based organisation that "provide help and medical assistance to communities through campaigns".

Patients are then told about Christianity through evangelism to bring not only medical but spiritual help to the people.

One of the foreign doctors, Atef Twafik, an Egyptian-born American, received his training in Egypt and America and is registered to practice in South Africa, because of the campaign, said Mr Herbst.

Dr Tawfik said: "It's rewarding for us to meet with our South African friends. It's a joy, because they may be small people, but they have big hearts."

His American colleague, Dr Helen Laib, said: "We know that people in Lavender Hill have a difficult life in many ways. And we feel that the church needs to be an expression of caring and love, because that's what Jesus was." "We know that even after we have given people medication, they must still be hungry and have no jobs and have inner hurts due to abuse and other family difficulties. But whatever their needs are Jesus is there to comfort them, and so we are trying to meet some of those needs."

The founder and president of Crossroads International, Kent Kelly, said his organisation offered compassion in meaningful and tangible ways, as well as offering a message of spiritual salvation to people.

The organisation worked in youth ministries, medical missions and fed children in HIV-Aids orphanages in South Africa, he said. He added: "We are opening a preschool in Durban this year. We are working to develop a child sponsorship programme, which will make it possible for the poorest of the poor to have a solid education."- Raphael Wolf

There may be no lavender in Lavender Hill, but there are big hearts, that's for sure. The ladies' group of the congregation outdid themselves making food for over 200 people a day. We managed to get Pick n Pay on board who sponsored us with bread and other groceries. Addidas sponsored shirts for each of the doctors and their staff, as a token of our appreciation for their work. Morningside Hospital on the Blue Route lent us portable hospital beds for each of the eight or ten cubicles. Doctors and surgeons also performed minor operations and one whole day was set aside for eye testing and giving free glasses. Willem's office at the church was converted into a doctor's lounge where we served them coffee and sandwiches throughout the day.

On one of the days a prominent gang leader arrived. He received medical attention. He was a big man, covered in tattoos from head to toe. After hearing the Gospel he began to cry uncontrollably but in the end was not able to commit. Months later we heard that a man matching his description did come to Christ and turn his life around. He lived in fear of his life. Once you are in a gang it is very difficult to leave.

The experience we gained at the various conferences together enabled us to pull off this one-off amazing event. Cape Town's mayor got to hear about it too and came to visit our little church a bit later with his lovely wife. How Lavender Hill enjoyed that!

The church in Pinetown donated the youth Bibles and we started a Bible reading programme together in the evenings for the youth. A large group of kids came, and we were able to tackle behavioural problems so prevalent in the area just by discussing the Word as they read. One of the OM ships came into Cape

Town harbour, and we took a big group see and tour the ship and learn what a missions ship looks like. I always encouraged them to realise that the world around them is bigger than the environment they found themselves in and to recognise the myriads of opportunities that waited for them out there.

Faith, Hope and Love were rare commodities in a drug torn world, where perhaps every family had a member in prison or has been to prison. Teenage sex and motherhood were on the rampage as well as lack of self-respect and lawlessness. So, we took every opportunity we could in the church to build up self-respect and clean living. Therefore, when we heard that one of our sister churches was running a course of Bible Studies produced by Dr Richard Bewes from All Souls Church in London, we invited ourselves to it. 'Old Rusty' rocked all the way there and back to songs of praise. It gave this wealthy church a chance to serve their much poorer neighbours and our youth an opportunity to develop social skills to cope in the world out there. At the end of the course each one of our youths received a certificate, personally presented by Richard Bewes who had flown in from London for the event.

One evening, just after we had dropped off one of the last little girls at her home, we had a flat tyre. Willem managed to get us to the church where he commanded me to stay in the Kombi. He was undoing the nuts to the wheel, when a very fancy Mercdes Benz people carrier stopped next to us, and several men jumped out. We were terrified. Then we heard: "Pastor! What can we do to help you?" These druggies, which is what they were, treated us so well. They could not do enough for us. The church was the one to bury them when there is any gang warfare and that happened with frequent monotony! There was hardly a Sunday when we didn't hear the shots go off and the whole congregation would hold their breath hoping it would not come nearer.

On another occasion after church in the afternoon, I went to give support and comfort to a widow who had recently lost her husband. After much tea and talk, I emerged from the unit and had just opened the gate to the road when a bullet whizzed past my head. With trembling knees, I reversed and went back inside. An hour later, I quickly got into the car and took off at high speed. The little Monza did me proud, even over the speed bumps.

Willem made some very dear and precious friends while we renovated the church for the medical crusade. One Sunday his best friend and his wife walked to church as they liked to do. He sat and waited for Willem who was unblocking drains again. But he did not look good. He was sweating profusely, and his breathing was laboured. Willem took one look and told me to get them to hospital as quickly as possible. That was not an easy thing to do considering all the speed bumps. I began to pray like never before. By this time the poor man was groaning. I drove straight to where the emergency ambulances stopped and ran inside for help. I was seconds too late. Willem's lovely friend passed away next to his wife in the back seat of our car. During the next ten years, Willem would lose several such wonderful friends.

Everything we did was an exercise in Kingdom building, Kingdom truth. But our time was coming to an end in Lavender Hill. Willem's father passed away at the age of 90. Willem's son needed him to help him in Mauritius and internal schisms emerged in the church due to the previous leadership inability to let go. Willem was also getting on in years and his diabetes was getting worse. So, we packed our bags and left for Mauritius.

MAURITIUS

Mauritius is a beautiful volcanic island set in the Indian Ocean not too far from Madagascar and the Seychelles. Here we supported Willem's son with whatever savings we had left of Willem's pension, and I in turn worked in his office helping where I could. I can't say I was very good at it. Will was running his own construction company and finding corruption on every level making it virtually impossible to make a profit. Colonisation had already taken all the island resources. Sugarcane, vanilla and tea plantations make up the crops, and together with tourism are the main sources of income. Almost every square inch of beach has a hotel on it offering five-star accommodation to the elite of Europe and South Africa.

In addition to whatever else that may have occurred, I believe the main reason for coming to Mauritius was that it was an opportunity for father and son to reconnect in a meaningful way, and for Willem and me to meet the grandchildren. I made friends with a large group of South African expats. We met up once a week for encouragement and prayer. On occasion, Willem preached at the local Presbyterian church. However, after almost two years we did not receive our residency, and we returned to South Africa.

Entering the Slough of Despond

For three or four months we lived in an apartment owned by a friend at the church. She was living with her father in Durban while undergoing cancer treatment. God stepped in and started to provide for us again. Willem got the job of running the Christian bookstore at our church and I got a job running an upmarket bakery delicatessen in Kloof.

After our tenants had eventually left, we were able to move back into our own home again, which looked as though it had been vandalised. During our absence the house had been broken into twice. First, when the youth minister was living there, the back door was hacked to pieces with an axe and all our electronic equipment stolen, including the TV and sound system. The second burglary happened when the O'Briens were there. In broad daylight a pickup truck screeched into the driveway in front of the back door. Our friend was in the garage working. He was bound and threatened that if he did not do as they say, they would rape and kill his daughter who was home at the time. They were going to rape her anyway but somehow, she managed to say to them: "I have

HIV-Aids, don't touch me!" They plundered the house and the garage and then took off with their vehicle also.

In the last ten years things in South Africa had deteriorated immensely. Crime was at its highest ever. Farmers were being murdered in gruesome and cruel ways including the aged, woman and children. It was as though the whole country had been taken over by perpetrators of organised crime. This was both political and nefarious at the same time. Our cousin, Remo Herrmann's mother (my father's aunt), was brutally murdered in Vryheid in the same year the children left, in her home by a young adult African, who was later caught and tried. But the effect rippled through our family. There was another attempted robbery at our home while we were at work. They tried to break in through the windows, but did not realise that we had steel rods going through the wooden cottage pane window frames. Both our front and back doors now had steel security gates.

"Vryheid Herald January 12th, 1996 – Brutal Murder

An elderly lady living alone in Commission Street was murdered in her home on the night of the 1st of January.

The body of Mrs Inge Herrmann (77) was found after her maid reported she couldn't get into the house when she arrived for work the following morning.

Entry was gained to the house and Mrs Herrmann was accosted while still in bed. She had been hit over the head and been throttled.

The community of Vryheid was shocked and upset by the senseless murder especially as Mrs Herrmann was a kind, shy person who was always so grateful for anything done for her. She is one of five sisters, all of whom live in Vryheid.

She is survived by her two daughters and two sons who live elsewhere.

Excellent investigatory work by the police led to the early arrest of a suspect on Tuesday, 9 January. He appeared in court yesterday."

Brutal Murder of Inge Herrmann (77) Vryheid Herald, January 12, 1996. Image researched and supplied by André van Ellinckhuyzen for the author 2023.

Gravestone of tante Inge Herrmann at Vryheid Cemetery. Photo taken by André van Ellinckhuyzen for the author 2023.

Ingrid was being bombarded by external circumstances as well as internal ones. Willem's health was steadily worsening, possibly due to his age. His 'get up and go' approach to life was dwindling and it worried me. But he was a determined man and always kept his wit and sense of humour going for him. Ingrid not so much. The collective emotional battering I have received throughout my life was threatening to get the better of me. Years of pent-up rage, anger, bitterness and unforgiveness came spilling out. Only my pillow could tell you the story of grief. The years of tension manifested itself in my muscles and spine. Already in Cape Town I had bouts where I could hardly walk when my muscles seized.

I put my head down and worked very hard in the deli. Those years during childhood reading books included many recipe books and the love of these continued throughout my life. I taught myself to cook and bake and make preserves. Mama was not a baker. It was my escape that I could take with me wherever I went. In Italy, while on our Tour de Herbst, I came across Anna Del Conte's book "From an Italian Kitchen" on the island of Pescatore right next door to Isola Bella, one of the most unlikely places to find a bookshop, let alone an English published cookbook. Then, while living in Italy, I added onto this everything Antoinetta taught me. I enjoyed the books of Gennaro Contaldo and his friend Antonio Carluccio who also lived in Borgofranco for some time as a child. Their books and many others all became my friends. I would read them like novels.

With the knowledge from reading all those recipe books, I got stuck into the deli, which was in a state of damage control after the previous owners ran it down. The new owner gave me carte blanche. I gradually added a wider range of products from the mediterranean and sourced imported goods from Italy. We got some new equipment and generally gave everything a good clean up. The staff were the most difficult to deal with and had been pilfering for years. But without their experience in the kitchen, it would be difficult to cope – I was caught between a rock and a hard place.

The owner agreed to send me for cookery lessons at a prestigious college in Durban, Christina Martin Cookery School. This gave me the finishing I needed and the necessary clout with the staff. Soon the business turned around, and people were beginning to take notice. And then on Christmas Eve the following year, I was left in the lurch cooking more turkeys than I could possibly handle on my own. With four turkeys to a baking tray, I was hauling them in and out the oven on my own until my lower back gave in. But still I pushed on. The owner and his family arrived, and all pitched in to make sure every last order was processed.

We had baked a record amount of Christmas cakes, puddings, mince pies and other confectionary too that year as well as almost selling out all the imported Panettone. Our own supplier of French Riette [Rabbit, duck and pork] did us proud. We had so much fun sourcing a chocolatier for Bouche Noel and a supplier for duck from in the Natal Midlands and brought in locally made artisanal cheeses. Ingrid was in her element, but her body gave in. Before long I could barely walk dragging my right leg behind me. I had lost feeling in my right foot and all the way up my calf, I was in excruciating pain.

I did my best to avoid surgery but ended up in Entabeni Hospital in Durban under the care of an excellent neurosurgeon for a spinal fusion. Childbirth was nothing compared to this. As I came too in the bay next to the operating theatre, I thought I was going to die. Next to me was an elderly lady coming out of anaesthesia after a hip replacement, groaning very loudly. I had no sympathy for her whatsoever and her groans were tipping me over the edge. They allowed Willem in to see me, who turned a whiter shade of pale when he saw me.

Fortunately, they soon wheeled me to the ward with a good dose of morphine. The next day I still dipped in and out of consciousness and topped to gills with pain medication. By the second day the physiotherapist had arrived and started to get me moving with exercises and methods of how to turn and get in and out of bed. I was not allowed to sit or drive for six weeks and only allowed out of hospital once I was able to climb a flight of steps. All meals were taken standing up. Mama arrived to come and take care of me so that Willem could continue to work. We were still getting on each other's nerves.

I went back to the deli for a few weeks to hand over the job to someone else. I got a job at the bookshop with Willem and here the Lord began to work in a deep way again in my life. I was working part time and then started my own little business from home baking for coffee shops and a gift basket company in Kloof. The idea was to convert the garage into a mini factory outlet so that I could do this full time from home. But my body began to give in again. My abdomen was swollen, and I was in much pain. They treated me for depression because it felt as if I was dragging my body behind me. I was also being treated for chronic gastritis after tests revealed that the lining in my stomach was being eaten away. Eventually the doctor sent me for a scan on my gallbladder.

The young radiologist sat down to do the scan very professionally, but as she got started, she could not help to gasp. She excused herself politely and hastily went to get the head radiologist. He sat down to have a good look and while his eyes grew wider, he very calmly told me to go straight back to my GP. All the test results were hastily completed and sent through to him. I did not have to wait long to see him. There I was told that my gallbladder was so impacted, that I had to be admitted into hospital as soon as possible. I also had an appointment with the surgeon. I was so relieved that keyhole surgery was possible, otherwise I was in for another horrible operation. The gallbladder was removed, and the surgeon visited me later and told me that the operation was done just in the nick of time. He warned me not to go home if there was any biliousness or vomiting. I smiled and said I was fine. As soon as he left the ward, I emptied my stomach in the basin. I lifted my chin, pulled my shoulders straight and went right back to work the same day at the bookshop as though nothing had happened.

The surgery count was starting to stack up. I had polyps removed, and later a hysterectomy during which an inexperienced nurse had inserted the catheter incorrectly into my bladder and the fluid was not able to drain. Eventually I was so uncomfortable blowing up like a balloon. The poor nurse on duty thought I was dying and ran to get the ward sister, who very hastily rectified the situation with a seething Ingrid. By then, I had four surgeries to my abdomen in addition to a tonsil's procedure and spinal fusion. Ingrid had had enough!

I wondered why I was experiencing these physical health challenges. When emotional and psychological issues in one's life are not dealt with correctly, they manifest in one's body and flesh. All those pent-up issues needed to be dealt with, and the first one was unforgiveness. The more you dig into the Word the more the Word digs into you. The Holy Spirit showed me in no uncertain terms that this was a major issue. I fell face down on the lounge room carpet and wept, forgiving everyone the Holy Spirit brought up into my recollection at that moment. I felt a huge weight lift off me and what felt like chains snapping and falling off. I learned that this is never a once off thing. You need to practice it every time a memory comes to mind. The evil one loves to do that. And I heard the Lord say: "Ingrid, how much do you love Me?" I answered, "Lord, with all my heart." "Then pick up your cross and follow Me!" "Father, teach me how. Lord, teach me how". And He did and still is. Over the last thirteen, fourteen years I learned a lot!

> "The Significance of Bread in the Bible
>
> Jesus connects bread and forgiveness. He says, "Give us this day our daily bread, forgive us of our trespasses as we forgive those who trespass against us." At the Lord's Supper He broke the matzah, which is the unleavened bread and said, "This is My body which is broken for you." Which is significant, for Jesus, Yeshua says, "I AM the bread of Life." Which is crazy. Where was Jesus born? Bethlehem, 'Beit Lechem' which means the House of Bread. But there is a deeper thing. Hebrew is alpha numerical. That means, that every letter has a numerical value. Bethlehem/house of bread has a numerical value of 490. Nativity has a numerical value of 490. To be perfect or complete

'Tamim' in Hebrew equals 490. Why is that significant, because Jesus born in Bethlehem 490, was the perfect Tamim (perfect complete) sacrifice 490. Peter comes to Jesus and asks, "How many times do I have to forgive? Seven times?" And Jesus says no, 70 x 7 = 490. Why did He pick that number?

You can't be perfect or complete unless you extend the bread of forgiveness." (@JesseSpeaks. https://www.youtube.com/shorts/3Gdjjot1vgk)

ON A LIGHTER SIDE

The work at the book shop was wonderful. Of course, I was surrounded by books! And I was as happy as a pig in a strawberry patch. Willem settled in as the manager and I was his gopher. Every nook and cranny, bookshelf and most importantly, books got my attention and then I applied all my business skills to promote and market the shop.

Every church was a marketing opportunity, and I invited them to come and meet with Willem and see how we could meet their needs. Before long we had a string of book tables set up at various churches catering to their particular needs at the time. Other churches were ordering all their Bible Study requirements from us. Minsters continued to come in and browse for their own resources and were always invited to join Willem at the Stamm Tisch for a cup of coffee and cake. We made many good friends here. Harold had been studying the GWC courses. Another student of theology came too and had his own table near the window. He later assisted in running the bookshop with a new manager when we left. Seminary lecturers came in too, and one was Dr R. Govender who had an insatiable love for books that outweighed Ingrid's obsession. I learned a lot from him.

Willem Herbst and Tom a close friend and evangelist at the bookshop in Pinetown, March 2012. Just prior to moving to Australia.

Rev. Willem Herbst at the 'Stammtisch' Christan Book Discounters Pinetown.

One Saturday morning two gentlemen walked in looking for a particular Bible. We fortunately had the one they were looking for in stock. Johann was a prayer warrior and intercessor. Willem was busy on the computer, so I continued to help our new guests. They had just driven down from Johannesburg and missed the turnoff to Pietermaritzburg, where they had intended to stop and buy the Bible. Then Johann says, "The Lord showed me where to come. He gave me the directions to come here. Neither of us have ever heard of this bookshop or been here before. I believe the Lord has a word for you!" By this time, I was totally intrigued. The date was 11 October 2011, ten past ten am. The Scripture reads as follows:

> "Arise shine for your light has come and the glory of the Lord rises upon you. *See darkness covers the earth and thick darkness is over the peoples,* but the Lord rises upon you and His glory appears over you. Nations will come to your light and kings to the brightness of your dawn. Lift up your eyes and look about you. All assemble and come to you; your sons come from afar and your daughters are carried on the arm. Then you will look and be radiant, your heart will throb and swell with joy, the wealth of the seas will be brought to you." – Isaiah 60 vs 1-5 NKJV

We spoke about many things and then just before he left, he said he would be praying for me for the next year. Wow! He did. Every week or so, I received a word in season from the Lord through him.

Earlier that year Willem celebrated his 70th birthday. Small health changes were continuing to manifest. Most were put down to age-related issues. But I was not so sure. His driving was affected, and he would walk almost like a crab to the side. We arranged a huge party for him with the help from my dear friend, Lovey. The community centre at her retirement village in Kloof was booked and packed with guests. He had a wonderful time. His daughter flew up from Cape Town. What joy! Ten years later Willem went home to be with the Lord.

I tried everything to get to Australia. For at least ten years I was on this quest. Now, with Willem getting older it became more urgent. But it was not easy, especially for Willem. Ingrid was the idealist and Willem the realist. We did not see eye to eye on everything. But I refused to give up. One day he would say yes, and the next day change his mind again. It was a torturous, emotional rollercoaster ride.

Out of the blue, we got a Skype call from our son in Australia to say he was getting married. Willem surprised me with a trip to Australia to attend the wedding. On our return the rollercoaster continued. Next, he booked us 'on his final holiday' – a bus tour of the UK. Something we really could not afford but he used emotional blackmail. On our return he changed his mind again.

Then Olga came to see me in the bookshop. She visited several times. She too came on a 'sent mission'. Her main message to me was "Ingrid you have a problem with obedience. You have to learn obedience." I was not too sure what she meant by that because we had obeyed the call to missions and ministry. The full implications of what she meant would only come home to roost in 2022/23. Three years after Willem passed away.

Next, a lovely lady and her mum came to visit me. Karen's mum was living in the retirement village opposite the bookshop where Ekka, my cousin was living too. They spent about two hours relating Karen's amazing testimony in Canada and her prayer ministry. Following her directions, we began a prayer meeting at the bookshop on the unused mezzanine floor. Every Friday afternoon for at least two hours we gathered a group of prayer warriors together, including Karen's mum, to pray for Pinetown. However, the bookshop was also a target for thieves and a group of three stole my handbag from behind the counter while another distracted me. The bag was dumped in a dumpster near a factory and returned to me with my wallet and ID. But all the cash was stolen.

Through a member of the prayer group, I was introduced to 'Open Doors', an international mission organisation that had originated in Holland. Open Doors had an office in Pinetown in those days and were very big on prayer. I began to attend their meetings too. Here I was learning about smuggling Bibles into closed countries and the power of prayer in a whole new way. Brother Andrew [Andrew van der Bijl] was the founder of this organisation. His testimony was an incredible one. In his biography, "God's Smuggler" he describes how he came to faith after sustaining bullet wounds in his ankle as a soldier in the Dutch East Indies during the Indonesian National Revolution and how God led him to smuggle Bibles behind the iron curtain during the Cold War. An amazing story I heartily recommend.

THINGS BEGIN TO GO SOUTH

Not long after that I met two retired Open Doors missionaries from the UK who happened to be in South Africa to start an orphanage. Jennifer and Margrite had many adventures together with Open Doors, smuggling Bibles into East Germany and getting caught by the Stasi after the Bibles had already been distributed. They were well seasoned and very brave ladies. Jennifer ordered many children's books for the orphanage in Hillcrest/Valley of the Thousand Hills, and Margrite at that time did counselling for traumatised African ladies. Both continue to reside in the UK and fly out to South Africa regularly to lead this new ministry – "Beauty from Brokenness".

I became a bit bolder in my warfare prayers and had discovered that my late father-in-law was a freemason. By then Willem and I had sold our house in Mariannhill and moved into a lovely cottage in Gilletts near Hillcrest. It was situated in a cul-de-sac in an upmarket neighbourhood. While his father was still alive, both Willem and his father had renounced freemasonry, but had not destroyed the regalia. Willem kept his regalia after his father passed away. I gathered what I could find and tried to burn it in the kitchen sink. It would not burn. I remembered what another friend told me after a similar experience, and eventually I poured some methylated spirits over it and nearly set the roof on fire. The backlash was almost immediate.

A couple of nights later I woke up very early, struggling to go back sleep. I decided to phone my daughter in Australia. In order not to disturb Willem, I sat in the dining room just in my pyjamas. Thomas, our very old cat needed to go out, so I let him out the front door. This part of the cottage was completely concealed from the road but if you were standing outside the dining room window in the backyard, you would be able to see the door slightly ajar. The dining room and the kitchen backed onto another property, so I didn't think anything of it. As I was talking on the phone, I felt something brush past me from behind. I looked around to find an intruder making his way to the kitchen and the back door, which was bolted with steel bars. I screamed so loud that it woke the neighbours on both sides of the cottage. Dogs began barking and before I could catch my breath, another intruder snatched the mobile phone from me, scratching me across the face.

My daughter had heard everything! She tried to call me back several times but, in the end, they switched off the phone. In the meantime, Willem woke up and came stumbling through. They began tying him up and punching him repeatedly. They took him back to the bedroom and I was terrified that they were going to torture him. He was fighting to try and come and save me. But there was a third intruder. I was commanded to remain seated at the dining room table, unable to get to the panic button.

It was lunch time in Brisbane. Our daughter phoned every police number she could find on the internet for Pinetown through to Hillcrest, including Kloof. Not one of those police stations in the area answered their phones. Eventually, in desperation she went to the police near her work in Brisbane. After listening to her, the officer on duty said there was very little that they could do to help her. She just broke down and cried. Our poor girl was terrified that we were being killed and wanted to do whatever she could to try and save us. They then supplied her with Interpol's contact details. Later I heard that our son had been alerted too, and he asked old family friends in Pinetown to come and check up on us. However, by the time they drove by the police had already arrived.

Back in Hillcrest, the second intruder returned to the dining room, and with my hands tied behind my back, I was being frogmarched into the bedroom. At this point Willem went berserk. The third intruder began to dismantle the TV and all equipment they could lay their hands on and carry it out the cottage to the back fence into the neighbour's yard. In the bedroom, we were being threatened with serious bodily harm if we did not give them what they demanded. From my handbag they discovered a safe key. However, this key was for the safe at the bookshop in Pinetown, but the thieves did not know this and refused to believe us. They were convinced we had a safe with weapons and cash. I just knew something very bad was about to happen. I looked over to the bedside table and saw my Bible and began to pray out loud. I was going to fight with whatever weapons I had at my disposal. There was no way we were going concede victory.

Suddenly the neighbour's dogs began to bark on the driveway just outside our bedroom window and we heard voices of people walking past the bedroom. The night patrol man from the local security company had also arrived on the scene. The neighbours on the one side had activated their alarms, while the neighbours on the other side contacted the police.

By then, Willem and I were gagged and tied up to the bed. The two intruders bolted and joined their accomplice jumping the fence into the back yard and got away with almost everything we had of value, including jewellery, money and keys. Willem and I managed to free ourselves from our tethers and call for help.

Within minutes after the police arrived, Willem had to rush down to Pinetown to secure the store, change the locks and bank whatever money was in the safe. I was left behind to field a never-ending stream of police officers and give a statement. As one lot of police officers left another lot came, including forensics. There were no useful fingerprints! Interpol had contacted the local police chief in Pretoria, who in turn contacted the local commander to organise everything for us. In the end, four or five different groups of police had been sent from both Hillcrest and Pinetown and I had to repeat my statement every time to someone else. Nothing ever came from all this bustle. I think they were just ticking the boxes because of Interpol.

Lovey arrived and helped me get changed as soon as the last lot of police finally left. She drove me to the nearest bank in Hillcrest so that I could cancel all my cards. As we walked past a coffee shop, I heard my name being called. It was Jennifer and Margrite. I had completely forgotten that we had made an appointment to meet up for coffee that morning. It turned out Willem and I were not the only ones with problems. Another man in Hillcrest sustained heavy bodily harm from an axe attack. And the two girls experienced a very bad spiritual attack from the local sangomas the night before.

Willem and I were very fortunate to survive the home invasion as lightly as we did. Many victims are murdered. Most are tortured before dying and sometimes wives are raped while their husbands are forced to watch. Sometimes boiling hot water is poured over them or they are forced into baths with boiling water. This includes children. A family friend of Willem found his wife hacked to death by an axe murderer. He has never recovered from the trauma, even though he now lives in Queensland, Australia.

Three weeks later I woke up cold. It can get nippy in the early hours of an autumn morning. The bedroom window above my head was slightly ajar and the breeze a bit too fresh for me. All the windows were heavily burglar guarded. I kneeled on the bed to close the window and then I saw the same three men running down the fence line towards the back of the cottage. They must have entered over the fence near the garage. I shot out of bed to make sure all the doors were secured, especially the back door, since they had keys. The steel bars were in place. They could not get in and then gave up jumping the fence when they heard the alarm being activated. These gangs of three are highly organised crime syndicates. They wait for the insurance to pay out and then strike again when new items were bought to replace the stolen ones. Finally, after this incident, the owners of the property installed a security door for our front door and razor wire fencing all around the property. This is never a pretty sight but a very necessary one.

We managed to get hold of the children to let them know we were okay. Shaken up for sure but okay. But this was not the first home invasion. While married to my first husband, Peter, our house was broken into while we were at work. Next, our car was stolen one evening outside the library. I took the children to the library at least once a week after picking them up from daycare. We came out and the Ford Estcourt Panel van was gone. In those days without mobile phones, it took much longer to get hold of people to help and then get a lift back home. Also, public transport was non-existent. There was no such thing as an Uber. The police eventually found our car, very damaged and spraypainted black around the windows. It looked horrible. Mind you, the original avocado green was not much better.

But perhaps one of the worst experiences for me was the bank robbery. I was working as a teller for a building society when two robbers burst in with guns in our faces, forcing us face down onto the floor while they emptied the tills. I was in shock for some time after that. Negotiating burning rubber tyres to and from work was nothing in comparison, while the masses were dancing and chanting, what we call 'toy toying'. I am just very grateful that I never saw the tyres around a human body.

My brother in Johannesburg had similar incidents with break-ins while they were away from home. He was also car jacked one evening after work. His boss had invited him and his wife for dinner that evening. They were on their way to Eddie's home to pick up Sua (his wife). Along the way they had to stop at a traffic light. Eddie was following his boss when three armed men stepped out in front of Eddie's car. One on the left, one on the right and one in front. He was commanded to keep his hands where they could see them and to vacate the vehicle without trying to take anything with him. The instructions were explicit'

"Try anything and we will shoot you!" In those days most vehicles were fitted with tracking devices. Within hours of the vehicle taken, armed response units located his car in Soweto and returned the vehicle using a spare key Eddie had provided. This trauma stayed with him for some time.

This is everyday life in South Africa. People are leaving in droves to relocate to Australia, New Zealand, UK, America and Canada. And the little nefarious men sit back and laugh. Divide and conquer!

Just prior to us visiting Australia, we received a phone call from our son, very distressed. His friend was arrested for manslaughter. We agreed to pray for him. I began to search the Lord for answers for my desire to be reunited with the children. You cannot do things relying on your own strength; it always goes pear-shaped if you do. Johann was praying for me and so were others. Our garage caught alite and we just managed to rescue some of the things a friend had stored in it from going up in flames. We had no insurance.

I wanted to know what ministry the Lord had chosen for me. The answer came in a word: chaplain! I wondered about that and went to speak with our Rector, Dr Warwick Cole-Edwards, who was also an army chaplain. That was the only thing I could think of at the time. He asked me if I would be able to hold a gun, let alone shoot if necessary. He did not know that Peter had me shooting his 9mm Browning years ago and taught to make bullets. But somehow that did not seem right. Preaching to men in an army camp and being a chaplain are two different things.

Then, one night I received a message for Willem. I did not like it. "Tell Willem he has left his first love." I knew instinctively that this was the one message that would get his attention. I did not have the courage to tell it to him to his face, so I sent him an email. Only a few minutes later he jumped up from his desk at work looking like thunder and lightning. As he marched out the door, he told me he would be a few hours. Two hours later he came back and commanded me to sit at the Stamm Tisch. I made us each a cup of coffee and sat down very quietly folding my hands before me and looking down. I was going to be read the riot act from page one to the end! Instead, what came out shocked me. "Right, we will go to Australia, but not as civilians. We will go as missionaries!" "We will be prison chaplains!" Within hours he had a response from Jan at Prison Fellowship in Queensland. This was early 2012. We arrived in Australia 2 April 2012.

> To many South Africans, for example, it is inexplicable that their country should now be threatened with worldwide sanctions, where the apartheid policy of "separate development", ostensibly the greatest evil of this country, has in fact for years been undergoing demolition at an increasingly rapid rate. They cannot understand why an international world press, and consequently so-called world opinion, should damn them root and branch, while they have demonstrably achieved the highest standard of living for their black compatriots in all Africa, built schools and universities for them and given them the best medical care available.
>
> Nor can they understand why the governments of Great Britain and America helped the Marxist dictator Mugabe into power in neighbouring Rhodesia, now Zimbabwe, in very fishy circumstances and by manipulated elections, after simply rejecting the moderate black Bishop Muzorewa who had already been democratically elected. And now Mugabe is waging a genocidal war against the Matabele people, which so far, according to trustworthy estimates, has caused the loss of fourteen thousand lives. Yet Mugabe continues to receive support, while South Africa is constantly accused of all manner of violations of human rights.

Many South Africans find it an impenetrable mystery that "friendly" Western governments, such as Great Britain, should send military officers to train former FRELIMO terrorists in Mozambique next door to enable the communist government there to cling to the reins of power.

They really cannot understand why the big international banks should refuse any further credits to South Africa, the soundest and most reliable payer in Africa, and demand immediate repayment of all outstanding credits; which has had the inevitable effect of plunging the country into its deepest depression since the thirties; while at the same time granting thousands of millions to communist states and banana republics in South America and black Africa without the faintest prospect of ever being repaid.

It is completely incomprehensible to them that the World Council of Churches in Geneva should stab in the back what many missionaries regard as the most Christian nation in the world, while giving moral aid and comfort and financial support to Marxist-controlled "liberation movements" through the device of their Programme to Combat Racism, which is then used to wage a terror war against the god-fearing Boers.

Taken separately, all these and many more are the little pieces of a worldwide political jigsaw puzzle that many find baffling, and few can make out as a coherent whole; for they are only fragments of a world-revolutionary drama, which unknown to the ordinary peoples of the world towards the end of this our century is heading at an ever-accelerating speed for its undeclared goal. This confusion and apparent incoherence of events, however, is not accidental; it is managed by powerful forces behind the scenes. As Benjamin Disraeli (1804–1881), a former Prime Minister of Britain, put it:

The world is ruled by persons who are quite different from what those who cannot see behind the scenes think.

Solzhenitsyn calls them "the powers of evil" which have now gone over to the final attack. Particularly since the beginning of this amazing century they have by craft and stealth plunged mankind into a succession of wars and bloodshed unprecedented in all human history. In the course of the years, as the jigsaw puzzle gradually took shape, it became clearer and clearer to me that there was a huge design being put into effect behind the scenes of the world stage, whose purpose is to change that world completely, with all its old established orders. It is a conspiracy with the objective of exploiting and enslaving all mankind and achieving atheistic totalitarian domination of the world; in fact, of establishing a world government, to which all the peoples of the earth shall be forced to submit.

Since of course the nations of the earth would never willingly submit to such a plan, an enemy-image, an "East-West confrontation", had to be created. It is perfectly obvious that the instrument of the conquest and subjection of the nations is imperialistic soviet communism, which the conspirators themselves created with their instigation of the October Revolution in 1917 and have ever since kept in being with enormous credits, shipments of grain and the technical and military know-how of the West.

South Africa is merely a new pawn in this cynical game of chess, which is now being put through the revolutionary wringer so that another and particularly important obstacle may be got out of the way to the New World Order, as they call it. The concentrated attack on South Africa now taking place everywhere is, therefore, as we shall see in later chapters, not just a matter of getting rid of apartheid, more human rights or votes for the black citizens of South Africa (however desirable that might be) but plainly and simply to install a socialistic Marxist black regime which would be firmly anchored in the camp of the One-Worlders, that band of internationalist conspirators. We shall hear more about them too.

It is in the very nature of the case that a conspiracy should work away secretly and covertly; nevertheless, it is inevitable that now and again, here and there, some incident should give the game away and allow the alert observer to get a glimpse through the thing, and with further study to discern the total design.

The principal evidence of the existence of a deliberate conspiracy to destroy the anti-communist and pro-Western countries is to be found in the continuity and similarity of events in different countries, where "revolutions" and subversions have all followed an identical pattern. We need think only of Cuba, Vietnam, Iran, Nicaragua, Cambodia, Rhodesia, Mozambique, Angola, the Philippines and others.

And it is hardly conceivable that the similarities of these events could be purely accidental, when the same factors and the same external influences operated decisively.

As Franklin Roosevelt (who undoubtedly knew what he was talking about) said:

Nothing happens by accident in world politics. Everything is well prepared, carefully planned and deliberate.

South Africa, and with it the rest of the free world, is confronted with an enemy who exerts perilous influences and powerful blackmailing pressures on all the governments of the world with diabolical cunning and deception through manipulation of the mass media that he controls, and with almost unlimited financial resources at his disposal. By these means governments can be induced to pass measures and carry out "reforms" that often entail their own destruction, as we have seen from other examples.

"I pray to God that the peoples and the politicians of South Africa may be imbued with the wisdom to recognize the real enemy behind the mask of communism. Only if they can see through this greatest political intrigue of our century will they be able to make an effective stand against the enemy. If this book can provide a modest contribution to that end it will have fulfilled its purpose" (Vaque 1989).

In *Behind the News* (January 1985), Ivor Benson writes:

The revolutionary changes which have swept the world since the beginning of this century and now appear to be headed for a grand climax had their origin in a revolutionary change which occurred in the realm of high finance.

For a long time after the beginning of the modern industrial era, finance capitalism – not to be confused with private ownership capitalism – existed almost entirely in national concentrations; there was a British finance-capitalism, answerable to a British government which was in turn answerable to an electorate; a German finance-capitalism, a French one, a Dutch one, etc, each one joined to a national government and finally answerable to a national electorate. Last century and well into the twentieth, these national concentrations of financial power were in vigorous competition.

What then happened was that the many national concentrations of finance-capitalism were drawn into coalescence to form something new in history; namely, an **international finance capitalism** fiercely resolved to free itself from answerability to any national government and its electorate.

This process of coalescence had already begun at the time of the Anglo-Boer War but only began to exert a major influence in world affairs in the next two decades. One of the last national concentrations of finance-capitalism to capitulate was that of the United States; this occurred in the middle 1930's when the multimillionaire American pioneering families, led by J.P. Morgan, finally lost their supremacy in Wall Street to the internationalists, as recorded by Dr Carroll Quigley.[106]

In *Tragedy and hope: a history of the world in our time*, Carroll Quigley (1966) writes as follows:

There can be no doubt that a major factor in bringing about revolutionary changes in the realm of high finance was the existence within the different nations of Europe of banking families or dynasties which had always specialised in transnational operations. "The story of how these financial families consolidated their power on an international basis is told by Dr Quigley in his *History of the world in our time – tragedy and hope*. He writes: *The greatest of these dynasties, of course, were the descendants of Meyer Amschel Rothschild (1743–1812) of Frankfort, whose male*

---

[106] Quigley, C. 1966. *Tragedy and hope: a history of the world in our time*. New York: MacMillan.

descendants, for at least two generations, generally married first cousins or even nieces. Rothschild's five sons, established at branches in Vienna, London, Naples and Paris, as well as Frankfort, co-operated together in ways which other international banking dynasties copied but rarely excelled.

Dr Quigley names as some of the other international banking families: Baring, Lazard, Erlanger, Schroder, Seligman, Speyers, Mirabaud, Mallet, Fould and Morgan. This list could easily be extended – Warburg, Wallenberg, Kuhn, Loeb, Schiff, etc. There is no need to enquire deeply into the genealogies of these internationally dispersed banking dynasties which, as Dr Quigley put it:

In time brought into their financial network the provincial banking centres organised as commercial banks and savings banks, as well as insurance companies, to form all of these into a single financial system on an international scale which manipulated the quantity and flow of money so that they were able to influence, if not control, governments on the one side and industries on the other.

All the major changes which have occurred in our century – the Bolshevik Revolution and its aftermath, the precipitation of World War II, the dismantling of the colonial empires and the creation of a bogus 'world parliament', etc. – all of these and much else can be explained as having been dictated by the needs and ambitions of the new international financial power; for there was obviously no way in which the prosperity and security of this Jewish-controlled money power could be reconciled with the continued existence of strong governments in Europe and Russia to which it would have to be responsible and answerable.

When we consider the conflicts and revolutions of this century in many countries, it becomes conspicuous that:

a) every revolution or overthrow of a government has followed almost the same pattern;

b) every new regime has been either socialist-Marxist or at least *strongly centralized and dictatorial in its nature*, and in nearly every case more brutal, corrupt and oppressive than the government that was overthrown ostensibly on those very pretexts;

c) the regimes overthrown were strongly nationalist, anti-communist and particularly autonomous or independent;

d) although the new clique in power were more brutal than the former rulers and trampled human rights underfoot, after a little while they were recognized by practically all the Western governments and supported with credits and material aid;

e) officials of the American State Department had a hand in all these subversions.

In his book, *Behind the Scene* (1976) Douglas Reed writes:

Hatreds, passions and prejudices are to some extent innate in man and may be reduced by wise leadership or inflamed by bad. As I have gone along I have seen that they are incited, in all countries, by organized forces from outside for the purpose of setting up the World State on the ruins of Christian nations. That key once found, the dark origins of our twentieth century wars and the strange doublings their courses take are alike plain to understand.

It is not possible within the compass of [this book] to reveal the full extent of the global conspiracy in detail. Many excellent books have been written on this subject, and it is recommended to the interested reader to acquire the books listed in at the end of the list of references.. Many of the big booksellers might, however, be reluctant to stock such books, for fear of reprisals.

Although the plans of the world-rulership conspiracy go far back in time, as far as the occult notions of the Novus Ordo Saeculorum of the eighteenth-century Illuminati and the Freemasons, the ideas of Adam Weishaupt, Giuseppe Manzini and others were taken over by Karl Marx for his Communist Manifesto and then put to use by powerful high-finance groups for the furtherance of their world rule.

Never before has any nation been exposed to such a heavy and incessant barrage of vituperation from the establishment media all over the world, for decades on end, as this country; it can be compared only to the conjoint press campaign against the German Third Reich in the thirties. (Could that be a portent of coming events in South Africa also?)

While South Africa can hardly stem the flood of black refugees from the "liberated" neighbour countries, an ill-informed world public sees it as the very embodiment of racist oppression and exploitation. Unprecedented diplomatic pressures are exerted on the country. Total sanctions and economic boycotts are threatened and have actually been put into effect by many former trading partners. Ten members of the EEC have ordered their ambassadors back. Australia has withdrawn its embassy; Norway and Denmark have shut down their consulates. The US State Department has put South Africa on its list of "hostile foreign powers" – the first country in the free world to receive that honour. The American Congress resolved to introduce thorough-ongoing economic sanctions.

The picture formed by the man in the street in the West from the media is one of total confusion; for how is all this hostility to South Africa to be reconciled with the fact that Yugoslavia, Angola, Red China, Mozambique and other totalitarian self-styled Marxist states are still treated as friendly allied powers worthy of aid and support, while the Russian invasion of Afghanistan is apparently forgiven and forgotten?

In Diagnosen (no 1/86, p. 26) Ivor Benson, a former adviser to the Rhodesian government, writes:

The first fact of decisive significance is that the real history of what is happening in South Africa is only one episode of a widespread scenario that is essentially devised for the whole world and all mankind. That means that only by understanding what has happened and is happening in the world in general can we hope to find out the truth about what is going on in South Africa at present. To put it briefly. South Africa has become one of the main targets of the worldwide revolutionary movement that started at the beginning of our century and has rapidly gained impetus since the end of the Second World War. *Its goal is the centralization of political power, which is in line with its increasing, by now almost completed, centralization of financial power.*

So, all the talk about "apartheid" and "human rights" is mere camouflage for a political war drama, and its purpose is to conceal the identity of those who want to soften up South Africa preparatory to its incorporation in the planned new international economic order, which will in due course turn out to be a new political order: the unitary world that the UNO is assiduously working towards.

Above all we must realize that it is not communism in itself that is the chief enemy to be repelled, but the forces that lurk behind it, that control it and use it as a wedge to drive for the attainment of their goal of world domination.

Hitler fell into that trap when he mobilized his armies against Bolshevism. While he was giving the German troops their marching orders for the East, the bankers in the West were mobilizing the forces of the governments that they controlled for the attack on Germany. They had no wish to see the fruit of their labours, the Red Empire, destroyed. Their plans were well thought out and carefully executed. On the one hand the predominantly Jewish Zionist bankers deviously supplied Hitler with credits to make Germany capable of waging war; whereupon they manipulated events in Europe in accordance with their own intentions. They were well aware of Hitler's feelings about the Jews and Bolshevism. If they could induce him to persecute the Jews on a vast scale and expel them from Europe, and then to invade Poland and the Soviet Union, they would have killed several birds with one stone: the state of Israel long envisaged by the Zionists would gain official support from all over the world as a home for the Jews driven out of Europe, their communist empire would be strengthened, Germany would be destroyed, and Europe would be divided and enfeebled.

As we now know, General Eisenhower, Supreme Commander of the American forces in Europe, on orders "from above" stopped his advancing troops, thus allowing Eastern Europe to fall into the hands of the communist hordes, which America had been supplying with enormous quantities of weapons and other material.

The bankers' objectives had thus come true according to their plans.

In his book *National suicide*, Professor Antony Sutton, a scientist at the Hoover Institute, Stanford University in America, cites irrefutable evidence that:

During the past five years we have on the one hand threatened Russia and communism with the sword, while on the other we have secretly given aid to the Bolsheviks on such a colossal scale that without it the communist despotism in Russia would probably have collapsed. In 1944 Stalin admitted that about two-thirds of all large industrial undertakings in the Soviet Union had been accomplished with American aid or technical assistance.

Professor Sutton proves that the remaining third had been built by the other Western states; that the tank factories, the aircraft factories, the explosives and munitions factories came from America; that 90 to 95 per cent of Russian technology since 1918 had come from the USA and its allies; that we built, sold or gave to the communists plants for the production of copper wire, motor vehicles, tanks, missiles and calculators; that the Russians now have the largest merchant navy in the world, with about six thousand ships, two-thirds of them built abroad.

Why did the super bankers build the biggest steelworks in the world in Russia? Why did they build the biggest tanks factory in the world in Russia? Why did the Roosevelt government not only betray the secrets of the atomic bomb to the Russians but also send them at the same time the materials necessary for its production?

Question upon question that admit of only one conclusion: There has long been in existence a conspiratorial network of secret forces that spins its web in the shadow of the officially elected governments and controls them so as to manoeuvre all mankind into a collective world state. Nowhere can that be seen more clearly than in the attack on South Africa (Vaqué 1989).

Australia: Prison Fellowship

The appalling thing in the revolution is not the tumult but the design. Through all the fire and smoke we perceive the evidence of a calculating organisation. The managers remain studiously concealed and masked but there is no doubt about their presence from the first. Lord Acton (1834–1902)

Sometimes there is just enough oil on the blade that you don't know you have been nicked until the blade is back in its sheath (Author's own thoughts).

Arrival and Survival

I have the good fortune, or misfortune, depending on your personal perspective, to have lived long enough to compare "then" to "now". Having been born and raised in the golden era of South African history, thereby having experienced the type of freedom most western countries can only dream about. However, as I discovered while working in aged care, many in Australia – particularly those living in rural areas – still remember those days too.

Willem and I were met at the airport by Candice and our begrudging son. To be fair, it was an ungodly hour of the morning. We were to spend the first few months with our son, while we got settled in. I experienced an immediate culture shock – which was odd, given my mission background: there were no high fences, no razor wire and dogs were being kept as pets.

The forthright manner of South Africans is often seen as rude, and you have to adjust to a more diplomatic way of criticizing others while keeping a smile on your face. In this way, you can lie, cheat people and do almost any atrocious thing, as long as you do it politely.

Naïve foreigners are often caught out in this way; particularly in business transactions or with their visas. It is simply a way of life to which I have not gotten used to. There is never an apology, and they will never admit they are wrong.

We soon discovered that we had become *persona non grata*, despite both our children being Australian citizens. It was incredibly difficult to find accommodation.

Willem was in permanent holiday mode, wanting to explore every nook and cranny of Brisbane without a care in the world, while I was watching every dollar disappearing into the ether. Our saving grace was discovering a lovely church not far from where we lived, where numerous South African expatriates also gathered. Soon, we had a great group of friends and began to feel a little more at home.

This was where we met Dirkie, who asked us to join him in his home where he was living alone at the time. This gentle giant had a heart of gold. He graciously gave us the master bedroom in his large, three-bedroom house in Bray Park. Willem could not have wished for a better place to live. The two of them got along so well. Through friends, we soon managed to get our own second-hand car, which made life easier. Since I was Jack of all trades and master of none, it was particularly difficult to find employment and, yet again, the church and our connections helped a great deal.

Prison Fellowship

We applied for Prison Fellowship Australia as chaplains and for participation in the Kairos Prison Ministry on arrival. Many years later, I was to meet the leader of this group and his lovely wife again in Killarney. It so happened that they were going into Arthur Gorrie Correctional Centre that year. We discovered that the friend of our son was held there and, although we tried to make contact with him, we did not succeed. When our applications for chaplaincy with Prison Fellowship Australia came through, we did the training, as well as all the security checks. The only prison requiring two chaplains for Prison Fellowship at the time was in Woodford. After our induction, we settled down to the routine of weekly visits and scheduled Sunday preaching services, which came around about every six weeks.

I think we slotted in quite well. The spiritual warfare was rather intense, which was to be expected. The security extreme, which was also to be expected. One day, while perusing through the nominal roll, I discovered the name of my son's friend. I had to do a mad dash to the other side of the complex, which was not easy. On arrival, I had to introduce myself tactfully, as I did not want to scare him off.

He looked so relieved to have someone he could talk to. Willem and I ministered to him on and off for more than a year. When his parole came up with heavy restrictions, a new wave of insecurity hit him. Would he ever be able to settle down to a normal life again? Would he be able to find someone who would accept him? He really wanted to get married and have a family of his own. It took time and patience to encourage him, but by the time he left, we could see that he was ready for life on the outside.

It turned out that he made a great effort and found a lovely girl to whom he got engaged. They were going to have a baby. However, I heard through the grape vine that he had been involved in a fatal motorbike accident and died. Life can be so very cruel sometimes.

Through the Prison Fellowship's Sycamore Tree Programme, I was introduced to Martin Howard, the Programme Director. I volunteered to attend the programme at the Southeast Queensland Correctional Centre (SEQCC). This amazing programme takes crime victims and participating prisoners through a programme of understanding one another as people. It encouraged victims to open up, allowing themselves to be vulnerable and to show the effect and trauma of crime on an individual and their families, thereby giving them the chance to heal. As it happens, healing often does not occur right away. Many victims participated on a regular basis and systematically experienced healing, while others, like me, found healing in one course.

The greatest benefit of the program was being able to extend forgiveness and assistance to the prisoners. Once they saw that they were harming people – not simply targets – genuine repentance and regret occurred, thereby facilitating their transformation. Again, not every participant goes through this programme and finds instant transformation.

Some of them had to go through this programme repeatedly, but, unfortunately, that was not always possible. Many were transferred to other prisons before getting their parole, and if the chaplains in those prisons had not undergone the training, they were not necessarily able to slot in with what the participant had learned. As a chaplain, I found this course highly helpful.

Martin Howard was also deeply involved with Art on the Inside – another programme offered by Prison Fellowship. Every year, a large exhibition was held of the magnificent art created by the inmates. We spent many an hour watching the men drawing and painting, while gently talking to them. There were so many young folk, who should never have been incarcerated, but through foolish choices, they found themselves on the wrong side of the law. These broke my heart, because they often tended to lose hope. Therefore, I saw my task as giving hope and encouraging them not to give in to despair. In those conversations, we could easily talk about the Gospel of the Kingdom. Explaining it often helped them to have an "aha" moment. When that light bulb moment happens, it is such a joy to see the light come back into their eyes and hope returning.

It is wonderful how the Lord brings the right people into your life. Martin agreed to do the graphic design for the cover of this book, and an awesome job he did too.

About two years into our chaplaincy, I found a job as a local retirement village manager. It was a good job that offered us accommodation on site. At first, Willem was apprehensive because he would miss Dirkie, but after a while he settled down and began to enjoy meeting and chatting with the residents. Both of us had a wonderful time at this facility. We learned a great deal about Australia and the culture. We still saw Dirkie and our friends at church on a weekly basis and at various other meetings.

Our children were also exceptionally good to us. On arrival, our daughter sent us away for a night at a B&B near Suncorp Stadium. She surprised us with Reds' scarves, tickets to a rugby union match that weekend, and a bottle of champagne. I think it was against the Natal Sharks or Stormers. We had an absolute blast, cheering until we were hoarse.

Another time, she treated us with cricket tickets at the Gabba and joined us for the day. Despite getting scorched under the Brisbane sun, we savoured every moment of the match. Willem loved sport: the more the better. Apart from Rugby Union, which of course was what he played himself, he had also played soccer, cricket and did karate.

His soccer team was Liverpool, but mine remained Juventus, although the team was notoriously bad at the time. Willem and I enjoyed social tennis in South Africa, but we did not continue with it in Brisbane. His knee was giving him trouble and was swelling quite badly. If the television was not on sport, it was on the news. Candice enjoyed coming over to visit when a good rugby match was on, or the Grand Prix. We were all great Ferrari fans and, of course, Schummi[107] was the cream of the crop, until his terrible ski accident. Our village was situated between the two kids; so neither of them had too far to drive.

I was offered another part-time role as Pastoral Carer with the same company, but at an aged care facility not far from the retirement village, actually just up the hill. Willem and I were barely making ends meet on a half day wage, but with full-time employment, it became much easier. Our biggest expense was the high private health insurance premiums, since we did not qualify for Medicare.[108] With the extra income, I made sure that we had top cover to make provision for all eventualities. I was beginning to notice subtle changes in Willem, but without a full diagnosis, we assumed that his diabetes and those old sports injuries were the reason for the troubled knee.

A lovely lady from church had a great gift of bringing people together and entertaining. They lived on an acreage near Samford. It was here that I met and got to know one of the most influential women in my life – Anna – a true gift from God. From our first meeting, she wove herself in the fabric of my life, dedicating time and energy to our friendship week after week. She maintained this unwavering support for more than five years, until I moved to the country after Willem's passing.

I was a slow learner, and she required much patience with me. The journey towards complete surrender is far from simple or easy. One would think that, after decades as a missionary and a pastor's wife, surrender would come naturally, but let me tell you, nothing can be further from the truth. I would even venture as far as to say that most folk in the ministry struggle with this, let alone everyone else in the pews.

---

[107] Schummi is short for Michael Schumacher, the German Formula One racing driver.
[108] Medicare is the Australian universal health care.

This was one-on-one discipleship into practical spiritual walking that I had not experienced in the denomination from which I came. It was a very humbling experience, but I was up for the challenge and hungry to learn. Anna taught me deliverance and spiritual warfare on a level I had not known before and, in this way, I experienced deep healing from old wounds and received understanding – not only knowledge. As a result, my wisdom deepened too. I longed to be baptised, but I knew that Willem was not on the same page as me yet.

Another friend introduced me to Healing Rooms Australia, whose team proved invaluable in supporting Willem and me. During our time there, we performed a final renunciation of generational curses linked to our family's Masonic history. Moved by their compassion, I asked to be baptised. The leaders were a lovely, retired couple. He was a doctor.

They invited me into their home in the middle of a cold wintry blast, which meant that baptising me in their pool was ruled out. They had filled their spa bath with hot water and plunged me in. I was wondering how long he was going to keep me under and beginning to panic slightly, when suddenly he lifted me up again, and as I gasped for air, she announced out loud, "Your name is Grace! Ingrid did you hear? Your spiritual name is Grace". Such a beautiful name that describes so well the amount of grace Christ has lavished over me throughout my life. She had been waiting to hear from the Lord what my name was and did not realise how long it was taking, while I was still under the water.

WILLEM

Several months later, Willem also wanted to be baptised. I agreed to go with him. He opted for our local paster to baptise him in a pool. As it turned out, there were at least four pastors present as witnesses, five including Willem. It was a good thing that I was in the water with Willem, as he could not swim.

Soon after this glorious day, Willem began to experience mobility issues. He had many falls, some of which occurred in the afternoons, while I was out. I was sure he did not tell me about those. Getting into prison became increasingly challenging for him; particularly the steps up from the car park to the main entrance. He could no longer walk around the entire facility; so he would visit one section and stayed there for the remainder of our time. Despite his mobility struggles, he was still determined to go. Hell-fire and damnation could not keep him away. When a walking stick became useless and we struggled to get him in and out of the car, I realised that something had to be done soon.

For the first time, we did not attend the annual Prison Fellowship conference in February that year and, after close to four years of service, we resigned from Prison Fellowship. Someone from the village offered us a stay in a beach apartment on the Sunshine Coast for a weekend. We had a lovely time driving through Malany and the Glasshouse Mountains, taking our time and enjoying the beautiful scenery. Willem had never been a great friend of hospitals, but on our return, we made an appointment with our general practitioner to have Willem's knee seen to, and he finally agreed to a knee replacement, if necessary.

After consultation with our doctor, additional scans were required, and an appointment was scheduled with the surgeon. However, our doctor insisted on seeing Willem again before sending him to the surgeon. Even in the space of a month, Willem's mobility deteriorated significantly. He was leaning very heavily on me to get up or to sit down and we got him a walker.

Our doctor insisted on testing him again for neuropathy in both legs. Although he had previously cheated and peeked, this time, I made Willem close his eyes properly. The neuropathy was extremely severe. Right up to his knees, he had no feeling in his legs. This time, the doctor was taking absolutely no chances with Willem and ordered him to go to hospital.

He had already summoned an ambulance and made all the arrangements with a specialist on duty. Being his normal, ornery self, Willem refused point blank. The ambulance was cancelled. On our way home, the specialist kept phoning to find out where we were. Eventually, Willem politely told her that he would come on the Monday, after the weekend. This was probably a new experience for the specialist, who was not impressed at all. On the Monday, Willem was admitted to hospital.

Antagonising the specialist was a serious mistake on Willem's part. She made sure that every single test and scan that was needed was done on him. He was even taken by ambulance to another hospital for further MRI scans. When we arrived for the afternoon visiting hour, the surgeon saw me first. Willem's knee did have some cartilage damage, but nothing that warranted an operation. However, they discovered that Willem had narrowing of the spine around the spinal cord in his neck. He had probably had this condition for quite some time, and he was referred to a neurosurgeon, which, of course, Willem refused. Both the surgeon and the specialist could not establish which condition was actually responsible for the neuropathy – his diabetes or the Cervical Myelopathy. When I saw the specialist, she dropped the bombshell: Willem was terminally ill. She had already had a conversation with Willem before I arrived. The prognosis was not good. If Willem did not wish to see a neurosurgeon, there was no longer anything they could do for him.

Somehow, we always convince ourselves that we would be able to handle bad news. However, Ingrid did not handle the bad news about Willem's condition well at all. Inwardly she was struggling to cope, but she squared her shoulders and chose to face the situation head-on. It was recommended that Willem be transferred directly from the hospital straight to aged care, as he would require 24/7 care and support from that point on.

Given the nature of the illness, it was hard to determine how much time Willem had left. He refused point blank to go into aged care, even though we were offered a fantastic, newly renovated room that would have ensured that I could keep working full-time, while seeing him every day. There was no way to change his mind. Although she agreed reluctantly, the specialist demanded that she would only release him on condition that he used a wheelchair.

There was no time to involve an occupational therapist, and that evening, I rushed around, looking for a wheelchair to borrow and spent the night researching the best option to buy. Fortunately, I was able to claim the new wheelchair from our private healthcare, because the wheelchair was a requirement for Willem's discharge from hospital. I still had hurdles to overcome, though: nothing in this chaos was easy; it felt like navigating a massive storm.

I do not know what I would have done without Candice. She was a tremendous support throughout this entire ordeal, from beginning to end. She is truly a remarkable human being with an incredibly generous heart. She had just met her husband, Michael, and she managed to arrange a trip to Adelaide and the Adelaide Hills, where Willem could explore the wineries and quaint German Villages. It was to be his last holiday. God alone knows how we got him on and off the plane, because stand transfers were becoming impossible. They hired a car for wheelchairs and, the entire time that we were there, Michael drove the car and pushed Willem in the wheelchair. Willem loved every single moment of it!

After our return from Adelaide, Willem completely lost his mobility, and we scrambled to find a hoist. Candice paid for the rental. Our new doctor, whose consulting rooms were slightly closer to where we lived, introduced us to an organisation that gave assistance in eventualities like these. We made an appointment for an assessment. A lovely, registered nurse (RN) came to meet with us for about two hours or more. We discovered help that we never thought we would have. Willem received access to maxi taxis, a Seniors Card and a package for home care.

The nurse provided us with all sorts of free equipment and incontinent aids to bridge the gap before the package kicked in. I had to buy a hospital/aged care bed, so that we could put Willem in the lounge room. Even with the hoist, wheelchair access to the bedroom would have been impossible. Fortunately, there was a company that sold these beds just up the road from where we lived. Our wonderful home church in Bray Park helped with the balance of the payment. Once the package came through, we received a new hoist and slings. In the meantime, I did all the nursing and care myself.

The level three package provided care every morning, which was wonderful. The nurse was a young married man from Spain, who was a trained intensive care unit (ICU) nurse and a soccer coach, and he and Willem got on famously. He arrived early each weekday morning; bathed Willem; and got him ready for breakfast and, if there was enough time, he would take him for a brief walk in his new wheelchair to get some fresh air. Over the weekends, we had another, equally lovely nurse.

For the rest of the day, until late at night, I took over Willem's care. We had put a chair next to his bed so that I could sit with him, until he fell asleep. We talked and watched some television shows together. In the afternoons, I read to him from those missions' biographies I mentioned before and from Scripture. During this time, I thought I was helping him, but in a very subtle way, he was investing into my life also.

I contacted his son, Will, in Mauritius and his daughter, Lisa, in the Cape, urging them to visit him. Lisa and her daughter, Cara, came and stayed with Candice and Michael in New Farm. They had a good time with Willem over Easter. In May, Will arrived on a surprise visit from Mauritius and nearly gave me heart failure when he suddenly walked into my office. He wanted to surprise his dad. He too hired a wheelchair-friendly car and took Willem all over the place. They went for long walks, talking non-stop. I am so glad his children spent time with him while he was alive, creating beautiful memories.

The following year, Willem celebrated his 80th birthday in February 2019 with all his amazing friends from church and from Prison Fellowship. None of us knew that, in a little over a month, Willem would be taken away from us for good.

It was the same routine as usual. His appetite was normal during the day, he was lucid but began flagging a little earlier in the evening. I thought he was just having an off day. He complained that he was not feeling very well and wanted to go to bed. I got him settled in bed and leaned over to kiss him goodnight. Shakingly, he raised his arm and hugged me, thanking me for taking such good care of him. He declined any dinner, which was unusual, but because it was the first time, I did not think anything of it. I gave him his medication for the night and promised to sit with him for as long as he needed, which I managed until about 12 o'clock.

At about 4 am, I suddenly woke up, immediately realizing that the unit was far too quiet. Normally, I could hear his breathing from the bedroom. He suffered from light apnoea; so, I waited a few seconds thinking, "Breathe, Willem. Breathe". Nothing. I got out of bed without turning on the light and quietly crept into the lounge room. I gently touched him to see if he was okay. I called out to him, but there was no response. When I touched his bare arm, he was already ice cold. I knew at once he was gone. Willem had gone to sleep very peacefully that night. By the time I had left for bed, his breathing was even, and he was in a deep sleep. It was as though he waited for me to leave before he passed, for his body had completely cooled by the time I woke. It was 27 March 2019.

We had three funeral services for him. One service was at the retirement village where I managed to get hold of Rev. Dug Wannenburgh, who was now living in Brisbane with his wife and family. He spoke beautifully. It was a wonderful service for all Willem's friends at the community. The second service was held at the church in Bray Park for all our friends and family. This was a real celebration of his life. Dirkie spoke beautifully, Candice had prepared all the hymns and songs, and Michael read the Scriptures. Lisa and Will made contributions too and the service was live streamed to several countries. The third service was held at the end of the year at the University of Queensland, for Willem had donated his body to medical science.

> May the Lord bless you and keep you: May the Lord make His face shine upon you, and be gracious unto you: May the Lord lift up his countenance upon you and give you peace.

Willem went to sleep with this blessing every night. Anna had sent a beautiful audio version of it, specially for him. I would hold it close to his ear, so that he could listen to it, after which we would pray, before I dimmed the lights for him to sleep.

The Pandemic

The size of the storm that hit me began before the enormity of the pandemic had been established. It was no more than ten days after Willem's funeral service at the church that I received a phone call from South Africa.

Eddie was phoning from his car with his new bride, Helena, next to him. "Ingrid, Mama is very sick. We had to take her to hospital. She has been vomiting since last night". As the volume rose, I could sense Eddie's annoyance growing. He was exasperated, convinced that Mama was deliberately not following the doctor's advice and skipping her medication. "Ingrid, they have to operate, because they think there is a blockage in her colon, but Mama is refusing any intervention. You have got to help talk to her". With my heart sinking to my knees, I asked Eddie to calm down. They were on their way to the hospital, and within a few minutes, he got hold of me again. Mama was being wheeled to theatre making an enormous fuss. She was obviously scared, but our mother was also a highly determined woman. Eddie thought that she might listen to me. For some or other reason, she calmed down when she heard my voice. She listened and they wheeled her off to surgery.

The next thing I heard was that she was in the intensive care unit (ICU), in an induced coma, receiving a very high dosage of antibiotics. During the surgery, they established that her gall bladder had ruptured, and that she was in septic shock. Later, it was reported that she was responding well to the treatment and that it appeared that she was fighting the infection. Everyone sighed in relief.

Mama would not be able to return to her unit at the retirement village: her macular degeneration had become too advanced, and she was a high fall risk. For years, she had struggled on her own, refusing help of any kind. She was determined that she would manage on her own. As it turned out, she was not.

Eddie asked me to come and help with the mammoth task of clearing out Mama's unit at the retirement village. However, during Willem's illness, our South African passports had expired, and I simply could not renew them, as we only had enough funds to do the one. I was knee-deep in paperwork with Willem's stuff – death certificates and government notifications for both Australia and South Africa – and now I had to apply for a new passport through the South African consulate in Canberra as well.

I was caught in a quandary, which is why Candice and I consulted a migration lawyer. They take notoriously long to process these applications in South Africa. I could possibly travel on an emergency passport, although the chances were that Pretoria would not provide the new passport for collection in South Africa before my return flight.

There was also the likelihood that Australia would not allow me back into the country without a valid passport. So, I had to let Eddie and Helena know that I would only be able to travel once the new passport arrived in Australia. There was a minimum wait of six months.

In the meantime, this was not the end of the storm. Within a week or so of Mama having her surgery, I got another phone call from Eddie: "Hi Ingrid, I just want to let you know that I am going into hospital next week for a small operation. Tests have come back, and I have Stage 1 cancer of the colon. They are just going to cut out a small piece of the colon and I should be fine". Famous last words.

By the time he was having his surgery, Mama was being transferred out of ICU into a ward. She required rehab therapy, because she had lost a significant amount of weight and could no longer walk. She needed a walker from there onwards. They sent her for rehabilitation, where she relapsed with another infection and was sent back to hospital.

In the meantime, Eddie found himself in the intensive care unit too, in the same hospital as Mama. Although the surgery had been successful, there was an infection causing severe problems. Eddie almost died. Eventually, the doctors established that there was a leak. It took several surgeries and an entire year of recovery before Eddie was finally better.

Helena was tested to the very brink of her faith. Apart from the fact that she was also caring for her ageing parents at home, she had both her new husband and her mother-in-law going through life and death situations. And Ingrid was unable to be there to help. What an amazing woman!

After clearing Mama's unit, she got her into aged care, for Mama was suffering from post-operative dementia and she was seeing "little rhinos" all over the place. Eventually, they managed to get Mama into a lovely home, where she was fairly well looked after. Eddie took her to a geriatrician, who prescribed the correct medication to stop her from taking glasses of water and dowsing it over other, unsuspecting residents.

In the midst of all of this, the "plandemic" – as I prefer to call it – arrived full force. Both Eddie and Helena got COVID and followed the FLCCC[109] protocols immediately. They were both working from home and required no venti-

---

[109] FLCCC = Front Line COVID-10 Critical Care Alliance

lation or hospitalisation. His father-in-law from his late wife, Sua's side also got ill. Although he required oxygen, he recovered well, without being admitted to hospital. As it turned out, my passport arrived just as all the borders closed and I was forbidden from visiting Mama, who could not understand why she could not be taken out for her usual weekly tea and toasty or Chicken Lickin.

Not long after Willem had passed, I was given my job back as pastoral carer at the same aged care facility as before. I threw myself into work and was clocking approximately ten hours a day. The isolation of the aged placed a greater weight of duty on the shoulders of the pastoral care team. Together with the diversional therapists, we worked like demons to make the time for the residents as comfortable as possible.

However, despite all our efforts, I could see the light leaving the residents' eyes, which concerned me deeply. In an attempt to give them the much-needed joy and hope, we developed our own version of "Songs of Praise", modelled on the songs of praise from the BBC in the UK. I had found that many loved that show. I worked until late at night creating playlists on various themes like hope, joy, peace and love on YouTube. We managed to get a new large flat screen television set for the hall, mounted on the wall and bundled in as many residents as we were allowed at a time and gave them a show. I think we did this once a month and it was very well received. We did the same for Christmas. This time, the show went on for over two hours and no one wanted to leave for tea. Eventually, we had to usher them back to their rooms. Against all protocols, we had the hall filled to the rafters – and no one got sick.

Most of us were burning the candle at both ends. I was carrying my family back home on my knees. At the village, I became creative, making sure that each resident had a lovely birthday celebration despite everything. When things relaxed a little and we were able to use the community hall again, I gave them a Christmas celebration to remember. Anna came in and helped with the decorations. During those nights at Willem's bedside, I began crafting handmade decorations – hearts and covered baubles with fancy cloth and ribbons, etc.

We had renovated the community centre, and it looked grand. I also made playlists for Advent and a group of residents attended and enjoyed the Christmas songs of praise on Sunday evenings and lighting the candles.

However, my time at this organisation was nearing an end. I had refused to take the vaccine and, before I knew it, I was given two weeks to vacate the unit. There was no large payout from Willem, as all our savings had gone, but he did have a small insurance policy in South Africa, which took forever to be sorted out. In the end, I gave all that money to Eddie to help with Mama's care.

KILLARNEY

During the pandemic, Candice and Michael bought a property in Killarney and then they got married on a farm nearby. Rev. Dug Wannenburgh did the nuptials. The house was empty at the time, and I needed somewhere to live. The Southern Downs was going through a mouse plague, and the house was overrun with the critters. Candice was highly pregnant with baby Jack and was very sensitive to the faintest whiff. They opted to stay in their unit at New Farm.

God raised Candice for such a time as this. She has been a Joseph and an Esther, placed in a position to help her brother and then Willem and myself. And now she was helping me again. I could clearly see the hand of God in everything, and I praise Him for it. After moving into the house, lock stock and barrel, I gave it a good clean. And then I crashed.

The A Team. Candice with Michael and baby Jack.

There were days I could not lift my head off my pillow. Blood was dribbling from my mouth, and I had taken on a grey look. While I was still in Brisbane, Anna had walked beside me every step of the way. She would come and see me every Friday afternoon to encourage me and pray for me. Once I had left, God brought Teresa into my life. She was my partner in pastoral care and had left a couple of months before me to move to New South Wales. For the last two and half years, we had been keeping in touch and telephone each other on a weekly basis to encourage each other and pray.

God never leaves you alone in the valley. He is always there beside you. Sometimes He sends people.

Psalm 23 – Young David, Angel Studios

Even if I walk through the valley / Even if I'm lost in the shadows
I will not fear for / I know you are with me

The Lord is my Shepherd

I have everything I need / I lack nothing at all
He leads me beside quiet waters / to a place I can lie down and find rest for my soul
He restores and revives my life / Never leaves my side
* Even if I walk through the valley / Even if I'm lost in the shadows

* I will not fear for I know / You are with me
Surely goodness and mercy will follow / follow me wherever I go
* I will not fear / for the Lord is my Shepherd
You are / You are my best friend
Like an eagle, you renew my strength / For all of my days
You are good! / and your heart is for me / and will guide me in
the path of righteousness / for the honour of your name
* Even if I walk through the valley / Even if I'm lost in the shadows
* I will not fear / for I know you are with me
* Surely goodness and mercy will follow / You will follow me wherever I go
* I will not fear / for the Lord is my Shepherd

I spent many hours in the mornings having my breakfast and quiet times with the Lord looking out over the paddocks enjoying nature and the swishing of the horses' tails. Systematically God healed me from the inside and then the outside from burnout and grief. I gradually began to make new friends in the little Christian community here. I had my moments in this village that were not always that nice. I cannot get used to the trade in information for one. I had a vision one morning and saw salvoes of spears and fiery darts flying from one side of the valley to the other.

As the last of my savings became depleted, my financial situation dire. I tried everything I could think of to find a job. In the meantime, Eddie had contacted me again and said it was time to fly back home. Mama, who had deteriorated quite rapidly, was in frail care. Using the little that I got back from the Australian Taxation Office (ATO), I booked my ticket and bundled up Willem's ashes with my luggage. It was eleven years since I had last been home to South Africa. After helping me with my "visa permission to travel", Candice took me to the airport.

Nothing could prepare me for what I was about see on my arrival at Oliver Tambo Airport. The place was derelict in comparison to when we left. I suppose the pandemic had much to do with it.

Eddie and Helena came to collect me and drove me straight to the frail care facility, where Eddie had been told that Mama might not make it through the night. It was evening when I walked in, but I could not see her. She had changed so much that I did not recognise her at all. Even with hearing aids, she was totally deaf, and she was blind from the macular degeneration. It took a little while for me to find my voice, as tears were streaming down my face. When Eddie tried, there was a response. She took hold of my arms and held on to me so tight, not daring to let go. She did not utter a word. This was 31 December 2022.

She rallied round for another six days before passing away very quietly and without any fuss. Before she died, we had all gathered around her bed, where we prayed together and sang hymns. Eddie read a beautiful piece of Scripture while we held hands. Then Eddie, Helena, Eckhart and Jaydene left, and I remained with Mama. I was determined to be with her until the end. The staff brought me a lovely armchair and a rug to keep me warm. I was drowsing, thinking of all the phone calls and conversations we had over the last eleven years. Without fail, I had called her every week, and we would chat for hours. It was really the only reason why I had a mobile phone. When she became too deaf, Eddie and Eckhart had a job and a half to help her hear when I called, until we all gave up, because it was simply too hard for her.

She turned back to the Lord in her late seventies, along with her beloved sister, Friedel. She reached out to ask for forgiveness from both Willem and me. While Willem was so ill, she thanked him for guiding her on the right way. After making peace with her Saviour, she spent the remaining part of her days praying for her family, her children, grandchildren and all her great grandchildren whom she so desperately wanted to see.

I was just closing my eyes, nodding off, when I felt a tap on my shoulder. I looked up, but there was no one there. When I looked at Mama, I saw her last breath give way. Goodbye, my beautiful vivacious Mama. Go home, safely into the arms of Jesus.

> There is therefore now no condemnation to those who are in Christ Jesus, who do not walk according to the flesh, but according to the Spirit. For the law of the Spirit of life in Christ Jesus has made me free from the law of sin and death. For what the law could not do in that it was weak through the flesh, God *did* by sending His own Son in the likeness of sinful flesh, on account of sin: He condemned sin in the flesh, that the righteous requirement of the law might be fulfilled in us who do not walk according to the flesh but according to the Spirit. (NKJV Romans 8:1–5)

The next two weeks were occupied by going through all Mama's stuff and sorting through her documents. Mama was cremated and we had a small, simple family service for her at the funeral parlour. Both Eddie and I spoke. We created a collage of photos and arranged appropriate music videos. Tea and refreshments were served at Eddie's home. Thereafter, both Mama and Willem got interred at the Dutch-Reformed Church in Benoni.

Soon I was on my way back to Australia. Panic set in. My body was giving up on me again. I could hardly walk without limping. The bursitis in my hip and advanced chronic arthritis were getting the better of me. My metabolism was shot and, therefore, I had also put on more weight than I cared to think about. After Willem's death and before Killarney, I had further surgery too. They found a lump on one of my ovaries. After all the scans, it was decided to rather err on the side of caution and to remove both ovaries, as it is very difficult to diagnose ovarian cancer – which is a highly aggressive type of cancer – in time for intervention.

I was booked into North West Private Hospital and, lying in my hospital bed, I decided that fear was not of the Lord and I started praying, happy to leave things at the feet of Jesus. The operation took much longer than anticipated, and a second surgeon's help was called in. When I came to, both the anaesthetist and the gynaecologist came to see me. They were rather flabbergasted. The surgeon discovered extensive scar tissue from all my previous operations that needed to be cleared. When she finally located the problematic ovary, which was in an entirely different position than the scans had shown, it became evident that there was no sign of cancerous tissue.

They did remove the ovary for good measure but failed to locate the left ovary altogether. They were standing at my beside, shaking their heads in confusion, but Ingrid just smiled, knowing full well where her answer had come from.

The same was not true of my back. Now, after all this time and much prayer by myself and others, I am fine with that too. The Lord asked me, "Ingrid, how much do you love Me"? And I replied, "Lord with all my heart", to which He responded: "Pick up your cross and follow Me". And I pick up my cross and I followed Him.

New scans were done, and I was given steroid injections bilaterally in my spine and hip to help with pain and mobility. It has given me relief for now, but for how long? All of that is in the Potter's hands.

At the Cross (Love Ran Red) – Chris Tomlin

There's a place
Where mercy reigns
And never dies

INGRID HERRMANN

There's a place
Where streams of grace
Flow deep and wide

Where all the love
I've ever found
Comes like a flood
Comes flowing down

At the cross, at the cross
I surrender my life
I'm in awe of You
I'm in awe of You
Where Your love ran red
And my sin washed white
I owe all to You
I owe all to You Jesus

There's a place
Where sin and shame
Are powerless
Where my heart
Has peace with God
And forgiveness
Where all the love
I've ever found
Comes like a flood
Comes flowing down

At the cross, at the cross
I surrender my life
I'm in awe of You
I'm in awe of You
Where Your love ran red
And my sin washed white
I owe all to You
I owe all to You

Here my hope is found
Here on holy ground
Here I bow down
Here I bow down

Here arms open wide
Here You save my life
Here I bow down
Here I bow down

At the cross, at the cross
I surrender my life
I'm in awe of You
I'm in awe of You
Where Your love ran red
And my sin washed white
I owe all to You
I owe all to You

I owe all to You
I owe all to You
Jesus (oh)

Where Your love ran red
Your love ran red

THE BEGINNING AND THE END OF THE BOOK

What an incredible journey this has been. I can see light at the end of the tunnel. Today is one of those grey winter days in Killarney. The property has just been assessed for the umpteenth time and I wonder what the outcome is going to be. We could use some rain. Everything is dry and the garden in general disrepair. Sad. It is like reaching the end of a lollypop.

I had spent the last three weeks in Brisbane helping my son, who is recovering from yet another surgery. During the past two years, he has had more surgeries than I can count on my two hands, and he is looking down the barrel of yet another. It was a healing time – in more ways than one.

In Brisbane, I could reconnect with my old friends. Charlotte took me for breakfast, and we chatted for a long time, I can always count on her for a good debate. I also met Anna again. Wow! We had so much to share that we got together again two days later. On the Tuesday, she gave me a card, without knowing what I had been facing since March, followed by another card for my birthday, with Scripture verses and encouragement.

This journey, which essentially began 33 years ago, is finally nearing an end. Yet, the bulk of the work has been done over the last twelve months. I had one of those light bulb moments, when you realise circling the mountain leads you nowhere. When you reach the end of your rope, and you do not know what else to do, go back to the last thing the Lord asked of you. So, I buckled down, stood tall and started writing around July 2023. I reorganised my mountains of research, relying heavily on the Holy Spirit to guide each decision – a challenging feat with zero income.

The Dream Team 2023 - used with permission.

This is what it means to trust in God, even when you are sitting at the empty brook, to pick up one's cross and follow Him at all costs. Obedience is not cheap. After all, His walk to the cross cost Him His life.

In January 2024, Eddie and his entire family came to Australia for a visit. They took a few days off the beaten track and to visit Killarney too. Towards the end of his holiday, Eddie promised to support me financially until the end of June. This time, it was my jaw that hung open. He kept his promise, even remaining faithful for a while longer at a much-reduced amount. Like Paul, I have learned to be grateful for so much and for so little and to be content with both. Who knows when I will see my brother again. He had been declared five years cancer free; praise God. They have sold their house in the crime-riddled Benoni and moved up North to a little village, where it appears to be safer.

Along the way, my wonderful friends in Killarney pitched in too to help me, not to mention the magnificent two and their families. Just on four weeks ago, I got a call from my son, asking if I would be happy to have his car "White Betty". Would I ever! I loved my little Mazda, and she has done me proud for two years, but it was time to say goodbye to her. I am hoping for a good price. When the kids came to deliver the Toyota Yarris over the weekend, he quietly whispered in my ear, "Mum, don't ask too much for her", pointing to the Mazda. My beautiful boy is back! My heart is overflowing.

I missed the anniversary of Willem's passing this year. It has been five years. I was distracted by love and taught the value of a broken heart. My hunt for lavish goodness, lavish loving kindness came in an unexpected form. Forever cherished.

Looking back over the history of this book and my story in it, I realise this is what I have learned through this journey – the lavish grace and love of the Lord, the resilience that all my beautiful ancestors had found too. It was at the Cross that they too had found their roots to weather every storm life threw at them. His lavish love for us has always been the antidote to that brooding darkness and that loveless way of living.

Looking at this house and those around me, built with little foundation on the sand, I feel some concern – especially as we live on a hill. Should we not build our foundations on a rock? My heart aches. Over the months, there have been few days when I have not shed tears. I cried tears of joy, reuniting with family and friends I had not seen for so long, followed by the sadness of having to part ways again.

I shed tears of deep gratitude for an unexpected kindness, an unexpected gift, and I had shed tears for the suffering of my family and my own personal grief. However, like Jeremiah, I shed tears for those who have been duped by the brooding darkness and it is endless lies.

I cannot help but wonder what is to become of them – those who do not know Him – when their illusions are shattered by the realisation that they have been building their houses on nothing but shifting sand; when the supernatural of the Bible collides with their unreality. What is going to happen when their self-righteousness and their ideology of perfectionism fall to the ground?

We are steadily entering dangerous times. Are you ready?

Postscript (PS)

You may wonder what has happened to the Gevers family? While I was reading portions of the book to her one day, my friend, Barbara, in Killarney mentioned, "Ingrid, remember I talked about Hermannsburg in the Northern Territories"? She had been to Hermannsburg for a visit and she could not stop raving about the spiritual atmosphere of the place. By chance, she discovered that the wife of one of the missionaries had the maiden name Gevers. Despite my skepticism, Barbara became convinced that this woman must be connected to my family. I dismissed the idea entirely, not being able to see the possible connection.

While writing, I have been asking the Lord for the perfect ending to the book. While I was waiting for His answer, I consulted a genealogical Facebook page, trying to find more information on the connection of the French Gevers side to the German family. If only I could find that link!

I got a reply from Mark Albrecht, who could not find any connection either, although he indicated that he had done quite a bit of research into the Gevers family from Germany and, after looking into my Geni account, he managed to get all my Gevers family together. He had a book from Germany with all the Gevers, dating back to 1656. My mother used to have the book, Mark was referring to, but it got lost with all the moving around. I have been hunting for a copy, but without any success. Mark was kind enough to send me a PDF version of the book as a gift.

After establishing that Mark was living in Adelaide, Australia, I asked him if he was a Gevers and if he was related to the Gevers family from Hermannsburg. "Yes", he responded: "That is my family"! By this time, my heart was pounding, and I wrote back, "Are we related?" Again, the answer came back as a resounding Yes! "We are seventh cousins". Within a short time, he created a diagram of our family tree, showing our connection. I had to eat humble pie, admitting to Barbara that she has been right all along. She could not resist pointing out, "I told you so. I knew you were". My heart's desire is to meet up with Mark and his uncle, Martin, who still has strong connections with the work in the Northern Territory. It would be amazing if we could all meet up at the mission.

HERMANNSBURG NT AUSTRALIA

Minna Gevers and Friedrich Wilhelm Albrecht. Used with permission.

Through a mutual friend of Barbara, Vicky, I was given the following book to use as a resource: *Seeing the centre: the art of Albert Namatjira, 1902–1959*, written by Alison French. Vicky had been to visit the mission at Hermannsburg too, where she bought the book at an exhibition. Albert was one of her favourite artists. I quote:

> Elea (or Llea), who was to become known as Albert Namatjira, was born at Ntaria on the Finke River Mission Station at Hermannsburg on the 28th of July 1902, the year that his

parents had moved from 'out bush'. He received the name 'Albert' in a baptismal ceremony on Christmas Eve in 1905 (French 2002).

From the web page of Hermannsburg Historic Precinct [2024]:

The Albrecht Years 1926–1952

Pastor Friedrich Wilhelm Albrecht and his wife Minna Maria Margaretha (née *Gevers*) inherited the task of implementing Pastor Stolz plan to make the mission more financially independent. This was the time of assimilation polices in Australia and the focus was on equipping people for a modern world.

Through horrendous droughts and difficulties, the Albrecht family faithfully served the Lord. I encourage the reader to trace a part of their story on the web page, which includes a photo of the family. On their retirement, both Friedrich and his wife, Minna, were gifted a painting by Albert. These paintings have been passed down to Mark and his uncle, Martin.

When my children left with their father to Australia, I had hardened my heart against the country that stole my children. Grief turned into bitterness, resentment and even hatred. Being a chaplain and a pastoral carer involves psychological supervision. During my final two years as a pastoral carer, our church highly recommended the services of Illona, a South African lady practicing in Brisbane. Through our many meetings, I came to recognize Illona's remarkable insight. She saw through all my defenses and, after diagnosing me with post-traumatic stress disorder (PTSD), she gently and patiently put my fragmented pieces back together, guiding me towards wholeness.

I am here by grace. It has been a hard journey living in a "perfectionist" society. It was a bitter revelation to discover that what we had so fiercely opposed in South Africa had already taken root here. This tide has swept across every nation, leaving no one untouched. Churches everywhere are shutting their doors, forced to close either through pressure or non-attendance of dwindling congregations. Yet, the Hermannsburg Mission endures, nearly two centuries later. God faithfully preserves His remnant.

POST-POSTSCRIPT (PPS)

I asked my lovely friend, Karen, in Canada to write a review of this book. She peppered me with questions. In the end exclaimed, "Ingrid, you're a missionary"!

Behold Our God (Who has held the oceans)
by Sovereign Grace Music

Who has held the oceans in his hands?
Who has numbered every grain of sand?
Kings and nations tremble at his voice.
All creation rises to rejoice.

Behold our God, seated on his throne
Come, let us adore him.
Behold our king, nothing can compare.
Come, let us adore him.

Who has given counsel to the Lord?
Who can question any of his words?
Who can teach, the one who knows all things?
Who can fathom all his wondrous deeds?

Behold our God, seated on his throne.
Come, let us adore him.
Behold our king, nothing can compare.
Come, let us adore him.

Who has felt the nails upon his hands?
Bearing all the guilt of sinful man
God eternal, humbled to the grave.
Jesus, Saviour, risen now to reign

Behold our God, seated on his throne
Come, let us adore him.
Behold our king, nothing can compare.
Come, let us adore him
You will reign forever (let Your glory fill the Earth) x8

Behold our God, seated on his throne
Come, let us adore him
Behold our king, nothing can compare
Come, let us adore

Behold our God, seated on his throne
Come, let us adore him

REFERENCES

Alexander, P. 2019. *The Anglo Boer War and the Bambatha Rebellion.* Facebook entry, 30 August 2019.

Antelman, M.S. 2002. *To eliminate the Opiate. Vol. 2, Zahavia.* The Zionist Book Club.

Barruél, A. 2017. *Memoirs illustrating the history of Jacobinism. Part III. Vol. III: The antisocial conspiracy.* Hidden Light.

Bäschlin, B.C. 1987. *Die Protestantischen Kirchen im Sog des Kommunismus.* 4. Auflage. Tegna, Switzerland: Selvapiana-Verlag.

Benson, I. 1985. *Behind the news,* January 1985.

Brown, R. 1992. *He came to set the captives free: a guide to recognizing and fighting the attacks of Satan, witches and the occult.* New Kensington, PA: Whitaker House.

Bulpin, T.V. 2014. *Natal and the Zulu country.* Hatfield, Pretoria: Protea Boekhuis.

Cawcutt, R. 1986. *The Citizen,* 30 April 1986.

Chamish, B. 2005. *Shabtai Tzvi: labor Zionism and the Holocaust.* Modiin House.

Chung, C. 2024. Cynthia Chung Calgary: P2-Templars to Jesuits & Vatican: how occult underground shaped world history. Canadian Patriot Press. https://youtu.be/p74yBzmKYtQ?si=5xT8ywPwQNaX-zJC (Accessed: 14 January 2025).

Dalton Woman's Institute. 1973/4. Dalton & district area anals.

De Courcelles, M.L. 1826. *Histoire généalogique et héraldique des pairs de France : des grands dignitaires de la couronne, des principales familles nobles du royaume et des maisons princières de l'Europe, précédée de la généalogie de la maison de France*. Paris. [De Courcelles].

De la Chesnaye Desbois, F.A.A. 1770-1778. Dictionnaire de la noblesse. Paris: Schesinger freres.

De Poncins, L. 2015. *Freemasonry and Judaism: secret powers behind revolution*. EWorld.

Doveton, D.E. 2010. *The way of Balaam*. Port Elizabeth, South Africa: Cadar Press.

Eloff Commission. 1984. *Commission of Inquiry into The South African Council of Churches held at Pretoria on 23 May 1983*.

Erinnerungen an Glückstadt, 1908–2008: Gluckstadt Primêre Skool Gedenkalbum, 1910–1985.

Fey, E. & Rouse, R. 1974. *Geschichte der ökumenischen Bewegung, 1948–1968*. Göttingen: Vandenhoeck & Rupert.

Fouché, L. 2020. The Anglo Boer War and Bambatha Rebellion. Facebook, 1 December 2020. https://www.facebook.com/groups/2248402385422011/.

French, A. 2002. *Seeing the centre: the art of Albert Namatjira, 1902–1959*. Australian Government Publishing Service.

Gehrig, J.M. 1818. *Goldene Äpfel in silbernen Schalen, oder Wahrheiten in schöner Form*. Bamberg.

Harms, T. [n.d.]a. Heimatgeschichtliche Erzählungen by L. Harms, compiled by T. Harms.

Harms, T. [n.d.]b. Life work of Pastor Louis Harms: Pastor of the Church and Mission in Hermannsburg.

Hermannsburg Historic Precinct. [2024]. The *Albrecht years, 1926–1952*. https://www.hermannsburg.com.au/stories/albrecht-years (Accessed 28 October 2024).

Hilali, A.Z. 2006. *Cold war politics of superpowers in South Asia.* https://qurtuba.edu.pk/thedialogue/The%20Dialogue/1_2/4_Mr.%20Hilali.pdf (Accessed 1 September 2024).

Holy Bible. New King James Version (NKJV). 1990. American Bible Society.

Homuth, N. 1983. *Vorsicht Ökumene! Christen im Strudel der antichristlichen Eindzeitkirche.* Selbstverlag.

Homuth, N. 1984. *Diagnosen 10.*

Hurley, D. 1981. Interview with Archbishop Hurley. *Misereor Provincial Magazine.*

The Kairos document: a theological comment on the political crisis in South Africa. 1985. London: Catholic Institute for International Relations.

Kauffenstein, P.J. 1985. *ProTEST, No. 3/4.* Kenmare, Johannesburg: Information Service of Kreuz im Süden.

Kauffenstein, P.J. 1987. *ProTEST, No. 5.*

Kierkegaard, S. 2009. *Works of love.* Harper Perennial Modern Classics.

Leiss, A.C. (ed).1965. *Apartheid and United Nations collective measures: an analysis.* New York: Carnegie Endowment for International Peace.

Lilje, D. [2024]. History of the early Christianisation of Northern Germany [unpublished historical account].

Lily of the Valley. 2024. *Hope for 120 children.* https://childrensvillage.org.za/ (Accessed 18 October 2024).

Lutherans, Germans: Hermannsburgers. 1992. *Natalia* (22), 1992.

Martin, Fritz. [19--?]. *War memoirs of a German-Afrikaner in the Boer War of 1899 to 1902.*

Muller, H. 2017. *German churches Northern Kwa-Zulu Natal.* The Heritage Portal, 23 November 2017.

Musée virtuel du protestantisme. Musée protestant. [s.a.] Martin Luther, translator of the Bible. https://museeprotestant.org/en/notice/martin-luther-translator-of-the-bible/

Nehru, J. The *discovery of India*. https://ahmednagar.nic.in/en/about-district/history/

Nel, C. 2002. Friedrich & Johanne Schumann: Arbeiter im Weinberg Gottes im Zululand 1887-1923, dargestellt mit Hilfe von Aufzeichnungen, Akten, Briefen und Berichten. [s.l.]: C. Nel.

Nel, C. & Horz, U. [n.d.]. F. Fröhling: Missionar: Ein Botschafter des Evangeliums im Zululand 1862-1887, dargestellt mit Hilfe von Tagebuchaufzeichnungen, Briefen und Berichten. [s.l.]: C. Nel & U Horz.

Nicolini, G.B. 1854. *History of the Jesuits: their origin, progress, doctrines and designs*. London: Henry G. Bohn.

Olivette, A.2001. *Città dell'uomo*. Einaudi.

Operation Mobilisation (OM) International. 2024. https://www.om.org/int/home.

Oschadleus, H.J. 1992. Lutherans, Germans: Hermannsburgers. *Natalia*, 22:27–38.

Pape, H. 1986. *Hermannsburger Missionare in Südafrika: 221 Lebens und Arbeitsberichte mit Bildern: ein Beitrag zur südafrikanischen Missionsgeschichte.* Eigenverlag.

Pinetown Gala Committee. 1952. *Pinetown favoured for the future.*

Prince, D. 2023. Witchcraft unveiled: witchcraft exposed and defeated. Derek Prince Ministries. https://cdn.prod.website-files.com/5f6406a0f4666a9c-79d0742e/60e3b655dc0d664ba2122935_Witchcraft_Exposed_and_Defeated_WD1ol.pdf.

Prince, D. 2024. *The Cross nullifies Witchcraft.* Derek Prince Ministries. https://www.derekprince.com/sermons/475.

Quigley, C. 1966. *Tragedy and hope: a history of the world in our time.* New York: MacMillan.

Readman, K. 2023. *Woden, not Odin: strange Anglo-Saxon derivation of a pagan God?* Historic Mysteries, 5 July 2023. https://www.historicmysteries.com/myths-legends/woden/34621/.

Reed, D. 1976. *Behind the scene.* [S.l.: s.n.].

Roberts, A.E. 1972. *Victory denied.* Committee to Restore the Constitution.

Robison, J. 1998. *Proofs of a conspiracy against tall the religions and governments of Europe, carried on in the secret meetings of Free Masons, Illuminati and Reading Societies.* 4th ed. Edinburgh: W. Creech.

Rundgren, P. 2020. *The Siege of Ladysmith and the two battles in the Rietfontein area.* Talana Museum, Facebook entry, 23 October 2023.

Rushdoony, R.J. 1973. *The institutes of Biblical law.* Vol. 1. The Presbyterian and Reformed Pub. Co.

Savchuk, V. 2024. The power of prayer: making a difference in your life. https://www.youtube.com/watch?v=uULY8AB9SSk.

Schaeffer, E. 1993. *Affliction: a compassionate look at the reality of pain and suffering.* Baker Books.

Schaeffer, F.A. 1968. *Escape from reason.* London: Inter-Varsity Fellowship.

Schumann, F.W.J. 2016. Statte van die Zoeloe-Konings. *Huisgenoot,* 24 Julie 2016.

Schumann, K. 1992. *Aus dem Leben eines Süd-Afrikanischen Taugenichts.* Notebook Publications.

Schütte, H. 1967a. *Die Klingenbergs in Südafrica, 1859–1997: Familienjubiläumsbuch.* Pretoria: Afrika-Post.

Schütte, H. 1967b. *Nach Hundert Jahren: Familien Buch der Klingenbergs.* Vryheid Gazette Printers.

Schütte, H. 1973. *Aus Dem Leben Unser Voreltern Umhlangeni.* Literature Centre.

Sepehr, R. 2015. *1666 Redemption through sin: global conspiracy in history, religion, politics and finance.* Encino, CA: Atlantean Gardens.

South African Catholic Bishops Conference (SACBC). 1982.

Sproul, R.C. 2009. *The Prayer of the Lord.* Sanford, FL: Reformation Trust Publishing.

Sutton, A. 1973. *National suicide.* Arlington House.

The New Nation, 10(86), 19 June 1986.
The New Nation, 10(86), 22 June 1986.
Theron, F. & Joyce, C. 1987. *The French Huguenots*. Cape Town: C. Struik Publishing.
United Christian Action (UCA). 1986. *UCA News* 11/86.
Van Schoor, M.C.E. 1983. *Die bannelinge: A.B.O.-Boerekrygsgevangenes, 1899–1902: 'n gedenksbrosjue*. Bloemfontein, South Africa: Die Oorlogsmuseum van die Boererepublieke.
Vaqué, K.D. 1989. *The plot against South Africa*. Varama Publishers.
Volker, W.V. [n.d.] Deutsch-Afrikanisches Geschlechterbuch. Band XVII: Der alten Niedersächsischen Familie: Gevers/ Gebers (c.1650-2007).
Volker, W.V. [n.d.] Deutsch-Afrikanisches Geschlechterbuch. Band XX: Fortmann (1724-2007).
Volker, W. [n.d.]c. *Nachkommen Von Johann Christlieb Martin (1801–2007)*.
Volker, W.V. 2006. *The Cotton Germans of Natal = Die Baumwol Deutschen von Natal: From Bramsche to New Germany, 1848 – 2006*. W Volker.
Volker, W.V. 2024. The Cotton Germans in Natal, 1848-2023: presentation to the eGSSA/ eGGSA. Available: https://youtu.be/BQyzRkaA05c?t=3520.
Voster, J.D. [n.d.]. *Christianity under communist attack*. Pretoria: Christian League of Southern Africa, Pretoria.
Vryheid Tourism Association. 2014.
War Museum of the Boer Republics. (p. 190).
Wikipedia: the free encyclopedia. 2024. https://en.wikipedia.org/wiki/Main_Page
Winkler, K. 2024. Instagram, 28 May 2024. https://www.instagram.com/kyle-jwinkler/?hl=en (Accessed 12 October 2024).
World Council of Churches (WCC).

FURTHER READING FOR THE CURIOUS (AS MENTIONED IN THE TEXT):

Matt Ehret and Cynthia Chung. They have both written numerous books and are to be found on Amazon. Their podcasts and videos are on Telegram, Rumble and Substack.

Free Burma Rangers: David Eubank and family; missionary and soldier. Their website and testimony are also available on YouTube as well as on Deidox Films. Mission in Burma and helping other war-torn nations.

Eddie has recommended: Dr Peter Hammond missionary and soldier from Frontline Fellowship in Cape Town. This mission organization has some excellent resources on their web page as well as on YouTube. Their mission is primarily the continent of Africa.

Counciloftime – www.counciloftime.com. Also known as Mike from COT or MFATW (Mike from around the world). Also rebroadcast by permission on Youtube on the Daily Excellence Channel. This 'Organization was founded on the principles of Jesus Christ; the non-altering truth originally given by Christ which has not and does not change regardless of the changing times'. This is for those who want to do deep dives. My personal favourite.

APPENDIX TABLE OF CONTENTS

Appendix A: Gevers Genealogist Diagram 481

Appendix B: Gevers Plaat 483

Appendix C: Statte Van Die Zoeloe-Konings 485

APPENDIX A: GEVERS GENEALOGIST DIAGRAM

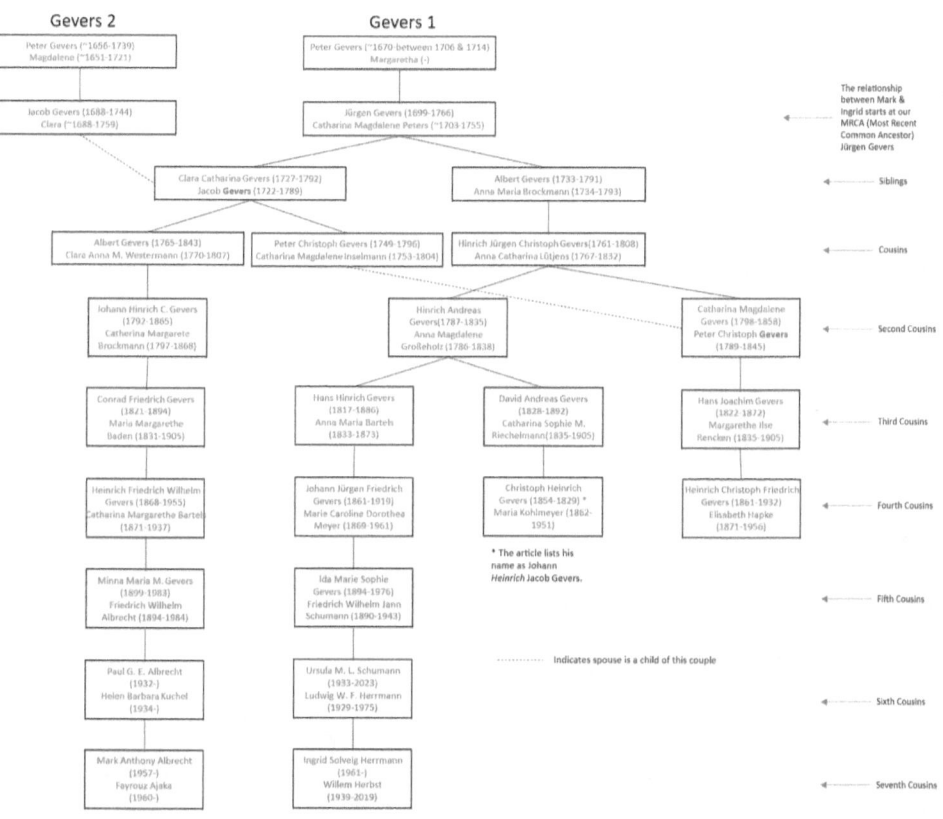

(Source: Created by Mark Albrecht – Adelaide Australia)

APPENDIX B: GEVERS PLAAT

GEVERS (PLAAT 29 EN 30).

Van dit voormaals Fransch geslacht, dat zijne bezittingen *) had in de Brie Champenoise aan de oevers der Ourcq, heeft zich ten tijde van Philips, Hertog van Bourgondie, Graaf van Champagne en van Brie, een tak hier te lande nedergezet, aanvankelijk te Delft, later te Rotterdam, alwaar de afstammelingen bijna zonder uitzondering hebben gewoond tot in het begin der 19de eeuw.

De eerste, die zich in Holland vestigde, was de vader van *Karel Gevers*. Deze Karel, geb. 1496, had een zoon, *Abraham Paulus*, geb. 1540, schepen in het baljuwschap van Schieland, gehuwd met zijne nicht Anna. Uit dit huwelijk sproot, 1569, *Jan Gevers*, kommandant der schutterij, enz. Hij had tot echtgenoote Maria Nysse †). De eenige stamhouder, *Paulus*, geb. 1599, had verscheidene kinderen, waardoor allengs twee takken ontstonden.

De jongere stierf uit. De tweede zoon van Paulus, *Hendrik*, geb. 1634, kapitein der schutterij en schepen te Rotterdam, geh. met Anna Ida de Witt, had slechts één mannelijken telg, Mr. *Witte Gevers*, burgemeester aldaar, wiens eenig overgebleven zoon, Mr. *Hendrik Gevers*, heer van Piershil, lid van verschillende regeeringscollegiën en eveneens burgemeester te Rotterdam, in 1761 kinderloos overleed.

De oudere tak plantte zich voort door het huwelijk van den in 1629 geboren zoon van voornoemden Paulus, *Abraham*, schepen te Rotterdam, enz., met Aletta Hallingh. Diens zoon, *Paulus*, schepen, hoofdofficier, enz., was geh. met *Adriana Leuven*.

Alle thans levende leden van het geslacht stammen af van den oudsten der beide zoons uit dit huwelijk: Mr. *Abraham*. De kinderen van den jongsten, *Arnout*, schepen te Rotterdam, geh. met eene dochter van den schepen Adriaan Brouwer en jonkvr. van der Werff, zijn op jeugdigen leeftijd overleden.

Mr. *Abraham Gevers*, in 1712 te Rotterdam geb. en 1780 overl. op zijn buitengoed Crooswijck §) nabij Kralingen, raad in de vroedschap en presideerend burgemeester te Rotterdam, gecommitteerd door de Staten-Generaal tot Raad ter Admiraliteit, meesterknaap in het jachtgericht over Holland en Westfriesland, enz., liet *vijf* mannelijke afstammelingen na: twee uit het huwelijk met *Kenau Deynoot*, dochter van burgemeester Adriaan Pietersz. Deynoot, en drie uit dat met Catharina Wilhelmina, dochter van den burgemeester van der Staal van Kethel en Spaland.

Uit het *eerste huwelijk* van Mr. Abraham Gevers (met Kenau Deynoot):

I. *Paulus Gevers*, ambachtsheer van Noord-Nieuwland, geb. te Rotterdam 1741, gest. op Noord-Nieuwland 1707, bewindhebber der O. I. Compagnie ter Kamer Rotterdam, raad in de vroedschap en hoofdofficier, een man van bijzondere energie, die, als patriot verbannen, later resident werd in Indië, en in 1795 in Holland terugkeerde. Hij was geh. met Jacoba Maria, dochter van den burgemeester Cornelis de Groot. Diens oudste zoon, *Abraham*, bekleedde velerlei betrekkingen, waaronder die van lid der Nationale Vergadering, van dat jaar (het eerste Gevers-wapen op Pl. 30, met de wapenspreuk *Hora ruit*), grondeigenaar op Java, die twee kinderen had: Jkvr. *Gertruda*, geh. met Mr. F. A. G. Graaf van Limburg Stirum-Noordwijk, en Jhr. *Hugo*, uit wiens huwelijk met Jkvr. Rendorp van Marquette kinderen, waaronder twee zoons.

II. *Adriaan Gevers Deynoot*, geb. 1742, schepen van Schieland, raad in de vroedschap en kolonel der schutterij te Rotterdam. De oudste zijner drie mannelijke nakomelingen uit het huwelijk met Anna, dochter van den syndicus van Groningen J. H. Lohman, was *Willem Théodore*, schepen van Schieland, maire, later president-burgemeester te Rotterdam, ongeh. overl. in 1819. De jongste, *Cornelis Johan*, lid der Provinciale Staten van Zuidholland, hoogheemraad van Schieland, had, uit zijn echt met Jkvr. Beelaerts, twee zonen, van welke de oudste, *Anne Adriaan*, geb. 1810, met Jkvr. de Mey van Alkemade is gehuwd, doch geene kinderen heeft.

NB *) Deze gingen in het begin der 16en eeuw, door het huwelijk van Jeanne Françoise Ceuillette de Gevers, over aan een tak van het geslacht Potier, welks leden 1e als Baron, enz., later als Hertog de Gevers, bezeten hebben tot 1794, toen de laatst overgebleven geguillotineerd en het kasteel verwoest werd. De ruïne ligt op den rechter Ourcq-oever, niet ver van het dorpje Gevres (*Dict. de la Noblesse* van DE LA CHESNAYE, 1734; *Histoire généal. et héráld. des Pairs de France* door COURCELLES, Tome VI, 1826; en andere werken.)

†) De het eerst alhier gevestigde leden waren nog niet met Nederlandsche vrouwen getrouwd. De vader van Anna, met name Pierre, huwde te Noyon Marie Cornets, kleindochter van Jacques (zie hiervóór het artikel *Cornets de Groot*, en EXPILLY, *Dict. des Gaules*, 2e dl., Tome II). Maria Nys of Nysse behoorde tot den tak van een oud Silezisch geslacht, voormaals gevestigd op het kasteel Ark in Henegouwen.

Van de Rotterdamsche regeeringsgeslachten, met welke de vermaagschapping daarop, zonder uitzondering, plaats had tot in de tweede helft der 18e eeuw, zijn de meeste, o. a. het destijds oud en aanzienlijk geslacht Hallingh, uitgestorven of voor meer aldaar aanwezig.

§) De ambachtsheerlijkheid Crooswijck of Crouuigh, voormaals aan de van Cralingens behoord, was omtrent 1455 tot de grafelijkheid teruggekeerd. Het kasteel, oudtijds Reusenhuys genaamd, waarvan de oorsprong onbekend is (vóór 1065 een verdedigingstoren bij de sluis in de Rotte), kwam later met bijbehoorende goederen, aan het geslacht van der Duyn en daarna aan dat van Gevers, waarin het sedert erfelijk is gebleven. Het werd in 1817 verkocht, gesloopt en het terrein in 1830 ten deele tot begraafplaats bestemd.

132

INGRID HERRMANN

De talrijkste tak *Gevers Deynoot* sproot voort uit het huwelijk van Adriaans tweeden zoon Mr. *Abraham Gevers Deynoot*, met Margaretha Catharina Wijckerheld Bisdom. Geb. te Rotterdam 1776, vice-president der rechtbank aldaar, verheven tot den adelstand bij Koninklijk besluit van 19 Oct 1837 (zie het wapen op Pl. 30) en overl. op zijn landgoed Rusthoek nabij Loosduinen in 1845, had hij vijf zoons, waaronder: 1° Jhr. Mr. *Dirk Rudolf Gevers Deynoot*, geb. te Rotterdam in 1807, ongeh. overleden op Rusthoek in 1877, lid der Provinciale Staten van Zuidholland, kantonrechter en kolonel der schutterij te Rotterdam, ter wiens nagedachtenis de Hollandsche Maatschappij van Landbouw een monument oprichtte aan den straatweg nabij Loosduinen; 2° Jhr. Mr. *Willem Théodore Gevers Deynoot*, geb. in 1808, ongeh. overl. te 's Gravenhage 1879, officier honorair der jagers, dijkgraaf van Schieland, wethouder te Rotterdam, lid van de Tweede Kamer der Staten-Generaal enz. *); 3° Jhr. *Adriaan Willem Anne Gevers Deynoot*, geb. te Rotterdam in 1811, generaal-majoor, inspecteur van het wapen der artillerie, geh. met Jkvr. Jacqueline Quarles van Ufford. Van hunne beide zoons, eveneens officier, heeft slechts de oudste, luitenant der veld-artillerie, nakomelingen, waaronder één zoon; 4° Jhr. Mr. *François Gerard Abraham Gevers Deynoot*, geb. te Rotterdam in 1814, lid der Provinciale Staten van Zuidholland en sedert 1858 burgemeester van 's Gravenhage, geh. met Margaretha Gravin van Limburg Stirum. Van een aantal kinderen zijn er drie geh., waaronder een zoon, Jhr. Mr. *Pieter Hendrik Gevers Deynoot*, geb. in 1848, referendaris bij het Kabinet des Konings, met Jkvr. Huydecoper van Wulperhorst.

Uit het *tweede huwelijk* van Mr. Abraham Gevers (met Catharina Wilhelmina van der Staal, vrouwe van Kethel en Spaland):

III. Mr. *Dirk Cornelis Gevers van Endegeest* van Kethel en Spaland, geb. te Rotterdam in 1763, verheven tot den adelstand bij Koninklijk besluit van 31 Dec. 1827 en diploma van 17 April 1828 (het laatste wapen op Pl. 29), overl. op Endegeest 1839, schepen van Schieland, hoogheemraad van Rijnland, commissaris-generaal van 's Rijks waterstaat, presideerend burgemeester van Leiden, lid der Gedeputeerde Staten van Zuidholland, enz., geh. eerst met Maria Benudina Barones Rengers, waaruit Jhr. *Marius Benudinus Holenus Wilhelmus Gevers van Kethel en Spaland*, garde d'honneur onder Napoleon I, referendaris bij den Staatsraad, lid, later president der Algemeene Rekenkamer, enz., overl. op het huis te Werve onder Rijswijk 1873. Hij was geh. met Jkvr. Johanna Cornelia Mollerus. Van zijne kinderen bleef ééne dochter in leven, *Meline*, geh. met Willem Anne Baron van Pallandt, kamerheer des Konings.

Uit het tweede huwelijk van Mr. Dirk Cornelis G. met Maria Catharina, dochter van Mr. D. C. de Leeuw, raad in de vroedschap te Utrecht, waren twee zoons: 1° Jhr. Mr. *Daniel Theod. Gevers van Endegeest*, geb. te Rotterdam 1793, geh. met Jkvr. Johanna Deutz van Assendelft, kinderloos overl. op het kasteel Endegeest 1877. In 1813—15 uitgetrokken als jager te paard der Garde du Corps van den Souvereinen Vorst, is hij later o. a. geweest: referendaris bij den Staatsraad, daarna bij het Departement van Binnenlandsche Zaken, lid en voorzitter van de Tweede Kamer der Staten-Generaal, president der commissie voor de droogmaking van het Haarlemmermeer, staatsraad in buitengewone dienst, lid van de Eerste Kamer der Staten-Generaal, minister van buitenlandsche zaken, president curator der Leidsche Hoogeschool, grootkruis van den Nederlandschen Leeuw, enz. †); 2° Jhr. *Adriaan Leonard van Heteren Gevers*, geb. te Rotterdam 1794, overl. te 's Hage 1866, geh. met Marie Barones Sirtema van Grovestins. Onder meer was hij eerste page van Keizer Napoleon I, luitenant der huzaren bij den veldtocht van 1812 in Rusland, agent van het Domein, lid der Staten van Holland en lid der Gedeputeerde Staten van Zuidholland. Van zijne drie zoons liet de oudste, Jhr. Mr. *Adolf Gevers*, geb. op Endegeest 1823, overl. in Indië 1859, één zoon na, geb. 1858. De anderen, Jhr. Mr. *Charles Gevers*, overl. 1873, en Jhr. Mr. *Alfred Gevers van Endegeest*, kamerjonker des Konings, bleven ongeh.

IV. *Arnout Johannes Gevers Leuven*, geb. 1767 op het huis Crooswijk, huwde 1793 te Chelmsford in het Graafschap Essex Louisa Elisabeth Parker §), zette zich in Engeland neder, werd bij Parlements-acte van 26 April 1796 genaturaliseerd en nam een werkzaam deel aan de maatregelen tot herstel der vorstelijke dynastie in Nederland. Hij overleed in 1826 hier te lande, waar zich ook zijne kinderen vestigden en zijne dochters gehuwd zijn met den generaal Graaf van Heerdt, ritmeester Bucaille en Baron Taets van Amerongen. Van zijne zoons zijn er twee wier descendentie in de mannelijke lijn zich tot meer dan één geslacht uitstrekt: *John*, geb. te Londen 1796, betaalmeester van 's Rijks schatkist, door diens eenigen zoon *Arnout Johannes*, officier bij de grenadiers, en *Theodore*, geb. te Tottenham 1801, luitenant-kolonel der jagers, uit wiens huwelijk met Suzanna, dochter van den minister van staat C. Th. Elout (zie hiervóór, blz. 107), één zoon, *Arnout Cornelis Théodore*, geb. te 's Hage 1830, majoor, later burgemeester, onder anderen van Doesborgh, enz. **). De kinderen van dezen voeren enkel den geslachtsnaam *Gevers*.

---

*) Mr. L. E. LENTING heeft hem eene necrologie gewijd in de *Levensberichten der afgestorvene medeleden van de Maatschappij der Nederlandsche Letterkunde* van 1880, en daarin ook zijne werken vermeld, waarvan wij hier o. a. noemen de *Beschrijving van het Hoogheemraadschap van Schieland*, waarvoor hem door het Bataafsch Genootschap te Rotterdam de gouden medaille werd toegekend, en de beschrijvingen zijner reizen in Algerie, Noord-Amerika en Java.

†) Tweemalen werd hij met eene gouden medaille bekroond voor verhandelingen over duinontginning en de behandeling van het houtgewas, terwijl hij over de droogmaking van het Haarlemmermeer een groot werk met kaarten en platen uitgaf.

Zijne uitvoerige levensschets van de hand van professor J. T. BUYS komt voor in de *Levensberichten der afgestorvene medeleden van de Maatschappij der Nederlandsche Letterkunde* van 1881.

§) Zie *The County Families of the United Kingdom*, by WALFORD; BERRY's *Encyclopaedia Heraldica*, enz.

**) Van zijne hand bestaat geschriften over militaire onderwerpen, waaronder wij vooral kunnen noemen het belangrijke en uitvoerige *Overzicht van Neêrlands verdedigingsmiddelen*, 's Gravenhage 1869, en verschillende opstellen in militaire en andere tijdschriften.

APPENDIX C: STATTE VAN DIE ZOELOE-KONINGS

STATTE VAN DIE ZOELOE-KONINGS

deur F. W. J. SCHUMANN

DAAR is vandag ongetwyfeld baie min mense, selfs onder die naturelle, wat weet op watter bouplan die Zoeloe-statte ingerig was. Die Voortrekkers het, vir sover my bewus is, geen sketse daarvan nagelaat nie, en die ou blanke bewoners van Natal het in hierdie opsig ook waardevolle geskiedkundige materiaal verlore laat gaan.

Wat die Zoeloe-geskiedenis betref, is die boeke wat tot duster onder my aandag gekom het, vol leemtes. Selfs die beste, dié deur eerw. Bryant, wat met die steun van staatsweë opgestel en uitgegee is, bevat tekortkominings.

Miskien het geen ander koning van die Zoeloes soveel statte of stede gebou nie as Chaka, die Napoleon van Suid-Afrika. Toe hy die heerskappy van sy vader, Seuzangakona, aanvaar het, het daar in Zoeloeland verskillende klein koninkryke bestaan. Maar dadelik het hy aan hierdie leenstelsel 'n end gemaak deur een koninkie na die ander te verslaan en by sy regering in te lyf. Sy magtigste teenstander was Zwidi, die koning van die Ndwanduwe-stam, wat oor die hele gebied tussen die Swart-Umfoloos en die Swaziegrens regeer het.

Nadat hy die hele Zoeloeland onder sy septer gebring het, het hy sonder versuim die Tugela oorgesteek. Die gerug van sy koms was voldoende om die stamme van Natal op die vlug te laat slaan, met die gevolg dat daar 'n ware chaos ontstaan het, want een stam het in sy vlug oor die ander geval en in 'n oogwenk en sonder noemenswaardige gevegte het Chaka in besit van die hele land tussen die Swaziegrens en die Drakensberge gekom.

As gevolg hiervan het hy op verskillende plekke in sy koninkryk koninklike statte gebou.

Na Chaka se verpletterende oorwinning oor Zwidi het eersgenoemde sy eerste stat aan die Swart-Umfoloos teenoor die Coza-berg gebou. Hierdie stat het hy Embeyebeye genoem (beter: Embelebele—moeite sonder einde).

Van daar het hy in die buurt van Mahlabatini (by die sand) 'n tweede stat opgerig wat hy Mabulewa (wat gedood word) genoem het, omdat Zwidi hom wou uitroei. Hy het vervolgens by Eshowe vertygetrek, oor die Enyezane gegaan en daar sy ander stat, Gingindhlovu (verslinder van olifante) gebou.

Hierrvandaan het hy met sy leër die Tugela oorgesteek en langs die kus op Dukuza (buffer), nou Stanger, sy hoofstat opgerig.

Maar sy oorvloedige energie het hom verder langs die kus by Etekwine (Durban) vertygedryf laat. Faku, die Mpondo-koning. Maar Faku het sonder teenstand voor Chaka gevlug. Nadat Chaka hom tot oor die Umzimkulu agtervolg het, het Faku hom baie beeste gestuur en hom gesmeek om die agtervolging te staak. Dit het Chaka aangeneem mits Faku sy onderdaan word. Faku het ingestem en Chaka het met 'n groot

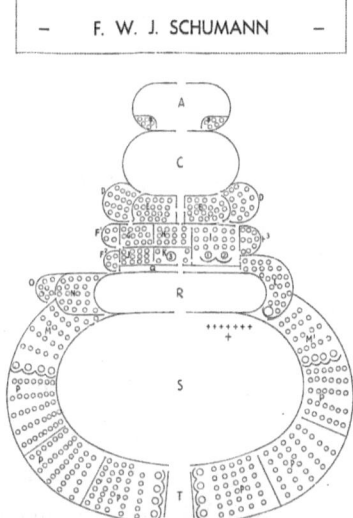

PLAN VAN 'N ZOELOEKONINGSTAT

A: Algemene beskraal. B: Strooise van die beeswagters. C: Die melkkraal. D: Die Koning se wagters. E: Die woning van die Koning se vroue en kinders. F: Koring- of koshutte. G: Dienaresse van die Koning. H: Dienaresse van die Koningin. I: Die jonkvroue (vrouens) van die Koning. (1) Koning se woonhut (2) Koning se slaapvertrek. J: Dienaresse (bierbrouers). K: Afdeling Koningin-moeder (3) Hut van die Koningin. L: Dienare. Koning se lyfwag. M: Seniore. N: Dienare van die Koningin. O: Besoekers en revisers. P: Solhtehutte. Q: Voorhof. R: Kraal vir die Koning se slagbeeste. S: Grootkraal of paradekraal. ++++: Sitplek van die Koning se lyfwag. +: Die Koning se sitplek. T: Hoofingang.

noordwaartse boog oor Pietermaritzburg teruggekeer. Op laasgenoemde plek het hy sy ander stat gebou, wat hy Umgungundhlovu (iemand wat 'n samewerking teen 'n olifant (Faku) gesmee het) genoem het.

Dit was hiervandaan dat Chaka sy bevelhebber Ndhlaka teen die Basoeto's gestuur het om hulle heeltemal uit te roei, omdat hy hulle weens hul rooi lippe nie as onderdane wou hê nie. Chaka het met sy lyfregiment na die kus teruggekeer en by Tongaat nog 'n stat gebou, wat hy die naam Utongati (iets het ek gesê) gegee het. Daarna het hy na Dukuza (Stanger) gegaan en daar sy paar geveting.

Maar sy impi kon teen die Basoeto's, wat in die berge posisie ingeneem het, niks of min uitrig. Die Basoeto's het die aanvallers met klippe bestook. So was die bult baie gering, en omdat Ndhlaka die koning se toorn oor die mislukking gevrees het, het hy op die terugpad na Dhlomodhlomo, naby Nongoma, gevlug.

Al die statte of krale van die koning is volgens 'n bepaalde skema of plan gebou. Net die omvang het verskil, omdat die Zoeloes geen maat- of gewig-eenhede gehad het nie. Daar is dus geen maatstaf nie, maar na skatting het die koningstat 'n middellyn van honderd tot honderd-en-vyftig tree gehad.

Die rye en getal hutte is ook net skematies. Dit staan egter vas dat elke stat 'n groot hut (3 op die sketsi) gehad, en die koning self twee hutte (1 en 2) bestaan het.

Ter verduideliking moet ek sê dat Senzangakona, die vader van Chaka, getroud was en baie vroue gehad het, sodat Chaka, Dingane en Mpande, wat stiefbroers was en een na die ander die troon bestyg het, oorgenoeg moeders gehad het om aan elke stat een te gee. Chaka het geen kinders gehad nie, want hy het al die swanger meide laat vermoor. Sy moeder, Inandi, het haar bes gedoen om van sy nakomelinge te versteek, maar Chaka het dit uitgevind en hulle van kant gemaak. Dis ook die rede waarom hy sy moeder gedood het. Hy self het van sy eie kinders opgetel en hoog in die lug gegooi, sodat hulle op die grond verbrysel is.

Dingane was nie getroud nie, maar Mpande was getroud toe hy koning geword het, en hy het 'n groot aantal kinders gehad. Dis hierdie kinders en hul moeders wat hulle verblyf in die afdeling E op die sketsi gehad het.

So het dan elke stat—behalwe die koning s'n—onder die beheer van 'n koninginmoeder gestaan. Buitendien was daar in elke kraal 'n hoof-indoena wat deur 'n klomp ondergeskikte hoofde en raadsliede bygestaan is.

Die vernaamste indoenas se wonings was altyd regs van die kraal se hoofingang (regs van die letter T). Links het die ondergeskikte hoofde gewoon.

Alle gewigtige tydings en berigte is eers aan die hoof by die ingang afgelewer, wat dit dan regs (met die stippellyn) na die afdeling L gebring het, om dan deur die hoof van die koning se lyfwag aan die koning self oorgedra te word. Dus was die regterkant van so 'n stat die belangrikste.

As die koning wette wou proklameer of 'n parade bywoon, het hy uit sy hut deur die hekkies van K, gestap, dadelik regs gedraai en daar met sy lyfwag gaan sit (sien x x x x x), terwyl op 'n gegewe teken die soldate, een regiment na die ander, deur die onderste hoofingang, beurtelings na regs en links gaande, stadig, singende en dansende langs die kraalmure boontoe beweeg het. Dieselfde bewegings is gevolg toe Dingane Piet Retief laat vermoor het.

In mooiweer het die koning gewoonlik uit sy hut deur die boonste hekkie uit sy afdeling na buite en langs die muur van D, C, B en A gestap om die buitelug en die warmte van die son te geniet of om sy melkkoeie en beeste in die krale C en A te besigtig.

Op die dag toe hy vermoor is, het Chaka die oggend vroeg, voor sonop, opgestaan en soos gewoonlik met sy klomp honde na buite gegaan om op die verwarmende son te wag. Daar het Nkabane, een van sy lyfwag, met sy volle wapenrusting en sy wilde gebare hom die skrik op die lyf gejaj; die honde van die koning, wat hom aangeval het, het Nkabane woes gesiaan. Chaka het toe langs die buitemuur na die hek terug gegaan en is deur sy twee broers, D'ngane en Nomhlangano, wat aan weerskante van die hek, binnekant die afdeling I,

(*Vervolg op bladsy 69.*)

Overview and Highlights of *Her Name is Grace* by Ingrid Herrmann

Review by Martin Howard

Her Name is Grace is a deeply personal and historically rich autobiography that takes readers on a journey through faith, heritage, and resilience. Through the lens of her German ancestry, Ingrid Herrmann weaves a compelling narrative that connects the Hermannsburg Mission, the migration of her forebears to South Africa, and her own life experiences across continents. This book is not just a personal memoir but a testament to the enduring impact of Christian faith across generations.

The book begins by exploring her Huguenot heritage in France and the migration of the Gevers families to South Africa. The story then shifts to Lutheran influences in Germany, detailing the work of Pastor Louis Harms and the establishment of the Hermannsburg Mission. These early chapters provide detailed historical context for the religious and cultural forces that shaped Ingrid Herrmann's ancestry.

As the narrative unfolds, we see how the author's forebears, such as Missionaries Friedrich Fröhling and Friedrich Schumann, played key roles in early missionary settlements. The book recounts the Zulu Wars, the Anglo-Zulu conflict, and the struggle of German settlers who sought to bring faith and education to local communities. Through historical records and family stories, these chapters vividly depict the sacrifices and extreme challenges faced by early missionaries.

Herrmann connects her family's experiences to pivotal events in South African history, including their insider accounts of the Boer War. Readers gain insight into the ways colonialism, war, and faith intersected, influencing her ancestors' lives. The book presents deeply personal accounts, such as the testimony of a woman involved in witchcraft, adding an intimate and thought-provoking dimension to the historical narrative.

The book also delves into the theme of harmful interference by colonial powers, international organizations, and secretive entities. It examines how the World Council of Churches, the United Nations, and pro-communist global foundations played roles in shaping the socio-political landscape of South Africa, often under the guise of humanitarian or diplomatic efforts. Herrmann critiques the consequences of these interventions, highlighting their impact on local communities, missionary work, and faith-based traditions.

The later chapters focus on Ingrid's own experiences, tracing her journey from Empangeni and Pinetown to mission work in Italy and Mauritius. She shares how her faith led her into prison ministry, her work with Prison Fellowship in Australia and the Sycamore Tree Project (where I first met Ingrid). These personal reflections offer a touching conclusion to the book, showcasing the ongoing legacy of faith and service in her life.

Her Name is Grace is more than just a family history—it is a moving account of faith's endurance through time. Ingrid Herrmann's storytelling is both intimate and historically enlightening, making this book a valuable read for those interested in Christian missions, German-South African heritage, and personal testimonies of faith and resilience. With its rich historical detail and personal warmth, this book is a compelling exploration of how grace weaves through generations, shaping lives in profound ways.

Review by Adam Schoenmaker, Lead Pastor at Oasis Church, Brisbane, Australia

'Her Name Is Grace' by Ingrid Herrmann is a wide-ranging and far-reaching story about God's faithfulness across generations, continents, and individual lives. Part-history, part-memoir, part-theological treatise, this unique work traces God's guiding hand in the life of Ingrid Herrmann and her family, both past and present, weaving together a compelling story of joy, sorrow and redemption. Ingrid issues a clear and, at times, controversial call for believers to open their eyes to the 'brooding darkness', but without losing sight of God's good and wise sovereignty. Read this book; be moved by its story, challenged by its perspective, and most importantly, changed by the grace of God to which Ingrid so beautifully testifies.

Review by Charlotte Kruger

When Ingrid shared that she was writing a book spanning multiple generations of missionaries and colonists across three continents, exploring their battle between darkness and light, I wondered how she would make it an engaging read. Through her meticulous research, Ingrid crafted an absorbing story of survival, death, persecution, hardship, persistence, and faith during times when there seemed to be little hope. I was drawn into the book, and it challenged my thinking in many ways. Her personal journey – from a humble farmer's daughter to a devoted child of the Most High – moved me. This is a book I will revisit often, reminded of the truth that His mercy is for those who fear Him from generation to generation.

General Disclaimer:

1. References to sources are recorded as accurately as possible. In some instances, the original sources were not available for verification. Unless otherwise stated, all photos are in the possession of the author. All other images are used with permission.
2. Some passages are free translations and may not always accurately reflect the original meaning or intent of the primary author/speaker.
3. Any mistakes and omissions are my own and do not reflect the opinions of any other person or organisation.

www.ingramcontent.com/pod-product-compliance
Lightning Source LLC
Chambersburg PA
CBHW020631230426
43665CB00008B/127